Jan. 1983

ORGANIZATIONS
and organization theory

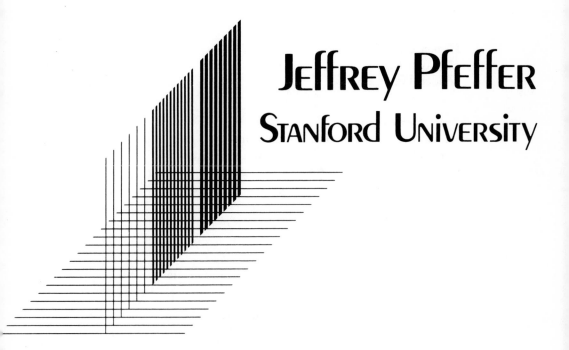

Jeffrey Pfeffer
Stanford University

ORGANIZATIONS
and organization theory

Pitman

Boston · London · Melbourne · Toronto

Pitman Publishing Inc.
1020 Plain Street
Marshfield, Mashachusetts 02050

Pitman Books Limited
128 Long Acre
London WC2E 9AN

Associated Companies
Pitman Publishing Pty Ltd., Melbourne
Pitman Publishing New Zealand Ltd., Wellington
Copp Clark Pitman, Toronto

© **1982 Jeffrey Pfeffer**

Library of Congress Cataloging in Publication Data

Pfeffer, Jeffrey.
   Organizations and organization theory.

   Bibliography: p.
   Includes index.
   1. Organization. 2. Organizational behavior.
I. Title.
HD31.P3983 1982   302.3'5   82-10154
ISBN 0-273-01851-5   AACR2

Manufactured in the United States of America

10 9 8 7 6 5 4 3 2 1

iv

PREFACE

In many respects, this book came into being because of the actions of Jim March and Charles O'Reilly, although neither of them could have anticipated the chain of events triggered by their behavior. In 1979, March received a telephone call from Gardner Lindzey asking if he would do the organizations chapter for the forthcoming new, third edition of the *Handbook of Social Psychology*. I am sure Jim gets many requests like these, and having other, more pressing things to do, he declined. For all, or any, of many reasons (a sense of obligation, a strategic move to direct Lindzey to someone else, a favor to me, a response to Lindzey's request for other recommendations, . . .) March told Lindzey that I would be an appropriate choice to do the chapter. Thus, also in 1979, I received an invitation to do a chapter on organization theory for the *Handbook*. Having, in the past, been talked into doing things I later decided I did not want to do, I begged for time to make the decision and, with that, went off to consult with someone whose judgment I respected about whether this was a sensible thing to do.

My erstwhile consultant and confidant was Charles O'Reilly. I can still remember approaching Charles, telling him about the invitation, and telling him I thought I was going to decline it because doing a review of the field seemed like both a singularly unrewarding and particularly taxing task. Charles thought I was making the wrong decision and, in his own inimitable way, persuaded me, in a series of conversations, to do the chapter. The persuasive techniques and brilliant arguments used in this endeavor are better left undisclosed, and I am not sure I remember them all in any event.

Thus, it happened that in 1980, with the first (of many) deadlines approaching, I sat down to do the chapter. My initial reaction was to regret that I had decided to undertake this activity and to think that I should have never let Charles persuade me to accept this assignment. The field of organization studies is both broad and diverse, and since I thought I should try to somehow capture as much of its essence as I could, I faced the tasks of organizing the field in a sensible fashion and then exploring numerous bodies of literature that represented its diverse components.

My initial reaction of dismay proved to be only partly valid as the project progressed. Although the task was indeed difficult, it also became clear that it was enormously useful. For in reviewing the various bodies of theory, comparisons and contrasts, points of overlap and points of discontinuity, and the pattern of research and idea development became clearer to me in a way that they had never been before. I could see similar themes played out at different levels of analysis, and I could also observe more clearly the effects of the social context on the development of knowledge about organizations through this overview of the various domains of the discipline.

Somehow in my academic career, I had never written a handbook chapter before and thus was unsure about the product when I had completed it. Following Festinger's theory of seeking social information and engaging in increased communication in the face of uncertainty, I sent the chapter off to O'Reilly (who could not escape the consequences of having persuaded me to do the chapter), Barry Staw, Jerry Salancik, and Dick Scott for comments. Their reaction to the effort was basically positive, although they had numerous suggestions for improvement and revision. With the chapter now revised, and with publication, given Lindzey and Aronson's task of pulling 32 chapters together, far in the future, I sent copies off to various other colleagues. Back came more kind words. I began to think that if a chapter was useful, a book might be even better; thus, I asked some colleagues whether they thought the task of expanding the chapter into a book-length treatment would be worthwhile. With encouragement to proceed in that direction, off I went.

At this point, I should probably let most of these colleagues off the hook, for the book as it took shape became less and less like a handbook chapter and more and more a critical review of the field of organization theory — where it had been, where it was, and where it might progress. It came to have, as one colleague noted, a "point of view." And, it paid increasing attention to the contextual effects on the development of organization theory, seeking to describe those social forces, values, and structural characteristics of this particular field of study that seem to have affected how theory and research have developed.

And what is the "point of view" that emerged? It is that a great deal of research has been done with, in many instances, little or no return in terms of the development of knowledge. One reasonable supposition is that the problem is not with the talent or motivation of those seeking to understand organizations but, rather, with the point of view, the perspective, the approach to analysis that has tended to dominate the field. This argument seems to require three elements for its demonstration. First, it is necessary to survey or overview the field of study, trying to point out what has been accomplished and where critical issues and problems remain. To provide an overview of a wide range of organization theory is the first objective of this book. It should be clear, however, that this is not primarily a review of the literature. It is a review of theoretical perspectives and approaches, an effort to focus attention on the underlying logics of the processes of inquiry that have been pursued, rather than on every detail of every study.

Second, as these streams of research are discussed, it is necessary to begin to articulate some reasons for how and why these approaches to organizational analysis have developed as they have. What is the social context in which organization theory has developed? Can we understand anything about the field and its approach to analysis by investigating this context? I think the answer is decidedly yes to this latter question. Thus, the second objective is to provide some sense of the social context of this field and its effects. At the same time, this is not a systematic, formal treatment of the sociology of organization theory. Particularly for those perspectives that have for so long dominated the field, I have tried to present some evidence and some logic as to how and why they have achieved their position. But much additional work remains to be done in understanding the sociology and ideology of organization theory.

Third, having reviewed where the field is and some of the forces that have gotten it there, I wanted to conclude by drawing some implications for where additional work might be productively focused, both in terms of perspectives and approaches already in place, as well as some new analytic points of view that seem particularly productive. The third objective, then, is to nudge gently organizational analysis in some new directions. These are the themes of this book: to review the major dimensions of organization theory from the perspective that what we know is very much a function of how the questions have been raised and phrased; how questions have been posed is a function of the social context of the field of study; and there is evidence that knowledge might be advanced more effectively if we were, collectively, willing to pursue some avenues that have been relatively unexplored and abandon some ideologically comfortable but theoretically bereft lines of inquiry.

The organizing principle for this book is based on distinctions among theoretical approaches differentiated on two dimensions: the level of analysis and the perspective on action taken. In the first case, I differentiate between those approaches that have treated organizations as wholes, as units (for example, structural contingency theory, population ecology, and the market failures approach), and those approaches that have analyzed individuals or subunits within the organization, including the numerous studies of individual motivation and task attitudes, operant conditioning, role theory, and political or coalitional perspectives. In the second instance, I distinguish among three perspectives on action. The first is the rational or quasi-rational approach, with its foundations in instrumentality theory and the utility maximization point of view. This perspective argues that action is foresightful and organized for the attainment of needs, goals, or preferences. The second perspective is the situationist or external control approach. This line of argument maintains that social units can be understood by looking at the conditions of their social context and that recourse to internal psychological states such as values, preferences, needs, goals, and so forth is unnecessary and not particularly useful. The third perspective, the emergent, almost random process, socially constructed view of behavior argues for the importance (for the most part) of intrapsychic processes, but maintains that behavior can be understood only by analyzing the unfolding of these processes over time. Thus, this perspective moves away from a stimulus-response logic to a focus on process and emergent meaning.

Three perspectives on action each examined at two levels of analysis leads to six chapters (Chapters 2 through 7). These six chapters form the core of the book and provide the overview and comparative perspective on approaches to organizational analysis. The first chapter (Chapter 1) sets the stage. It provides some understanding of the context of organizational behavior as a discipline, describes the two organizing dimensions in more detail, and highlights some of the themes and controversies that not only underlie much of the research but are important for understanding the material to follow. That chapter also briefly reviews some of the criteria by which theory may be evaluated, so that the reader can approach the subsequent material both with some understanding of the general context in which it was produced as well as some metrics by which it may be evaluated.

After the six chapters treating the three perspectives on action as used at the two levels of analysis, the last chapter concludes by drawing together some impressions that emerge, at least from my reading of this literature. Then, it suggests three additional analytical concepts that may be useful in helping knowledge advance at a more rapid pace. In many respects, these approaches as well as those that fare better in the earlier chapters all represent, in some sense, a back-to-basics philosophy. As Phil Mirvis so aptly put it, we have moved away from analyzing organizations as what we know them to be, physical entities with relational structures characterized by demographic processes such as entry and turnover. We have so enjoyed drawing figures on the ground, speculating and psychologizing about intrapsychic processes, and developing complex and convoluted concepts and measures that we have at times lost sight of the ground for all the figures we have drawn. Although the urge to draw is great, it seems that it is useful to review and prune somewhat from what has already been created and refocus on the basic attributes and characteristics of organizations.

As one surveys the field of *organizational behavior* or *organization theory* (in this book I use the terms interchangeably), one sees an immense increase in the number of publications and a growth in the diversity of points of view, theoretical perspectives, approaches to analysis, and so forth. This book is largely motivated by the conviction, acquired as I wrote and did the research for the *Handbook* chapter, that to move forward we need to examine carefully where we are and how we got there. We need to be much more self-conscious about issues such as the choice of units of analysis, perspectives on action, and the role of ideology and values in the development (or lack thereof) of social science knowledge. In many respects, then, this book seeks to raise the consciousness of those who think about, write about, and do research on organizations. It asks for some inspection and examination of modes of inquiry, of logical assumptions often left implicit, and of the social factors that have created the field of study as it is today. Such reflection, introspection, and critical thinking is not likely to be pleasant. Frankly, when I put on these particular glasses, I am not too pleased with a good portion of my own research. But, if we are to progress to develop valid and useful theories of organizations, we need to develop our critical faculties and comparative perspectives to a much greater degree. If this book moves us along at all in this direction, it will have been well worth the effort.

I owe special thanks to three friends and colleagues who generously and thoughtfully provided excellent comments on earlier versions of this manuscript. Charles O'Reilly, Dick Scott, and Phil Mirvis each provided unique and valuable insights. They sometimes saw what I was doing better than I did, and they often noted problems in the argument, in the literature covered, or in the presentation that I have tried to correct. If I could be certain this manuscript was of the same quality as their comments, I would be pleased indeed.

I also would like to gratefully acknowledge the absolutely wonderful typing assistance of Rose Giacobbe, Aimee Hamel, and Pauline Henault, as well as the support of the Division of Research at the Graduate School of Business Administration, Harvard University, that made such typing available. These three individuals met impossible deadlines with work of superb quality, and I am truly grateful for their help.

CONTENTS

	Page
PREFACE	v

Chapter

1 THE VARIETY OF PERSPECTIVES	1
Perspectives on Action	5
Prospective, Intendedly Rational, Created Action	5
The External Constraint or Situational Control Perspective	8
Almost Random, Emergent Process View of Action	9
Differences in Practice and Methodology	10
Levels and Units of Analysis	12
Methodological Issues in the Choice of a Unit of Analysis	14
The Individualist-Structuralist Controversy	18
The Social Context of Organization Theory	23
The Environment and Demography of Organization Theory	26
Theory versus Application in the Study of Organizations	33
Some Criteria for Evaluating Theory	37
Conclusion	40

2 MICROLEVEL RATIONAL ACTION	41
Expectancy Theory	44
Path-Goal Theory of Leadership	47
Goal Setting	48
Needs Theories and Job Design	54
The Status of Needs Theories	62
Political Theories of Organizations	63
Summary and Critique	71

3 THE EXTERNAL CONTROL OF INDIVIDUAL BEHAVIOR   80

   Exchange-Based and Informational Influence   83
      Exchange   83
      Informational Social Influence   85
   Operant Conditioning   86
      Schedules of Reinforcement   87
      Types of Reinforcers   89
      Applications   91
      Critical Questions   92
   Social Learning Theory   93
   Socialization   96
   Role Theory   98
   The Effects of Social Context on Behavior   102
   Retrospective Rationality   105
      Insufficient Justification Conditions   107
      Overjustification   109
   Social Information Processing   111
   Summary   117

4 THEORIES OF ORGANIZATION-LEVEL RATIONAL
   ACTION   121

   Incentives, Control, and Organizations as Units   124
      The Empirical Fact of Ownership-Control Separation   126
      The Use of Financial Incentives   128
      Organizational Rationality through Control   130
      The "As If" Argument   131
   A Market Failures Approach   134
      The Issue of Efficient Boundaries   137
      The M-Form Hypothesis   139
      Organizing the Employment Relation   141
      Conceptual and Empirical Issues   146
   Structural Contingency Theory   147
      Size   148
      Technology   151
      The Environment   155
      The Relationship between Strategy and Structure 157
      Strategic Choice   159
      Theoretical Issues   161
   Marxist Analyses of Organizations   162
      The Employment Relationship and the Organization
         of Work   163

Interorganizational Behavior   170
Summary   173

5   THE EXTERNAL CONTROL OF ORGANIZATIONAL
    BEHAVIOR   178

    Population Ecology   180
        Variation   183
        Selection   186
        Retention   189
        Population Ecology Compared with Other Theories   190
    Resource Dependence   192
        External Constraint from Resource Dependence   193
        Attempts to Manage Resource Dependence   197
        A Mechanism for Environmental Effects on Organizational
            Actions   202
        Resource Dependence and Other Theories   204

6   SOCIAL CONSTRUCTIONIST VIEWS OF INDIVIDUAL
    BEHAVIOR   208

    The Ethnomethodological Perspective   211
    Cognitive Theories of Organizations   214
    Language in Organizations   218
    Affect-Based Processes   221
    Summary   224

7   ORGANIZATIONS AS PARADIGMS AND PROCESSES   226

    Organizations as Paradigms   227
    Decision Process Theories and Administrative Rationality   233
    Institutionalization Theory   239
        Some Determinants of Institutionalization   241
        Institutionalization and Organizational Structure   244
        The Diffusion of Innovations   246
        Additional Topic Domains   249
    Summary   252

8   DEVELOPING ORGANIZATION THEORY   254

    An Overview   256
    Organizations as Physical Structures   260
        Measures and Dimensions   260

CONTENTS

Some Causes of Particular Physical Dimensions   264
Some Consequences of Physical Design   265
Organizations as Relational Networks   271
Measurement and Dimensions   272
Some Determinants of Network Characteristics   273
Consequences of Network Structures   276
Demographic Processes in Organizations   277
Dimensions and Measurement   278
Sources of Variation in Organizational Demography   280
Some Consequences of Organizational Demography   284
Conclusion   293

REFERENCES   295

AUTHOR INDEX   364

SUBJECT INDEX   374

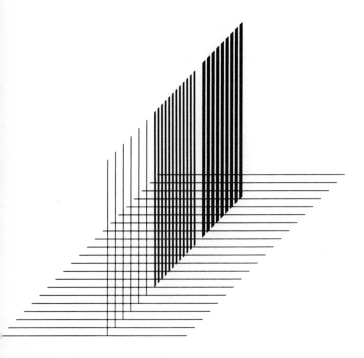

ORGANIZATIONS
and organization theory

1

THE VARIETY
OF PERSPECTIVES

The domain of organization theory is coming to resemble more of a weed patch than a well-tended garden. Theories of the middle range (Merton, 1968; Pinder and Moore, 1979) proliferate, along with measures, terms, concepts, and research paradigms. It is often difficult to discern in what direction knowledge of organizations is progressing — or if, indeed, it is progressing at all. Researchers, students of organization theory, and those who look to such theory for some guidance about issues of management and administration confront an almost bewildering array of variables, perspectives, and inferred prescriptions. To take just one example, Stogdill (1974) reviewed more than 3,000 studies of leadership, a major, much-studied topic. Yet, reviewing this literature, Stogdill concluded:

> A review of the preceding chapters suggests that some topics and research designs have been overworked while other important questions remain relatively unexplored. . . . The same period witnessed a wasteful repetition of testing shopworn hypotheses, accompanied by a general disregard for negative results. . . . Naive, uncritical theorizing is likely to retard the process of discovery (1974: 421).

1

What is the problem? It is not that the study of organizations is conducted by unintelligent people. Nor is it because organizational scholars are lazy or somehow unmotivated. Areas of inquiry such as leadership (Stogdill, 1974) and job satisfaction and job attitudes (Locke, 1976) represent topic domains in which a large number of intelligent, highly motivated, and committed individuals have invested immense intellectual effort. Rather, it can be argued that the development of better organization theory requires several things that have been missing in some of the extant research: (1) much more attention to the criteria of theory development and theory testing, particularly as the development of organization theory is distinguished from both the development of ideology that legitimates and supports organizations and current organizational practices, and advocacy of some favored theoretical orientation; (2) recognition and understanding of the range of perspectives and the different levels of analysis at which organization theory has been and can be developed, and some sensitivity to the factors that affect the choice of perspective and level and whether such factors hinder or advance theory development; (3) some understanding of the social context in which organization theory is developed, and how this context has influenced what has been studied; and (4) incorporation into theoretical work of some potentially powerful, but largely ignored, analytical concepts.

This book, then, is an attempt to advance the development of organization theory by doing the things that seem to be needed. Thus, one of its aims is to provide an overview of some of the major theoretical perspectives that populate the field. This overview is, quite often, critical. It is clear from the metaphor of the garden that a good deal of pruning and weeding is needed. The book will indicate how critical questions and issues can be highlighted for a number of theoretical points of view, to focus research in ways that make the development and refutation of theory occur in a somewhat more efficient and faster manner. It is also important to overview the various theories and perspectives to provide some understanding of the panoply of approaches to understanding organizations that currently exist. A second aim of the book is to provide some insight into how the context of organization theory has influenced its development. However, this is not a book primarily treating the sociology of organization theory and its development but, rather, the theories themselves. Hence, this point is alluded to on several occasions, but it is not the primary focus. Third, I want to highlight some comparisons and contrasts among the different points of view to bring the critical theoretical issues into somewhat sharper focus. And fourth, the book concludes by offering some alternative conceptualizations and variables for incorporation in the study of organizations. But, to get on with the new, it is useful to have a good understanding of what already exists.

The addition of just more ideas and perspectives can merely add to the theoretical tangle unless the reader is armed with some appreciation and perspective on the field as a whole as well as some conceptual apparatus to make sense out of the various theories of organizations.

This treatment of organization theory has three themes: (1) what we know about organizations is a consequence of how the questions have been phrased and raised; (2) how the questions have been posed is very much a function of the organization of the field and its size, growth, interdisciplinary nature, and so forth, and the social context in which the field exists, including the historical time periods in which organization theory has been done; and (3) there may be some more productive approaches to posing the questions to make the development of organization theory advance at a faster and more consistent pace. Given these three themes, in this chapter we begin to lay out a framework for surveying the field. There are two dimensions that are advanced as being heuristically useful for characterizing the various theories of organizations. The first dimension is the perspective on action taken, with three positions visible in the various theories: action as rational or at least boundedly rational, purposive, and goal directed; action as externally constrained or environmentally determined; and action as emergent from, and in, social processes. The second, the level of analysis at which activity is analyzed, distinguishes between those theories that treat the organization primarily as a unit and those that deal with smaller social units within the organization, such as individuals, coalitions, and subunits.

These perspectives on action and levels of analysis distinctions emerge from the social context of the field—the next subject to be explored in this introductory chapter. One element of that context is the fact that much of the study of organizations is today done in various professional schools. Thus, there is the issue of the extent to which theory has been or could be advanced or retarded by concern with issues of application and practice. This is an important enough subject to warrant some separate treatment, as it is a theme that will recur as various theories are examined in the rest of the book.

Finally, the criteria by which theories are evaluated are detailed. One might think that such criteria are both well known and obvious. The fact that so many of the theories to be reviewed violate several of the criteria, and yet are well regarded and accepted, indicates that some explicit focus on criteria for evaluating social science theory is useful. Thus, by the end of the chapter, the reader should see the organizing framework, how and where it came from in terms of the context of organization theory, and some issues to be considered in thinking about organization theories and their development.

Two other introductory notes are in order. First, the conceptual framework used in considering the myriad theories of organizations has some costs as well as benefits. The two benefits are its ability to encapsulate much, if not most, of the research of this field and its relationship to a number of contextual factors (such as disciplinary boundaries and applied versus theoretical focus) that are important in understanding why organization theory looks the way it does. One disadvantage is that it draws some boundaries where, at times, they may seem artificial. Thus, for instance, several perspectives consider action to be at once somewhat constrained but also purposive within such constraints. Several writers have developed theories that span levels of analysis. We have categorized theories into one cell or another, but we are cognizant of those that span perspectives and levels and will note them as appropriate.

The second disadvantage is to portray the field as somewhat disjointed and discontinuous — many separate theories taking somewhat different looks at different aspects of organizations from somewhat different points of view. There are clearly more unified, systematic treatments of organizations (e.g., Scott, 1981; Thompson, 1967). These treatments, however, give something up in terms of comprehensiveness, because the field is indeed diverse and somewhat diffuse. It should be recalled that this book is not a theory of organizations, or even a single perspective, but rather an attempt to map the terrain of organization theory as completely as possible, both to see what new directions may be useful and to review and critique the ground already covered. Thus, we have sacrificed some degree of cumulativeness for comprehensiveness.

The other point to be made is that this is a review of theoretical perspectives — and those that have enjoyed some prominence and continue to occupy researchers. It is a review that is both selective and that, of necessity, differs from that found in an *Annual Review of Psychology* chapter. Thus, for instance, Cummings (1982) describes the field of organizations in terms of topic headings such as task design, feedback, and structure, technology and control. Other reviews (e.g., T. Mitchell, 1979) have used headings such as job attitudes, motivation, and leadership. It should be clear that some of these are more topic headings than headings corresponding to some reasonably comprehensive, systematically developed theoretical perspective. The discussion here is organized by theory, not by topic. Some topics do not have much theory — they tend to be underrepresented in this presentation. Moreover, the purpose of the book is to illustrate as well as demonstrate the type of critical scrutiny to which research should be put and to provide an overview of the scope of organization theory that is comprehensible. Thus, the major boundaries and patterns are sketched; some of the detail is, of necessity, missing. Nevertheless, the treatment does draw together a number of disparate approaches and perspectives. Through the juxtaposition, hopefully, it will serve to sharpen thinking about, and analysis of, organizational issues.

PERSPECTIVES ON ACTION

A critical dimension distinguishing among theories of organizations is the perspective on action adopted, either explictly or implicitly, by each theory. The three perspectives seen in the literature are: action seen as purposive, boundedly or intendedly rational, and prospective or goal directed; action seen as externally constrained or situationally determined; and action seen as being somewhat more random and dependent on an emergent, unfolding process, with rationality in the second and third perspectives being constructed after the fact to make sense of behaviors that have already occurred. This distinction among perspectives on action is similar to that advanced by other writers. Van de Ven and Astley (1981: 428) distinguish among theories based on the emphasis placed on "deterministic versus voluntaristic assumptions about human nature." Thus, they distinguish between "the view that human beings and their institutions are . . . determined by exogenous forces" and the position that human action and institutions "are autonomously chosen and created by human beings" (Van de Ven and Astley, 1981: 429).

This distinction, while important, omits yet a third view of human behavior. Both the situational constraint and individual choice views of behavior are, essentially, stimulus-response (S-R) views of understanding behavior (Tuggle, 1978). That is, both seek to understand the behavior, the response, in terms of the antecedent stimulus conditions that produce the behavior. The situational constraint perspective seeks such antecedent stimulus conditions in the context or environment of the social entity, while the rational, proactive choice perspective seeks such antecedents within the social unit, in concepts such as preferences, values, personality, needs, or goals. The third perspective on action, the emergent, process perspective, rejects the S-R paradigm and argues for the importance of the unfolding process in understanding action.

Prospective, Intendedly Rational, Created Action

The Judeo-Christian tradition and the philosophical underpinnings of much of American life and culture venerate and idealize the concepts of free will and conscious choice. For this important reason, and because such a perspective is more proximately tied to a focus on application and practice, the perspective on action as rational and foresightful has dominated theories of organizations. This perspective has several critical elements. First, behaviors are construed to be chosen. Second, such choice is presumed to occur according to a set of consistent preferences. Allison (1971: 11) has noted that rationality presumes that events are "purposive choices of consistent actors." Thus, behavior is determined by and presumably reflective of conscious, purposive action. Allison (1971: 13) has stated that "behavior reflects purpose or intention." Third, as implied by the above, choice is presumed to occur prior to the action itself — rationality is prospective rather than retrospective in that actions are consciously chosen in the light of some anticipated consequences. Fourth, action is goal directed. Friedland (1974) has argued that *rationality* cannot be defined apart from the existence of goals. Choice, then, is value maximizing.

The presumption that actions are consciously undertaken to attain some goal or set of goals means that preferences can be inferred from the choice. Allison (1971) has illustrated this inference process in the realm of foreign policy analysis, in which the actions of nations are scrutinized to infer from them what the underlying goals and motives of the nations are. The problem, however, is that "an imaginative analyst can construct an account of value-maximizing choice for any action or set of actions performed" (Allison, 1971: 35). In a similar fashion, the choices of individuals may be employed, after the fact, to construct statements about the needs and goals of the individuals that would be consistent with such actions. Indeed, the ability of observers to construct readily such statements concerning personal dispositions after the fact to account for any observed behavior may be a factor underlying the widespread acceptance of personal, dispositional theories of organizational behavior (e.g., Salancik and Pfeffer, 1977a).

The maximizing model of rational choice employed in economics (Simon, 1978) has been criticized as being insensitive to the cognitive limitations possessed by individuals and organizations. Thus, a subset of theories of rational choice has emerged emphasizing the boundedly rational nature of decision making (Simon, 1957). Bounded rationality encompasses choice "theories which incorporate constraints on the information-processing capacities of the actor" (Simon, 1972: 162). Such theories incorporate the notion of "satisficing" (Simon, 1957), the fact that the search for alternatives stops when an option is available that is satisfactory — in the sense of meeting the actor's aspiration level rather than necessarily being the optimal or the best choice. Furthermore, boundedly rational choice recognizes explicitly that search is costly (Simon, 1978) and that heuristic procedures for decision making arise that are based on experience and that economize on information-processing requirements. One decision-making procedure consistent with the boundedly rational view of action is incrementalism (Lindblom and Bráybrooke, 1970), defined by Padgett (1980: 355) as "a pattern of marginal change in final allocation outcome relative to some base, which frequently is the previous year's allocation outcome." Incrementalism has been used to explain budget allocations, particularly in governmental organizations (Wildavsky, 1979). Boundedly rational choice also forms the foundation for behavioral theories of decision making (e.g., Cyert and March, 1963).

Bounded rationality in some versions represents a slight modification of rational choice more generally but, in other versions, takes on elements of the emergent, process-dependent perspective on action. In some versions, the basic assumptions of the rational model are left largely intact: decisions are still made prospectively, choice is value satisficing (if not value maximizing), and preferences are presumed to be exogenous to the choice and consistent and to guide the choice. Furthermore, bounded rationality is a theory that appears to be very time dependent — as new decision technologies are uncovered and new information-processing systems developed, the bounds of bounded rationality are pushed back. Indeed, the task implicitly set out by this perspective is the development of new decision technologies to increase the capacity for taking rational action.

In other versions, the effects of bounded rationality on producing the use of rules, standard operating procedures, and routinized, habitual patterns of acting are emphasized. These versions stress the analysis of behavior in terms of these routinized, automatic processes and, in this sense, are consistent with an emergent, process-dependent view of behavior. The distinction between the approaches is whether choice is emphasized or whether the automatic, rule and procedure-oriented nature of action is stressed.

The critical distinguishing feature of organization theories taking the rational perspective is the element of conscious, foresightful action reasonably autonomously constructed to achieve some goal or value. Examples of such theories at the individual level of analysis include expectancy theory, an approach that looks much like a model of the maximization of subjective expected utility in decision theory (W. Edwards, 1961, 1962); the path-goal theory of leadership (House, 1971), premised on expectancy theory; goal-setting theory (Locke, 1968), which argues that people's behavior is governed by the goals they are seeking to attain; and most versions of needs theory and task design theory, which tend to argue that persons evaluate situations in the context of their needs or work values and then react to situations accordingly. At the total organizational level of analysis, the various approaches that argue that organizations act intentionally and rationally to achieve some goal, such as efficiency or higher performance, fall within this perspective's domain and include structural contingency theory, the market failures or transactions cost approach (Williamson, 1975), and even Marxist approaches to organizations, which presume foresightful, intentional behavior — in this case on the part of the capitalist class or the owners of capital.

The External Constraint or Situational Control Perspective

The second perspective on action has been called "situationism" (Bowers, 1973) by psychologists. Situationism, or the external constraint perspective, tends to ignore individual or organizational factors, such as personality, preferences, goals, and information processing, or at least to see them as less important than the primary impact of the external stimulus or effect (Harre and Secord, 1972). In this view, action is seen not as the result of conscious, foresightful choice but as the result of external constraints, demands, or forces that the social actor may have little control over or even cognizance of (Pfeffer and Salancik, 1978). Behavior may have little to do with the values or preferences of the actor taking the action but instead reflects the constraints of external elements. Action results from the pattern of constraints, contingencies, or demands confronting the social unit.

When cognition is considered by theories in this domain, the role of cognition is viewed as a mechanism for making sense of or rationalizing behavior that has already occurred. Cognition is used to provide meaning and a sense of control to the world, but this meaning is developed after the fact of the behavior, rather than guiding the behavior prospectively. Thus, the external control or situational constraint perspective talks to the issue of retrospective rationality — of reasons constructed after the fact to explain what has occurred.

The key element distinguishing theories taking this perspective on action is the analysis and explanation of action using variables or descriptors of the social entity's environment and not incorporating any entity-specific descriptors (such as goals, values, needs, or personality) in the understanding of behavior. Thus, population ecology (Hannan and Freeman, 1977) seeks to explain organizational form or structure not in terms of the choices made by managers to enhance efficiency or performance given some contextual factors — the approach taken by structural contingency theory — but in terms of the inevitable, selection-induced fit that emerges between characteristics of environmental niches and forms that can survive in those niches. And, in a somewhat similar fashion, operant conditioning (e.g., Luthans and Kreitner, 1975) seeks to account for the behavior of individuals not in terms of their cognitions, goals, needs, or personality but in terms of the reinforcing properties of the environment. Relatively few of the theories using this perspective ignore or delimit choice quite this severely. Other theories included in this perspective emphasize the importance of situational constraints but tend to allow for some proactive behavior within such constraints. Such theories include role theory, social influence and social information processing, socialization perspectives on individual behavior, and the resource dependence perspective on organizational behavior. But, these perspectives still tend to focus analytical attention on factors of and in the environment, rather than in the entity taking the action, as the most productive means of understanding behavior.

Almost Random, Emergent Process View of Action

The third perspective on action is not as homogeneous as the first two. This view of behavior fundamentally denies either an internally directed or an externally determined rationality of behavior. Some variants of this perspective, decision process theories (e.g., Cohen, March, and Olsen, 1972; Mackenzie, 1978; March and Olsen, 1976) stress the sequential, unfolding nature of activity in organizations. Because participation in organizational decisions is both segmented and discontinuous, because preferences develop and change over time, and because the interpretation of the results of actions — the meaning of history — is often problematic, behavior cannot be predicted a priori either by the intention of individual actors or by the conditions of the environment. Rather, organizations are viewed as contexts in which people, problems, and solutions come together, with the results determined importantly by the process and constraints on that process. Rationality cannot guide action in this view, because rationality, goals, and preferences are viewed as emerging from the action rather than guiding action. March (1978), for instance, has argued that one of the purposes of behavior is to discover preferences through experiencing various outcomes. Furthermore, there are too many different parties involved with fluid participation to predict resulting actions even if preferences could be specified. And, knowledge of external constraints and forces is insufficient to predict action because of the ambiguities and uncertainties involved in registering these external demands within the organization and incorporating them in language and meanings shared by the various organizational actors.

Other variants of the third perspective emphasize the socially constructed nature of organizational realities. These cognitive perspectives on organizations (Weick, 1979) view the organization as a system of shared meaning, in which much of the organizational work consists of symbol manipulation and the development of a shared organizational paradigm (Brown, 1978). Action is governed by the systems of meaning that emerge and develop within the social structure to provide understanding of the social world, and through the development of a shared perspective and negotiated order, they provide stability and cohesion for those within the system.

Differences in Practice and Methodology

The three perspectives on action imply very different views about the fundamental nature of organizations and about the task of administration. In addition, they have tended to be associated with somewhat different research methodologies and procedures. It is important to understand these differences to comprehend how differences in methodological tastes and in orientations toward practice tend to produce research of one type rather than another.

The rational, goal-directed perspective on action presumes that administrative activity impacts firm performance. The fact that there are almost no studies on the effects of managers on performance (e.g., Lieberson and O'Connor, 1972) attests to the fact that the assumption of administrative potency is just that — an assumption, rather than a hypothesis to be empirically investigated. The task of management is viewed as figuring out what to do to enhance organizational goal attainment. Problems of organizational design or the design of incentive and control systems for individuals within organizations are viewed virtually as engineering problems (Pfeffer, 1978). This perspective on action is quite compatible with the various normative choice models and planning procedures that have emerged from management science and economics, such as linear programming, economic order quantity inventory planning, and strategic planning and analysis.

The second, the external control or situational constraint perspective, views both organizational actions and the outcomes of such actions as being either somewhat or largely outside the control of administrators or others in the organization. This perspective has recognized the numerous constraints on leaders (Pfeffer, 1977) and views the administrator role as being either relatively unimportant or, at best, one of registering the environmental constraints and demands and attempting to align the organization with external pressures. The image of the manager is that of a person engaged in the activity of coalignment (Kotter and Lawrence, 1974), aligning the organization with the environment, in those theories that stress managerial action at all.

The third perspective can potentially encompass a sophisticated integration of the first two points of view (Pfeffer, 1981a: chapter 6), in which the organization is viewed as externally constrained and administrative action is focused around creating the illusion of competence and control to maintain support both internally and externally for what the organization or other social entity is required to do to survive. The manager is viewed as having a symbolic, legitimating, sense-making role, providing assurance of the controllability of events even in the absence of such control. This view of the social construction of reality process is, however, not one shared by all those writing on this third perspective. With its emphasis on the relativistic nature of social reality and the focus on randomness and unpredictability, the third perspective would appear to deny most possibilities to manage organizations proactively as well as the capacity even to forecast the course of organizational behavior over time. In some versions (e.g., Meyer and Rowan, 1977), the administrative task would be seen as a ritual role, designed to provide the appearance of conforming to social expectations about rational management even in the absence of the ability to change or manage the operations.

There are also some methodological differences associated with the three perspectives on action that have tended to make their comparative evaluation difficult. The social construction of reality view has been generally studied either through the use of case analysis and natural language (Daft and Wiginton, 1979) or through the use of computer simulations, as in the instance of some of the decision process theories (Cohen, March, and Olsen, 1972). There has been little of the kind of quantitative, comparative empirical work more commonly found in examining either of the other two perspectives, though such approaches are clearly possible (e.g., Axelrod, 1976; Bougon, Weick, and Binkhorst, 1977). This difference in methodology has led to some tendency for methodological preferences to drive perspectives on organizational action, not the healthiest situation.

Attempts to distinguish the perspectives empirically, and the conditions under which each is more or less a valid descriptor of reality, are notable by their rarity. There have been attempts to apportion variance in individual behavior to person versus situational factors in the psychology literature (e.g., Sarason, Smith, and Diener, 1975), but, as we shall see in subsequent chapters, some of the assumptions underlying this work are open to question. More important, the controversy over the perspectives on action has barely been felt in the organizations' literature. Yet, the perspectives do appear to be empirically differentiable, at least in theory. The external constraint approach argues that action is (1) predictable a priori from (2) conditions measuring the dimensions of the social environment. The rational, purposive action perspective would appear to argue that action is (1) predictable a priori but (2) requires knowledge of the goals, needs, personality, or other dispositional characteristics of the social entity under study. The emergent action perspective would seem to suggest that (1) action is not predictable, at least to any great extent, from the knowledge of a priori conditions but that (2) knowledge of the unfolding process is critical for predicting and explaining behavior. The first two approaches suggest the examination of fundamentally different types of variables and their relative effects in explaining behavior in different circumstances, while the latter perspective suggests that prediction of behavior in any kind of S-R paradigm is not going to be successful.

Whether the perspectives are inherently incompatible, or whether they can be combined — as in thinking about taking rational action in the context of a socially constructed world — must await the development of the perspectives into somewhat more refined and specific models of action. This kind of empirical specification has begun in the more limited domain of decision models (Chaffee, 1980; Padgett, 1980), in which the dimensions that distinguish among decision-making theories and the empirical outcroppings of such distinctions have been formulated, so that empirical disconfirmation is possible.

In Table 1-1, the two dimensions along which we have chosen to categorize organization theories, as well as the theories to be reviewed, are displayed. The discussion of the basic differences among perspectives on action and levels of analysis, as well as how such distinctions arise and are maintained (the topic of this chapter), should be useful in facilitating some understanding of the various approaches to organizational analysis and how they interrelate.

LEVELS AND UNITS OF ANALYSIS

The second dimension useful in characterizing theories of organizations is the level of analysis at which activity is analyzed. This dimension distinguishes between those theories that treat the organization as a unit, as an undifferentiated collectivity, and those that deal with smaller social units within organizations. Although some treatments of organizations (e.g., Leavitt, 1978) consider three distinct levels of analysis (individuals, groups, and organizations as wholes), we follow Van de Ven and Astley (1981) and distinguish between the microlevel of individuals and substructures within organizations and the macrolevel at which organizations as units and populations and networks of organizations are examined.

There are two issues of importance in considering the unit and level of analysis issue. The first is methodological and scientific and involves problems in inference and analysis that occur when a unit of analysis is chosen that is inappropriate, given the theoretical propositions being examined. The second is somewhat more a matter of taste and philosophy and in-

Table 1-1. CATEGORIZATION OF THEORETICAL PERSPECTIVES IN ORGANIZATION THEORY

PERSPECTIVES ON ACTION

LEVEL OF ANALYSIS	Purposive, Intentional, Goal Directed, Rational	Externally Constrained and Controlled	Emergent, Almost-Random, Dependent on Process and Social Construction
Individuals, Coalitions, or Subunits	Expectancy theory Goal setting Needs theories and job design Political theories (Chapter 2)	Operant conditioning Social learning theory Socialization Role theories Social context effects and groups Retrospective rationality Social information processing (Chapter 3)	Ethnomethodology Cognitive theories of organizations Language in organizations Affect-based processes (Chapter 6)
Total Organization	Structural contingency theory Market failures/ transaction costs Marxist or class perspectives (Chapter 4)	Population ecology Resource dependence (Chapter 5)	Organizations as paradigms Decision process and administrative theories Institutionalization theory (Chapter 7)

13

volves the selection of dependent variables and theoretical processes that are defined at different levels of analysis on the assumption that one level rather than another is inherently more productive in generating useful and theoretically important scientific theories. The choice of the appropriate unit and level of analysis turns on both issues — thus, both are examined.

Methodological Issues in the Choice of a Unit of Analysis

The issue of the appropriate unit of analysis (J. Freeman, 1978) has both theoretical and statistical aspects. The statistical issue arises because, under certain conditions (particularly when the model being tested is misspecified, as, for example, by leaving out important predictor variables), the process of aggregating to a larger social unit inflates the estimate of the true relationship between the variables (Hannan, 1971). Of course, one never wants to leave out important predictors, in part because this can result in variance being inappropriately attributed to included predictor variables that are moderately correlated with those omitted. However, the problem of misspecification and omitted variables is made worse by aggregation to larger social units in which the amount of variance apparently being explained is inflated. As an example, consider a study that seeks to relate student achievement to educational expenditures. The amount of money spent on education may reflect the socioeconomic characteristics of the community as well as how important education is viewed by the voters in that community. Both of these factors — socioeconomic status and emphasis on education — can have independent effects on achievement in addition to their effects on funding. Thus, studies should control for these other factors to examine the relationship between funding levels and achievement. But the drawing of inappropriate conclusions from leaving out such control factors is statistically much more likely if the data are aggregated to higher and higher levels of analysis.

This phenomenon is conceptually related to the ecological fallacy (Robinson, 1950). The classic example of this fallacy is relating variables measured at an aggregate level as a way of investigating the relationship between the same two variables at an individual level of analysis — for instance, examining the correlation between the proportion of a state's population that is nonwhite and the median educational level in the state. Finding a relationship at the state level of analysis does not permit one to make any inferences about the effect of race on educational attainment at the individual level of analysis.

An organizationally relevant example of the aggregation problem is Bidwell and Kasarda's (1975) attempt to examine the effect of some administrative properties of school districts on district effectiveness, defined in terms of the average achievement level of students in certain grade levels. They reported that district level pupil/teacher ratios, administrative ratios, and measures of average teacher qualifications all had effects on average pupil achievement. Hannan, Freeman, and Meyer (1976), using individual student data, demonstrated the impact of aggregation bias on estimates of administrative effects. In virtually every case, a correctly specified model including controls for input quality such as student ability and social background, and estimated at the individual level of analysis, yielded smaller (and frequently insignificant) estimates of school administration effects.

The unit of analysis should correspond to the level of the theoretical mechanisms that are presumed to be affecting the dependent variables. Hannan, Freeman, and Meyer (1976: 138) contrasted estimating the effects of school properties on student learning or achievement, an individual-level process, with estimating the effects of schooling on the rationalization of labor markets by a signaling function (Spence, 1975), a process that occurs on a societywide basis and that would require analysis at the level of economic systems.

The choice of a unit of analysis requires the exercise of judgment, and it is not a simple issue. For instance, an alternative heuristic to the one just specified argues that the level of the dependent variable should determine the level of the unit of analysis: dependent variables defined at the individual level require analysis at that level; dependent variables defined at the organizational level require analysis at that level; and so forth. The problem with this heuristic is that it potentially does not tell us anything at all. Any set of characteristics can be aggregated to any level and called a property of the collectivity. In fact, this is the central argument in the response to the Hannan, Freeman, and Meyer (1976) comment. Bidwell and Kasarda (1976) responded that they were not studying student achievement, clearly an individual-level phenomenon. Rather, they were studying organizational effectiveness, an organization-level phenomenon, and their aggregated measures of student achievement were indexes of organizational effectiveness, an organization-level property. In a similar fashion, one could argue that the level of strike activity in an industry is an indicator of an industry-level property (Britt and Galle, 1974), even though strikes occur for the most part at the level of the firm or plant. Thus, the heuristic that seems to be the most ultimately useful, even if it is somewhat harder to apply, is to match the unit of analysis to the level at which the theoretical processes underlying the phenomenon being studied are operating.

There has been a lack of sensitivity to unit of analysis issues in organizational research, with some unfortunate results. That is because, as seen in the Bidwell and Kasarda (1975) study, the choice of an inappropriate unit can affect the conclusions drawn. Pennings (1975) attempted to study the effects of variation in the environment on organizational structure, using a sample of stock brokerage offices. But, as J. Freeman (1978: 347) noted, the sample consisted of 40 local offices from a single company, studied at a single point in time. Most variations in the environment, such as the level of the stock market, trading volume, and securities regulations, would vary longitudinally, not cross-sectionally. Furthermore, it is likely that the local offices were not free to adjust internal structures at will. Consequently, the finding of no environmental effects on structure and no support for the effect of structure-contingency matching on performance may speak more to the sample and the choice of units — how the theory was examined — than to the correctness of the theory itself.

Meyer's (1972a, 1975) studies of state and municipal finance departments also raise the question of whether the appropriate hierarchical level and unit are being investigated. Meyer (1972a) investigated the relationship between size and structural dimensions. Subsequently, he investigated whether the predicted patterns of association between size and structure, particularly measures of differentiation, held for all departments equally or whether such effects were found more strongly for departments that experienced a recent change in leadership. Meyer (1975) observed that the predicted size-structure relationships held more strongly when leadership had changed in the finance department. However, one might wonder whether agency chiefs have the authority to change structures within the finance agency and whether the structural changes accompanying changes in finance department leadership are peculiar just to the finance department or reflect larger political change. As J. Freeman (1978: 338) has noted, "The answer to this question affects the locus of causation. If one's research is conducted at the local level, one may be missing the most important causal variables."

It is clearly critical to define units of analysis inclusively enough to incorporate the variation of interest. Meyer's studies of finance departments and Pennings's study of the stock brokerage offices treated as independent units subunits that were potentially under the influence of hierarchically superior control. By neglecting to attend to the effects of these larger structures, important sources of variation may be missed. J. Freeman (1973), in an early study of the effects of the environment on the size of the administrative component, noted that care must be taken in studying subunits of organizations as separate units. Changes in the administrative intensity of the unit may reflect either the effects of environmental variables on the amount of administration required or where that administration is performed. Administrative tasks may be moved from headquarters to subunits, or the reverse; correlating the administrative component's size with other variables can be misleading if attention is not given to where the administrative functions are performed.

This problem of considering subsidiaries without considering the effect of the parent organization on the subsidiary is exacerbated in the sample used in the Aston research (e.g., Pugh, Hickson, and Hinings, 1969) in which subsidiaries were treated as separate units along with entire firms. Some variation in structuring and in the relationship between factors of context and structure could easily be due to the mixing of units of various types in the same sample. Clearly, one would expect more consistent relations between context and structure for units in which such decisions on organizational design can be made without regard to the demands of the parent organization and its managers. And, the type of functions performed, as well as how they are organized, could differ among headquarters or entire firms and subsidiary units.

Organizations are, of course, hierarchical in the sense that they are comprised of smaller units (Simon, 1962) such as individuals and groups. This fact suggests that research spanning multiple levels of analysis may be both useful and necessary (Roberts, Hulin, and Rousseau, 1978). Lincoln and Zeitz (1980) have argued that it is necessary to separate individual from organizational effects to test theories that may operate at both levels. They further suggested that an analysis of covariance framework affords an appropriate mechanism for accomplishing this. Using Hauser's (1971) path-analytic approach to covariance analysis, Lincoln and Zeitz demonstrated how effects operating at the individual level could be distinguished from those operating at the organizational level. Using data from 20 social service organizations, they estimated a model in which decentralization was the dependent variable; lateral communications and administrative intensity were intermediate dependent variables; and size, the amount of division of labor, professionalization, and change in the task environment were exogenous variables. The important finding was that estimates of total effects in some instances hid differences in processes that were operating at the individual as contrasted with the organizational level of analysis.

The choice of the level of analysis focuses attention and affects the types of variables considered in the analysis. By far the majority of the studies contained in the domain of organizations and organization theory have proceeded using the individual as the unit of analysis. Thus, in a typical study of motivation, employees in a single organization may be surveyed to assess their perceptions of job characteristics, their growth need strength, and their attitudes and motivational states (e.g., Hackman and Oldham, 1975). The analysis considers each individual observation as independent. Because the focus is on the individual, attention is given to individual-level variables such as individual demographics, needs (Alderfer,

1972; Maslow, 1943), and attitudes. The effects of more inclusive variables such as the normative context as well as the technology, economic conditions, and so forth that might affect individual reactions to work are often neglected. Although it is not inevitable that the choice of the unit must delimit the kind of variables used to explain the phenomenon under investigation, a limited focus is almost always the consequence of selecting some units rather than others. Thus, the critique of task design and job attitudes literatures as being too preoccupied with needs theories and neglecting contextual effects on the assessment of job characteristics and the development of job attitudes (Salancik and Pfeffer, 1978a) reflects the limited set of variables and limited perspective adopted by researchers in the literature. This focus is, in part, a consequence of the attention-focusing properties of the choice of a particular unit and level of analysis.

The Individualist-Structuralist Controversy

Thus far, we have talked about issues of good scientific practice, that is, of units of analysis problems that impact the validity of the conclusions drawn from data. However, there is, as noted previously, another aspect to the levels of analysis issue—at what level explanation is most productively focused. The question involves fundamental epistemological beliefs about the nature of human interaction and social structure.

One position, the individualist position, has been that organizations do not behave, people do (Weick, 1969). Weick explicitly rejected the notions of organization and structures as being too static and too abstracted; rather, he emphasized organizing, the process by which individual behaviors become interstructured, organized, and interdependent (e.g., Allport, 1962). For Weick, the fundamental element was cycles of behavior, action followed by reaction followed by further interaction. Organizations, and organizational processes, could not be understood except by considering the organizing process, and that was a process accomplished through the interactions among people, continually reaccomplished and renewed.

In a similar vein, Argyris (1972) took organizational sociology to task, arguing that analyzing larger collectivities in terms of their structural properties has led to an unwarranted neglect of the processes that occur within such units that produce the observed results. Collins (1981) has also argued that descriptions and analyses of macrostructures should be grounded in microanalysis of behavior:

> . . . there is no such thing as a "state," an "economy," a "culture," a "social class." There are only collections of individual people acting in par-

ticular kinds of micro-situations — collections which are characterized . . . by a kind of shorthand . . . a series of tacit summaries between the actual life experiences and the way in which they are finally reported . . . if macrophenomena are made up of aggregations and repetitions of many similar micro-events, we can sample these essential microcomponents and use them as the empirical basis of all other sociological constructions (1981: 988).

Thus, Collins maintained that concepts could be made empirical only by "grounding" them through samples of the microevents that make up the macrophenomena. It is necessary, according to his position, to translate all such macroconstructs into their microevent equivalents, much as Weick (1969) translated the macrophenomenon of organization into the micro-events of interlocked cycles of behavior.

Collins's second argument was that

. . . . the *active* agents in any sociological explanation must be micro-situational. Social patterns, institutions, and organizations are only abstractions from the behavior of individuals and summaries of the distribution of different microbehaviors in time and space. These abstractions and summaries do not *do* anything . . . *the dynamics as well as the inertia in any causal explanation of social structure must be microsituational; all macroconditions have their effects by impinging upon actors' situational motivations* (1981: 989–990).

An excellent example of the kind of analysis that appears to be consistent with Collins's position is that undertaken by Schelling (1978). Schelling (1978: 13) provided numerous examples of a kind of analysis that "explores the relation between the behavior characteristics of the *individuals* who comprise some social aggregate and the characteristics of the *aggregate*." Schelling, in other words, sought to translate how individual motivations might combine to produce macroevents and how macroconditions impinge on individual motivations to further affect both individual behavior and the resultant aggregate of that behavior.

Collins did not argue that the macroconcepts of organization, culture, class, and so forth should be eliminated completely in theories of behavior. He noted, "It is strategically impossible for sociology to do without this kind of macro summary. It would take too much time to recount all the micro-events that make up any large-scale social pattern, and a total recounting in any case would be tedious and unrewarding" (Collins, 1981: 988). But although these macroconstructs might be useful as summaries, as aggregate theoretical constructs, Collins argued that they are insufficient as empirical explanations of social processes. He argued:

> . . . the ultimate empirical validation of sociological statements
> depends upon their microtranslations. By this standard, virtually all
> sociological evidence as yet presented is tentative only. This . . . does not
> mean it may not be a useful approximation. . . . Success at some degree of
> microtranslation . . . is the test of whether the macro statement is a good
> approximation or a misleading reification (1981: 988).

What this line of argument means is that statements like "size causes
differentiation" (Blau, 1970; Meyer, 1972a), "environmental uncertainty
causes decentralization" (Burns and Stalker, 1961; Lawrence and Lorsch,
1967), or "the degree of routineness of the organization's technology causes
the degree of formalization and decentralization" (Hage and Aiken, 1969)
are not permitted at all, or are permitted only as first approximations. Since
it is presumably individuals who act, it is necessary to develop some
understanding of the *processes*, presumably mediated by individuals, that
link increasing size to increasing differentiation, environmental uncertainty
to decentralization, or routine technologies to more formalized and centralized systems. Indeed, some would define concepts such as formalization
and decentralization in terms of individual behaviors, and others would
argue that such concepts are not useful because they are abstractions and
aggregations of individual-level behavior and processes that should be the
ultimate focus of the analysis.

The other position, the structuralist position, is that collectivities, such
as organizations, can be understood by relying on structural concepts and
without necessarily considering or studying the microprocesses that occur
within them. This point of view argues that there is an enduring, empirical
reality to macrostructural concepts such as role, formalization, centralization, and organizational structure. Collectivities and macrostructural constructs are more than just the aggregation or sum of the individuals or activities that constitute them. This position is represented most strongly in
sociology in which the study of social psychology within the discipline is of
diminishing prominence and status.

One argument mounted for the structuralist (as contrasted with the individualist) position is that individualists have confused questions with
answers. Thus, instead of asking the question of whether a focus on the individual level of analysis is more productive for analyzing behavior, the individualist position asserts the answer of the primacy of individual-level
phenomena without really exploring alternatives. Thus, Mayhew noted:

> Individualists, with their focus on individuals and individual activity, do
> not have a question, they have an answer. They carry this answer around
> until they encounter a question and then restate this question *in terms of
> their answer* without regard to how weak the answer may be or, indeed,

without regard to whether the answer has anything at all to do with the
question in the first place. . . . The question is: What explains social
phenomena? The question is not: How does the behavior of individuals explain social phenomena (1980: 363).

Mayhew argued that individualists commit a logical fallacy in arguing
that because macrostructures are comprised of individuals and individual
behavior, they must be analyzed solely in those terms:

> It is a fallacy to claim that because X is present in or part of Y, then the ex-
> planation of Y must involve X. Otherwise, one could argue that because
> the average hair length of individuals in a group is always present in and
> part of the situation to be explained, then the average hair length of group
> members must be *taken into account* in any explanation of what happens in
> the group. Leslie White . . . noted this fallacy long ago (1980: 363).

There is yet another problem in the individualist position on
understanding social phenomena. That is, in arguing that social entities
must be studied in terms of their underlying processes, one embarks on a
process of reductionism from which there is no logical stopping. Concepts
such as attitudes, conflict, values, goals, and so forth, which are regularly
used in individual-level explanations of behavior, are themselves hypothetical constructs and in many cases aggregates of even more molar
behaviors. Thus, the process of arguing that behavior must be understood
in terms of its microprocesses can lead to the study of behavior in almost
biological terms. Mayhew has again stated the position:

> Structuralists generally consider that there are two fields of study relevant
> to understanding human society: biology and (the structural version of)
> sociology. They fail to see any psychic (mental) phenomena falling in be-
> tween these two. . . . Structuralists tend to agree with Kunkel that
> sociologists have made too many unwarranted assumptions about human
> beings. Structuralists consider that the human brain is a biological
> phenomenon and that its electrochemical processes are the subject matter
> of biology. . . . Human organisms are conceived as information and
> energy processing machines. . . . Accordingly, structuralists do not assume
> that people think, that people are conscious, or have a mind as these terms
> are defined by individualists. . . . From the structuralist point of view,
> what individualists call "being conscious" is an electrochemical configura-
> tion not unlike the one projected on a television screen (1980: 346-347).

The structuralist critique of the individualist position is, therefore, (1)
that the presumed requirement for using individuals as the unit of analysis
because organizations are comprised of individuals and individual behavior

incorporates a logical fallacy; (2) that those adopting this perspective have confused a question as to what is the most productive level of analysis in terms of developing theory with the assertion of an answer to this question, the individual level of analysis; (3) that the logic underlying the individualist position leads to reductionism that must, logically, result in attempting to account for behavior in essentially biological terms; and (4) that the individualist approach to understanding organizations and other social phenomena ultimately tends to involve reliance on hypothetical constructs that are not directly observable or measurable but that largely reside in the heads of people. This means it requires the cooperation of the objects of study to learn about them, and this further requires sharing a language and coming to speak about behavior not necessarily in the theoretically most useful terms but in language that can enable the researcher and the subject to converse. This reliance on unobservable, hypothetical constructs residing within the heads of people makes some researchers uncomfortable.

> What individualists call psychology is for the structuralist either a part of biology, or it is an item of data in a culture which posits psychic phenomena (in the same sense that witchcraft is an item of data in a culture which posits witches). To the structuralist, people who talk about self-concepts are like people who talk about witches . . . psychology is contemporary civilization's witchcraft and psychologists are its corresponding witchdoctors (Mayhew, 1980: 346).

Although Mayhew intentionally overstated the argument as part of a debate, he makes an important point. Theories that rely on unobservable variables lodged in individual minds and with strong ideological overtones may be as much religion as social science. Indeed, March (1976) explicitly used the metaphor of religion in describing models of individual rational choice.

The structural alternative to the individual level of analysis calls for analyzing collective structures using variables and measures that capture important dimensions in theoretically meaningful and usable ways. As Mayhew (1980) explained structuralism:

> In this view, the individual is never the unit of analysis in either research or theory construction. Rather, in this *structuralist* conception of social life, sociologists are studying a communication network mapped on some human population. That network, the interaction which proceeds through it, and the social structures which emerge in it are the subject matter. . . . In studying organization, structuralists are concerned with at least two kinds of phenomena: (1) aggregated properties of populations and (2) *emergent* (purely structural) properties of organization itself (1980: 338).

Thus, for instance, structuralists might study the degree of differentiation, the degree of stratification, the extent of specialization or division of labor, and the properties of networks (such as their interconnectedness or centrality). Structuralists do not take their task to be that of studying individual behavior per se, rather that of studying social structures such as organizations:

> Structuralists do not study human behavior. The behavior they do study is that of the variables which define various aspects of social organization, its population, environment, ideological and technological subsystems. . . . From my structuralist point of view, the psychological concerns . . . do not bear on questions of social structure and organization, and at best would have only a secondary relevance to them. . . . If one assumes the structure of society in order to examine its impact on the immediate acts, thoughts, and feelings of individuals, one has assumed most of what has to be explained (Mayhew, 1980: 339).

The point of this discussion is that the choice of units and levels of analysis is too important to be left to unconscious belief, ideology, habit, or empirical convenience. First, the choice of a unit can have important implications for the analysis of data and the testing of theory. Second, the issue of the most productive level of analysis in terms of the development of a theory of organizations has yet to be examined or considered really systematically. With the possible exception of some of the work of Blau (1970, 1977) and population ecology (Hannan and Freeman, 1977), organization theory has yet to pay much attention to the analysis of organizations from a structural perspective.

THE SOCIAL CONTEXT OF ORGANIZATION THEORY

It is apparent from Table 1-1 that the study of organizations is diverse in a number of dimensions. But, the diversity of the field and its organization can be tied quite directly to various contextual aspects. First, consider its overall diversity. It can be argued that the proliferation of various theories at different levels of analysis with different perspectives on action reflects both the relative youth of the field and its interdisciplinary character. The interdisciplinary nature of the field means that there will be variety in every dimension of the theories brought into the field. The comparative youthfulness means that there will not yet have been the time required for the development of a critical focus and the paring down of the various perspectives that have been imported.

As to the youth of the field, there can be little doubt that the study of organizations as a distinct, albeit interdisciplinary, subject matter is fairly recent. As J. Freeman (1982) has noted, a review of the *American Journal of Sociology* index from the time of that journal's founding in 1895 until 1947 revealed no entry for organizations or formal organizations. The index to the *American Sociological Review* published in 1955 had but six entries on "bureaucracy." Not until the next index of the *American Journal of Sociology* appeared in 1965 did the subject of organizations emerge as a distinct category in the discipline of sociology.

Of course, industrial psychology has a tradition that goes back at least to the early 1900s; and much of the study of organizational behavior today has its roots in that tradition. However, again it seems that the development of organizational psychology, as distinct from industrial psychology, is a relatively recent occurrence. Leavitt (1962) has distinguished industrial psychology from organizational psychology as follows:

> Organizational psychology occupies itself with the study of organizations and organizational processes. It is as much descriptive as normative; as much or more basic as applied; as much interested in developing theories of organizational behavior as ways of improving organizational practice . . . the most unique aspect of organizational psychology is its two-wayness . . . industrial psychology has been applied psychology, carrying psychological wisdom to real industrial organizations. In contrast, organizational psychology views organizations as . . . deserving of research; and is therefore as much concerned with the nature of systems and the nature of human decision making as with any applied problems . . . the second differentiating characteristic of organizational psychology — its address. It tends very often to be finding a home in business schools (1962: 26-27).

The change in the name of Division 14 of the American Psychological Association from Industrial Psychology to Industrial and Organizational Psychology in 1970 has more than symbolic significance; it recognizes some distinct and unique aspects to the study of organizations that have emerged in the recent past.

> In summary then, a distinguishable new area of psychological teaching and research already exists. It is allied to classical industrial psychology and to human relations psychology, but it differs from both of them in its greater concern with descriptive and experimental research; its emphasis on understanding organizations as well as improving them; its central location in business schools rather than in psychology departments or industry itself; and its proximity to certain areas of teaching and research in economics, sociology, and mathematics (Leavitt, 1962: 29).

There is additional evidence of the newness of the field. Scott (1981:8) has written that "until the late 1940's, organizations did not exist as a distinct field of . . . inquiry." The *Administrative Science Quarterly*, an interdisciplinary journal devoted exclusively to the emerging field of organizational behavior and administration, began publication in 1956. The *Academy of Management Journal* began publication at that time also. It was in the mid-1950s that Leavitt's *Managerial Psychology* (1954) and March and Simon's *Organizations* (1958) appeared. With two journals and with the emergence of the first texts, the field of organizational behavior began to establish itself.

Although the field is relatively young, it has expanded fairly rapidly. At least one course in organizational behavior is required in virtually all M.B.A. programs, in most undergraduate programs in business, and in many programs in educational, hospital, and public administration. Estimates vary, but there are now somewhere between 125,000 and 200,000 students in the United States taking at least one course in organizational behavior in a given academic year.

And, the study of organizations is indeed interdisciplinary. Courses covering some aspect of organizational analysis and research on organizations as a distinct focus of study occur in anthropology, political science, economics, psychology, and sociology departments, as well as in various schools of administration, including business, public, hospital and health, and programs of educational administration. Indeed, there are relatively few professional schools that do not have courses and research on organizations. City planning programs, library schools, and even some industrial engineering programs all have the study of organizations represented within them.

As Roberts, Hulin, and Rousseau (1978) have noted, one consequence of the interdisciplinary nature of the field has been the focus on different levels of analysis. For the most part, sociologists have been interested in the study of organizations as units, while psychologists have taken an approach focusing on the individual as the unit of analysis. Economists, political scientists, and anthropologists have also tended to focus more on the macro-structural aspects of organizations, though with some exceptions. Thus, the different units of analysis visible in the disciplines become mirrored in the different levels of analysis incorporated into organizational research. The perspectives on action are not, however, identified with disciplines as strongly. Within both psychology and sociology, one can readily find examples of theories that take a rational, conscious choice or an external, situational constraint perspective on action. Rather, differences in the perspective on action come, it would seem, from other kinds of social forces.

The Environment and Demography of Organization Theory

It is clear that the unit of analysis used to explain organizations as well as the perspective on action adopted does not vary randomly across departments or disciplines or over time. We have already noted some disciplinary differences in the level of analysis. But, more than disciplinary distinctions are involved. The study of organizations is inextricably bound up with the study of the management and control of organizations. As organizations have come to employ larger and larger segments of the work force, and as people have tended to be increasingly employed in larger organizations, the study of organizations has become the study of an important social institution that has a number of effects on individuals. Faber (1973) has summarized some of the data on the change in the arrangements of work:

> The trend of the past 70 years or more, and particularly in recent years, has been a decrease in small independent enterprises and self-employment, and an increase in the domination of large corporations and government in the workforce. In the middle of the 19th century, less than half of all employed people were wage and salary workers. By 1950 it was 80%, and by 1970, 90%. . . . Out of 3,534,000 industrial units employing 70% of the civilian labor force, 2% of the units accounted for 50.6% of the employees, and more than 27% of the employed were accounted for in 0.3% of the units (1973: 21).

Organizations are important not only as objects of study in their own right, then, but also for their effects on individuals and the economy. It has been argued, for instance, that organizations have effects on the development of individual personality (e.g., Argyris, 1957), the degree of satisfaction with life (Campbell, Converse, and Rodgers, 1976), the extent to which stress and tension are experienced (Kahn et al., 1964), the earning of income and one's place in the occupational structure (e.g., Granovetter, 1981), and even on health and mortality (e.g., Caplan, 1971; Levinson, 1964). Thus, the perspective on action taken and unit of analysis adopted varies depending on whether one is interested in understanding the impacts of organizations on society (Aldrich, 1979), the impacts of organizations on individuals (Argyris, 1957), or how to manage and control persons who work in organizations (Ouchi, 1981). Furthermore, the research perspective, in terms of both levels of analysis and point of view on action, will vary depending on whether an action-oriented point of view is taken, whether the perspective of managers or workers is adopted, and whether one underlying ideology and belief system or another motivates the investigation.

The social context of organization theory has varied, first of all, over time. In an example of an analysis of the effects of time and context on a discipline, Cartwright (1979) has explored the development of the field of social psychology. He noted that concern with democratic versus authoritarian leadership styles, research prominent in the 1940s and early 1950s, could be traced to the migration of a number of German social psychologists to this country around the time of World War II. The interest in attitudes, often focused around racial attitudes, and the question of whether attitudes led to behavior or the reverse, could be traced to the early efforts at integration occurring in the 1950s and, particularly, the integration of schools mandated by the Supreme Court's decision in the *Brown* case. Cartwright (1979) argued:

> It is true . . . that the substantive content of the knowledge attained in any field of science is ultimately determined by the intrinsic nature of the phenomena under investigation, since empirical research is essentially a process of discovery with an internal logic of its own. But it is equally true that the knowledge attained is the product of a social system and, as such, is basically influenced by the properties of that system and by its cultural, social, and political environment (1979: 82).

Because organization theory is a relatively young field, we do not have a long time period to consider. However, it is possible to argue that the emergence of the field itself can be related to changes in the structure of work over time. As several authors have noted, the first large-scale enterprises used systems of internal contracting rather than hierarchical control (Braverman, 1974; Williamson, 1975). As Braverman noted concerning these internal contracting systems, they

> . . . bore the marks of the origins of industrial capitalism in mercantile capitalism, which understood the buying and selling of commodities but not their production, and sought to treat labor like all other commodities. . . . The subcontracting and "putting out" systems were plagued by problems of irregularity of production, loss of materials in transit and through embezzlement, slowness of manufacture, lack of uniformity and uncertainty of the quality of the product. But most of all, they were limited by their inability to change the processes of production (1974: 63).

The substitution of internal contracting with hierarchical control introduced new and unfamiliar problems — problems of management:

> In the workshops of the Medieval "master," control was based on the obedience which the customs of the age required. . . . With the advent of the modern industrial group in large factories in the urban areas, the whole

> process of control underwent a fundamental revolution. It was now the
> owner or manager of a factory . . . who had to secure or extract from his
> "employees" a level of obedience and/or cooperation which would enable
> him to exercise control. There was no individual interest in the success of
> the enterprise other than the extent to which it provided a livelihood (Ur-
> wick and Brech, 1946: 10-11).

R. Edwards (1979) noted that this control process went through three
phases. In the first phase, there was hierarchical control. This was exercised
chiefly through the relatively arbitrary power of bosses or their foremen to
hire, fire, and discipline workers. By passing favorable jobs to those who
cooperated, by firing or physically disciplining those who resisted control,
and by hiring persons likely to be susceptible to control (such as immi-
grants), control over the work force was obtained, although at the cost of
some very violent strikes. In the next phase of control, technical control, the
control process was embedded more in the technology of the work itself,
with the classic example being the mass production assembly line. This process of technical control accelerated the separation of work into the planning of the work, an engineering task, and the doing of the work, a relatively mechanical activity (Braverman, 1974). This led to some deskilling of the
work force (Braverman, 1974) and a consequent loss of power on the part of
workers. However, although the workers had lost power individually, they
had gained it collectively. It was easier to disrupt the highly mechanized, se-
quentially interdependent production lines; thus, technical control was a
relatively brief phase and was augmented quickly by bureaucratic control.

Note that in the early forms of control, the emphasis was on the hiring
and firing of individuals as the control strategy. Thus, the early concerns of
industrial psychology with identifying traits or characteristics of individuals
that would make them both capable and willing to do the work were consistent with the control task faced by organizations. Concerns with the administration of discipline, the selection of workers for mechanical skills,
and the selection of people who would be reliable were the concerns consistent with the organization of work at that time period and tended to be the
concerns reflected in the research done then. Recall that the Hawthorne
studies were originally intended to be examinations of the effects of physical
aspects of the workplace (such as the level of lighting) and incentive systems
on worker productivity.

Braverman (1974) has noted the close relationship between problems of
the workplace at that time and the development of a science of the psychology of the worker:

> Shortly after Taylor, industrial psychology and industrial physiology came
> into existence to perfect methods of selection, training, and motivation of

> workers. . . . The cardinal feature of these various schools . . . is that . . .
> they . . . concern themselves . . . with the conditions under which the
> worker may best be brought to cooperation in the scheme of work organ-
> ized by the industrial engineer (1974: 140).

Even in its initial stages, industrial psychology was very much attuned to
the needs of managers and to issues of practice. Thus, there was not much
concern with the structure of work. Rather,

> . . . most orthodox social scientists adhere firmly, indeed desperately,
> to the dictum that their task is not the study of the objective conditions of
> work, but only of the subjective phenomena to which these give rise: the
> degrees of "satisfaction" and "dissatisfaction" elicited by their questionnaires
> (1974: 141).

The initial simple organization of work involving control through hierarchy — and, later, technical control of the workplace — led to relatively simple and straightforward tasks for a psychology that was to be of use to management in the process of control. Writing of an early psychologist, Hugo
Munsterberg, Braverman (1974: 143) noted, "He sees the role of psychological science in industry as the selection of workers from among the pool offered on the labor market, and their acclimatization to the work routines
devised by 'civilization.'"

As R. Edwards (1979) noted, the subsequent emergence of bureaucratic
control has changed the relations in the workplace:

> Hierarchical relations were transformed from relations between (unequally
> powerful) people to relations between jobholders, or relations between jobs
> themselves, abstracted from the specific people or the concrete work tasks
> involved. "Rule of law" — the firm's law — replaced rule by supervisor com-
> mand (1979: 145).

With both changes in state and federal labor laws — including laws facilitating the formation of labor unions, safety and wage and hour regulations,
and, even more recently, laws concerning hiring and dismissal — coercive
control over the work force and a control policy based heavily on selection
mechanisms were no longer viable. Bureaucratic control and associated in-
ventions such as job ladders required job analysis, an increased concern
with issues of motivation, and an approach to leadership that relied less on
brute force or charisma and more on the development and use of authority
within a bureaucratic structure. Edwards has dated the introduction of
bureaucratic control as occurring in the 1940s. It is not, perhaps, surprising
that organizational behavior as a distinct field emerged shortly thereafter to

work on the numerous and more complex problems and issues that confronted managers using this new and more complicated control structure.

In the early years of organizational behavior, several problems confronted work organizations. First, in the 1950s, the work force was comparatively small. The Great Depression and World War II had hindered the formation of families and diminished fertility. In the context of labor scarcity, the early concerns within the field were focused very strongly on attracting and retaining those workers the firm did have and obtaining as much production as possible from these employees. Second, the emphasis on productivity and profit was consistent with the basically pro-business environment that prevailed in the 1950s and early 1960s. This was a time in which the social legitimacy of corporations was not very much questioned, in contrast to those periods around the turn of the century, during the Great Depression, or the period to follow in the 1970s. Business values of productivity and performance were emphasized — and emphasized also in the study of organizations.

The late 1960s and the Viet Nam War saw two changes that were reflected in the study of organizations. First, the post-World War II baby boom began to enter the work force. Thus, labor scarcity became a situation of labor surplus. More attention on issues such as careers, career plateauing, and the motivation of persons through incentives other than movement up a hierarchical career ladder (e.g., intrinsic motivation) drew increasing concern in the field of study. Second, American society was, to some extent, radicalized and politicized by the war, the urban riots of the middle 1960s, and the declining economic opportunities (Easterlin, 1980) confronting persons entering the labor force during the late 1960s and 1970s. These effects were also visible in the development of organization theory.

Perhaps the classic example of the impact of the times on research can be seen in the research of Staw. Staw's (1974) insightful treatment of the effects of commitment and justification on attitudes used the draft lottery as a natural randomization and samples of ROTC cadets as subjects. His studies of escalating commitment to a chosen course of action even in the face of apparent problems with the policy (Staw, 1976; Staw and Fox, 1977; Staw and Ross, 1978, 1980) draw heavily on the analogy of the escalating commitment of troops to the war in Viet Nam in the presence of evidence indicating that the policy was not achieving its desired objectives.

Two other themes can be seen to have emerged as a consequence of these social events. First, there was less respect for authority, in general, and work organization authority, in particular. Work organizations could no longer be justified solely in terms of productivity, or profits; rather, new emphases came to be placed on their effects on the total human experience;

emphasis grew on the quality of working life and, finally, the role of the workplace as a kind of substitute for other forms of affiliation such as families and communities (Ouchi and Jaeger, 1978). Second, with the increasing focus on politics in society came renewed attention to issues of power and politics in organizations (Bacharach and Lawler, 1980; Pfeffer, 1981a).

Clearly, this description of some important trends misses many other crosscurrents. Yet, in a fashion similar to that of Cartwright (1979) in the case of social psychology, it is possible to trace how shifting social contexts produced or were reflected in shifting concerns in organizational behavior research, as well as, perhaps, in the very birth and growth of the field.

Differences across disciplines can be seen, too. Industrial psychology (Baritz, 1960) had, from almost the beginning, been an applied field. This association between industrial psychology and psychology, as well as the tendency to focus on the individual as the level of analysis, tended to make psychology closer to the dominant concerns of organizational behavior as practiced in professional schools — how to manage and control individuals in organizational contexts. The study of organizations in business and other professional schools tended to be associated with taking a perspective on action that emphasized the role and potency of the administrator — this was the prospectively rational perspective. Managers and administrators were being trained, and a perspective on action that emphasized what they could do, and that legitimated the formal, rationalistic models that were taught in professional schools, was the one almost universally adopted. There was also a tendency to take an individual level of analysis perspective, in part dictated by the administrative focus and in part dictated by some ideological blind spots. The focus on practice implied that one should be able to tell practicing managers what to do, and few managers are in positions to redesign entire organizations, let alone interorganizational and economic systems. Rather, most managers spend most of their time interacting with their bosses, peers, and subordinates (Mintzberg, 1973). A focus, therefore, on such interaction, as embodied in topics such as conflict, leadership, motivation, and group processes, grows naturally from concerns with what one can tell individual managers about doing their jobs.

By contrast, some different issues emerged in the study of organizations from a sociological perspective. First, various studies have indicated that sociologists tend to have a somewhat more radical political orientation (e.g., Ladd and Lipset, 1975). The focus on social systems or organizations as units tended to make sociological research less proximately relevant to managerial concerns. Thus, sociological research has emphasized more the relationship between organizations and other social institutions, such as the state, and social processes, such as stratification. There is less concern with the practice of administration, though whether such sociological research is, in fact, any less practical in terms of its implications is less clear. The European approach to organizations has been, in general, closer to the sociological than to the industrial psychological-professional school model. With a strong tradition in critical theory (e.g., Clegg and Dunkerley, 1980), and with an emphasis on conflict and politics arising in basic disciplines as well as in industrial relations, the European perspective has been, on the whole, substantially less practice focused and more concerned with issues such as the relationship between work organizations and other social institutions as well as conflicts among and within organizations.

Some of the differences between contexts have been imported into the professional school, and particularly business school, context as a result of the change in recruitment practices. As developed in more detail elsewhere (Pfeffer, 1981a: chapter 9), several forces combined to increase the recruitment of persons trained in the basic discipline departments onto business school faculties in most subject areas, and certainly in organizational behavior. Such factors included the publication of the Gordon and Howell (1959) report, which called for more systematic and fundamental research and more training in the basic skills; the expansion of graduate programs in the arts and sciences that occurred in the early 1960s, which wound up producing many more graduates than the discipline departments themselves could absorb; and increased availability of research funding and the consequent growing emphasis on research in American universities generally during this period. With the recruitment of more people from the basic disciplines, and particularly psychology because of its close connections on both levels of analysis and practice-focus dimensions, research in business schools changed. Whereas the original research coming from schools of administration had tended to be quite prescriptive and oriented toward developing general principles (Barnard, 1948; Gulick and Urwick, 1937) or had consisted of relating various case or clinical experiences (e.g., Barnard, 1938), research became, over time, more quantitative (Daft, 1980), more systematically comparative, and more grounded in questions arising from the disciplines. This heterogeneity brought some increased conflict among paradigms within professional schools, leading to differences of opinion within individual schools and to a division of labor between schools, with some taking a more applied, practice-oriented, managerial focus, rejecting the influence of the disciplines, while others adopted a more disciplinary orientation, in effect becoming applied social science departments.

The simplest conclusion from this discussion is that if one wants to understand the perspective on action, level of analysis, and even the methodology that is likely to characterize a person's work, knowing (1) when that individual was trained for entry into the field, (2) what department he trained in, and (3) where the person works now can provide information that will enable a fairly accurate prediction of the individual's research along those dimensions. The differences visible within the field across cohorts and academic disciplines and between disciplinary departments and professional schools are all explicable in terms of the context of those doing organizational analysis.

THEORY VERSUS APPLICATION IN THE STUDY OF ORGANIZATIONS

This emphasis on the effects of context on the study of organizations becomes particularly important if such differences in level of analysis or perspective on action come to have effects on the development of knowledge. One of the more important effects of context, as seen in the preceding discussion, is whether research tends to focus on concerns of organizational managers or whether research focuses on the development of theory qua theory without regard to immediate applicability. This debate has implications for the level of analysis and perspective on action issues — those who focus on practice tend to take a rational perspective most often at the individual level of analysis. The debate also has implications for how to go about enhancing our understanding of organizations.

The position of those who argue for grounding organizational research or other social science inquiry in the concerns of practice is either that description and understanding are inevitably value laden and ideological — and, thus, the development of pure theory, untainted by practical concerns, is a mirage; or that attempts to develop a theory of organizations free of concerns of application or practice are inevitably unproductive even for the intended aim of the acquisition of scientific knowledge. Gergen (1978) has argued that there is an inevitable intrusion of values, ideologies, and practical concerns into research, because, first, research is not value free and scientifically neutral by its very conduct and, second, people have interests in the particular substantive implications that result from research.

For Gergen, the very selection of concepts, variables, and what is to be studied is an act with ideological and practical consequences. He noted that "understanding may also entail 'assigning a meaning' to something, thus creating its status through the employment of concepts" (Gergen, 1978: 1344). As Unger (1975: 32) has argued, what are perceived as facts, and what is distinguished from other phenomena inevitably results from the particular theoretical position one has adopted before one begins the study. Thus, for Gergen, there is no such thing as pure description or pure understanding. The very act of choosing concepts and distinguishing among events involves the researcher in the construction and interpretation of the events, and this is never a value-free or intellectually neutral process for the very fact that judgment is required — judgment applied by the individual researcher or a group of researchers. As Gergen argued:

> . . . activity appears in a state of near continuous motion, its forms are infinitely variable, fresh patterns may emerge at any point. Under such conditions, the conceptual standpoint of the observer may become an extremely powerful determinant of what is perceived. . . . Each perspective may operate as a lens through which experience is served up in differing form (1978: 1348).

Gergen also argued that the very methodology of the social psychological experiment, as well as of other hypothesis-testing procedures, tends to produce support for the hypotheses being tested. Thus, the methodology of science itself is not objective, value free, and unencumbered by external influences. Inevitably, one measures according to one's theoretical predispositions, analyzes the data accordingly, and thus, tends to produce support for the initial conjectures. Gergen wrote:

> To the extent that the relationship between theoretical terms and empirical operations is an ambiguous one, the investigator's latitude of choice for testing any given hypothesis is increased . . . securing anticipated results speaks far less to the empirical status of the hypothesis than it does to the investigator's familiarity with the shared meanings and mores of the subjects under test (1978: 1352).

Gergen also argued that what is selected for study, as well as the theoretical concepts used to address the phenomenon, is a result of ideology and beliefs held by those doing the investigating. Thus, to pretend scientific inquiry is value free is to be intentionally misleading. The view that science is free of values had, according to Gergen, several negative effects on the conduct of that science:

> . . . the scientific paradigm treats the individual solely as an object to be acted upon, thus denying him his subjecthood or status as a free agent . . . in their underlying epistemology, positivist formulations obliterate the critical issues of social ethics; such formulations appear to be nonevaluative and, as such, resist questioning on ethical or ideological grounds . . . with fundamental questions of value obscured, the critical problem of ends is replaced with the relatively superficial concern with means . . . we find that the fruits of neutrality are passionate in their consequences (1978: 1355).

Gergen argued that what is needed was what he called "generative theory." Ideological commitments and advocacy are important parts of the scientific process, and "undermining confidence in commonly shared assumptions represents a positive goal for scientific theory" (1978: 1356). Such commitments and advocacy are mobilized, he implied, around specific substantive concerns. Gergen's position is close to that of Argyris's, who on numerous occasions has argued for the need to ground organization theory in practical issues. Argyris (1968, 1972) has maintained that the best way of overcoming problems arising from the use of static correlational analyses and contrived variables and situations with no external validity was to develop and test theory in clinical settings, as part of a consulting or change effort. Argyris has articulated the second reason for having a practice focus — that only by focusing on real, substantive problems can valid theory be developed.

Argyris (1972) noted that there were several ways to test theory in field settings:

> The first is to derive predictions from the theory about what one should find under given conditions, then go to the non-contrived world, locate such conditions, and note if the predicted consequences actually occurred. A second method is to make *a priori* predictions of what one would find under a differential set of conditions. This includes comparative studies. . . . It also includes the study of change over time that is created by forces not under the direct or indirect influence of the researcher. The third, and most rigorous test of a theory, is to be able to increase the conditions hypothesized; to create the variables, and to predict *a priori* what should happen. The third mode is the most rigorous because it involves the researcher in generating, managing, and controlling the variables under consideration (1972: 85-86).

It is only by testing theories in actual applications, Argyris maintained, that valid knowledge could be developed. He argued, "The applicability and utility of knowledge are criteria that should be integrated and given equal potency in the development of behavioral science theories and the execution of such empirical research" (1972: 83). By confronting real situations and the constraints of providing usable, practical knowledge to guide ongoing organizations, Argyris believed that theory would be not only more useful but also more valid as a descriptive statement of the world as it exists as apart from the world of the scientist's mind.

While Gergen and particularly Argyris have argued that social science theory — and in the latter case, particularly organization theory — has not been enough focused on applications and practice, others have argued that it has been *too* focused on managerial concerns, with resulting harm to the development of knowledge. Nehrbass (1979) has commented on the ideological content of some streams of organizational research, such as participative decision making and the quality of working life movement. Nehrbass argued that this ideological content inhibited the ability of the field to learn from empirical data. Nehrbass believed that because of ideology, data that yield results contrary to that ideology are systematically ignored. Thus, knowledge develops from empirical research with great difficulty. Not only are Gergen's (1978) arguments about the self-fulfilling prophecy aspect of the research process apropos, but even when contradictory findings emerge, they are ignored in those domains in which there is a strong ideological component.

Baritz (1960) has criticized industrial psychology, one of the more applied subspecialties within psychology, because of its close association with industry. He argued that the close association between the scientists and industry, either through direct employment relationships or through indirect linkages such as consulting or research support, hinders the development of knowledge:

> . . . the usual industrial social scientist, because he accepted the norms of the elite dominant in his society, was prevented from functioning critically, was compelled by his own ideology and the power of America's managers to supply the techniques helpful to managerial goals. In what should have been a healthful tension between mind and society, the industrial social scientist in serving the industrial elite had to abandon the wider obligations of the intellectual who is a servant of his own mind (1960: 194).

The problem is that working on applied problems tends to lead to considering only those variables that are defined as relevant by management, using their definitions and their conceptual constructions (Pugh, 1966). Thus, potentially critical factors may be neglected. For instance, commenting on Elton Mayo, the founder of the human relations movement and an influential figure in the development of organization theory, Baritz (1960: 200) noted, "Mayo throughout his inquiring and productive life ignored labor, power and politics."

Calder's (1977) critique of the leadership literature follows a similar logic. Calder argued that one of the problems with that literature was that it often failed to move beyond first-level, common-sense concepts and constructs. This problem is a result of the applied focus of that literature (Gordon, Kleiman, and Hanie, 1978). Calder (1977: 182) noted that he did not deny that intuition and everyday language and observation could be sources of sound theory and insight, only that "the constructs and logic of everyday language can be accepted as scientific without additional support." Similarly, Mechanic (1963) argued that the dearth of theory in much organizational research could be attributed to the selection of variables not on the basis of their potential for theory building but on their familiarity and importance to practitioners. Mechanic (1963: 145) noted that concepts useful to administrators "may prove sterile to researchers." Gordon, Kleiman, and Hanie (1978) have argued that one of the reasons for the lack of theory in industrial psychology has been the too close concern with practical implications.

Thus, there are two principal arguments mustered by those favoring downgrading practical or applied concerns: the ideology associated with application and service to management dulls the critical faculties and makes it difficult to advance knowledge from empirical research; and adopting managerial definitions of what are the important problems, what are the important variables, and sometimes even how to measure the variables may lead to the neglect of important explanatory factors and to the phrasing of issues in ways that make them scientifically useless.

Both sides in this debate have telling arguments. It is clear that Gergen's comments on the self-fulfilling nature of the research process and on the inevitable intrusion of ideology are valid. It is also clear that without the constraints of applicability, abstracted, jargon-filled theoretical constructions can emerge with no scientific or practical utility. Yet, it is evident that the practice focus clearly delimits what is studied, how it is studied, and what theoretical perspectives are employed. To leave this much control implicitly in the hands of others is to assume that the scientists have no particular insights or skills that afford them a comparative advantage; they become collectors and distributors of managerial wisdom but not generators of insights of their own. The ideology of management comes to color what they do and how they do it. Although the intrusion of ideology may be inevitable, it is not clear that management ideology, and solely management ideology, is a healthy foundation on which to rest a science of organizations.

SOME CRITERIA FOR EVALUATING THEORY

Before embarking on a closer examination of the theories represented in Table 1-1, it is useful to consider what criteria might be kept in mind in evaluating them. For we want to understand these approaches to organizational analysis not only as products of the context in which they are created but also, if possible, in terms of their relative usefulness as conceptual levers.

There are a number of criteria by which theories can be evaluated. Mayhew (1981), for instance, proposed three:

> . . . there are three related and fundamental criteria which can . . . be invoked to examine the tenability of a position. These are: (1) clarity, (2) parsimony, and (3) logical coherence . . . no viewpoint can be appreciated . . . if it is stated in such obscure language that we cannot decide what is being discussed. Sometimes a lack of clarity boils down to a refusal to discuss certain critical questions, questions which must be answered for the theory to be intelligible . . . parsimony is critical to the development of any theory. . . . A theory that is too complex to be understood (or too complex to permit the implementation of research on critical questions) is no more than an appeal to incomprehensibility, a claim that what is being studied cannot be understood . . . logical coherence is a *sine qua non* of any intellectual enterprise (1981: 629).

In addition to these three, one might add two others: refutability and consistency with empirical data. Theories must not only be clear, parsimonious, and logically coherent, they should also be able to account for at least some of the variation observed in organizational behavior — they should, in other words, be consistent with empirical observation. And theories should be refutable. The logic of strong inference (e.g., Mackenzie and House, 1978) suggests that knowledge is gained only as ideas are *disconfirmed*. Because of the biases described by Gergen (1978), disconfirmation is a stronger test than confirmation. But whatever one's position on the issue of theory advancement through refutation, it is the case that a theory that is true by definition or for which the converse is very implausible is a tautology, not a theory. Without disconfirmability, empirical research is both unnecessary (for it can never shed light on the veracity or inaccuracy of a theory) and useless.

These five criteria might appear to be reasonably self-evident, but they are far from universally applied. Gergen (1969) has made the argument that another characteristic of theories, particularly theories of social behavior, is whether they fit prevailing social norms, values, and beliefs. On more than one occasion, I have heard students and colleagues describe theories as either good or bad because they seemed to be right — i.e., they fit prevailing views about organizational behavior. The problem with this as a criterion for evaluating theory is that prevailing norms and beliefs are as much lodged in ideology as in empiricism, and good values and beliefs may make very bad social science. Nevertheless, the criterion of fitting prevailing norms and expectations is one of the more potent criteria that is applied to evaluating theory, even if it is not a reasonable yardstick.

Thus, Kelley (1971) has noted that in developing causal explanations for behavior lay social scientists seek explanations that are not only correct but that also provide the sense of control over events. The desire for control is evidenced in Langer's (1975) illusion of control experiments, in which subjects were more willing to be in situations in which they engaged in activities that gave them a (false) sense of efficacy — e.g., picking the card from a deck or picking marbles of a given color from a jar, rather than having these objects selected for them. This desire for control manifests itself in the building of theories of organizations that encompass assumptions, often implicitly, of administrative efficacy. This does not mean that administrators are necessarily not efficacious — only that because of the existing social norms and biases in favor of control, theories that do not presume such efficacy start out with several strikes against them because of the potency of the fitting social beliefs criterion. Another bias of naïve observers is the attribution of causality to dispositional characteristics of the individual rather than to effects of his or her context (Jones and Nisbett, 1971; Ross, 1977). Thus, a person performing poorly on a task will be assumed to be incompetent or unmotivated even if task performance is entirely out of the individual's control. In a similar fashion, research that indicates that organizational performance or organizational structure is under the control of external factors is likely to be resisted — as seen in the substance of the critique of population ecology offered by Van de Ven (1979).

The criterion of parsimony means that theories that are simpler in their explanations, presuming fewer causal variables and more simple causal mechanisms (e.g., direct effects rather than multiple interactions), should be preferred, other things being equal. In fact, many of the theories turn this principle on its head, and some colleagues argue that theories should be evaluated according to whether they are "interesting." To intelligent people, *interesting* often means convoluted and complicated. Thus, the rule of parsimony is violated on a regular basis by many of the theories reviewed in this book. Clarity and comprehensibility imply that theories should be stated in a way that makes the operationalization of the concepts possible and makes understanding the argument a reasonable intellectual task. This criterion, unfortunately, flies in the face of another, held by some, which argues that if theories are so incomprehensible as to be virtually untestable, this tends to ensure long life for the theory (Shearing, 1973). Although in the particular instance in question this argument was cited in a facetious fashion, as we shall see, some of my colleagues have taken this advice to heart. And, we shall also see examples of widely held theories that persist in spite of the inability to find confirming evidence, or much of it in any case, as well as examples of tautologies. The reader is advised to watch out for all of these characteristics. If we are to build social science theories of any power or value, we will need to begin to pay much more attention to these criteria for evaluating knowledge structures. A good place to start is the evaluation of those theories currently in use for analyzing and explaining organizations.

CONCLUSION

Now equipped with some sense of the social context of organization theory, the outline of the dimensions to be used in arraying the various theories, and some concerns to be noted in evaluating theory and methodology, it is time to plunge into the thicket. The choice is to consider contrasting perspectives at the same level of analysis before moving on to the higher level of analysis. Thus, in Chapter 2 we describe some of the theories that treat individual or subunit behavior in organizations from a rational or at least quasi-rational perspective. In Chapter 3 we consider some situational and external constraint perspectives on individual behavior, as well as some perspectives that try to integrate the two approaches. In Chapter 4 we move up to the organizational level of analysis, considering various theories of rational action at the total organizational level, while in Chapter 5 the two perspectives that address external constraint and the external control of organizations are described and compared. In Chapter 6 we examine the emergent process explanations of organizational phenomena focused on microlevel behavior, while in Chapter 7 the same perspective as a framework for analyzing organization-level properties is explicated. Finally, in Chapter 8 we emerge from the underbrush to see what has been learned and to describe some potentially profitable, but thus far largely neglected, avenues of inquiry that might be of use in building better organization theory.

It should be clear that the two areas of controversy noted in this chapter, the individualist versus structuralist and theory versus practice disputes, are related to this overview of the domain of organization theory. The individualist versus structuralist dispute is relevant to the choice of the level of analysis, while the theory versus practice dispute tends to be associated with the perspective on action, but not inevitably, as there have been numerous applications of behavior modification (Luthans and Kreitner, 1975), an external constraint approach. Each of these positions is, in turn, asociated with the context and demography of those studying and practicing organizational analysis. Keeping these themes in mind can help in understanding the various theories to be examined.

2

MICROLEVEL
RATIONAL ACTION

Most of the research domain of organizational theory, and virtually all of that research that has emerged from a social psychological or industrial psychological tradition, had adopted a focus on the individual as the unit of analysis and proceeded from the premise of conscious, foresightful action guided by intent or purpose (Cummings, 1982; T. Mitchell, 1979). Several of the theories of this form are reviewed in this chapter. Expectancy theory (e.g., Vroom, 1964) argues that people undertake actions according to the probability that these actions will lead to some instrumentally valued outcome; goal theory (Locke, 1968) argues that people undertake actions to achieve their goals; needs theory argues that people act purposefully to fulfill their needs or to overcome need deficiencies (Alderfer, 1972; Maslow, 1943); and political theories assert that individual action is motivated to achieve some desired outcome such as more resources, promotion, or additional power (Pfeffer, 1981a).

The theories each share some common elements: (1) analysis proceeds from the basis of essentially individual-level concepts, such as preferences, goals, values, or needs; thus, social action is presumed (often implicitly) to be the result of some aggregation of individual-level behaviors and behavior-determining processes; (2) the behavior is the operation of a rational value- or utility-maximizing choice process; and (3) this process is based on the attainment of some valued needs, goals, preferences or the taking of action consistent with some attitudes, beliefs, or value judgments; thus, in each instance, the rational calculus is presumed to operate over some individual-level dispositional property. Calder and Schurr (1981) have described one variation of this dispositional view of behavior:

> The attitude concept has traditionally been one of a stable positive or negative disposition learned through experience. Once formed, an attitude guides behavior. Also, an attitude remains in effect unless the individual is persuaded to change his or her attitude. That is, attitudes persist unless the individual is presented with information causing attitude change. At any point in time, the attitude exists as a fixed characteristic of the person (1981: 284).

The rational model of choice is so ubiquitous in all of the management sciences that we take most of its elements for granted. After reviewing these perspectives, we will discuss several problems with them, including (1) their presumption of the preexistence of purpose or intent; (2) their tendency to ignore the effects of context on behavior; (3) their use of individual-level constructs to build theories of collective or macrolevel behavior; (4) their heavy reliance on cognitive, information-processing assumptions about the causes of human activity; (5) their reliance on hypothetical constructs that reside largely in people's heads and thus that are problematic to observe and measure; and (6) their fundamentally tautological nature, which makes them somewhat theoretically suspect.

There are probably several reasons for theories of this structure to be so pervasive and resistant. First, the earliest analyses of behavior at work adopted a rational perspective with a focus on individuals. Taylor's scientific management proceeded from an attempt to rationalize the doing of work and from presumptions that individuals were conscious and rational, so that better methods of work would be adopted once they were demonstrated if proper rewards were given. Thus, Taylor (1911), to increase the rate at which pig iron was loaded, offered the workers about 60 percent more money, after first insuring that they were, indeed, interested in the money:

> Schmidt, are you a high-priced man? . . . What I want to find out is whether you are a high-priced man or one of these cheap fellows here. What I want to find out is whether you want to earn $1.85 a day or whether you are satisfied with $1.15. . . . If you are a high-priced man, you will load that pig iron on that car tomorrow for $1.85 . . . you get $1.85 for loading a pile like that every day right through the year. That is

what a high-priced man does, and you know it just as well as I do (quoted in Braverman, 1974: 104-105).

In effect, this is the path-goal theory of leadership in action, as well as an illustration of expectancy theory. The leader, in this case, Taylor, has shown the worker, Schmidt, how to achieve one of his desired objectives — being a high-priced man and earning $1.85 a day — with certainty by following directions and loading a certain quantity of pig iron according to directions given by a foreman. Thus, the rational actor approach to understanding organizational analysis has a long and venerable tradition, extending back to the roots of management in the operations of Taylorism.

Second, the focus on individual rational action leads directly to prescriptions, and prescriptions that are implementable, for enhancing performance. The prescriptions are illustrated in stark form in Taylor's description of pig iron loading. Essentially, these involve finding out what someone wants and showing how increased effectiveness at work can lead to acquiring these valued outcomes, or, in more general terms, making the performance of work lead to something valued (in this case, more money) by the worker. In contrast to operant conditioning or other perspectives on reinforcement, the rational actor view indicates that people will work harder on the expectation of higher rewards. The fact that, at least initially, there were people who worked harder for the higher rates, in spite of continual downward rate adjustments instituted by management (much to Taylor's dismay), indicates that expectations can, in fact, produce behavior.

Third, the perspective on individual rational action maintains a focus on the individual as the source of behavior. Problems are defined in terms of individual motivation, needs, predispositions, or expectancies. By contrast, there is no focus on conditions in the economic system as a whole or on the workers or jobs as more collective entities. Certainly, class consciousness is a concept inconsistent with the focus on individual-level explanations for behavior as being derived from expectations, preferences, and needs. This focus on the individual and away from characteristics of the system is both at once politically conservative and consistent with the view of mankind as possessing free will (Sampson, 1981).

And finally, the view of management that emerges from this perspective is one of creating opportunities for need or goal fulfillment. The focus is away from the malleability of human activity and the important situational constraints on behavior. People are viewed in these theories as autonomous social actors, with free will and rational decision-making capacities. Theories of need fulfillment or subjective utility maximization almost never assume that managers work to change the needs or utilities themselves. Rather, the task is always viewed as one of finding relationships or connections between work that is desired by the organization and the values, preferences, or needs of individuals. The control process becomes less overt and much more sanitized. Workers are autonomous decision makers; management merely creates conditions under which, by doing the work desired by the organization, these autonomous, preexisting needs or goals can be fulfilled.

Thus, somewhat ironically, even as technical control over the work increased and the separation of planning of the work from its execution reached new heights, the existing theories of motivation have tended to emphasize not the reality of external control but the myth of the autonomous, decision-making worker. Indeed, reading much of the literature, it is as if the organization were constrained to find incentive systems or reward stuctures that would somehow manage to induce autonomous workers to undertake those tasks specified by the organization and necessary for production. This view is in sharp contrast to the historical accounts provided by Braverman (1974), R. Edwards (1979), and others who have examined the reality of control in the workplace and its evolution over time.

EXPECTANCY THEORY

Expectancy theory, originally presented in detail by Vroom (1964), is an example of an instrumentality theory (Mitchell and Biglan, 1971). Instrumentality theories "are distinguished by the hypothesis that the behavior of an individual is in part determined by (a) his expectations that the behavior will lead to various outcomes and (b) his evaluation of these outcomes" (Mitchell and Biglan, 1971: 432). Instrumentality theories have also been used in developing theories of attitudes in two ways: as a way of conceptualizing the attitude concept and as a way of developing predictions of behavior from attitudes (e.g., Ajzen and Fishbein, 1969). Most of the use in organizational behavior has been associated with the development of theories of motivation.

According to Vroom's formulation, there were two components to understanding the force to perform some behavior. The first component was a model predicting the valence of some outcome, and the second component was a model predicting the force motivating an individual toward some behavior. According to Vroom, valence was the anticipated satisfaction with an outcome, or an individual's positive or negative affect toward it. "The valence model states that the valence of an outcome . . . is a monotonically increasing function of the algebraic sum of the products of the valences of all other outcomes and his conceptions of the specific outcome's instrumentality for the attainment of these other outcomes" (Mitchell and Biglan, 1971: 445). The force toward behavior was then conceptualized as "a monotonically increasing function of the algebraic sum of the products of the valences of all outcomes, and the strength of his expectancies that the act will be followed by the attainment of these outcomes" (Mitchell and Biglan, 1971: 445). This distinction between first-level outcomes, or the immediate result of the act, and the second-level outcomes, the value or valence assigned to these first-level outcomes (for instance, the value attached to a promotion or a raise) in terms of more fundamental goals, has been further developed by Galbraith and Cummings (1967), Graen (1969), and Lawler (1973). The valence model can be used to predict job satisfaction:

> In essence, the model says that the worker's satisfaction with his job results from the instrumentality of the job for attaining other outcomes and the valence of those outcomes (Mitchell and Biglan, 1971: 445).

The second model in which valences and expectancies are combined to predict the force to perform some action has been used to account for behavior, performance, and choice, such as occupational choice.

The testing of expectancy theory has developed over time. Prior to the mid-1970s, respondents were typically asked to rate the importance of a number of outcomes, sometimes from a list provided by the experimenter, sometimes from lists culled from earlier responses from the subjects. Lawler and Porter (1967), for instance, had respondents rate the importance of pay, promotion, prestige, security, autonomy, friendship, and opportunity to use skills. Then, subjects would be asked to what extent job performance or effort might produce those outcomes. Ratings of effort and performance were obtained sometimes from the subjects alone, sometimes from superiors or company records, and sometimes from multiple sources. The model was evaluated by determining the extent to which the various links posited by expectancy theory actually were empirically valid. The correlations were computed across individuals within the same organization.

The results from these studies tended to find support for expectancy theory, but the results were not strong. Lawler and Porter (1967) found support for the expectancy x importance ratings for their seven outcomes and correlations with superior, peer, and self-ratings of effort, but the amount of explained variance was small. Not surprisingly, given methodological considerations, the largest amount of explained variance was obtained for self-ratings of effort. Hackman and Porter (1968) found that the products of expectations and valences for a set of some 14 outcomes correlated with a series of effectiveness measures, but, again, the correlations were not high, with at most about 16 percent of the variation being explained.

T. Mitchell (1974) criticized much of this early expectancy theory research on two fundamental grounds. First, it is clear that the original Vroom (1964) formulation required a within-subjects rather than an across-subjects design. The model predicts the choice of an action from among those available to an individual, but unless one is willing to make claims for the comparability of the outcome valence and expectancy estimates across subjects, no across-person comparisons are possible. Second, Mitchell (1974) noted that there were problems with the dependent variable. Some people were attempting to predict effort, the variable proposed in the original formulation. Many, however, used some indicator of job performance that could be affected by numerous factors (such as ability) besides the individual's level of effort. A third issue was raised by Schmidt (1973), who noted that the multiplicative model advanced in expectancy theory required ratio scale measurement to be tested. Following Mitchell's (1974) criticism, several studies did employ a within-subjects design (Matsui and Ohtsuka, 1978; Parker and Dyer, 1976), with results generally supportive of the expectancy model. Arnold (1981) used a within-subjects design and a procedure to overcome scaling problems, finding support for a multiplicative formulation.

L. Peters (1977) has noted that in expectancy and other cognitive theories of motivation there are, in fact, three links. First, there is the overall link from environmental conditions to the observed behavioral responses. Second, there is the perceptual link from environmental conditions to the individual's belief system, as in the link from the actual pay-performance contingencies to individual beliefs about the pay-performance relationship. And finally, there is the link from the belief system to the behavioral responses. Peters argued that expectancy theory, predicting the force to perform some act, explained only this latter link, from the belief system to the behavioral response. Given Lawler's (1967) findings, for instance, concerning employees' misperceptions of organizational pay policies, the reason why there was only mixed support for the link between environmental conditions and behavioral responses could be due to misperceptions of environmental factors, not due to failings of the expectancy model itself. Using an experimental paradigm, L. Peters (1977) found support for all three links in the model.

The applications of expectancy theory have typically involved recommendations to (1) clarify behavior-outcome linkages, as in making certain that employees know that effective performance will be rewarded, and (2) find out what outcomes have the highest valences and provide these outcomes as rewards. Thus, there have been recommendations to use cafeteria-style compensation schemes in which the employee is allowed the option of choosing particular pay, retirement, and other benefit trade-offs, subject to an overall budget constraint.

Expectancy theory research has evolved over time to use designs both more consistent with the theoretical formulation and less prone to producing priming and consistency response artifacts. However, several problems have continued to plague the research. First, in spite of Mitchell's (1974) criticism, across-subjects designs are still used (e.g., L. Peters, 1977) even though the theory is a within-person choice theory.

Second, expectancy theory has not followed other instrumentality theories in incorporating terms representing the influence of normative, social control. For instance, Dulany (1968) has developed a theory of propositional control that maintains that

$$BI = [(RHd) (RSv)]w_0 + [(BH) (MC)] w_1,$$

where BI is the subject's behavioral intentions; RHd is the person's hypothesis that the occurrence of the response will lead to a certain event or class of events; RSv is the subjective value of the reinforcement, or the subject's attitudes toward those events; BH is the subject's behavioral hypothesis, or his belief as to what he is expected to do; MC is the subject's motivation to comply, or how much he wants to do what is believed to be expected; and w_0 and w_1 are standard regression weights (Mitchell and Biglan, 1971: 434–435). As Mitchell and Biglan noted:

> This theory says that a subject's behavioral intention is determined by an instrumentality component and a social component. The instrumentality component is (RHd) (RSv). . . . The second component deals with the normative or social influences on the subject's behavioral intention: (BH) (MC). . . . The subject's actual response is caused in part by his behavioral intention (1971: 435).

Fishbein's (1967) theory of the attitude-behavior link also includes terms similar to Dulany's representing normative or social influences. Thus, it is only in the case of expectancy theory, of the three types of instrumentality theories reviewed by Mitchell and Biglan, that a term representing the effects of social influence is not included. One reason why instrumentality or expectancy theories of motivation may have been less successful than comparable theories of attitudes and verbal reinforcement in accounting for variation in behavior could be the omission of these normative and social influence considerations.

Path-Goal Theory of Leadership

There are numerous theories and studies of leadership, many of which have been reviewed by Stogdill (1974). The path-goal theory is highlighted here

because it is a direct extension of the type of instrumentality theory that expectancy theory represents. House (1971) argued that subordinate performance and job satisfaction could be improved if the leaders clarified the
paths to various desired outcomes and provided valued outcomes when
goals were achieved. In other words, House conceptualized the leader's task
as one of working on the various links in the expectancy theory framework
to enhance subordinate performance and satisfaction. House's approach
suggested why the traditional leader behavior approaches, focusing on the
dimensions of consideration and initiating structure (Fleishman and Peters,
1962), might not produce consistent research results. House predicted that
the consideration behaviors would be more effective in situations with well-
defined goals and technologies, or in unambiguous settings. Initiating structure behaviors, which organize and direct task activity, would be more effective in situations evidencing high ambiguity and task complexity. In
other words, when the task itself provided direction, the leader's role was
one of providing social and emotional support. When the task was ambiguous, more leader direction was effective.

House (1971) further argued that the subordinate's preferences for various kinds of leader behavior would determine satisfaction. Subordinates
who valued consideration behavior and support would respond well to
those leaders who exhibited such behaviors, while those subordinates who
preferred more direction would be more satisfied under leaders who exhibited more initiating structure behavior.

The evidence for the path-goal theory is more consistent with the predictions of satisfaction than with predictions of performance (Evans, 1970;
House, 1971), but even for this variable the results are mixed (Downey,
Sheridan, and Slocum, 1975; House and Dessler, 1974; Stinson and Johnson, 1975). Again, however, note that performance may be an inappropriate dependent variable, as effort may be the variable that is explained, given
the structure of instrumentality theories from which the path-goal theory is
derived.

GOAL SETTING

Locke (1968) proposed a model of rational, consciously chosen, motivated
individual behavior emphasizing cognitive processes. Locke's theory of goal
setting is another excellent example of a version of an approach emphasizing individual-level cognitively mediated rational action. Locke suggested
that it was an individual's conscious intentions that regulated actions. Goals
were defined in terms of what the individual was trying to accomplish. Ban-

dura (1977) has also emphasized the importance of rational cognitive information processing for understanding behavior. He argued:

> If human behavior could be fully explained in terms of antecedent inducements and response consequences, there would be no need to postulate any additional regulatory mechanisms. However, most external influences affect behavior through intermediary cognitive processes (1977: 160).

For Bandura, goals were an important part of the motivational process:

> Self-motivation requires standards against which performance is evaluated. When individuals commit themselves to explicit goals, perceived negative discrepancies between what they do and what they seek to achieve create dissatisfactions that serve as motivational inducements for change. The motivational effects do not derive from the goals themselves, but rather from the fact that people respond evaluatively to their own behavior (1977: 161).

In Bandura's framework, the three key goal dimensions were goal specificity, the level at which the goals were set, and goal proximity, or how far into the future the goal was projected. Locke also emphasized the importance of setting specific goals (as opposed to the more general, "Do your best") and further argued that more difficult goals, if accepted, tended to produce higher levels of performance than easier goals. Locke argued that it was goal setting that affected how individual performance was mediated by monetary incentives, knowledge of results, and participation in decision making. Since behavior was viewed as the result of conscious intention, attempts to change behavior, according to this view, should proceed from attempts to change the individual's goals.

Locke's goal-setting theory spawned a great deal of empirical research for several reasons. First, the basic concepts of the theory, goal specificity, goal difficulty, and even the activity of goal setting, are relatively straightforward to measure and understand. Second, both goal specificity and difficulty are fairly readily controllable by management, making Locke's theory of great potential utility to organizations. Indeed, this utility may be one of the reasons why this theory is notable for its extensive testing in field settings using quasi-experimental designs. This much intervention in work settings reflects at once both the theory's ease of implementation and its perceived potential utility.

Some of the earlier research was correlational in nature, leaving open alternative interpretations for the results. Carroll and Tosi (1970), for instance, reported that perceived goal difficulty was positively correlated with the self-rated effort of managers, although this relationship was found only for managers who perceived rewards to be contingent on performance and for managers who were high in self-assurance and maturity. Dachler and Mobley (1973) found significant correlations between employees' stated goals and performance, though the strength of the relationship differed significantly between the two organizations studied. In both cases, Weick's (1969) arguments about the retrospective nature of goals and Bem's (1972) self-perception theory offer another interpretation of the results. High-performing managers might assume or infer that they had high goals, when asked about them. Thus, one cannot tell whether the higher goals caused performance or were inferred after the fact to make sense of the performance. Interestingly, Steers (1975) observed no correlation between supervisors' perceived goal difficulty and the rating made by the supervisors' bosses in a study of female first-line supervisors. Steers's results indicate that, as frequently occurs in the literature, one obtains weaker results when independently derived measures of the dependent and independent variables are used.

Most of the studies in this literature are, however, quasi-experimental and, thus, avoid the causation and self-perception issues. Stedry and Kay (1966) assigned 19 foremen in a nonrandom fashion to conditions that varied goal difficulty along two criterion dimensions. Performance improvement was measured as the difference between average performance during the 13 weeks before the experimental treatment and the 13 weeks afterward, and goal difficulty was defined by reference to the average level of performance achieved during the preceding six months. Stedry and Kay found that total perceived difficulty for both goals was significantly associated with a composite index of performance improvement. Latham and Kinne (1974) randomly assigned pulpwood producers and their crews to either a one-day program on goal setting or to a control condition. Data on production, absenteeism, and turnover were collected for a 12-week period. The data indicated that those with training in goal setting experienced a decrease in absenteeism and an increase in production. Latham and Baldes (1975), using a sample of unionized truck drivers, implemented goals to increase the net weight of logs carried. A specific, difficult goal resulted in substantial improvement in performance, and this improvement persisted over a nine-month period. Latham and Yukl (1975b), reviewing goal-setting studies, concluded that the evidence supported the importance of setting specific goals. Further evidence on the relative effectiveness of setting specific goals has been provided by Ivancevich (1976, 1977), Kim and Hamner (1976), Terborg (1976), and White, Mitchell, and Bell (1977).

Locke's emphasis on the primacy of goal setting led him to downplay the importance of monetary incentives. He argued, "Offering an individual money for output may motivate him to set his goals higher than he would otherwise, but this will depend on how much money he wishes to make and how much effort he wishes to expend to make it" (1968: 185). In a series of experiments, Locke (1968) reported that once goal level was controlled, incentives did not affect task performance. However, Pritchard and Curtis (1973) criticized the studies as not offering sufficiently large incentives to test their impact. On the basis of another experiment, Pritchard and Curtis concluded that incentives affected performance independently of the level of the goal and goal commitment. Dachler and Mobley (1973) found that tenure mediated the relationship between goals and performance but that this occurred primarily because employees with longer tenure in the organization perceived outcomes to be contingent on task performance. Terborg and Miller (1978), London and Oldham (1976), and Latham, Mitchell, and Dossett (1978) also provided data consistent with the position that subsequent performance is increased more in goal-setting treatments when rewards are contingent on performance. Latham and Yukl (1975b: 835) concluded that the perceived contingency between goal attainment and positively valued outcomes moderated the effects of goal difficulty on performance. Their interpretation was that this contingency relationship affected goal acceptance. However, alternative explanations stressing the independent, reinforcing effects of incentives are also consistent with the data.

Because the effects of goal setting depend on the acceptance of the goal (Steers, 1975), how to obtain goal acceptance has become a focus of the research. The customary prescription is to have goals set participatively rather than unilaterally. However, evidence on this point is inconsistent with Latham and Yukl (1975a) and Arvey, Dewhirst, and Boling (1976) finding positive effects for participation, but other studies finding no difference between participatively set or unilaterally set goals (Carroll and Tosi, 1970; Ivancevich, 1977; Latham, Mitchell, and Dossett, 1978; Latham and Yukl, 1976).

Although there has been a substantial amount of research on goal setting with reasonably consistent results, four issues remain to be resolved. First, goal-setting theory illustrates the problem of being so concerned with application that the more precisely formulated issues of the theory are overlooked. The prescriptions deriving from the goal-setting research are relatively straightforward: participatively set specific, difficult goals, with rewards contingent on goal attainment, and have feedback provided on performance. There has been only limited effort to disentangle the relative effects of the various components of the goal-setting process. This task is important because of Locke's (1968) explicit statements concerning the primacy of goal setting over other aspects such as rewards and feedback.

Most goal-setting treatments include feedback or knowledge of results. There is substantial evidence that feedback, even in the absence of goal setting, can impact behavior (Annett, 1969; Erez, 1977; Nadler, 1977; Seligman and Darley, 1977). Thus, one would want to know: Is it the goal setting that produces the change in the attitudes and behavior or the feedback? Latham and Yukl (1975b: 836) reported that field studies that independently manipulated goal setting and feedback did not exist. In an analogous fashion, there is the issue of the extent to which goal-setting effects are mediated by contingent rewards. If goal setting works only through reward expectations, then alternative theoretical explanations ranging from expectancy theory to social learning theory (Bandura, 1977), and even versions of operant conditioning, could account for the results.

The second issue in goal-setting research has to do with the dependent variable. In some cases, actual performance measures were employed as dependent variables (Blumenfeld and Leidy, 1969; Latham and Baldes, 1975; Latham and Kinne, 1974; Stedry and Kay, 1966). In other instances, effort (sometimes self-rated) was used (Carroll and Tosi, 1970; Steers, 1975). In still other cases, measures of attitudes such as satisfaction were the dependent variables (Ivancevich, 1977; Kim and Hamner, 1976; London and Oldham, 1976), although these studies also generally included measures of performance. Performance is a function of both effort and ability (Vroom, 1964). Therefore, studies that have emphasized performance have used an inappropriate dependent variable unless ability is relatively constant across the subject population; otherwise, without explicit controls for ability, the results are difficult to interpret. Clearly, goal-setting theory speaks to the prediction of effort, not necessarily to the performance that might result from that effort.

Anderson and O'Reilly (in press) presented data that indicated the relevance of the preceding points. First, in a study in which both job satisfaction and performance (supervisor's ratings) data were collected, the correlation between the two measures was only 0.11. This indicates that whether one focuses on attitudes or performance (and presumably, or on effort) is a consequential decision for the results of the study. Collecting separate measures of the various components of goal-setting theory, they used multiple regression analysis to try to assess which of the variables had significant independent effects. They found that goal difficulty and feedback were both significantly associated with performance, though neither was associated with job satisfaction; in their multiple regression equations, only reward contingency significantly affected satisfaction. This particular result, however, may have been due to the collinearity among the various goal-setting dimensions. The possibility of an interactive or multiplicative formulation, which is what is implied in some variants of the theory, was not investigated. And no measure of effort was collected. However, the study is notable in its explicit attempt to untangle the relative effects of the various components of the goal-setting process as they relate to various outcome measures.

The third area needing attention is distinguishing goal-setting from other theoretical mechanisms. Salancik (1977) has argued that commitment (Kiesler, 1971) offers an alternate explanation for the goal-setting results. His argument is that in a goal-setting treatment, once the goal is set and the individuals involved acquiesce by not objecting, they are deemed to have chosen the goal. Specific goals are, presumably, more explicitly directed to the implications of behavior and, hence, are more committing than general goals. Many goal-setting treatments occur in public in the sense that the individual either works with his or her supervisor in the goal setting or goals are promulgated in a public meeting. Thus, with many of the components of commitment processes in place (choice, explicitness, and publicity), the individuals are bound and committed to the specified behaviors. Furthermore, the commitment perspective has something to say about participatively set versus unilaterally set goals as well. Although commitment theory might be expected to argue for the relative advantage of participatively set goals, since presumably there is more choice in this case, the critical issue is the extent to which choice was perceived in both situations. It is quite possible that the act of assenting or agreeing to the unilaterally set goals constitutes a sufficient choice manipulation.

The goal-setting perspective would argue that variables such as choice, explicitness, and publicness merely impact the extent to which goal acceptance has occurred and that goal acceptance remains the critical mediating variable. Indeed, one might argue that the differences between the two theories are more a matter of semantics than substance. There are, however, differences between the perspectives. Commitment theories tend to presume that insufficiently externally justified (underrewarded) behavior is more binding (Salancik, 1977; Staw, 1974), while goal setting argues for either the irrelevance or the positive effect of increasing contingent incentives. Also, commitment perspectives are less consciously rational than goal-setting theory. It seems evident that disentangling the two perspectives, if that is possible, is not a trivial task. However, given the differences in the fundamental theoretical orientations of the two theories, distinguishing between them is important.

The fourth area of further work involves remedying the neglect of considerations of the organizational context in studies of goal setting. Dachler and Mobley (1973) found that the correlation of stated goal with performance across employees was 0.46 in one organization and only 0.16 in the second. One possibility is that differences in reward contingencies may be responsible for the results. Another possibility is that the normative structure of the organizations differed with respect to how adequate performance was defined and what performance meant. If we are to make sense of the different results that sometimes occur when similar treatments (such as goal setting) are applied in different settings, more explicit consideration must be given to analyzing the context in which such treatments are embedded.

Although related to expectancy and instrumentality perspectives on behavior, Locke's goal-setting theory differs in some important respects. The theory argues that behavior is to be understood solely in terms of goals — their specificity, difficulty, and degree of acceptance. There is no consideration of expectancies or the strength of the linkage between behavior and the likelihood of goal attainment. Also, how goals come to be valued, or the source of goal valence, is not considered. It is, however, in the omission of expectancies that goal setting differs most importantly from expectancy theory, and in the neglect of normative constraints and situational influences that it differs as well from other instrumentality theories.

NEEDS THEORIES AND JOB DESIGN

As Alderfer (1977) has arugued, needs theories, in general, do not require assumptions about rational, foresightful choice; nor do expectancy-type theories of rational choice necessarily require the concept of needs. However, as the field of study has, in fact, developed, the two perspectives are closely interconnected. Needs — and in particular, higher-order or growth needs for interesting, autonomous, and responsible work — have been postulated to be important objectives or goals sought by individuals in work settings; thus, satisfaction and work performance have been argued to be a function of the extent to which the demands of the job facilitate the attainment of these needs as a consequence of the nature of the work. For example, Griffin, Welsh, and Moorhead (1981) noted:

> A paper by Hackman and Lawler (1971) laid the foundation by developing a task design framework from expectancy theory (Vroom, 1964). This initial framework . . . suggested that employees work harder to the extent that their individual needs and organizational goals are congruent . . . all outcome variables, including quality of work performance, "are expected to be more positive for jobs with high-motivating potential" (Hackman and Oldham, 1976: 259) (1981: 655–656).

According to most variants of needs theory, individuals are motivated to seek fulfillment primarily from their jobs or work environments. As

Strauss (1974) has argued, this is only one possibility, as individuals could come to view work as filling merely instrumental requirements such as earning enough money to enable them to fulfill their needs in other settings. However, the expressive as well as instrumental nature of work and jobs is an assumption taken for granted in virtually all of the current literature.

Various needs have been postulated to reside in individuals, ranging from the five needs of physical, safety, social, esteem and competence, and self-actualization needs proposed by Maslow (1943, 1954), the existence, relatedness, and growth needs postulated by Alderfer (1972), and the power, affiliation, and achievement needs advanced by McClelland (1961). Most theories argue that a satisfied need is not a motivator of behavior, which means that as more of the basic needs have been satisfied, it is incumbent on the organization and its managers to provide jobs that facilitate the satisfaction of higher-order needs. In arguing that behavior is directed to satisfy needs, it should be clear that these theories are, in essence, drive-reduction models of behavior.

Since it is often assumed that higher-order needs for feelings of competence and self-actualization are best satisfied by the job itself (Herzberg, Mausner, and Snyderman, 1959), needs theories are closely entwined with the large literature on job design and its effects on workers' attitudes and behavior (Hackman and Oldham, 1980). This literature (e.g., Hackman and Oldham, 1976) has emphasized the importance of changing dimensions of the task to enhance worker satisfaction and effectiveness.

In Figure 2-1, the basic dispositional or needs model of job attitudes and behavior is displayed. Note that in this model job attitudes are pre-

Figure 2-1.   A Need-Satisfaction Model of Job Attitudes and Behavior

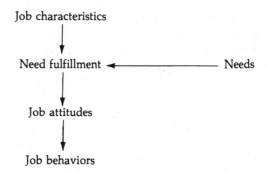

SOURCE: Adapted from Salancik and Pfeffer (1977a: 429).

sumed to follow directly from the interaction of needs or other individual dispositions and the characteristics of the work environment and that behaviors are presumed to follow from these attitudes. Thus, for instance, there are numerous instances of attempts to predict job turnover (e.g., Mobley, 1977; Mobley, Horner, and Hollingsworth, 1978; Porter et al., 1974), absenteeism (e.g., Johns, 1978, Nicholson, Brown, and Chadwick-Jones, 1976; Porter and Steers, 1973), and job performance (e.g., Brayfield and Crockett, 1955; Schwab and Cummings, 1970; Vroom, 1964) from job attitudes and the attitudes themselves from the interaction of job characteristics with individual traits or needs.

It is critical to recognize that the theory as outlined in the literature posits an interaction between dispositions and environmental attributes. It is in many respects a contingency theory at the individual level of analysis. Thus studies that find no consistent relationship between task attributes and task attitudes (Hulin and Blood, 1968; Turner and Lawrence, 1965) or between needs or other personal constructs and job attitudes or behaviors are not inconsistent with the theory; rather, they simply do not test it. Tests of the theory involve those studies that have hypothesized moderator variables that affected the job attribute-job attitude relationship, with particular emphasis on higher-order need strength, sometimes called growth need strength.

A large number of such studies have been conducted. Hackman and Lawler (1971), Brief and Aldag (1975), Stone, Mowday, and Porter (1977), Steers and Spencer (1977), and Ganster (1980) all investigated the extent to which individual need strengths moderated the job design-job attitude relationship, with the hypothesis being that enriched jobs, higher on variety, autonomy, task significance, and feedback, would be positively associated with favorable attitudes and work outcomes primarily for those individuals who had stronger levels of the more growth- and competency-related needs.

The evidence for the predicted interaction between personal dispositions or traits and task characteristics in affecting either attitudes or behaviors is quite weak. White (1978) reviewed more than 30 articles investigating the relationship between personal attributes, such as needs, urban-rural background, education, and locus of control, and other demographics on the job scope-job attitude relationship. He concluded:

> Nineteen years of theory building and empirical research have not provided much hope in finding generalizable individual difference moderators of the relationship between job quality and worker responses (1978: 278).

In Hackman and Lawler's (1971: 279) study, they compared the one-third of their subjects with the highest growth need strength with the one-third with the lowest growth need strength. This procedure, in which one-third of the subjects are discarded, is methodologically suspect. Nevertheless, there were almost no significant differences in the correlations between job attributes and job attitudes for the two subsamples. The Brief and Aldag (1975) replication of this study produced generally similar results. Only 3 of 32 correlations were statistically significantly different between the high and low growth need strength groups at the $p < .05$ level. Ganster (1980) reported no interaction effects of individual differences moderating the job scope-job attitude relationship.

Griffin, Welsh, and Moorhead (1981) recently reviewed 13 studies examining the relationship between perceived task scope and employee performance. In general, there were not consistent main effects, or there was no consistency for task attributes (as perceived) to be correlated with performance. In about 50 percent of the studies, an effect was observed. The evidence for interactive effects is even less supportive of the needs theory approach. In 11 of the 13 studies, absolutely no significant differences were observed between the relationship between job attributes and performance for persons higher as contrasted with lower in growth need strength. In one of the remaining studies (Sims and Szilagyi, 1976), three of the six pairs of correlations were different in the expected direction, with one difference being statistically significant; however, the remaining three pairs of correlations were significantly different in the direction *opposite* to that predicted. Thus, of 13 studies the only one that showed the expected moderating effects of individual characteristics was Steers and Spencer's (1977), who used need for achievement (rather than growth need strength) as the moderating variable. Although Griffin and coworkers (1981) argue that part of the problem lies with how performance has been measured, an alternative interpretation for the findings is that the theory is simply incorrect.

Salancik and Pfeffer (1977a) have criticized the basic theoretical structure of needs models as well as how they have been tested. In terms of empirical testing, these authors noted that studies have most frequently involved the use of questionnaires in cross-sectional designs, which led to correlating perceptions with perceptions at the same point in time. Recently, various experimental and quasi-experimental studies in which jobs were actually changed and then attitudes measured have been conducted, which partially overcome this particular problem (e.g., Hackman, Pearce, and Wolfe, 1978). Orpen (1979) found a significant main effect for a change in job content on a variety of attitudinal (though not on performance) results. However, Orpen found few of the predicted differences in the effects of the job changes on attitudes of persons with high rather than low growth need strength. Thus, Orpen's results are fundamentally inconsistent with the theory. As we will discuss in more detail below and in the next chapter,

there are numerous alternative interpretations for the main effects uncovered by Orpen. Moreover, recall that this theory emerged from an expectancy theory perspective, which requires that responses be consistent
with the preexisting dispositions, values, goals, needs, or attitudes of the
persons. Enriched jobs should produce favorable responses only for those
who have goals or objectives that are instrumentally served by such jobs,
not for everyone.

Salancik and Pfeffer (1977a) also noted that needs models were almost
impossible to refute, thus violating the condition of falsifiability, which is important for evaluating a theory. In Table 2-1, their table showing possible
combinations of needs, job characteristics, and attitudinal reactions is
shown. The table indicates why, by chance alone, the model is likely to find
support. Salancik and Pfeffer noted:

> In condition 1, individuals have the same needs, face the same job charac-
> teristics, and have the same reactions. This outcome is consistent with the
> need-satisfaction model. But so are the conditions in which the individuals
> have different needs, face the same jobs and have different attitudes; face
> different jobs, have different needs, and have the same attitudes; or face
> different jobs, have different needs, and have different attitudes. Further,
> the need-satisfaction model is compatible with the condition in which in-
> dividuals have the same needs, have different jobs, and have different at-
> titudes (1977a: 439).

Even in conditions 3 and 5, versions of needs theories could be constructed
to be consistent, because there is no necessary tight coupling between needs,

Table 2-1. POSSIBLE COMBINATIONS OF NEEDS, JOB CHARACTERISTICS, AND
ATTITUDES FOR TWO INDIVIDUALS, AND THEIR CONSISTENCY WITH NEED-
SATISFACTION THEORIES

Needs	Job Characteristics	Attitudinal Reaction	Consistency with Theory
1. Same	Same	Same	Consistent
2. Same	Same	Different	Inconsistent
3. Same	Different	Same	Partly consistent
4. Same	Different	Different	Consistent
5. Different	Same	Same	Partly consistent
6. Different	Same	Different	Consistent
7. Different	Different	Same	Consistent
8. Different	Different	Different	Consistent

SOURCE: Adapted from Salancik and Pfeffer (1977a: 438).

job characteristics, and responses in the sense that some needs may be irrelevant to producing attitudinal responses and some job characteristics
may be similarly irrelevant.

In a further critique of such models, Roberts and Glick (1981) have
argued that many of the tests of task design theories mixed within-person
and person-situation relations. Job design theory argues, in essence, that it
is the objective nature of the job or task environment, interacting with individual characteristics, such as needs, that determines motivation and job attitudes. Yet, few of the studies even measured task characteristics separately
from how they were perceived by respondents, and those that did (e.g.,
Hackman and Lawler, 1971) tended to use such measurements only to provide evidence for the validity of the perceptual measures. In several instances, the measurement of the "objective characteristics" of jobs was
accomplished by having assistants of the researcher, who almost certainly
were well versed in the theory and the hypotheses, observe the jobs and
make independent ratings of the various job dimensions. Such a scheme
scarcely can be said to tap objective job dimensions. Roberts and Glick
(1981) argued:

> Based on the observation of within-person relations between task percep-
> tions and job responses, researchers often jumped to the conclusion that a
> person-situation relation also held and suggested objective job changes to
> change job responses (1981: 196).

Thus, not only are the concepts themselves such as needs and job characteristics open to a variety of theoretical interpretations, but many of the
properties being investigated have not been measured in a way consistent
with the theoretical model being tested.

A critical problem derives from the fact that most of the studies use
data collected from only one or a very few locations — firms or departments.
Even in those conditions in which a quasi-experimental design was employed
(e.g., Hackman, Pearce, and Wolfe, 1978), the individual was the unit of
analysis. In Figure 2-2A, the causal model implicit in the task design literature is diagramed. This is a simplified version of the model shown in Figure
2-1. However, suppose that the perceptions of job characteristics, need
statements, and attitudes toward the job were being shaped by informational social influence (Festinger, 1954) and conformity pressures (Kiesler
and Kiesler, 1969), certainly not an unreasonable assumption, given the interactions among people in work settings. These effects will be described in
detail in the next chapter. Then, an alternative explanation for any observed relationship among the variables is possible, as diagramed in Figure
2-2B. This model suggests that any observed association between task char-

acteristics and task attitudes may be a spurious result of the fact that both are consequences of the prevailing normative and informational structure of the work environment.

There is evidence for the effect of social influences on both work attitudes and task perceptions. Herman and Hulin (1972), Herman, Dunham, and Hulin (1975), and O'Reilly and Roberts (1975) all reported data indicating that job attitudes were more strongly related to organizational position, identified by departmental or divisional affiliation, than to various background and demographic characteristics. Pfeffer (1980) observed a subunit effect on both attitudes and need statements. O'Reilly, Parlette, and Bloom (1980) examined differences in perceptions of task characteristics in a sample of nurses who were, by all available evidence including job analyses, doing the identical task. These authors found that perceptions of job characteristics were systematically related to the nurses' frame of reference, which included things such as education, tenure, orien-

Figure 2.2 CAUSAL MODEL OF NEEDS THEORY AND AN ALTERNATIVE INTERPRETATION

Needs Theory

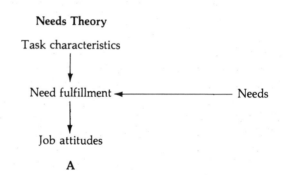

A

An Alternative Interpretation

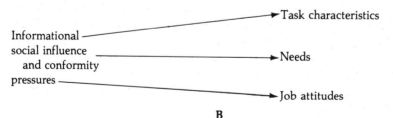

B

tation toward professionalism, and income. Most important, overall job satisfaction influenced perceptions of job dimensions, calling into question the direction of causality usually assumed in this literature. O'Reilly, Parlette, and Bloom (1980: 129) concluded that "the results are . . . consistent with the social construction of task characteristics."

It is clear that distinguishing between the models in Figure 2-2 is relatively straightforward. First, evidence that there are social or contextual effects on needs would provide support consistent with the alternative interpretation and would provide data not anticipated in the first model. Furthermore, although both models are consistent with an association between task characteristics and job attitudes, only the needs theory approach posits an interaction between needs and task characteristics in determining job attitudes. Thus, finding such an interaction would provide support for that version, while finding an association between job attributes and job attitudes does not permit one to distinguish between the models. In this regard, it is interesting that it is much more common to find significant job attribute-job attitude associations in the literature than it is to find the interaction between job attributes and needs. This evidence also tends to support the alternative formulation. In any case, distinguishing between the models will require additional evidence that will permit the estimation of the effects of context, which is what is required by the formulation of the model in Figure 2-2B.

In addition to testing needs theories through the examination of task design issues, more direct tests of needs theory have also been made. First, there have been studies that investigated the extent to which there is evidence for the hierarchical arrangement of needs (Blai, 1962; Goodman, 1968). Studies have also investigated the extent to which unsatisfied needs motivate behavior. And there has been research examining whether once some needs are satisfied, new needs emerge (Hall and Nougaim, 1968; Wofford, 1971). As summarized by Wahba and Bridwell (1976), these studies in general offer virtually no support for Maslow's need hierarchy theory. A more recent study using longitudinal data to test needs theory (Rauschenberger, Schmitt, and Hunter, 1980) also failed to find evidence consistent with theoretical predictions.

The literature on needs theory and task design may be the archetypical example of a theory being accepted regardless of the empirical evidence. Commenting specifically on Maslow's need hierarchy theory, Wahba and Bridwell (1976) made a statement that is equally applicable to most of the perspectives reviewed in this section:

> Maslow's need hierarchy theory . . . presents the student of work motivation with an interesting paradox: The theory is widely accepted but there is little research evidence to support it (1976: 212).

But the lack of supporting evidence has not hindered the efforts to take the theory into the field. The quality of working life movement and the associated activities of job redesign and evaluation brought needs theories into the world of practice (Lawler, Hackman, and Kaufman, 1973). Prescriptive writings have argued for the efficacy of job redesign as a solution to a variety of motivational and behavioral problems and have provided guidance on how to implement task redesign to increase chances of success (Hackman et al., 1975; Hackman and Oldham, 1980; Lawler, 1974). Yet, the evidence on the effectiveness of the quality of working life interventions is distinctly mixed (Strauss, 1974), in part because of the numerous contextual and political factors such reforms overlooked.

The Status of Needs Theories

The status of needs theories and other dispositional approaches to understanding behavior is presently uncertain. Such theories offer a trait-based conception of human behavior that fits those attributional biases that emphasize personal as contrasted with situational explanations of behavior (Jones and Nisbett, 1971; Kelley, 1971). As noted by Salancik and Pfeffer (1977a), need-satisfaction models are consistent with other models that have proceeded from the premise of human rationality:

> By suggesting that individuals develop preferences according to the manner in which states of the world satisfy their needs, it is suggested that individual responses are rationally linked to the environment. The idea suggests that people pursue their interests and shape their behavior and attitudes to achieve their goals (1977a: 437).

Rationality is not only a model of man but a valued social ideal (Parsons and Smelser, 1956), and thus such theories are consistent with some important social ideology. In addition, the perspective offers a relatively simple picture of human behavior and affords readily implementable prescriptions for attitudinal and behavioral problems confronted in organizations. Indeed, there is a growing technology, if not an industry, of job redesign and evaluation. Finally, such a perspective offers nice political language (Edelman, 1964; Pfeffer, 1981a: chapter 6) in which to couch the management activity: management is seen as changing the environment to better fit or match the requirements of the dispositions or needs of the individuals in the workplace. These are all strong factors that tend to cause this perspective to persist.

On the other hand, the theories imply a requirement for changing jobs and work arrangements that may impact the organization's basic power and governance system, causing resistance on the part of managers who see their control eroded through worker involvement in the task design process and through greater worker autonomy (Hackman, 1978). Also, the theory suffers from a lack of empirical support, or support that is often as equally interpretable as consistent with alternative formulations. Alternative perspectives to needs theory have arisen (e.g., Calder and Schurr, 1981; Salancik and Pfeffer, 1978a) that provide concrete examples of different ways of analyzing behavior in organizations.

Given the frequent lack of support for the theory in spite of the numerous methodological artifacts that favor finding support, one might question whether in fact further research is necessary. Yet, the issue is not completely decided. When such research is undertaken, the required focus would seem to be around distinguishing needs theory from its alternatives and, in particular, distinguishing between the social construction of task perceptions and the possibilities of social influence on task and need statements versus the effect of individual dispositions and objective task characteristics on the development of motivation and job attitudes. The research of O'Reilly (O'Reilly and Caldwell, 1979; O'Reilly, Parlette, and Bloom, 1980) is an example of the type of analysis needed, although his research paradigm must be expanded to include measures of needs and other individual traits to test fully the relative predictive utility of the two formulations diagramed in Figure 2-2.

POLITICAL THEORIES OF ORGANIZATIONS

The last theoretical perspective reviewed in this section, a political approach to organizational analysis, is different from the preceding in several respects. First, this perspective considers groups within organizations as well as individuals as the unit of analysis. More fundamentally, political theories have tended to be less managerial and less prescriptive in orientation, focusing more on the description of activities within organizations than on developing normative guidelines for management. Furthermore, in the sense that political perspectives on organizations neither assume nor prescribe goal homogeneity within the organization, they depart from assumptions of rationality as defined at the organizational level. This is because consistent preferences that guide action are fundamental elements in theories of rational choice (Allison, 1971; Friedland, 1974; March, 1976). Although they are not models of organizational rationality, political models belong in this section because they are models that presume intentional, rational action on the part of individuals or subunits within the organization.

Such social actors are presumed to act in their own self-interest and to engage in strategic action in pursuing this interest. The final difference is that although other perspectives on behavior considered thus far have at times considered outcomes or actions, they have also focused heavily on attitudes as dependent variables (Bem, 1967). By contrast, political models have tended to focus on the decisions and allocations that result from the interaction of interdependent, competing political actors. Thus, there have been studies of the allocation of budgets (Hills and Mahoney, 1978; Pfeffer and Leong, 1977; Pfeffer and Salancik, 1974; Pfeffer, Salancik, and Leblebici, 1976), changes in curricula and programs of study (Baldridge, 1971; Manns and March, 1978), succession to administrative positions (Zald, 1965), increases in university tuition (Baldridge, 1971), the choice of a particular computer (Pettigrew, 1973), and the organizational structure that results from the interplay of political interests (Pfeffer, 1978, 1981a).

The various political theories view organizations as pluralistic, divided into interests, subunits, and subcultures. Action results "from games among players who perceive quite different faces of an issue and who differ markedly in the actions they prefer" (Allison, 1971: 175). Because decisions are the result of bargaining and compromise, the resultant choice does not perfectly represent the preferences of any single social actor. Political models further presume that it is power that determines whose interests are to prevail more in the conditions of conflict. Power "is an intervening variable between an initial condition, defined largely in terms of the individual components of the system, and a terminal state, defined largely in terms of the system as a whole" (March, 1966: 168–169).

Thus, the concept of power is fundamental in political theories. *Power* is defined most often in terms of the capacity of the particular social actor to overcome opposition (Blau, 1964; Dahl, 1957; Emerson, 1962; Salancik and Pfeffer, 1977b). Power is one of the more controversial of the social science concepts. March (1966) has argued that the inference of power in decision-making situations is extremely difficult and that power is often used in a way conceptually similar to needs or personality to construct explanations for otherwise unexplained variance after the fact. March (1966) argued that to infer that power was a valid concept operating in a particular decision situation, one should observe consistency in patterns of outcomes over time, or else the outcome could have been produced by a chance process instead of by power. Furthermore, March argued that power would be more useful to the extent that it could be experimentally manipulated with predictable results and to the extent that power of social actors was itself explainable from a theory of the sources of power.

Most problematic to March (1976) in power models is the underlying assumption of conscious, rational, strategic action taken on the part of various social actors to obtain their preferences in situations of conflict. He has argued (March, 1978) that preferences are not nearly that well formed or consistently held. This issue is indeed central to political models of organizations, for as J. Nagel (1975) has indicated, power can be virtually defined by the relationship between the preferences of an actor and the outcomes achieved. If preferences are themselves problematic, the validity of the political model is open to doubt.

Power has been measured typically by interviews (Perrow, 1970a; Pfeffer and Salancik, 1974) in which actors are asked to rate the power of other units in the organizations and, less frequently, by unobtrusive indicators, such as departmental representation on important committees (Pfeffer and Moore, 1980; Pfeffer and Salancik, 1974). In those situations in which both types of measures were used, good convergence was observed. The use of archival or less obtrusive measures of power is important to allow one to study power historically as well as to avoid some of the criticisms of reputational measures of power that have emerged in the community power research (Polsby, 1960).

Political theories of organizations address the issues of what determines the power of the various social actors, what are the conditions under which power is used, and what various strategies there are for the development and exercise of influence. The source of power is typically argued to be the ability of the social actor to provide some performance or resource to the organization that is valued and important and the inability of others to obtain such performance or resource from alternate sources. Sometimes this critical performance is the ability to cope with important organizational problems or contingencies. Thus, Crozier (1964) argued that the power of maintenance workers in a French factory was derived from their control over the one remaining organizational contingency, the breakdown of machines. Hickson et al. (1971) also argued that power accrued to those units that could successfully cope with the most central, pervasive, and critical uncertainties. A study of seven organizations by Hinings et al. (1974) supported this formulation. Arguing that the power of academic departments came from their ability to provide important resources to the organization, Salancik and Pfeffer (1974) found that departmental power was strongly related to the amount of grants and contracts brought in. Pfeffer and Moore (1980), examining a different university, also found evidence for the importance of grants and contracts as well as student enrollment levels as sources of power.

The bases of individual, as contrasted with subunit, influence in organizational decisions have also been investigated, using somewhat different concepts. French and Raven (1959) argued that there were five bases of individual power: reward power, punishment power, expert power, legitimate power, and referent power. The first two are based on the ability to provide inducements or sanctions for behavior; the third basis relies on expertise and the ability to achieve the reduction of uncertainty. Legitimate power is the power that derives from occupying a certain role in the social structure that conveys the authorization to exercise influence. Referent power is power derived from the individual's personal characteristics that make others identify with and want to emulate the person. Patchen (1974) studied 33 purchase decisions in 11 organizations. He found that the most frequently mentioned reason for a person's influence was that the individual was affected by the decision in some way. The second most mentioned source of influence was characteristics bearing on expertise, with the third most mentioned reason being the posession of formal responsibility or authority. Interestingly, the most important reason for influence uncovered by Patchen's research, decisional involvement, was not included in the French and Raven classification.

Allen et al. (1979) surveyed managers attending an executive program and asked them their beliefs about the personal characteristics of effective political actors. The five most frequently mentioned characteristics were articulateness, sensitivity, social adeptness, competence, and popularity (Allen et al., 1979: 80). Because the word *political* probably triggered an association with the exercise of influence outside of normal channels, characteristics of referent power or identification, such as popularity, social adeptness, and sensitivity, were represented more frequently. Although intelligence and logical ability were mentioned, they were down on the list. One problem with this study is that, as Pfeffer (1981a: 134) has argued, the responses, "may reflect widely-held stereotypes and myths as much as any empirical reality."

Most of the studies have been cross-sectional in nature, but Pfeffer and Moore (1980) studied both power and budget allocations over time. Controlling for initial budget and changes in enrollment over the period, these authors found that power did account for budget allocations some ten years later. Controlling for the initial levels of departmental power, they found that grants and contracts and enrollment levels predicted power. These results provide some answer to March's (1966) argument concerning the need to study power and political processes dynamically.

Power is not used equally in all situations, and, thus, what March (1966) termed *force activation models* have developed, specifying the conditions under which power is more or less likely to be employed. Salancik and Pfeffer (1974), examining allocations of four additional resources, found that subunit power was more strongly related to the allocation of the more critical and scarce resources. Hills and Mahoney (1978) found that power accounted for more of the allocation of incremental budgetary resources at a university in times when resources were more scarce. Thus, scarcity seems to be one condition associated with the use of power. Another condition is uncertainty or disagreement either about goals or technology, the connections between actions and consequences. Conceptualizing the level of paradigm development as a measure of technological certainty in a scientific discipline (Lodahl and Gordon, 1972), evidence has been presented indicating that power is used more in paradigmatically less developed fields to allocate federal research funds (Pfeffer, Salancik, and Leblebici, 1976), positions on editorial boards (Yoels, 1974), jobs (Hargens, 1969), and journal publication access (Pfeffer, Leong, and Strehl, 1977). Therefore, uncertainty and disagreement appear to be conditions associated with the use of power. Salancik and Pfeffer (1978b) presented experimental evidence suggesting that secrecy, both concerning the information used in decision making and the identity of the decision makers, might be associated with the use of power. Although the range of conditions for power use has been far from fully explored, the existing empirical work does suggest that concepts of power activation are important in understanding organizations from a political perspective.

Research on strategies of power acquisition and use, including the determinants of the choice of strategies and the effectiveness of different strategies in different circumstances, is somewhat less developed. Pettigrew (1972), examining the decision to purchase a computer, found that control over the flow of information permitted the individual with such control to affect the decision outcome. This suggests that information control is one important political strategy. Salancik and Pfeffer (1974) found that department heads tended to favor basing allocation on criteria that favored their subunits, and Pfeffer and Salancik (1977) found that, after controlling for departmental power and objective bases of allocation, the selective advocacy of criteria favoring one's subunit was correlated with allocation outcomes. Plott and Levine (1978) have argued that the agenda, or the order in which decisions are considered, can affect the results, a point further developed by Pfeffer (1981a). Since power is seldom concentrated enough to have one social actor make the decision without the support of others, the development of coalitions is another important element of political strategy (Bucher, 1970). And the obtaining of political support through strategies of cooptation (Selznick, 1949), such as appointing committees and having powerful interests represented on such committees, is a strategy used to obtain support within organizations as well as from the organization's environment.

More personal actions of influence have also been investigated. Patchen (1974) reported that influentials were reported to be active in prodding others to act. The other activity mentioned with any frequency in his study of influence in purchasing decisions was information-gathering or technical activities. Mowday (1978) studied the exercise of upward influence by school principals and examined the strategies of threats, persuasive arguments, rewards, manipulation, and the use of legitimate authority to see whether the use of these strategies differed over decision issue, over the stage in the decision process, and between more effective and less effective principals. Mowday reported that influence strategies did differ depending on the stage of the decision process and the type of decision. He found that there was a greater tendency to go outside of channels later in the process and for reclassification of position as contrasted with budgetary decisions. He did not find any evidence, however, that the use of more severe influence strategies, such as threats, increased during the latter stages of the decision process. He also found that the method of influence differentiated between high and low effectiveness principals:

> . . . manipulation was the method of influence that most consistently differentiated between principals having high and low effectiveness. For the three budgeting decisions, it was found that high-effectiveness principals were more likely to indicate they would use manipulation. . . . In the special projects decision, the use of persuasive arguments differentiated the principals of high and medium effectiveness from those rated low in effectiveness. High-effectiveness principals were also . . . more likely to indicate they would use manipulation (1978: 152).

One of the issues confronted by research on strategies of power use is how to dimensionalize and conceptualize differences in strategies. Kipnis, Schmidt, and Wilkinson (1980) recently addressed this problem. First, they asked 165 lower-level managers taking evening business courses to write essays describing an incident in which they succeeded in getting someone in their organization to do something. Content analysis was used to sort the influence tactics into 14 categories. These categories and the relative frequency of their use are shown in Table 2-2. They then correlated the use of specific tactics with the reason for exercising the influence and with the relationship between the subject and the target of the influence (boss, subordinate, or peer). They found that

> . . . in organizational settings the choice of influence tactics is associated with what the respondents are trying to get from the target person, the amount of resistance shown, and the power of the target person. Combining these findings suggests that administrative sanctions and personal negative actions are more likely to be used when the target is a subordinate who is actively resisting the request of the manager and when the reasons for exercising influence are based on the respondent's role in the organization (1980: 443).

Table 2-2. CATEGORIES OF INFLUENCE TACTICS AND THEIR RELATIVE FREQUENCY OF USE

Category/Tactic	Percentage of Total Influence Tactics Reported
Clandestine	8
Challenged the ability of the target	
Lied to the target	
Acted in a pseudodemocratic manner	
Puffed up the importance of the job	
Manipulated information	
Made the target feel important	
Cajoled the target	
Showed understanding (pretended) of the target's problem	
Personal negative actions	8
Fait accompli/went ahead on own	
Chastised the target	
Became a nuisance	
Slowed down on the job	
Held personal confrontation with target	
Threatened withdrawal of help	
Blocked target's actions	
Ignored target	
Administrative negative actions	3
Filed a report with supervisor	
Sent target to superior for conference	
Gave unsatisfactory performance evaluations	
Gave no salary increase	
Threatened with unsatisfactory performance ratings	
Threatened job security	
Threatened loss of promotion	
Exchange	8
Contributed in exchange for compliance	
Compromised	
Offered to make sacrifice	
Offered to help to get the job done	
Invoked past favors	
Persistence	7
Repeated reminders	
Argued	
Repeated previous actions	
Surveillance	

Table 2-2. (Continued)

Category/Tactic	Percentage of Total Influence Tactics Reported
Training	6
Explained how it was to be done	
Showed how to do it	
Reward	2
Verbal reinforcement	
Salary raise	
Gave benefits	
Self presentation	5
Demonstrated competence	
Performed well, then asked	
Waited until target was in the right mood	
Was humble	
Was friendly	
Direct request	10
Weak ask	6
Showed dependency	
Weak request	
Demand	7
Invoked rules	
Ordered	
Convened formal conference	
Set time deadline	
Told target that it must be done as I said or better proposed	
Explained rationale for request	17
Gathered supporting data	6
Coalitions	7
Obtained support from coworkers	
Obtained support informally from superiors	
Obtained support from subordinates	
Threatened to notify an outside agency	
Made formal appeals to higher levels	

SOURCE: From Kipnis, Schmidt, and Wilkinson (1980: 442).

In a second study, 58 items were developed to measure the tactics identified, and these items were given to 754 employed respondents. Three forms of the survey were administered to distinguish among influence tactics used to influence bosses, subordinates, or peers. Factor analysis was used to try to combine the items into identifiable factors. Eight factors were identified: assertiveness, ingratiation, rationality, sanctions, exchange, upward appeal, blocking, and coalitions. Kipnis, Schmidt, and Wilkinson (1980: 449) found that the choice of influence tactics was affected by the status of the influence target and the reasons for exerting influence. They also found that the choice of influence tactics was related to the level in the organizations, the size of the work unit, and the presence of unions, but there were no significant relationships between the choice of influence tactics and the sex of the respondent.

This work by the Kipnis group provides an instrument for measuring influence tactics and some indication of the categories along which influence in organizations can be dimensionalized. Furthermore, their results are quite consistent with Mowday's (1978) findings concerning the situational specificity governing the choice of particular influence strategies.

Two important issues confront political perspectives on organizations. First, Chaffee (1980) has argued that it is, in fact, quite difficult to distinguish among political, bureaucratic, chance, and rational models using the procedures that have been typically employed — regressions in which indicators supposedly representing the various models are included in the equation. For instance, the fact that budgets tend to be incremental and stable over time (Wildavsky, 1979), which is sometimes taken as support for a model of bounded rationality and incrementalism, could reflect that the power distribution that determines the budget is stable over time, or even could be consistent with a more rational, optimizing model (Williamson, 1966). Chaffee (1980) suggested that it would require attention to both process and outcome to diagnose the use of power and politics in organizations. The explication of procedures for testing and assessing the use of power as contrasted with alternative perspectives on decision making remains an important task.

The second problem, closely related to the first, involves issues in the measurement of power. As Dahl (1957) has noted, it is important to be able to distinguish between those with actual power and those that just follow along (satellites) or are able to guess which side is going to win and line up behind that position (chameleons). By chance, in any single instance one actor could be on the winning side, and thus consistency over time is important. But that is not enough, as it is important to be able to distinguish power from foresight or following another powerful actor. Clearly, the measurement of the power of social actors in a way that distinguishes that concept from others and produces reliable empirical results is an activity that requires additional effort.

SUMMARY AND CRITIQUE

Most of the research in organizational behavior, in terms of numbers of articles, probably falls in the domain covered in this chapter—analysis of behavior and attitudes at the individual level of analysis adopting a perspective emphasizing rational, or at least intendedly rational or boundedly rational, cognitive processes. Such perspectives lodge the explanation for organizational actions and outcomes in terms of the behaviors of single persons or small collectivities. Furthermore, these perspectives all assume some preexisting goals, needs, attitudes, or intentions, which are to be served by the selection of some actions from a set of possible options. Thus, all presume foresight, intention, and attitudes and behavior that are largely cognitively mediated.

Although fundamentally similar, there are some distinctions among the perspectives reviewed. In particular, expectancy theory presents one of the more elaborated models of the development of both attitudes and behavior in the context of desired goals and estimates of the relationships connecting actions to these goals or desired states of the world. Goal-setting theory, on the other hand, predicts action solely in terms of intentions or goals, without the intervening calculus of expectations and instrumentalities. Thus, it would seem that one critical element distinguishing expectancy theory is its complex, interactive formulation. Unfortunately, this has not often been tested against simpler alternatives, and, indeed, doing such a test is difficult because the interaction term created (for instance, by the value of an outcome multiplied by its expectancy) is going to be highly correlated with the individual terms (such as the goal or valued outcome itself). Political theories, with their emphasis on relating outcomes to power, imply rather than directly argue for intentional action; to this time they have also tended to ignore issues such as estimates of the likelihood of attaining some valued outcome given a proposed or intended course of action. Political theories have, in many cases then, tended to analyze more aggregate-level outcomes rather than individual attitudes or behavior that are more the focus of the other theories.

Although this perspective—individual-level rationality—is the dominant one at least in much of organizational psychology, this is unfortunate because the perspective suffers from a number of serious shortcomings. In addition to the specific issues raised with each of the theories considered, it is appropriate to conclude this chapter by discussing several important problems that plague all of these perspectives and others in the individualist, rationalist tradition.

The first problem is the assumption of unidirectional causality that characterizes virtually all of these approaches. This is seen clearly in Figure

2-1 — needs and environmental dimensions are causally exogenous; their interaction together determines the degree of need fulfillment and consequently attitudes and, then, the behavior people engage in within organizations. This problem has been articulated by Bandura (1977):

> . . . internal personal factors and behavior also operate as reciprocal determinants of each other . . . people's expectations influence how they behave, and the outcomes of their behavior change their expectations. The major weakness of the traditional formulations is that they treat behavioral dispositions and the environment as separate entities when in fact, each determines the operation of the other . . . the environment is only a potentiality until actualized by appropriate actions; it is not a fixed property that impinges upon individuals. . . . Thus, behavior partly determines which of the many potential environmental influences will come into play and what forms they will take; environmental influences, in turn partly determine which behavioral repertoires are developed and activated. In this two-way influence process, the environment is influenceable, as is the behavior it regulates (1977: 195).

What this means is that behaviors determine attitudes (Bem, 1970), needs, and environments, not just the reverse as implied in the figures. The environment is created not only by action but also through an attentional or enactment process (Weick, 1969). Although Bandura does not suggest this, we would argue that personal dispositions are similarly created in a process in which behavior is causally attributed to various kinds of internal states such as attitudes or needs. The idea that environments need to be reconstructed (typically by others) for the individual "ultimately denies persons the creative capacity to cope with their environment, in part, by constructing meaning that makes the context more satisfying, and, in part, by redefining the situation and attending to selected aspects of the situation" (Salancik and Pfeffer, 1977a: 440). By assuming some relatively stable goals, attitudes, or needs, the view of individuals developed is one of persons searching for environmental circumstances in which these preferences can be satisfied. Although such proactive behavior does occur, it is also the case that people spend more time with the consequences of their actions, typically, than they do planning them, which means that theories of behavior need to incorporate the adaptation process as well as choice.

The second general problem concerns the neglect of the context in virtually all of these theories. The context provides the reward contingencies, or the action possibilities, but, beyond that, the processes of choice and action are essentially individual and free from considerations of social influence, imitation, and other macrostructural influences. Such an assumption is the only one that can justify treating the individual as the unit of analysis and neglecting any estimates of contextual effects, which is what occurs in virtually all of the studies reported in this chapter. It is somewhat ironic that the most potent forces continually observed in social psychological studies — group effects and conformity pressures — are somehow systematically ignored in the vast majority of the literature that attempts to explain individual attitudes and behavior. It is little wonder that such literature has been (and will continue to be) notoriously unsuccessful.

This theme, that context has been too much overlooked, has been echoed recently in critiques and reviews of social psychology more generally. Pepitone (1981: 983), for instance, has noted that "the major consequence of individualistic-reductionistic social psychology has been the neglect, in several interdependent social and physical contexts, of sources of social behavior that lie outside the individual." Pursuing a similar theme, Neisser (1976: 7-8) wrote, "We may have been lavishing too much effort on hypothetical models of the mind and not enough on analyzing the environment that the mind has been shaped to meet." The including of context effects may be difficult while maintaining the individualist, rationalistic orientation that has so long dominated the field. Pepitone has sounded this pessimistic note:

> . . . it would appear that a major lesson from history is that . . . social psychology . . . theories cannot adequately deal with the influences on personality and social behavior that originate in the objective environment, including especially the social structures and normative systems in which individuals are embedded and psychologically subscribed. The essentially intrapsychic dynamisms at the core of the most dominant theories in social psychology since the field was labeled as such do not implicate the objective social environment beyond the arousing or directing functions of "stimuli" or cognitive "representations." Such theoretical conceptions cannot account for the origin of objective social forces, nor for the conditions under which they become operative on and in individuals (1981: 983-984).

Not only are there the context effects of the immediate social environment, there is also the effect of the history of the interaction. The European sociologists (e.g., Karpik, 1978) have taken modern organization theory to task for developing theories and analyses that are quite ahistorical and culture free. Crozier (1964) provides an example of the alternative type of analysis, one in which the features of the organization are tied to the history and culture of the society in which the organization is embedded. The strategic contingencies' approach to analyzing intraorganizational power has been criticized for its neglect of factors such as the rules of the game and the meanings and norms that evolve in a specific organization and that exist because of the particular society in which the organization occurs (Clegg,

1975). Thus, the neglect of context, it is argued, leads to the development of theories that do not have the potential for understanding development and change over time or for understanding the subtle nuances of interaction that are critical in apprehending what is really occurring.

Calder and Schurr (1981) also have emphasized understanding dispositions, such as attitudes, in context:

> . . . the concept of attitude outlined here implies that one cannot simply "measure" attitude as a predictor variable. Measurements of attitude must be predicted [sic] on an understanding of how attitudes are created. Otherwise, the attitude measured is likely to reflect the measurement context rather than the organizational context (1981: 291).

They cited the Regan and Fazio (1977) study in which by experimentation and by survey the following finding was uncovered: attitudes predict behaviors much better when the attitude being measured refers to something about which the subject has experience. Thus, for instance, in one of the studies, attitudes toward playing with puzzles were more strongly related to subsequent behavior of choosing to play with the puzzles for those people who had actual experience with the puzzles. People will answer a questionnaire about anything. Whether this affective response means anything in terms of subsequent behavior is related to whether the attitudes being tapped have more or less foundation in experience.

The theories outlined in this chapter tend, for the most part, to begin with the goal, preference, need, or attitude. Little attention has been paid to how such dispositions develop or change or how they are affected by history and the social context in which the individual is embedded. In some sense, many of these theories take for granted elements such as environmental characteristics and the existence of needs or goals that are critical sources of variation in behavior and affect. Attention to the context in which dispositions and perceptions of the environment are formed is a critical deficiency in the various perspectives of individual rational choice, though such a deficiency is clearly remediable.

The third problem is that theories of prospective individual or subunit rationality, in common with theories of retrospective rationality, are heavily cognitive. Thus, they rely on a large number of hypothetical constructs related to the cognitive processing of information. Such concepts as instrumentalities, expectancies, goals, preferences, attitudes, and needs, and the various combinatorics by which such things are combined to produce attitudes or behavior, are essentially unobservable except through the interrogation of the subject(s). The epistemological difficulties posed by this problem are enormous. First, one may be creating the very phenomena by

asking about them. Salancik and Pfeffer's (1977a) critique of the job characteristics research is applicable to all research that relies on arbitrary, hypothetical constructs that exist only in a person's mind:

> When one sees well-developed lists of job characteristics, one is tempted to
> take such lists as descriptions of reality and forget to ask how the lists were
> developed in the first place. Saying that a job has certain characteristics
> orients the reader and the researcher to the characteristics, and the
> characteristics therefore become real and meaningful. However, if one asks
> the question of how did particular characteristics come to be identified with
> a job, one recognizes that the characteristics are defined into the situation
> by someone (1977a: 445).

The dimensions of needs, personality, goals, and so forth are just as arbitrary. Much more caution is required than is customarily observed in the
literature in which if something is measured on a questionnaire, it is assumed
that somehow it is both a real and useful construct and measurement of that
construct.

Second, as Webb et al. (1966) noted some years ago, measurement of
the constructs may alter them. One's attitude or needs may change when
one is interrogated about them. Such is particularly likely to be the case
when the conditions under which such questioning occurs are not considered. Asking people about their job attitudes or their characterizations of
their jobs may produce different responses if one asks as part of an announced,
job-redesign effort, as part of a union-organizing effort, or at home as part
of a general life satisfaction survey.

Third, because of its heavy reliance on questionnaires, much of the
research on rational individual choice in organizations is subject to the various kinds of problems well enumerated by Salancik (1979a) in his plea for
more field stimulation methodology. By imposing the researcher's concepts
and language on the subject through questionnaires, one largely determines
that the result will be consistent with those concepts and measurements. It is
unclear as to how much of the results of research are determined by the way
the questions are asked, but it is clear that it is enough to cause concern for
research dealing with essentially unobservable hypothetical constructs in
which the potential for the imposition of the researcher's frames of reference
is large. It is not clear, simply put, whether the results of much of the research in this tradition tell us anything about the world of organizations or
those who populate that world, but they certainly tell us a lot about those
who study organizations and how they view the world.

In addition, as cognitive theories, and rational theories at that, these
perspectives are all subject to the criticisms of those who have questioned

either the prospective nature of rationality (March, 1978; Weick, 1969) or the amount of cognitive work done by people in organizations at all, whether such work is retrospective or prospective (Collins, 1981). In the first tradition, Weick (1969), following Schutz (1967), has argued that meaning may be retrospectively inferred from action and that goals are formed from action rather than guiding such action prospectively. Similarly, March (1978) has argued that action may be undertaken to uncover preferences, rather than having preferences guide the action prospectively. Weick's (1980: 119) statement, "How can I know what I think until I see what I say?" summarizes this point of view quite well.

The ethnomethodological critique of the rationalist cognitive approach calls into question even the concept of retrospective rationality, arguing instead that much of life is taken for granted and is not thought about either before action or after it has occurred. Collins (1981) has summarized this line of argument:

> Much of the classic ethnomethodological research was oriented toward showing that the basic everyday life stance is to take it for granted that meaningful activities are going on. Garfinkel's (1967) breaching experiments indicate that to question or violate the usually tacit aspects of behavior upsets people. They assume there are aspects of life which they should not have to explain . . . it is in fact impossible to explicate all the tacitly understood grounds of any social convention, and the effort to do so quickly shows people the prospects of an infinite regress of discussion. . . . These results imply that meaningful cognitions do not ultimately guide social behavior; rather cognitive meaning is usually given to events retrospectively, when some difficulty has arisen which is to be remedied by offering an "account" (Scott and Lyman, 1968) . . . people are rarely able to verbalize many social rules guiding their behavior . . . immediate situations do not have to be explicitly defined in order for people to act in them (1981: 990-991).

Collins has further argued that affect or sentiment, rather than information processing, may have more to say about understanding behavior in organizations. This theme will be developed in more detail in Chapter 6 in which more phenomenological approaches to organizational analysis are considered. For the moment, the reader should recall that there is sentiment and affect, as well as cognition, that the two may not be closely connected, and that sentiments and affect offer an alternative basis for explaining and understanding behavior.

There are two more problems with these perspectives that are, perhaps, even more serious than those already enumerated. The first is the potentially tautological nature of the rational choice perspective. Summarizing the work of numerous theorists such as Parsons (1951) and Homans (1962), as well as research on the explanations of individual fertility behavior (Rind-fuss, 1978; Rivers, 1916), Mayhew (1980) noted that the basic position adopted for understanding human behavior from this individualist, rational-ist perspective was as follows:

> So: (1) values occur arbitrarily in space and time; (2) values tell people what they *want* to do; (3) people's behavior is generated by their values; and this makes it possible to say that (4) people do things because they want to. . . . The individualists do not seem to have grasped the elementary principle that one does not explain a set of data by simply repeating it. To say that *people do things because they want to* is not an explanation (nor even an interpretation) of what people do: it is a restatement of the . . . data. It is not different from saying people do things because they do things (1980: 354-355).

Thus, goal-setting theory (Locke, 1968) argues that people undertake ac-tions to achieve their goals; expectancy theory (Vroom, 1964) argues that people act to attain their highest subjective expected utility; and political theories assert that political action is motivated by the desire to achieve some end state or valued final outcome — in each instance, there is a cir-cularity present that is troublesome, to say the least. It may be possible to formulate rational choice perspectives to escape this circular reasoning, but it will require more effort than has yet been evidenced in much of the pub-lished research.

The final problem arises when other than individual action is to be ex-plained — for instance, incidents such as strikes, riots, panics, or other col-lective behavior. How are the attitudes and behaviors of individuals to be aggregated to derive an explanation of these collective phenomena? Not easily, according to Mayhew (1980, 1981). To see this problem, consider Martin and Murray's (1981) attempt to apply equity theory and distributive justice-social comparison approaches, formulated at the individual level, to understanding things such as race riots. Not only must such an approach employ the attitude-leads-to-behavior assumption (or cognition-leads-to-behavior), which is both a part of the theories just considered as well as an assumption of very dubious validity (e.g., Calder and Ross, 1973), but the argument must be implicitly made (though not explicitly stated) that these collective actions are the simple aggregation of the individual decisions made in the privacy of each person's mind. Thus, to explain collective action on the basis of perceptions of injustice studied and described at the indi-vidual level is to assume that such collective behavior represents the sum-mation of each individual's perceptions of injustice and willingness to act on those perceptions. Not only is there a neglect of factors such as resources and social influence, which Martin and Murray acknowledge, but, more fundamentally, there is no consideration of how (or why) collective action originates and whether it is the sum (or something else, including independent) of individual cognitions and choices.

But, organizations are collective entities, embodying and involving collective action. One might well wonder whether theories that begin by building up from the level of individual rational cognitions can ever really hope to explain the aggregation of behavior that occurs in larger social systems. It is at least a question worth posing.

These six issues — (1) the presumption of purpose or intent occurring in advance of the action — that behavior is foresightful rather than retrospectively rational, (2) the reliance on information processing (as contrasted, for instance, with sentiment-based) explanations of attitudes and behavior; (3) the neglect of the effects of context and the possibility that the perspective is structurally incapable of incorporating context very well; (4) the tautological nature of the explanations; (5) the reliance on hypothetical constructs that reside largely in people's heads, with consequent problems for observation and measurement; and (6) the use of individual-level constructs to try to explain collective or macrolevel behavior — pose a set of fundamental challenges for the theories of behavior reviewed here and the many similar types of theories that we have not even covered. The perspective being critiqued has come to dominate not only the field of organizational behavior but many other social sciences as well. This dominance does not seem to be warranted either by the data or by the fundamental problems confronting such an approach.

3

THE EXTERNAL
CONTROL OF
INDIVIDUAL BEHAVIOR

The basic premise of the external control or constraint perspective is almost deceptively simple. If one assumes that individuals (or organizations, as discussed in Chapter 5) are adaptive to their environments, then to understand behavior it is both necessary and largely sufficient to consider only the characteristics and constraints of the environment in which these social actors are embedded. To argue that individuals are adaptive presumes the question, Adaptive to what? If the answer is the environment, it is to the environment that one must look for explanation and prediction of behavior; the setting determines the behavior that is emitted.

Two examples should make the point clear. The archetype of external control or constraint is the customary social psychology experiment. Some variants of a treatment are devised—giving subjects choices from four rather than two soft drinks (Reibstein, Youngblood, and Fromkin, 1975), asking them to write essays counter to their initial attitudes toward some issue for more or less extrinsic justification (Festinger and Carlsmith, 1959), and so forth. Subjects are randomly assigned to treatments; in most studies, no individual difference measures (such as of needs, goals, values, or prior attitudes) are collected or analyzed. The results are presented in terms of the effect of the treatment, the setting or context, on the subjects' attitudes or behaviors. This analysis asks whether there are differences across subjects in responses determined by the external situation *regardless* of the various traits or characteristics of the subjects. The very success of many such experiments in producing differences across groups of people according to which external situation they are exposed attests to the reasonableness of the assumption that settings and treatments can be devised that are potent enough to create differences in responses across groups of individuals without regard for individual characteristics, traits, or goals.

Or, consider the response to a situation of poor work behavior on the part of a group of department store employees, where such poor work behavior might include being absent from the work station and standing around idle rather than waiting on customers or restocking shelves. Consider the prescriptions that might emerge from the perspectives discussed in the last chapter. One approach would be to measure the characteristics of the employees' jobs, to measure their growth need strength, and then to redesign jobs to involve more variety, autonomy, feedback, and so forth to the extent that this was possible and consistent with the degree of higher-order need strength possessed by the individuals. Many recommendations would focus on a survey of the employees' attitudes to assess what they liked and did not like about the job, their supervision, and so forth. The recommendation would be made to work on improving those aspects of the work setting that were sources of dissatisfaction. This approach proceeds from the premise of the stability of attitudes, the connection between attitudes and behavior, and the need to change attitudes to change behavior (Calder and Schurr, 1981). Yet another approach might involve setting high and specific goals for their behavior, while another prescription would be to find out what the employees valued and then show them how desirable work behavior would lead to their obtaining these desired outcomes.

In contrast to these approaches that focus on changing the cognitions, attitudes, and sentiments of employees to have them change their behavior, an external constraint approach might involve any one or a combination of the following: change the contingencies of their behavior, in particular, providing reinforcement for persons when they engage in desired actions; expose the employees to a thorough and protracted inculturation program in which the desired behaviors became internalized; provide the employees with information indicating how interesting, challenging, and important their jobs are, as well as information indicating that most persons in the job in fact do what they are being asked to do; and create task-based and social interdependence with others who will request that the employees do what is being sought. In each of these instances, some aspect of the environment — its reinforcement patterns, its informational content, or the structure of interactions — is changed for all the employees regardless of their paticular individual traits or dispositions. Moreover, these changes are designed to restructure the environment (not change the employees) to produce new behaviors and attitudes. The assumption is, as in the case of the archetypical social psychology experiment, that changing the environment in which the behavior occurs will change that behavior, without necessarily paying much attention to the individual differences and dispositional characteristics of the people involved.

It should be clear that the external control of behavior perspective tends to downplay the role of cognitive processes and foresightful, rational action as determinants of individual action. Rather, to the extent cognitive processes are considered at all, they are often argued to follow, rather than precede, action. Thus, in contrast to the rational choice approach seen in the last chapter, the external control approach argues that rationality is often retrospective, with goals, attitudes, and values developing *after* the behavior to make sense of what has already occurred, rather than serving primarily to guide behavior prospectively.

In this chapter, several prominent external control of individual behavior approaches are presented. We begin with operant conditioning, the most explicitly externally focused, and then consider social learning theory, which reintroduces cognition while maintaining the emphasis on the importance of reinforcement. Next, socialization, the internalization of external control, is considered, and then the effect of roles and role pressures. Procedures for measuring and assessing the effects of the social context are described. Then, the role of rationalization, the process of retrospectively creating rational action, is considered and its implications for understanding and predicting behavior are explored. We conclude the presentation of substantive theories by presenting the social information processing approach (Salancik and Pfeffer, 1978a), which integrates several of these approaches as well as some of the material from the preceding chapter. The chapter concludes by considering some of the critical issues confronting the external control of individual behavior perspective, particularly as this approach is contrasted with that developed in Chapter 2. Before beginning the discussion of the specific theories, however, it is first necessary to understand the two fundamental forms of external influence that are embodied in all of them.

EXCHANGE-BASED AND INFORMATIONAL INFLUENCE

Two different mechanisms are generally presumed to be responsible for the effect of context or the environment on individual behavior. One effect proceeds from a mechanism of social exchange in which behavioral compliance on the part of the individual is exchanged for something, which is perceived to be contingent on the individual's behavior. The other effect posits a mechanism of informational influence through uncertainty reduction in which ambiguity is resolved through reliance on shared judgments and perceptions, and through such reliance on the judgments and perceptions of others, the individual comes to be influenced. It should be clear that these effects are not mutually exclusive and that both can and do operate in the same situation.

Exchange

Blau (1964), Emerson (1962), and others have proposed a theory of exchange that argues that a given social actor A is dependent on some other actor B to the extent that B controls some resource or performance valued by A and to the extent that A cannot obtain this resource or behavior from alternative persons. Furthermore, Emerson (1962) proposed that power was the obverse of dependence — or to the extent that A was dependent on B, B had power over A. This power could potentially be used by B to have A do something that B wanted her or him to do. Thus, from the exchange perspective, behavior of an individual becomes controlled externally when others in that person's environment have power over him and make requests for behavior based on that power. Both Emerson and Blau argued that situations of asymmetric dependence and, hence, asymmetric power were not stable in that the less powerful actor would be led to undertake activities to redress the power imbalance. Such activities could involve things such as finding alternatives to what B provided, finding or developing some behavior or resource that A controlled that B wanted, or leaving the exchange relationship. For Blau (1964), one of the important behaviors A could perform to rebalance the exchange was deference. Thus B received deference and status and, in turn, provided A with the resource or performance needed. For instance, in a study of a law enforcement organization (Blau, 1955), persons with more skill or expertise in the complicated work of the agency were often asked for help by others in the office. This exchange was balanced by the status and deference they received from those for whom help was provided.

In social contexts such as organizations, one of the important items of exchange is acceptance into the group. Indeed, most of the work on conformity in groups has emphasized the importance of acceptance and membership as a basis for acquiescing to conformity pressure. *Conformity* has been defined as "a change in the behavior or belief toward a group as a result of real or imagined group pressure" (Kiesler and Kiesler, 1969: 2), a definition that highlights the differences between the group's position and the individual's and the pressure exerted by the group on the individual to conform. Individuals, of course, do not accede to the pressures of all social influences, rather only to those exerted by important groups to which they belong or want to belong. These groups are called reference groups and are defined by the following characteristics:

> . . . 1) the person is aware of the others, 2) the person defines himself as a member, or would like to be a member, and 3) the person feels that the others are significant to him (emotionally or cognitively) (Kiesler and Kiesler, 1969: 27).

Groups exert pressure on individuals to conform to central and important attitudes and behaviors. This pressure results from the fact that the group itself must be continually reestablished. What constitutes or defines a group is typically more dense communication within the group than across its boundaries and a similarity in orientation that distinguishes the group from other social actors in its environment. Groups consist, as do organizations, of interlocked cycles of behavior (Allport, 1962; Weick, 1969). These cycles of behavior must be continually renewed and reaffirmed to provide continuing assurance and evidence that the group exists as a distinct social entity. Deviance, particularly on behaviors or attitudes that are central to the group's definition, threatens the maintenance of the group. Thus, deviation is met, first, with increased communication to bring the deviant back into line and, then, with exclusion or expulsion from the group if pressure fails to ensure compliance (Schacter, 1951).

Groups serve two functions for the individual (Kelley, 1952). One function is a normative function. As Kiesler and Kiesler (1969) noted:

> . . . he may be motivated to gain or maintain acceptance. Seeking companionship, finding a mate, and showing off fall into this category . . . the group is in a position to award or withhold recognition to the person. To the degree that he conforms to the rules and standards of the group he may be rewarded. This type of group . . . encourages and enforces the enactment of acceptable behavior and belief . . . the person will be concerned with who likes whom, with avoiding rejection by the others, and with possible surveillance of his behavior (1969: 28-29).

Individuals comply, then, to group pressures in part because such compliance is necessary to maintain membership in and acceptance by groups that are important. An exchange is established. The individual complies with group norms and, in turn, he or she achieves membership and the social support that such membership affords, as well as possible goal attainment which can occur only through group action or group membership.

Informational Social Influence

In addition to normative social influence, mediated through exchange relations, there is informational social influence. Deutsch and Gerard (1955) have defined the two forms of influence as

> . . . *normative social influence* as an influence to conform with the positive expectations of another. An *informational social influence* may be defined as an influence to accept information obtained from another as *evidence* about reality (1955: 629).

Informational social influence is predicated on the assumption that people desire to be correct in their judgments and to understand the world around them. Festinger (1954) argued that when objective or physical reality was unavailable to anchor beliefs and judgments, persons relied on the information provided by others to form opinions and perceptions about the world.

In informational social influence, rather than there being any obvious pressure or force to comply, uniformity in group opinions emerges as each group member resolves his or her uncertainty by seeking to find a common judgment with the others in the group. P. Smith (1973) provided an excellent review of the concept of informational social influence and the experimental evidence supporting its effects. Smith argued that ambiguity was widespread in work organizations. A lot of time, particularly managerial time, is spent on relatively unstructured work and communication with others. Performance is often difficult to evaluate, and the outcomes of decisions may be only weakly linked to the decisions themselves. As March and Olsen (1976) have argued, organizations are frequently ambiguous. In such settings, informational social influence is likely to be both pervasive and important in understanding behavior.

Demonstrations of both conformity effects and informational social influence are too numerous to review. Theories of social comparison processes, including theories of relative deprivation (Martin, 1981), equity theory (Adams, 1965), and reference group theories (P. Smith, 1973), all presume that others in the environment anchor individual perceptions about issues ranging from the adequacy of one's compensation to how anxious one should feel (Schacter, 1959). All of these theories argue for the effects of the context or environment on individual attitudes and behavior.

OPERANT CONDITIONING

In terms of its focus strictly on the external determinants of behavior and its omission of any consideration of cognitive processes, operant conditioning (Skinner, 1953) represents perhaps the purest example of the external constraint on behavior perspective. Skinner argued that behavior was a function of its consequences. Therefore, behavior was under the control of, and could be understood by considering the, contingencies that were administered from the environment and that followed the emitted behavior. Behavior that was reinforced was emitted more frequently in the future; behavior that was either ignored (as in extinction) or punished would diminish in frequency over time. Thus, doing nothing (extinction) was also seen as one potential consequence of a behavior, with effects for subsequent behavior. Brought into the field of organizational behavior by Nord (1969) and then by Luthans (Luthans and Kreitner, 1975; Luthans and White, 1971), the basic premises of the perspective in terms of management were straightforward. Since behavior was a function of its consequences, it was important to diagnose the behavior-consequence connections in understanding behavior. For managers, the behavior-consequence linkage was an important target of attention. The very phrase, *contingency management*, became a part of the language (Luthans and Kreitner, 1974, 1975), encapsulating the idea that contingent reinforcement of behavior was the key technology for managing and changing that behavior.

The focus on the consequences of behavior, on reinforcement, and on the environment that characterized operant conditioning can be seen as a reaction to the focus on internal states and predispositions that had been characteristic of efforts to change behavior, particularly various types of behavior pathologies (Bandura, 1969). Bandura (1977) counterposed the two approaches as follows:

> . . . some theorists held that motivational forces in the form of needs, drives, and impulses, frequently operating below the level of consciousness, were the major determinants. Since the proponents of this school of thought consider the principal causes of behavior to be forces within the individual, that is where they look for explanations of why people behave as they do. . . . The inner determinants often were inferred from the behavior they supposedly caused, resulting in description in the guise of explanation (1977: 2).

By focusing on the learned, reinforced nature of pathological behaviors, Bandura (1969) argued for a focus on conditioning as a treatment modality rather than the continued emphasis on psychotherapy and other internally focused approaches.

There are some conceptual problems with operant conditioning, most notably its potentially tautological character. Reinforcers are defined in terms of their effects on behavior (a *reinforcer* is something that, administered after the behavior, increases its subsequent frequency or likelihood of occurrence); in turn, behavior is argued to be a function of its consequences (whether it was reinforced). The circularity of the argument is troublesome. However, operant conditioning makes some falsifiable predictions concerning the relative effectiveness of various types of reinforcers and various schedules of reinforcement. Moreover, in its focus on the behavioral effects of reinforcers, the theory is scarcely any more tautological than those approaches to behavior that account for the behavior by labeling it as the result of some trait (e.g., aggressive behavior is the result of the person being an aggressive personality).

Schedules of Reinforcement

There has been a relatively larger amount of research on schedules of reinforcement than on many other aspects of operant conditioning. This is probably because it is with respect to schedules of reinforcement that operant conditioning and expectancy theories of motivation make different predictions. As described by Jablonsky and DeVries (1972), reinforcement schedules can be continuous — in which each occurrence of the desired behavior is reinforced — or partial — in which some fraction of the desired behaviors are reinforced. Partial reinforcement can, in turn, be categorized along two dimensions: whether the reinforcement is fixed or variable and whether the reinforcement is administered on a ratio or interval basis. In reinforcement on a ratio basis, the basis for reinforcement is on the occurrence of a certain number of the desired behaviors; in interval-based reinforcement, the reinforcement is administered on the occurrence of the desired behavior after the given interval of time has elapsed. In fixed reinforcement, the consequences of the behavior are administered precisely every nth time (if a ratio) or the first time the behavior is emitted after a specific time interval has passed; in a variable reinforcement scheme, the reinforcer is administered more randomly, perhaps on the average of every nth time, but with variation so that it is not precisely the nth occurrence of the behavior that is reinforced.

The evidence indicates (e.g., Jenkins and Stanley, 1950) that the schedule of reinforcement makes an important difference in the characteristics of the behavior that is being conditioned.

1. Behaviors acquired under partial reinforcement continue for longer periods of time once the positive reinforcement is discontinued than do behaviors acquired under continuous reinforcement (e.g., Underwood, 1966).

2. To reach certain performance levels, partial reinforcement requires more trials but fewer reinforcements than does continuous reinforcement (e.g., Kanfer, 1954).

3. The response rate is more constant . . . under both variable ratio and variable interval schedules than under fixed ratio and fixed interval (e.g., Logan and Wagner, 1966).

4. The variable ratio schedule produces very high rates of responding and the steadiest rate of performance without breaks (e.g., Reynolds, 1968) (Jablonsky and DeVries, 1972: 344).

Thus, there is every indication from the operant conditioning literature that partial, variable reinforcement is more effective than either continuous or fixed reinforcement schedules.

This prediction is in contrast to that made by expectancy theory, which would appear to argue for the greater effectiveness of continuous reinforcement. As summarized by Berger, Cummings, and Heneman (1975), the argument is as follows:

> . . . while expectancy theory and the operant conditioning literature are in agreement that rewards should be contingent on desired behavior, expectancy theory does not explicitly predict one of the major findings of operant research: namely, that intermittent schedules of reinforcement . . . will maintain higher postacquisition performance . . . than will a continuous schedule . . . if the individual's subjective perceptions considered in expectancy theory do correspond to objective values, and if these values remain constant over time, then expectancy theory predicts that performance should be higher under a continuous rather than an intermittent schedule (1975: 288).

In expectancy theory predictions, anything that strengthens the link between behavior and the instrumental outcome to be received from engaging in the behavior should increase the force to perform the specific behavior. Increasing the probability that a given action will lead to a desired outcome should increase the force to perform that act (Vroom, 1964).

The existing empirical literature does not provide a resolution of the competing predictions. Some studies have found superior results for intermittent reinforcement (Yukl, Wexley, and Seymore, 1972), others have found no difference (Berger, Cummings, and Heneman, 1975; Deslauriers and Everett, 1977; Pritchard et al., 1976), and still others have found an advantage for continuous reinforcement (Copeland, Brown, and Hall, 1974; Zifferblatt, 1972). There are two problems that have plagued the research efforts to this point. In the first place, most operant conditioning approaches (e.g., Luthans and Kreitner, 1975) argue that more frequent or even continuous reinforcement is effective in obtaining the learning of a novel behavior and that the intermittent schedules are particularly effective in maintaining a behavior that is already firmly entrenched in the repertoire. The studies have, for the most part, not distinguished between well and poorly learned behaviors, although the tasks employed are all relatively simple and thus one might assume that the behaviors were already fairly well learned in all cases. More important, the distinctions in the reward levels are such as to make testing the various schedules of reinforcement problematic. In the Deslauriers and Everett (1977) study in which tokens were used to reinforce bus ridership, the difference was between giving a token worth 10 cents to every rider or to, on the average, every third rider. Thus, the difference was between 10 cents and 3.3 cents in the amount of reinforcement. Yukl and coworkers (1972) varied the payoffs between 50 cents and 25 cents, again a fairly small amount. It would seem to be useful to test the effects of varying schedules over a wider range of reinforcement to help distinguish between the expectancy theory and operant conditioning predictions.

Types of Reinforcers

According to operant conditioning, behavior is controlled by its consequences. There are four consequences of behavior (Luthans and Kreitner, 1975): positive reinforcement, negative reinforcement, extinction, and punishment. One way of viewing these possible consequences is shown in Figure 3-1, in which we distinguish between behaviors that are desired versus those that are not, on one dimension, and between the taking of some action versus doing nothing or ceasing to do something, on the other dimension. Thus, behavior that is desired can be either positively reinforced by doing something to provide a reward or negatively reinforced, as by taking away some aversive or noxious stimulus. For instance, the cessation of nagging on the occurrence of a desired behavior would be an example of negative reinforcement, the removal of something undesired upon the occurrence of the behavior to be reinforced. In the case of an undesired behavior, there

Figure 3-1. CATEGORIZATION OF FOUR CONSEQUENCES OF BEHAVIOR IN OPERANT CONDITIONING

Person Administering Conditioning Takes Action,
Does Nothing, or Stops Taking Action

		Action	No action or stopping action
Individual Does Something That Is Desired	Yes	Positive reinforcement	Negative reinforcement
	No	Punishment	Extinction

can be either action taken to suppress the behavior, as in the case of punishment, or nothing done, as in the case of extinction. Because unreinforced behaviors presumably disappear over time, extinction is one way of changing or shaping behavior.

Most behavior modification theorists have argued that positive reinforcement coupled with extinction for the undesired behaviors is more effective than the more frequently used punitive forms of control. The evidence on this point, however, is mixed. Bandura (1969) reviewed a number of experimental studies that seemed to indicate that punishment was ineffective in eliminating the undesired behaviors. However, he argued:

> The relative ineffectiveness of punishment in producing durable reductive effects in laboratory situations has probably resulted from the fact that, with few exceptions, the punished response constitutes the sole means of securing rewards. Hence, it comes as no surprise that in single-response situations punished behavior is performed for some time even though it incurs aversive consequences. . . . people generally have numerous options available in everyday life. Even though punishment may only temporarily inhibit dominant responses, during the period of suppression alternative modes of behavior may be strengthened sufficiently to supplant the original response tendencies (1969: 347).

O'Reilly and Weitz (1980), studying the disciplinary practices of managers in a department store chain, have argued that punishment can have important symbolic value and can positively impact performance. They argued that punishment, when administered on a clearly deserved basis, conveyed to the other employees the fact that the organization is concerned with performance; furthermore, the punishment makes clear the contingency between inappropriate behavior and the response to that behavior. Much of the literaure on punishment has dealt with how to administer it effectively (Miner and Brewer, 1976). There is evidence that indicates that discipline can be an effective performance-enhancing technique (Booker, 1969; Heizer, 1976; McDermott and Newhams, 1971). To test the propositions concerning the relative effectiveness of punishment versus positive forms of control, it would be necessary to compare the two strategies in a comparable setting directly. Most studies to this time have looked at the effectiveness of one or the other strategy but have not made such comparisons.

Applications

Hamner and Hamner (1976) detailed the generally successful results of the application of positive reinforcement/operant conditioning programs in ten organizations. The organizations included both public sector organizations (Detroit's garbage collection) and private sector firms and ranged from relatively small programs (28 persons in Standard Oil of Ohio) to larger programs covering a substantial portion of the firm's work force (2,000 employees in the program as part of a total employment of 5,500 at Michigan Bell-Operator Services). Most of the programs were focused on directly observable, fairly specific behaviors such as productivity, when that was readily measureable, and, more frequently, absenteeism, tardiness, and turnover.

Absenteeism interventions have typically used some type of lottery, game, or other variable ratio reinforcement schedule with good results. Pedalino and Gamboa (1974) reported on a study in which persons in a work group coming to work received a playing card, and the person with the best hand (in terms of poker) at the end of the week received $20. Using a reversal design (there is a baseline period, the treatment is administered and then the treatment is stopped while measurement continues), they reported excellent results from the program. Stephens and Burroughs (1978) compared two systems, one in which employees in a hospital were eligible for a cash drawing of $20 if they were not absent during a three-week period, and the second system in which subjects were eligible for the $20 drawing if they were not absent on eight dates randomly selected from a three-week period. Both interventions resulted in significant decreases in absenteeism, but there were no differences across the two systems in terms of their effectiveness. Nord (1970), Orpen (1978), and Kempen and Hall (1977) also have reported good results from using contingent reinforcers to decrease absenteeism.

Occupational safety was the target of one behavior modification intervention (Komaki, Barwick, and Scott, 1978). Desirable safety practices and behaviors were identified. The intervention was a presentation and explanation of the desired behaviors coupled with feedback. Using a reversal design, these authors found a significant increase in the observed behaviors during the period of the intervention, which fell to the baseline measure once the intervention was removed.

Operant conditioning has also been used to improve quality control (Adam, 1972, 1974; Adam and Scott, 1971) and to manage the performance of department store salespeople (Luthans, Paul, and Baker, 1981). This latter study relates to one of the examples with which we opened the chapter and affords some data relevant to examining operant conditioning versus goal-setting explanations of behavior — thus, we will consider it in more detail. In the study, 16 departments were randomly selected, with 8 each assigned to the experimental and the control groups. Observations were made of five categories of behavior: selling, stock work, miscellaneous activities related to work (such as referring customers to other departments, handling returns, and the like), idle time, and absence from the work station. The first three were called aggregate retailing behavior, and the last two were combined into an index of absence from doing work. For four weeks, observational measures were taken to provide a baseline. As one would expect, there were no differences between the experimental and the control groups. Subsequently, subjects in both groups were told that they would be observed on their performance, and both sets of people were given the same, more specific performance standards (e.g., the salespersons, except when excused, should be present within the department — i.e., within three feet of the displayed merchandise during working hours). In Locke's (1968) terms, they were given much more specific goals. Those in the experimental group were also offered paid time off and the opportunity to participate in a vacation lottery for attaining performance standards. After the four-week intervention period, the treatment was stopped.

Luthans and his colleagues found significant decreases in absence from the work station and idle time for the experimental group, compared with the control group, and a significant increase in aggregate retail behavior. Moreover, there was no difference in the behavior of the control group between the initial conditions and the period in which they were told they would be observed and were given much more specific performance goals. Thus, the data offer support for the operant conditioning approach but are inconsistent with Locke's (1968) goal-setting predictions.

Critical Questions

To some extent, operant conditioning is similar to goal setting in that, in practical applications, it is put into place with a variety of procedures that make it difficult to assess the extent to which the observed results are really the result of the positive reinforcement. As an example, consider the case of Emery Air Freight ("At Emery Air Freight," 1973). Emery, a freight-forwarding concern, was interested in improving its container utilization rates, as that saved it freight charges from the airlines. The firm implemented a self-monitoring program assessing container utilization and trained the supervisors to provide positive reinforcement, in the form of praise, for performance improvement. The program saved Emery millions of dollars in freight costs. Somewhat surprisingly, the results were almost instantaneous, occurring in one day.

Locke (1977) has argued that the program was really a goal-setting rather than a behavior modification intervention. The intervention involved setting specific, high goals and providing knowledge of results, whereas before performance was not well monitored and it was not clear if the goals for container utilization were either very specific or very high. Yet another interpretation of the results would be that it was the feedback on performance alone, independent of either the goal setting or the positive reinforcement, that produced the increase in performance (e.g., Seligman and Darley, 1977). The point is more than one of semantics. Goal-setting theory and operant conditioning differ substantially in terms of their focus on cognitive processes and their emphasis on individual, rational action rather than externally constrained behavior. Theories emphasizing the effects of feedback are different from both. To assess more precisely which of the theories are more or less accurate, or the conditions under which each is more or less likely to hold, it is clearly necessary to disentangle the various components that differentiate among the perspectives.

SOCIAL LEARNING THEORY

Operant conditioning approaches have been criticized for their neglect of the role of cognition in the learning process (Bandura, 1977). In operant conditioning, the assumption is that the behavior must be first emitted and then reinforced to be learned. Social learning theory, in contrast, admits a variety of learning processes. Such processes include vicarious learning, in which the behavior and its consequences for another person serve as information to the individual, and modeling, in which behavior is explictly presented for emulation, along with information about the likely consequences of engaging in that behavior.

Social learning theory departs from operant conditioning in two important respects. First, it emphasizes the importance of cognitive, symbolic activity:

The capacity to use symbols provides humans with a powerful means of dealing with their environment. Through verbal and imagined symbols people process and preserve experiences in representational forms that serve as guides for future behavior. The capability for intentional action is rooted in symbolic activity. Images of desirable futures foster courses of action designed to lead toward more distant goals. . . . Without symbolizing powers, humans would be incapable of reflective thought. A theory of human behavior therefore cannot afford to neglect symbolic activities (Bandura, 1977: 13).

Second, social learning theory emphasizes the self-regulatory nature of human interaction. "By arranging environmental inducements, generating cognitive supports, and producing consequences for their own actions, people are able to exercise some measure of control over their own behavior" (Bandura, 1977: 13).

As outlined by Davis and Luthans (1980), social learning theory is similar to operant conditioning in its emphasis on the consequences of behavior. This emphasis on the consequences of behavior, administered by the environment, is why social learning theory is categorized as a theory that stresses external control and constraint of behavior. However, social learning theory differs from operant conditioning in its emphasis on the role of vicarious learning processes such as modeling, the emphasis on covert, unobservable cognitive processes, and the part played by the self-control of individual behavior (Davis and Luthans, 1980: 283).

The fact that learning can occur through observation, as well as through direct experience, is to some extent the least theoretically threatening (to operant conditioning) of the three differences. Flanders (1968) has reviewed an extensive literature on imitation, and as noted above, the ability to learn symbolically is one of the consequences of the higher levels of cognitive development in man. Sorcher and Goldstein (1972) have developed training approaches oriented strongly around the use of modeling and vicarious reinforcement. In modeling, behavior is still strongly under the control of its consequences as administered by the environment; the only difference is that observational learning and higher-order cognitive processes are admitted.

The emphasis in social learning theory on cognitive processes that, by their very nature, are unobservable directly, represents a more substantial departure from the theoretical orientation of operant conditioning and begins to make social learning theory appear to be like expectancy theory. Bandura has emphasized the role of cognition in arguing that motivation is cognitively based. He maintained that "the capacity to represent future consequences in thought provides one cognitively based source of motivation" (Bandura, 1977: 161). Future outcomes function to motivate present behavior. "The widely accepted dictum that behavior is governed by its consequences fares better for anticipated than for actual consequences" (Bandura, 1977: 166). The data used to support this position are derived from experimental studies in which (1) the behavior being reinforced increases suddenly when the response contingencies are discovered through insight and (2) persons misinformed about the actually occurring reinforcement pattern respond differently from those who are correctly informed, even though in both cases the reinforcement pattern is identical.

The use of covert, cognitive processes is involved in the concept of self-control and self-reinforcement:

> A second cognitively based source of motivation operates through the intervening influences of goal setting and self-regulated reinforcement. Self-motivation requires standards against which performance is evaluated. . . . The motivational effects do not derive from the goals themselves, but rather from the fact that people respond evaluatively to their own behavior. Goals specify the conditional requirements for positive self-evaluation (Bandura, 1977: 161).

As noted by Davis and Luthans (1980), not only may the standards be self-created, but the consequences may also be self-created, as in feelings of accomplishment in writing, in which the reinforcing event of perceived completion of some work is largely self-created.

To consider anticipated consequences, symbolically represented, of potential action, as social learning theory does, comes very close to an expectancy formulation of motivation. Indeed, it is not clear that, in its more cognitive variants, there is much distinction between social learning theory and expectancy theory, except that the former pays much more explicit attention to the processes by which action-consequence contingencies are cognitively acquired. It is also clear that social learning theory has evolved over time. Initially proposed as a reaction to the use of traits and personal dispositions as explanations for behavior and emphasizing the external reinforcement of behavior, social learning theory has evolved over time to consider cognitive processes such as internal control and anticipated reinforcement. In a sense this represents a good example of the blending of perspectives on action in a single theoretical framework. It also illustrates the urge to reintroduce important elements of cognitive psychology into theories of behavior. Social learning theory has become quite representative of cognitive psychological approaches that recognize

> . . . a disparity between what is "out there" and its internal representation and argues that behavior is a function of the subjective world as transformed and represented internally. People respond to how they define

stimulus situations, not to the objective properties of those stimulus situations (Sampson, 1981: 730).

Although reasonable at first glance, the incorporation of individualist, cognitive elements into learning theory and operant conditioning approaches is both not quite consistent with the spirit of such approaches and inconsistent with the effects of social context on thought.

> Human thinking is not simply something inside the head of an individual; it is a social and historical product of collective endeavor. . . . Objective social practices and social relations constitute the forms and the contents of thought, which, in turn, participate in the maintenance of those very social objectivities (Sampson, 1981: 732).

Many of the other approaches reviewed in this chapter have been better able to maintain the social, contextual approach to understanding behavior while still incorporating some cognitive elements. In returning to some of the ideas and concepts of expectancy theory and motivation theory, social learning theory threatens to lose both its distinctive theoretical focus as well as the incorporation of external constraint and context as explanations for behavior.

SOCIALIZATION

Socialization represents a potent form of informational social influence. It is a process typically thought of as occurring at the time of organizational entry, though it occurs throughout one's career in some organizations. As a newcomer, a person is likely to be especially unsure about what are appropriate ways of doing things. Also, as a newcomer the individual is likely to be quite concerned about fitting in and being accepted in the new organization. Thus, the time of organizational entry is likely to be a time in which individuals are particularly open to the various forms of influence that constitute socialization.

The product of the socialization experience is intended to be an understanding of the organization's culture, way of doing things, and decision-making style that is internalized in the individual. This internalization presumably means that external constraint operated through surveillance and more formal exchange systems will be less necessary, as the practices and decision-making styles will have been internalized, will have become part of the individual. Socialization, as it involves learning and becoming a part of an organization's culture, is more important to the extent that the organization has a distinct, unique culture and, also, to the extent that internalization of control rather than surveillance or an emphasis on selecting people pre-trained or predisposed to the organization's ways is employed as the control strategy.

Dornbusch's (1955) description of the Coast Guard Academy provides a good overview of the stages of the socialization process. Initially, it is important to separate the new organizational entrant from previous sources of social support, which could serve to anchor or buttress preexisting beliefs and behaviors. This is often accomplished through physical separation and isolation. A certain amount of status degradation also occurs in this early part of the process. The underlying theory seems to be that by producing tension associated with past modes of behavior and thought, the target will come to realize the necessity of changing and adopting new ways. These new ways are inculcated through the provision of role models, the availability of literature illustrating the new principles to be adopted, and through constant exposure to various vicarious and direct feedback that illustrates the desired behavior and conduct. Thus, in the Coast Guard Academy, the upperclassmen serve as the role models, and cadets who deviate from prescribed practice are punished. In law firms, new associates are assigned to more senior work partners; similarly, in accounting firms, the new accountant is assigned to be part of a team in which he or she will learn both substance and conduct from those colleagues with whom one works.

The socialization process is also enhanced through the use of symbols of identification with the organization, such as uniforms, and through the belief that the organization one is joining is the best and that one can gain status through association with it. After the initial socialization is complete, follow-up is accomplished through the continued use of appropriate reading materials, meetings, and stories and sagas that both reinforce the greatness of the organization and make explicit the kind of behavior desired in the organization.

The empirical study of socialization in work organizations is relatively recent (Van Maanen, 1976) in spite of its apparent effectiveness as a control device. Edstrom and Galbraith (1977) presented data indicating that one form of isolation, involving the transfer of executives across national boundaries into foreign cultures, seemed to be associated with control efforts on the part of the organization and developed an organization-specific rather than a culture-specific frame of reference on the part of the employees. There has been increasing research attention to socialization as it is accomplished by and affects formal organizations (Feldman, 1976; Louis, 1980; Van Maanen, 1976), and occupational socialization has a long research tradition, including work on socialization into medical practice (Becker and Geer, 1958) and management (Berlew and Hall, 1966; Schein, 1968). The evidence from these studies is consistent with the position that, properly accomplished, socialization can lead to the internalization of occupational values for most of those undergoing the socialization experience.

Indeed, the effectiveness of socialization is one of its problems. When people enter an organization and begin to learn the ropes, they learn not only about the organization but also about a specific role, occupation, and perhaps subunit within the organization. Thus, one may be socialized to the occupation of engineering as it is practiced in the product design division of the Chevrolet division of General Motors. It is easy to think of instances in which socialization into a particular occupational role (engineer) or function or division (for instance, research and development) can lead to the adoption of beliefs and values (for example, state-of-the-art technical skills and development) that may be partly inconsistent with other values of the organization as a whole (for instance, profit). Thus, as a potent external control practice, the conduct of socialization requires planning as to what specific values and paradigms the individuals are to be trained.

ROLE THEORY

With the discussion of the socialization into organizational or occupational roles, the concept of role is introduced. Role theory and studies of role pressure provide yet another externally oriented perspective on the understanding of behavior in organizations. Role theory is similar to operant conditioning in its emphasis on the consequences of behavior—behavior in role, behavior that is expected, is reinforced in a number of ways; behavior out of role is typically punished or ignored. Moreover, as in many cases, role pressures are enforced both by exchange and by informational social influence that conveys to the role occupant what is required in the position.

As outlined by Kahn et al. (1964), role theory argues that individuals in work organizations occupy positions. Associated with these positions (or jobs) are sets of activities, including interactions with others, that are required or expected as part of the job. This set of activities, including interactions, constitutes the role of the individual who occupies that position. Because of the nature of organizations as systems of interdependent activity, the occupant of any given role is interdependent in his or her actions with others both inside and, in boundary roles, outside of the organization. These others with whom the individual is interdependent as a consequence of occupying a particular position in the organization constitute that person's role set (Merton, 1975). The very concept of interdependence means that performance of the individual's own role depends importantly on the activities of others in the role set; in turn, the performance of their jobs depends importantly on what the individual in the focal role does. Because of this interdependence — and particularly, the dependence of others in the individual's role set on his or her behavior — these others come to have role expectations for appropriate behavior. These behaviors get communicated to the role occupant and come to constitute role pressures. Role pressures as sent or communicated by various members of the role set need not, of course, be accurately perceived by the occupant of the focal role. Thus, there is a distinction between sent role demands and received role demands. Nevertheless, role pressures, enforced by various sanctions, form an important set of constraints on the behaviors of role occupants.

As seen by Kahn et al. (1964) and other role theorists (Gross, Mason, and McEachern, 1958; Merton, 1975), organizations are systems of mutual social constraint in which the activities of any given position occupant are determined by the demands and expectations of others in his or her role set. From this perspective, changing the focal role occupant, either by sending the individual to some training or educational program or by actually replacing the person with someone else, would be expected to have limited impact on the behavior of the person occupying the role. The individual or a replacement would still confront the same set of role pressures and role expectations from the same set of interdependent others and would, moreover, face the same information about what appropriate role activity was. Confronted with the same social demands and social information, behavior would remain similar to what it had been in the past. The image of organizations developed from role theory is of a net; because of the interconnections of the various nodes (through role pressures resulting from task interdependence), one can not lift the net or move the node very far without feeling the tug of the other points connected to that point in the network.

Roles and role pressures were viewed by Kahn et al. (1964) as important sources of tension and psychological stress in organizations, because although subject to a system of constraints and demands because of occupying a given position, there was no guarantee that the individual so constrained would be confronted with a consistent or feasible set of expectations and pressures. Kahn and his colleagues identified the following forms of role conflict: (1) intersender conflict, in which the demands of one member of the individual's role set conflict or are incompatible with the demands of another person in the set; (2) intrasender conflict, in which the demands of a single member of the role set are contradictory; (3) interrole conflict, in which the demands on one role occupied by an individual, such as employee, conflict with the demands of another role, such as family member; (4) person-role conflict, in which the expectations associated with fulfilling a role conflict with an individual's moral or ethical beliefs or self-concept; (5) role overload, in which the demands of the role are not contradictory per se but are so extensive and time-consuming that the individual cannot cope with all the role expectations; and (6) role ambiguity, in which the individual faces stress because of uncertainty about what behaviors are, in fact, required in the role.

The national survey undertaken by Kahn et al. (1964) uncovered the fact that a large proportion of the work force confronted various forms of role conflict. Furthermore, the data indicated that this role conflict was an important source of job-related stress and tension. Subsequent studies of role ambiguity and conflict (Bedeian and Armenakis, 1981; Hall, 1972; Rizzo, House, and Lirtzman, 1970) have provided further evidence on the effects of uncertainty and role-related stress in producing job dissatisfaction, turnover, and tension. The psychological and behavioral consequences of role stress and conflict provide further evidence for the potency and reality of role demands.

Lieberman's (1956) field study of workers in a plant is, perhaps, the classic demonstration of role effects. Lieberman measured the initial attitudes of plant employees. Subsequently, some of the workers were promoted to foremen, others became shop stewards, and others remained in their previous roles. Lieberman showed that there was no difference in their attitudes (e.g., toward the company, their jobs or the union) prior to the new positions being assumed. Thus, although one could not plausibly argue that there was random assignment of persons to roles, there was also no evidence that persons obtained their new roles (of foreman or shop steward) because of the differences in prior attitudes. Attitudes prior to the new positions and the new positions were uncorrelated.

After the people were in their new roles, Lieberman reexamined their attitudes. He found that there was systematic attitude change in a direction predicted by the role assumed. Foremen had developed more pro-company and other attitudes and beliefs consistent with their supervisory role; shop stewards had changed their attitudes in a pro-union direction; and those persons who had not changed roles did not evidence any change in attitudes. After these later measurements, the company encountered some financial problems, and some foremen were demoted to regular employees. Examining their attitudes yet again, Lieberman found that those back in their original roles as regular employees had reassumed attitudes identical to the other employees and different from their attitudes when they were foremen. Lieberman's time series design provides an excellent demonstration of the extent to which attitudes are changed and shaped by one's position and role occupancy.

In another study of role effects, Pfeffer and Salancik (1975) examined the effects of peer, subordinate, and supervisor expectations on the self-reported behavior of a set of managers in a state university housing office.

Behaviors were measured using items from the Leader Behavior Description Questionnaire (Stogdill and Coons, 1957). These authors found that both work-related and social behaviors could be accounted for by role set members' expectations. Work-related behavior was more heavily influenced by the expectations of the managers' boss, while social behaviors were more heavily influenced by the expectations of the managers' subordinates. In addition, Pfeffer and Salancik (1975) reported:

> . . . whether the supervisor attends more to the expectations of his boss or to those of his immediate subordinates appears to be a function of a) the demands to produce coming from his boss; b) the percent of the time the supervisor actually engages in supervision rather than in routine task activities; c) the number of persons supervised; d) the sex of the supervisor; and e) whether task decisions are made primarily by the supervisor, by his boss, or by his subordinates (1975: 152).

These factors relate primarily to the degree of social similarity between the supervisor and others in the role set and the amount of interaction (and thus, perhaps, interdependence) with them. Supervisors tended to conform more to the expectations of those with whom they were more similar and with whom they interacted more.

The fact that people conform, at least to some degree, to the expectations and demands of others is, of course, not news, given the extensive social psychological literature on conformity (Kiesler and Kiesler, 1969) as well as the literature on exchange theory (Blau, 1964). What is somewhat different about the role effects perspective, however, is that it argues that the demands and expectations for the behavior of the occupant of a given focal role are not strictly exogenous but emerge from the technological and task interdependence inherent in the division of labor designed to accomplish the work. Thus, role pressures and role demands are presumably amenable to the restructuring or reorganization of jobs and duties. Indeed, one might argue that successful occupants of roles in which previous occupants have failed use the occasion of their recruitment to the position to argue for and obtain just such restructuring. This change in job duties, job conditions, and job expectations prevents the new occupant from facing the same set of constraints and conditions that caused the predecessor difficulty.

The potency of role demands in constraining behavior has been used to explain the relative ineffectiveness of individually based change approaches (Campbell and Dunnette, 1968). Similarly, role constraints, and the image of the organization as an interlocked network of mutual role expectations, imply a need for systemwide approaches to changing behavior in organizations (French and Bell, 1973). Clearly, interventions such as team building and other work focusing on the group (Dyer, 1977) accept the critical nature of roles and role pressures in the determination of attitudes and behaviors in organizations.

The systematic study of role set determinants of behavior requires the collection of data on both behavior and expectations for that behavior from a large number of persons in the organization and then the application of some form of network analysis paradigm (e.g., Burt, 1977; Roistacher, 1974). Thus far, such research has not been carried out. Interestingly, network methodologies have been used in the study of constraints among formal organizations or economic sectors (e.g., Burt, 1980). Following that literature, one might define the autonomy of an actor in terms of the system of constraints to which he or she was exposed. One might argue that power was related to autonomy and, perhaps, attitudinal reactions to work as well, such as job satisfaction and the absence of job-related tension. It is clear that the concept of role and the idea of role constraints have been far from fully exploited in analyzing behavior in organizations.

THE EFFECTS OF SOCIAL CONTEXT ON BEHAVIOR

Both sociology and social psychology have emphasized the effects of the attitudes and behaviors of others in the individual's environment on his or her own attitudes and behavior. In the sociological literature, the search for the effects of context on attitudes and behavior occurred under the rubric of structural effects. Blau (1960) and Davis, Spaeth, and Huson (1961) called the effects of a group's composition on individual attitudes and behavior by that term, *structural effects*. The general model of such effects is:

$$Y = a_1 + b_1X_1 + b_2X_2 + b_3Z + u \text{ and } Z = f(X_1 - kX_2)$$

(Blalock, 1967). In the case of Blau's formulation, X_1 can be viewed as an individual's score on some variable (e.g., an attitude toward clients) (Blau and Scott, 1962), and X_2 represents the group mean on the variable. "The factor, Z, is . . . taken as a function of the difference between the individual score and that of the mean for his group, i.e., the degree of deviance or minority status" (Blalock, 1967: 792). Thus, the individual's score on some attitude or behavior is postulated to be an additive function of three variables: the individual's own independent attitude, the group mean attitude, and the difference between the individual's own preexisting attitude and the group mean. In the structural effects literature, it is presumed that the attitudes (or behaviors) of others in the individual's immediate environment impact the attitude (or behavior) exhibited in that environment, with there being a main effect for the group mean as well as an effect depending on the degree of deviation of the individual from that mean. No particular mechanism of effect was postulated — merely that social influence and group context effects were so pervasive and so potent that they could be analyzed directly.

As Blalock (1967) noted, there are identification problems with the formulation as originally developed that make estimation problematic. Hauser (1970) has recommended using covariance analysis and multiple regression analysis with dummy variables indexing group membership as a more appropriate way of assessing group or contextual effects than the methods used in the early research. Hauser (1970) noted that the early formulation inappropriately assigned variation to the effects of group composition because of the analytical procedures used.

Methodological considerations aside, there are a large number of theories that take the form of the equation above, recognizing the effect of group norms and the individual's context on the development of attitudes and behaviors by individuals embedded in these settings. Such a perspective is in contrast to the dispositional view of attitudes (Calder and Schurr, 1981), which views attitudes as stable positive or negative dispositions acquired through experience and guiding behavior. It is this dispositional view that has guided research on individual attitudes and behaviors in the work setting, for the most part, as reviewed in the previous chapter. As Calder and Schurr have perceptively noted, the contextual argument, taken to its logical conclusion, does not even need individual cognitive concepts such as attitudes or needs. "Rather, it is sufficient simply to understand the parameters of the social context" (Calder and Schurr, 1981: 287).

For most people working in organizations, the most potent and relevant contextual effect is that of the group with which they work. Groups are an important source of influence on individual behavior in organizations, a finding that emerged first from the Hawthorne studies conducted in Western Electric (Roethlisberger and Dickson, 1939) and that has been repeated many times since. The literature on the power of groups in influencing individuals within them is so large and extensive that it could easily encompass a book of its own. Thus, we will highlight only some of the major different group effects that have been observed.

Groups tend to enforce conformity on their members. In return for belonging, a person is expected to comply with the behavioral and attitudinal norms of the group, particularly when such norms are considered to be critical. Thus, the first group effect is attitudinal homogenization. Seashore (1954), for instance, noted that there was more uniformity of belief in more cohesive groups. Lipset, Trow, and Coleman (1956) in their study of the typographers union also observed group effects on attitudes toward union politics. They noted that

> . . . a group can place great pressure on its members to accept the
> salient attitudes and loyalties of the group — for example, the group's norm
> for production — and such acceptance is usually a condition for admission
> into the group. But a small group, in order to preserve good interpersonal
> relations and solidarity on matters of importance to it, need not and cannot
> enforce consensus with regard to all values and attitudes held by its
> members. A group may much more easily exert pressure on its members to
> *reduce* their interest or involvement in activities and attitudes which are
> peripheral to the group's own functioning and which may place a strain on
> solidarity if introduced into it (1956: 186).

Thus, there was less union political activity in small shops because of the
greater potential for cleavages to develop, which would threaten the solidarity of the group. And, in small shops where there was interest in and involvement in union political activity, the vote for one side or the other typically approached unanimity, indicating that consensus was enforced through
social pressure.

This tendency for groups to enforce conformity limits their effectiveness in some problem-solving situations. For instance, Davis (1969) argued
that one of the advantages of groups in some kinds of problem solving was
the ability to bring a number of different insights and knowledge bases to
bear on the problem. But, this advantage is often not realized in actual
groups, because there are pressures to avoid expressing deviant ideas or
disclosing data that are inconsistent with the theme of the discussion. Indeed, this problem of conformity has led to recommendations to use various forms of nominal groups (Delbecq, Van de Ven, and Gustafson, 1975),
in which the input of various individuals can get combined in an atmos-
phere free from some of the pressures to conform. Another example of a
group-based pathology is groupthink (Janis, 1972). In this condition, groups
operating under crisis conditions come to value conformity and consensus
greatly and define those who disagree as siding with the enemy. The group
begins to exchange increasingly inaccurate perceptions of the situation, and
without the ability to call these data into question because of the fear of ap-
pearing disloyal, processes of decision making that are premised on very inaccurate portrayals of reality can develop.

That group pressure can affect attitudes and behavior at this point in
time seems like an unexceptionable statement. But, embodied in that statement is the implicit argument that much of what occurs in organizations
happens as a result of forces residing outside of the single individuals who
so often constitute the units for our analyses. The first conclusion that must
be drawn from the literature on group effects is the empirical validity of the
external control perspective. For this literature suggests that one can learn
more about the attitudes of an individual or his or her production rate from

considering the context in which the individual works in terms of the norms for the attitudes and production in question than by examining the individual's beliefs, values, personality, or decision-making processes.

RETROSPECTIVE RATIONALITY

Some theories using the external control of individual behavior perspective, such as operant conditioning and some versions of the effects of context, are unconcerned about the cognitive processes that are involved. However, other theories consistent with the external constraint on behavior perspective have considered the role of cognition. Rather than arguing that behavior is prospectively rational, consciously chosen to obtain some goal, these theories argue that behavior is largely under some external control and that behavior is rationalized after the fact. As Aronson (1972) has put it, man is a rationalizing animal, not a rational animal. People act first and determine the goals of their actions later (Weick, 1969). The rationalizations developed for particular behavior can affect subsequent behavior by their focusing and committing effects. Thus, the type of rationalization developed can have implications for subsequent behavior — and usually has implications for the individual's attitudes toward the situation.

Bem's (1972) self-perception theory is a representative statement of the retrospective rationality view. Bem argued that when asked about an attitude toward some object, the individual would recall his or her behavior relevant to that object and infer the attitude from the past behavior. Thus, using Bem's (1970: 54) example, if a person were asked about an attitude toward brown bread, the individual would reflect on whether he ate brown bread. If he did, he would think, "I eat it and, therefore, I must like it"; if he did not eat it, the converse reasoning would apply. The argument of Bem and others implies that rather than preceding and guiding action, attitudes are an example of a construct used to make sense of the action that has already occurred.

In this process of retrospectively constructing explanations for events, the salience of different information is an important factor that can affect the explanation produced. As Salancik and Conway (1975: 830) have argued, "A natural extension of the cognitive theories . . . is the hypothesis that attitude inferences are not a function of behavior per se but of the information one has about one's behavior." Thus, by systematically affecting the information one has about one's behavior through cueing, different attitudes can be produced. Salancik (1974) demonstrated that by having some subjects recall intrinsically motivated behaviors (behavior motivated by, for instance, personal interest in the subject) toward a university course and others recall extrinsically motivated behaviors (behavior motivated, for instance, by the desire to get a good grade), the course attitudes of the intrinsically oriented subjects were related to the extent to which they did those intrinsic behaviors, while the attitudes of the extrinsically oriented subjects were related to the extent to which they did the extrinsic behaviors. This effect occurred even though there was no difference in the two groups' behavior or mean level of attitude toward the course.

Salancik and Conway (1975) demonstrated in two experimental studies that the level of attitudes could also be affected by impacting the salience of information. Since one of the studies involved course attitudes, the manipulation and its supporting logic is reported in some detail:

> The manipulation consists of having subjects answer whether a number of positive and negative behaviors apply to them. . . . Persons . . . review a number of their own behaviors by responding to a series of statements of the form *I do X*. If a person responds in the affirmative, it is assumed he will generate cognitions supporting his endorsement; if he responds in the negative, it is assumed he will generate cognitions supporting his nonendorsement . . . it should be possible to manipulate the cognitions that subjects generate by affecting their probability of endorsing or not endorsing statements of various forms. The particular device employed . . . is to pair either the adverb *on occasion* or the adverb *frequently* with the statement of the form *I do X*. It is likely that a person will have a higher probability of endorsing a statement, *I do X on occasion*, than a statement, *I frequently do X*. If the Xs are systematically varied to include behaviors that imply a positive or a negative orientation, then it should be . . . possible to manipulate the cognitive content available to a person from which he may infer or derive a judgement about his attitude (1975: 830-831).

Using attitudes toward religion in one study and attitudes toward courses in the second study, Salancik and Conway found support for their argument about the importance of information salience and the linguistic ways in which such salience can be affected.

In addition to information salience, two other factors affect the process of rationalizing past behaviors. The first is the extent to which the individual is committed to the behavior. Behaviors to which one is uncommitted are less likely to be rationalized; there is no need to explain something that one did not really intend to do or that does not have much meaning or relevance for subsequent behaviors. Salancik (1977) has argued that commitment is produced by the presence of four conditions: choice, irrevocability, publicness, and explicitness. Choice is probably the most critical factor. Without choice, there is no need to explain or justify one's behavior; one can simply maintain that one had to do the action. Actions that are irrevocable are more binding on the individual because they cannot be undone, and actions taken in public cannot be denied. Thus, there is more pressure for the individual to explain or rationalize such actions and to develop attitudes and beliefs consistent with such behavior.

The second factor affecting rationalizations is the logic or psychologic that is accepted and legitimate in the social context. As Salancik and Pfeffer (1978a: 231) noted, justifications for behavior must make sense and be accepted as being legitimate and reasonable by both the individual and by others. Justifications such as "I did it because I did not like doing it" are not considered to be logical or acceptable in this culture. Thus, doing behavior implies one likes it if the behavior was undertaken under conditions of choice and the other factors facilitating commitment were present.

The implications of the self-perception or retrospective rationality arguments for understanding behavior have been developed in two somewhat distinct but conceptually related literatures. One literature treats the consequences of engaging in some activity for an insufficient reward—the insufficient justification literature; the other literature treats the consequences of overrewarding behavior—the overjustification literature. Both literatures proceed from the basic premise that a person engages in some behavior for a level of reward and then makes sense of the behavior, with potential consequences for subsequent behavior, depending on the reward conditions. In this, both presume postaction rationalization in the context of the salient reward conditions.

Insufficient Justification Conditions

The basic insufficient justification paradigm emerges from the cognitive dissonance literature, although the findings are also consistent, for the most part, with the self-perception (Bem, 1972) interpretation of the effect. The argument is that persons who are induced to engage in some behavior for little or no external reward will adjust their attitudes to be more favorable toward the intrinsic aspects of the task they are doing. This attitudinal change results from a process of rationalizing why they engaged in the action. In the absense of external reward, they rely on internal constructs of positive affect and self-motivation to explain their activity. The difference between the dissonance and self-perception interpretations revolves around the motivational component of this process. While dissonance argues that persons are motivated to reduce discrepant cognitions (such as "I did X" and "I don't like doing X"), self-perception theory argues that the attitude change results from information processing rather than motivational effects. This difference, which has been explored in the social psychology literature, is not particularly important for our purposes since both predict the same result of insufficiently justified behavior.

Although most of the studies have been experimental (e.g., Brehm and Cohen, 1962; Comer and Laird, 1975; Festinger, 1964; Pallak, Sogin, and Van Zante, 1974; Weick, 1967; Zanna, 1973), there are some field studies also consistent with insufficient justification predictions. Staw (1974) studied ROTC cadets who had joined ROTC to avoid the draft. When the draft lottery was started, some subjects who had joined ROTC found out that they would not have been drafted, some found out that they would have been, and others faced a situation of uncertainty concerning their draft prospects had they not been in ROTC. Staw also distinguished between cadets who had joined under a committing contract and those who had joined under a two-year program that did not commit them to receive a commission and join the service at the end of college. First, as might be expected given their instrumental reasons for joining the program, cadets who were not bound to ROTC and who were unlikely to be drafted, based on their draft lottery number, dropped out of the program. For those cadets committed to the program by contract, the insufficient justification predictions held: those with low draft numbers (likely to be drafted) who had an external, instrumental reason for being in ROTC had less favorable attitudes toward ROTC and performed less well in ROTC courses than those with high draft numbers, who were not likely to be drafted and therefore no longer had any extrinsic reasons for being in ROTC, other than their committing contracts.

Pfeffer and Lawler (1980), using the Carnegie Council on Higher Education's survey of faculty, examined faculty attitudes as a function of their commitment (operationalized as being either tenured or untenured or by their years of service in the organization) and the sufficiency of their justification for being in the organization (operationalized as the deviation in actual salary from their predicted salary from a regression equation estimated on the entire sample). The dependent variables were a question asking about their satisfaction with their place of employment, a question asking about their intentions to quit, and a composite scale composed of both measures. In general, again insufficient justification effects were observed, although not in their strong form (Pfeffer and Lawler, 1980: 40–42). For the uncommitted group (untenured or fewer years of service), there was a positive relationship between the sufficiency of justification and attitudes toward the organization. For the committed group, this relationship was essentially zero. Furthermore, Pfeffer and Lawler reported that this effect was stronger for those who had a job inquiry or offer within the preceding two years, something that would affect the saliency of information about their situation and that would tend to cause them to engage more actively in a rationalization and justification process.

O'Reilly and Caldwell (1980, 1981) have examined the effects of choice and the sufficiency of justification on the attitudes and turnover of M.B.A. graduates. They argued:

> . . . subjects who have several job offers and who accept a job at a salary below the highest offered should have less extrinsic justification for their choice than those who either have only a single offer or who accept the top offer. When individuals who have fewer extrinsic justifications for their choice are made aware of this insufficient justification, one might predict that their commitment to the job would be higher. . . . For subjects who possess sufficient extrinsic justifications for their choice, making salient the reasons for their decision should result in less commitment (1981: 601).

The salience of the level of justification could be affected by their receipt of an outside offer or by any event that causes them to reflect on the sacrifices made to accept the lower-paying job. O'Reilly and Caldwell (1981) found evidence consistent with the interaction effect hypothesized between sufficiency of justification and commitment, in their case, assessed by the amount of choice the respondents had in choosing a job.

The evidence from the various field studies thus far appears to be consistent with the voluminous experimental literature. Both literatures indicate that postdecisional justification and rationalization is an important process (e.g., Staw, 1980b).

Overjustification

The overjustification literature suggests that, in a fashion parallel to the insufficient justification literature, if paying people too little or providing too few external reasons for their behavior increases their task interest and job satisfaction, providing too many rewards or paying them too much undermines task interest and job satisfaction. The argument is that persons confronted with salient extrinsic reasons for their activity will attribute their behavior to these external factors and, therefore, have less reason to justify their actions as being the result of the intrinsic nature of the task or situation itself.

Condry (1977) and Lepper and Greene (1978) have reviewed the numerous studies reporting an overjustification effect. Some studies have found that overjustification undermines the quality of performance on the task (e.g., Greene and Lepper, 1974; Kruglanski, Friedman, and Zeevi, 1971; Lepper, Greene, and Nisbett, 1973); other studies have found less reported interest in the task (Harackiewicz, 1979); in the original studies of overjustification, the evidence is that subjects who receive overjustification for engaging in the task during an experimental period show less interest in engaging in the task in subsequent unrewarded or "free periods" (Deci, 1971, 1972; Greene and Lepper, 1974; Lepper and Greene, 1975). This literature has led to a distinction being drawn between intrinsic and extrinsic motivation, with the argument being advanced that the rewarding of a task that would otherwise be intrinsically motivating leads to an undermining of this intrinsic motivation (Deci, 1971).

Again, most of the studies have been experimental, so there is the question of the extent to which the results will generalize to field settings. Although there is not much field evidence yet, the evidence is thus far consistent with the overjustification predictions. Caldwell, O'Reilly, and Morris (1981) examined the effect of an extrinsic reward, an educational subsidy, on the task interest and performance of students attending an evening M.B.A. program at Santa Clara University. These were all students employed during the day, and the subsidies were supplied by their employers and varied in the proportion of the tuition expenses covered. Caldwell and coworkers distinguished between subjects who were expressively motivated (by interest in obtaining knowledge for its own sake) and those who were in the program for more instrumental reasons (such as increasing their promotion or mobility opportunities). They observed an interaction between orientation and educational subsidy on task interest. For those with an expressive orientation, interest in the task was negatively correlated with the amount of the educational subsidy; for those students with more of an instrumental orientation, the larger the educational subsidy, the higher the interest in the task. There was, however, no main effect for the amount of subsidy on task interest or their measure of intrinsic motivation. One reason may be that there are norms that indicate that the payment of educational subsidies are appropriate. Staw et al. (1980) observed experimentally that intrinsic task interest was undermined by extrinsic rewards when these rewards were unexpected because they were not normal for the situation. In their field study, Caldwell and colleagues (1981) also observed an interaction between the norms for subsidy and intrinsic task interest.

Porac and Salancik (1981) have recently raised the issue of whether the terminology of intrinsic and extrinsic motivation is really helpful for understanding the process. Such distinctions in terminology are not made in the insufficient justification literature. There is some conceptual ambiguity concerning what are extrinsic as opposed to intrinsic rewards, even when psychologists are doing the categorizing (Dyer and Parker, 1975). Porac and Salancik argued that the issue was simply whether rewards were paired with one another, not whether they were extrinsic or intrinsic:

> If the intrinsic and extrinsic labels . . . are ignored, the research paradigm can be seen to involve the experimental juxtaposition of two conceptually

distinct rewards. One group of subjects receives two rewards during initial involvement with the task while another group receives only one. Following the reward manipulation, attention is then focused upon the value of the reward which both groups received. The overjustification effect, in general terms, is the reduction in the value of the common reward subsequent to its being paired with another during . . . a task (1981: 200).

Their experimental study indicated that one extrinsic reward (extra experimental credit) could undermine the value of another extrinsic reward (money), lending support to their general view of reward nonadditivity. The explanation for this finding is quite consistent with the justification and rationalization approach to behavior being discussed. The addition of a new, salient reward undermines the value of another reward because it provides some other reason for the person having engaged in the activity. Having paired the activity with the new reward, when that reward is removed, the reason for engaging in the activity is removed and performance, interest, or actual task-related behavior declines.

It seems clear, reviewing both the experimental and field evidence, that there is a great deal of evidence consistent with the retrospective rationality view of behavior. The evidence consistent with the external control of individual behavior perspective concerns the cognitive adjustment process. For the external control of behavior perspective to make sense, there should be some indication of postdecisional or postaction accommodation processes so that individuals come to terms with their environments and with their behavior. It is just this evidence that is provided by the insufficient and overly sufficient justification literatures. Although these literatures, by themselves, do not speak to the issue of the external control of behavior directly, they do so indirectly in two ways. First, they provide evidence for retrospective rather than prospective rationality, thus calling into question, at least to some extent, those perspectives on behavior (such as expectancy theory and its derivatives and variants) that argue from a prospective rationality point of view. Second, they provide evidence for the kind of postaction accommodation that would be supportive of an external control of individual behavior theory.

SOCIAL INFORMATION PROCESSING

Salancik and Pfeffer (1978a) have proposed an approach to understanding people's reactions to their work environment that incorporates many of the elements already described in this chapter. In Figure 3-2 their model of a social information processing approach to attitudes, behavior, and environmental characteristics is shown. Although developed with respect to

Figure 3-2. A Social Information Processing Approach to Attitudes, Behavior, and Job Characteristics

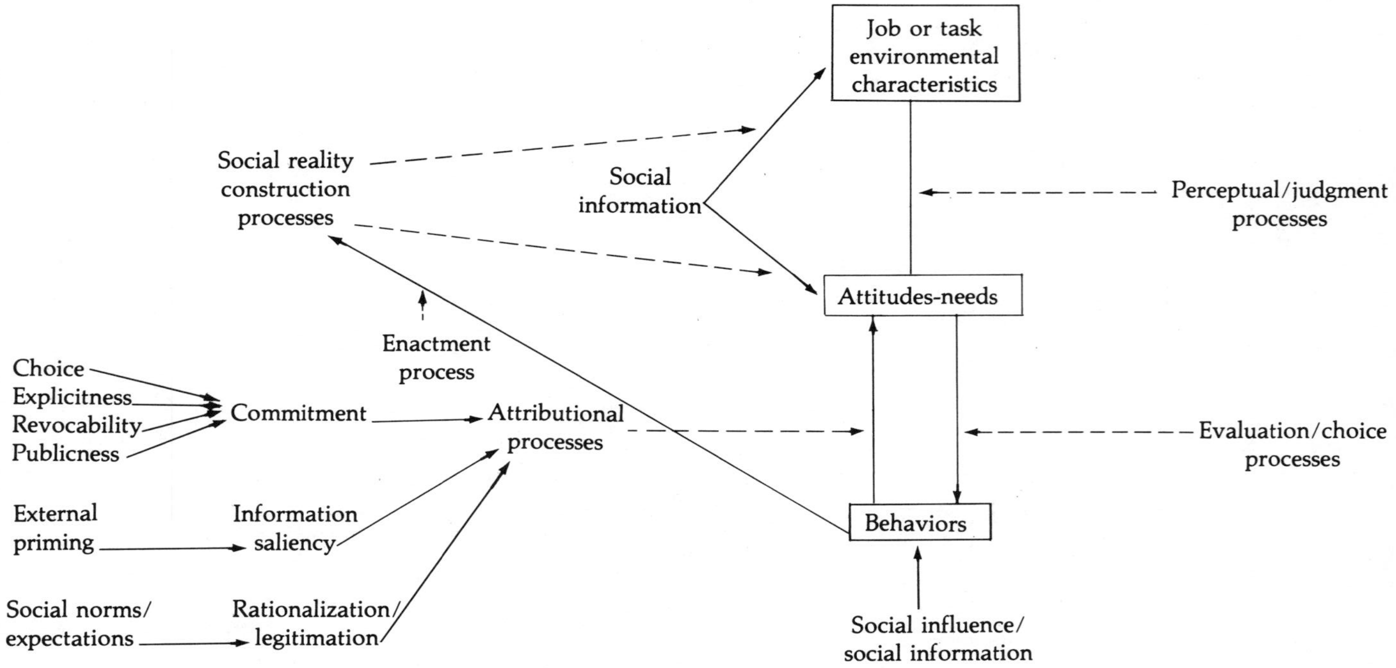

SOURCE: From Salancik and Pfeffer (1978a: 227).

the literature on job characteristics, the approach is a general one with respect to any environmental elements.

As Pfeffer and Lawler (1980) have noted:

> Their model had two major parts: 1) the effect of the social context on perceptions of the work environment, attitude and need statements, and the linkage between perceptions and attitudes; and 2) the effects of the individual's own past behaviors on self-perceptions of attitude, a process that is itself partly socially mediated (1980: 38).

We have already reviewed the literature indicating how behaviors are used to construct attitude and need statements, and how commitment, information saliency, and social norms and expectations about what are rational and legitimate explanations for behavior affect this process. James and Jones (1980) have provided evidence that affect toward the job can influence the perception of task characteristics. This is the second part of the model referred to above. The first part of the social information processing model is the most clearly social and the one that departs the most strikingly from dispositional or trait-based conceptions of behavior. Salancik and Pfeffer (1978a) argued that there were two effects of the social information and the social context: an effect in which the attributes of the work environment become defined and evaluated with the influence of others; and an effect through which attitude and need statements become determined directly from both information and social pressure exerted by others in the environment. There is empirical evidence consistent with both effects.

O'Reilly and Caldwell (1979) developed two versions of a task involving the processing of student application files, an enriched and unenriched version. Using a group of control subjects, these authors found that the two tasks did significantly differ on the fundamental job description dimensions (Hackman and Oldham, 1975). Subjects were randomly assigned to either the enriched or unenriched task condition. Simultaneously, subjects (students at the University of California-Los Angeles) were also assigned to either a positive or negative social cuing condition. In the positive condition, information was made available that implied that others who had done the task had found it meaningful, interesting, and worthwhile, while the reverse was implied by the negative cuing condition. O'Reilly and Caldwell (1979) reported that the social information had more effect on task perceptions and task attitudes than did the "objective" characteristics of the tasks. Although the study could be faulted for some of its demand characteristics, a replication by White and Mitchell (1979) provided substantially similar results using a somewhat different experimental methodology.

Indeed, the idea that job characteristics are, in part, perceptually filtered (Newman, 1975) is scarcely surprising. It is only a slight step from that position to recognize that these perceptions are influenced in important ways by the views of others in the work environment (Weiss and Shaw, 1979) and, therefore, that perceptions of the environment of the job are, in large measure, socially constructed. Griffin (1981) has recently undertaken an experimental field test of the social information processing approach that indicates the effects of supervisory behavior on perceptions of task characteristics and reactions to these perceived characteristics. Employees at two manufacturing plants in the Southwest were studied. In one plant, one half of the employees had nothing happen to them; they constituted the control group. The remaining employees in that plant were exposed to a social cuing condition. "Specifically, their supervisors received training in how to provide positive social and/or informational cues to their subordinates about their tasks" (Griffin, 1981: 13). In the other plant, one half of the employees had their jobs objectively changed along the core dimensions used by the traditional job design researchers. And, the other half of the employees in that plant received both the objective job change and social cuing treatment.

Griffin found that perceptions of core task attributes — task variety, task autonomy, feedback, identity, and interpersonal task attributes — dealing with others, and friendship opportunities — were all significantly affected by both the social cuing and objective task change treatments. Furthermore, in several instances, there was a statistically significant interaction effect between the two treatments. This indicates that there was some tendency for social cues and objective job changes to work together to provide even more change in task perceptions than would be expected from the individual linear effects of each treatment. Griffin further found significant main effects of both treatments on measures of satisfaction with intrinsic aspects of the job, extrinsic aspects, and overall satisfaction. Griffin also examined the effect of both treatments on productivity, measured as the average daily output during a three-month period prior to and after the treatments were introduced. In the case of this dependent variable, the objective job changes had a significant effect, while the supervisory cuing treatment had no effect. As Hackman and Oldham (1980) have noted, changing the objective design of jobs can have several impacts on productivity: employee motivation may be increased, as predicted by task design theory; inefficiencies in the use of time and support staff may be reduced; and the work itself may be simplified and the task process improved in terms of its technical characteristics through task redesign. Of course, it is impossible in the present instance to assess the extent to which the improvement in productivity resulted from any of these factors.

As Salancik and Pfeffer (1978a) have noted, objective changes in how tasks are organized and work gets done have to be introduced in some way, and this very introduction can produce a "Hawthorne effect" through the creation of social information and social cues indicating that the company cares about how the workers feel about their jobs and that changes will be made in the tasks to increase their motivating potential. In the present case, the involvement of consultants in the change (which must have been known by workers) would further indicate a commitment by management to improve conditions. Indeed, King (1974), in another experimental study, indicated that it was the expectations surrounding job changes rather than the specific nature of the changes themselves that resulted in differences in attitudes and behavior. Thus, distinguishing between social information and objective task design effects is not easy. One possibility would be to replicate the Griffin (1981) study but to introduce changes in jobs in the objective change treatment, which made the jobs *worse* on the core task dimensions, while doing the same process of introduction of these changes. If attitudes and productivity still improved, there would be more evidence for the social information component of objective job changes than for the nature of the jobs themselves as determinants of behavioral and attitudinal outcomes. Thus, Griffin's (1981) study provides support for the social information processing perspective, but it certainly does not provide the data that would yet enable one to reject the task design theoretical approach.

There are also other forms of social effects on task environment perceptions. As Salancik and Pfeffer (1978a) noted, others in the social environment can cue workers to focus on some dimensions of work rather than on others. If people talk about pay all the time, pay becomes an important dimension used in evaluating the job, and so forth. Daniel (1971) presented data that indicate that worker attitudes vary as the time for contract negotiations approaches. Not surprisingly, the approach of negotiations, accompanied by discussion of what the workers do not presently have on their job, results in focusing on those factors and a decline in worker attitudes.

In addition to providing information about what dimensions of the work environment are important, and how a given job measures up on those dimensions, people in one's environment help in the interpretation of events that occur in that environment. "A supervisor who disciplines a worker who is not doing an adequate job may be seen as lacking concern for the employee, or alternatively, as concerned for the success of the firm. Which interpretation develops may be socially determined: the more equivocal events are, the more social definitions will prevail" (Salancik and Pfeffer, 1978a: 230). Pfeffer (1981a: chapter 6) and T. Peters (1978) have both suggested that the interpretation of events and the use of symbolic activity and political language as part of that process are critical parts of the administrative task. Clearly, such interpretations occur continuously in the

work environment and provide information as to how that environment is
to be viewed.

Others in the work environment tell us not only about that environment but also about what we should want from that environment (what our
needs are) and how we should evaluate that environment (what our attitudes should be). This direct effect on attitude and need statements is also
important and empirically demonstrable (Kiesler and Kiesler, 1969). In spite
of the large literature on conformity, there have been almost no studies that
have tested the relative effects of social influences on attitudes against the
effects of individual traits, such as needs or personality dimensions.

Herman and Hulin (1972) attempted to account for individual job attitudes using individual characteristics (which might be correlated with
more basic individual traits) as well as the departmental and divisional affiliation of the employee. Herman and Hulin found that subunit membership accounted for attitudes better than did the various individual characteristics — age, sex, and time employed. Herman, Dunham, and Hulin
(1975) and O'Reilly and Roberts (1975) conducted replications that came to
the same conclusion. O'Reilly and Roberts (1975: 148-149) argued that "affective responses to work are predominately associated with organizational
characteristics rather than individual ones."

Examining the validity of the social information processing perspective, particularly in contrast to older theories of task design and motivation,
is not a simple task. For instance, the evidence just cited that job attitudes
are more related to organizational location than to individual characteristics
provides evidence consistent with a social information processing approach,
but the evidence is far from conclusive. Two possibilities are that the individual characteristics measured were not the right ones — for instance, more
attention should have been paid to needs rather than to demographic variables — and that the reason the attitudes varied was because the jobs performed in the various subunits varied.

A second problem is that an individual's own view of what his or her
needs are may result from behavior and from information provided by
others about what needs are appropriate and what are being fulfilled (Salancik and Pfeffer, 1978a: 239). Thus, needs and attitudes may be correlated
because both are derived socially. By randomly assigning persons with
presumably different needs to jobs that were identical except for their social
context and then seeing if individual attitudes could be predicted by that
social information, this problem can be partially overcome. The work of
O'Reilly, and Caldwell (1979), White and Mitchell (1979), and White, Mitchell, and Bell (1977) comes close to accomplishing this experimentally. The
existing evidence is supportive of the social information processing perspective, but the evidence is not as extensive as one might like.

Pfeffer (1980) studied 113 engineers and collected information on their needs, their perceptions of task characteristics, their attitudes toward their job and the organization, and their subunit membership as well as which of two companies they were in. He also gathered data on their length of employment, which may be related to coming to terms with their work environment, and how much choice they had and how difficult it was to get hired into their present organization. He found that there were effects of context (subunit membership) on the perceptions of task dimensions, on reported needs, and that there were subunit effects on satisfaction and intentions to leave the organization even when job dimensions and needs were statistically controlled. Although there was no random assignment of persons to subunits and one can assume that the jobs done in the various subunits differed, it is important that there were subunit effects on all of the predicted dependent variables and that there were subunit effects on attitudes even when job dimensions and needs were statistically controlled.

SUMMARY

One way of categorizing the various theories considered in this chapter that take an external control approach to the analysis of individual behavior is represented in Figure 3-3. Theories can be distinguished, to some extent, on the basis of which mechanism of social influence they postulate — exchange or informational social influence. Thus, operant conditioning explicitly involves the exchange of behavior for the reinforcer that follows the behavior, and role theories and some theories of group effects also postulate

Figure 3-3. A CATEGORIZATION OF EXTERNAL CONTROL OF BEHAVIOR APPROACHES

The Role of Cognition

		Acognitive	Retrospective Rationality
The Basis of Influence and Control	Exchange	Operant conditioning, Role theory Group pressures/ conformity	Insufficient justification Overly sufficient justification
	Informational	Socialization Social information processing Group effects	Social information processing

an exchange mechanism — compliance with group norms and role expectations in return for acceptance by the group and approval and resources from others in the individual's role set. Insufficient and overly sufficient justification perspectives also proceed from an exchange of resources for behavior and then proceed to examine the consequences of this exchange being too rich or too lean for subsequent attitudes and commitment. Socialization and social information processing, on the other hand, argue for informational social influence effects on individuals. People learn how to perceive things, how to make sense of things, and even what their preferences should be from those in their social environments. And, some of the effects of groups are informational in nature, such as providing information on the normatively acceptable rate of productivity and what attitudes are reasonable.

The other dimension on which these theories can be contrasted is their use of cognition and cognitive concepts. Here, we have contrasted those approaches that have focused on retrospective rationality with those that are relatively acognitive in nature. We have put social information processing in both categories, because in one part of the model it deals with issues of retrospective rationality and the inference of attitudes from behavior, while in another it deals with direct social influences. By *acognitive* we mean simply that cognitive mechanisms are often not postulated or explored as part of the theory. Thus, for example, the social context effects literature explores the impact of group norms on individual attitudes and behavior but does not really specify some intervening causal mechanisms through which such effects occur. Thus, under the acognitive category are theories that speak to effects of social context but that do not explore the hypothetical mental processes through which such effects occur. It should be clear, from the discussion in the last chapter, that this diminished emphasis on internal cognition is likely to be an advantage because of issues of testing for the existence of mental processes that are not directly observable. Acognitive theories of external effects include operant conditioning, role theories, theories of group pressure or group effects, socialization, and some aspects of social information processing.

It should be evident that with its focus on a priori cognitive mechanisms involving expectations and internal control, social learning theory really does not fit well into this class of approaches. Thus, although it originally developed from the same tradition that produced operant conditioning with its emphasis on reinforcement, in its more recent incarnations social learning theory has come to resemble more a variation of expectancy theory and, thus, might be more properly considered a theory of individual rational choice.

Also, as noted previously, exchange and informational influence mechanisms are not mutually exclusive, so in some sense competitive testing among the various theories is not likely to be productive. In many senses, these approaches are more complementary rather than competing. Of course, it would make sense to explore the circumstances under which exchange-based rather than informational forms of influence tended to predominate, and also the circumstances under which theories incorporating retrospective rationality offered advantages over explanations that were less cognitive in orientation.

However, these theories as a class do offer an alternative explanation for behavior to that developed by the rational actor approach described in Chapter 2. One manifestation of this controversy between approaches has been the reemergence of the dispute over the usefulness of the concept of personality. *Personality* (Epstein, 1979) has typically been defined in terms of cross-situational consistency in behavior; thus, the argument is made that persons behave similarly regardless of the situation, or, in other words, they are not adaptive to the constraints and contingencies of their immediate environment. Within psychology generally, there has been continuing debate concerning the relative importance of personal versus situational explanations for behavior (Sarason, Smith, and Diener, 1975), which has involved the issues of how to measure the characteristics of situations (Bem and Funder, 1978) and how to measure the characteristics of personality of individuals (Weiss, 1979). Mischel's (1968) original arguments that stable individual traits or dispositions are relatively ineffective in accounting for behavior has been met recently with new attempts to develop better measures of such traits as well as more thorough explorations of the personality or person-situation interaction.

Lest the reader get confused by all this controversy, two things should be kept in mind. First, neither the rational actor nor the external constraint perspective imply cross-situational consistency in behavior. Thus, the research on personality and other traits and dispositions as explanations for behavior is not quite germane to either approach. Bem and Allen (1974) have argued that it is the interaction of the person with the situation that accounts for most of the psychologically interesting variance. This approach is the one consistent with the rational actor perspective. If one examines the rational model of choice seriously, what is consistent across situations are the goals, values, predispositions, or needs of the individuals. Behavior would not be expected to be the same regardless of the situation; rational behavior is value maximizing and need fulfilling, but whether such behaviors are consistent over situations would depend importantly on the specifics of the setting. Thus, for example, if someone worked hard in one job and not in another, that would say nothing about the rational model of choice. It might be that one job provided an opportunity for need fulfillment or for attainment of instrumentally valued outcomes, while the other did not. A person with higher-order needs would be expected to act differently and have different attitudes, depending on the characteristics of the job; finding cross-situational consistency would be contrary to the theoretical predictions.

Therefore, looking for cross-situational consistency in behavior is not how to distinguish the approaches in Chapter 3 from those in Chapter 2. Rather, the argument posed by the external control or constraint perspective is that the situation is binding on individuals, tending to produce similarities in response regardless of any individual differences such as in goals, needs, or other personal characteristics. The external control of individual behavior perspective predicts within-situation consistency of behavior across individuals. The finding of significant personal disposition-situation interactions would be inconsistent with the external control perspective, and it is potentially consistent with the individual rational actor point of view. Indeed, it is the consistent failure to find such interactions (e.g., White, 1978) that provides evidence that calls the rational actor perspective into question, along with that evidence indicating the efficacy of the external constraint approaches in accounting for behavior and even attitudes without reliance on personal, dispositional constructs.

It is important to recognize that the controversy over the extent to which behavior is externally controlled or individually chosen touches both empirical and theoretical nerves and also basic assumptions about the nature of man embedded in religion and philosophy. Thus, the controversy is likely to be persistent and somewhat resistant to empirical results. Because the view of man as an active exerciser of choice and discretion fits the prevailing philosophical and religious tradition in the United States more closely, perspectives emphasizing external control and constraint have been somewhat less popular and well accepted.

4

THEORIES OF ORGANIZATION-LEVEL RATIONAL ACTION

The emergence of large-scale organizations almost demanded theories that would address these institutions as wholes and not just as environments in which individuals worked, were influenced, and obtained (or did not obtain) status, power, and the fulfillment of various needs and goals. As in the case of theories of individual behavior, there are several perspectives on action that can be taken. In particular, organizations can be viewed as rational, acting foresightfully and prospectively to obtain some collective ends; alternatively, organizations can be viewed as externally controlled or constrained, influenced by their environments and without much discretion or latitude in their behavior. The same ideological forces that would tend to favor explanations of individual behavior emphasizing free will and potency would be even more important in developing a view of organizations as purposive, foresightful, and in control. For, these larger social units are all the more powerful and socially important, and theories that emphasize the purposive control of such powerful agents can reassure the society that all is well and right.

The three approaches reviewed in this chapter — structural contingency theory, the market failures or markets and hierarchies perspective, and a Marxist, or class-based approach — each presume rational and conscious action, though each argues from a somewhat different motivational basis for understanding the behavior. The market failures approach (Williamson, 1975) has emphasized efficiency, the Marxist perspective has tended to emphasize the accumulation of wealth and economic and political power, and structural contingency approaches have implicitly posed an efficiency rationale for organizational behavior, though not stated as strongly or as uniformly as in the market failures approach. All three approaches also share the use of "as if" reasoning. Such logic takes an assumption (e.g., organizations attempt to make as much profit as possible), traces the implications of such an assumption for various behaviors and outcomes (e.g., profit-seeking organizations will seek to minimize costs, including transaction costs), and then sees to what extent such outcomes are, in fact, consistent with the data. The three approaches differ in the extent to which they pay attention to the details of how organizational goals and preferences, definitions of alternatives, and choices get created. Structural contingency and market failures approaches have paid almost no attention to internal processes, while several Marxist theorists have examined the processes by which collective action and the aggregation of the preferences of numerous independent actors get accomplished.

The legitimation of large, powerful, and relatively new social institutions is a nontrivial task. Thus, one might expect that there was and will continue to be more energy expended around advocating the two critical assumptions — that organizations are purposive, foresightful, and controllable and that such organizations seek goals of profit or efficiency that are in the general social welfare — for the organizational level of analysis rather than the individual level of analysis. Anecdotal evidence suggests that this is the case, although without a systematic content analysis of the ideology of the organizations literature, such a hypothesis must remain fairly speculative.

It is important to recognize how truly recent the appearance of large-scale economic organizations is. As R. Edwards (1979: 23) has noted, "Business in the nineteenth century was conducted by enterprises that, by today's standards, were very small." He reported that the Pullman Corporation employed only about 200 workers in 1870 and that only the railroads and the New England textile mills employed more than a thousand workers before the 1880s. The subsequent consolidation of capital proceeded fairly rapidly but, even so, left firms that were small by today's standards:

> The McCormick Harvesting Machine Company . . . required 1,400 work-
> ers and in 1899 more than 4,000. The Pabst Brewing Company . . . was
> regularly employing over 700 workers. . . . Edison, the predecessor of
> General Electric, employed about 1,000 workers in its factories in the early
> 1880s but had grown to 2,400 workers by 1890 and, through merger, to
> 10,000 by 1892. . . . By 1875, the workforce at the Pullman works alone
> was up to 600 men, and it grew to 2,700 by 1885 and 5,500 by 1893; em-
> ployees at all of the company's plants numbered over 14,500 by 1893 (Ed-
> wards, 1979: 27-28).

When one considers that today there are firms employing hundreds of thousands of workers, even 14,500 seems like a small number. Aldrich (1979) has reproduced census tables showing that the proportion of the work force working for others in large organizations has grown dramatically over this period. Whereas once most people were self-employed or worked in relatively small establishments, today a significant proportion of the work force and a significant proportion of the manufacturing and financial assets of the United States are in the hands of a comparatively small number of separate firms. One can argue that theories of organization-level rationality developed in response to the appearance of increasingly large organizations in which a higher proportion of the populace worked. With the appearance of large concentrations of economic and technical power, it was imperative for organization theory to address the operation and governance of these visible social actors.

Thus, the appearance and increasing power and prominence of large organizations dictated the development of a theory of them as units. Existing ideology and requirements for legitimation favored the development of a theory that argued for their beneficence and social utility as well as their controllability and rationality. If, after all, rationality is a valued social ideal (Parsons and Smelser, 1956), imbuing organizations with the property of rational action could only enhance their legitimacy. But theories of organizational rationality face a serious problem at the outset: how to account for the aggregation of individual actions, perceptions, and choices into action that is rational and goal directed from the point of view of the organizational level of analysis. As we shall soon see, the use of "as if" reasoning excused many theorists from trying to come to grips with this problem. Yet, this issue is serious, and there is evidence that overaggregation has hindered the development of organization theory in a number of ways. Thus, before reviewing each of the three perspectives that examine action at the organizational level of analysis from a rational choice point of view, we need first to consider the issue of how organization-level rational action can occur.

INCENTIVES, CONTROL, AND ORGANIZATIONS AS UNITS

Two problems immediately confront the researcher adopting the organizational level of analysis. One problem affects both external control and rational actor perspectives, and one affects primarily the rational actor point of view. The problem affecting any treatment of organizations as wholes is the internal differentiation of many large organizations, which makes the task of characterizing them along any set of dimensions almost impossible. Thus, for instance, Scott (1981: 226) has noted, "Efforts to relate technical and structural measures at the organizational level are extremely hazardous because organizations tend to employ a variety of technologies and to be structurally complex." Consequently, studies using organizations as the unit of analysis may include measures from departments, aggregated together, that are themselves quite distinct. The uncertainty or routineness faced by one division or one functional unit may differ significantly from that faced by another in the same company. Indeed, Lawrence and Lorsch (1967) argued that it was such internal differentiation of organizational subunits according to the type of subenvironment that each faced, coupled with effective integration, that made organizations more effective.

One attempted solution to this problem of differences in characteristics within, as opposed to just across, organizations has been to focus solely on the production subsystems of the organizations being studied (Khandwalla, 1974; Woodward, 1965). But, as Scott (1981) has argued, this still does not solve the problem, because even within a given department or division, there may be considerable variation in the technical characteristics of the work as well as in the type of control structures employed. Comstock and Scott (1977), studying patient care wards in a sample of 16 hospitals, found that the characteristics of the control system of the ward were more closely associated with "measures of complexity and uncertainty at the *ward* level," while "the predictability of the tasks confronting the nurses was more closely associated with the characteristics of the nursing personnel on that unit" (Scott, 1981: 228).

It seems clear that there are dangers in aggregating structural measures casually over individuals or subunits. Indeed, Scott (1981: 227) has argued that "given the great diversity and complexity of types of work and structures encompassed by most organizations, we should not be surprised to learn that many specific studies report varying and contradictory findings." It is also clear that the problem is likely to be greater in the case of actions or measures that are definable at the subunit or some other more microlevel of analysis, in contrast to measures that make sense only at the more macroorganization level. Decisions concerning vertical integration, composition of boards of directors, and, in many instances, policies of compensation are reasonably assumed to be organization-level properties. On the other hand, structures and the organization of work can vary greatly within organizations, and thus theories focusing on those types of dependent variables should be viewed with Scott's caution in mind.

The second problem, which affects primarily those theories taking a rational action perspective, is how the elements required for rational action, such as goals or preferences and definitions of alternatives, get produced at the organizational level of analysis. There has been some tendency for most organizational literature to, often implicitly, follow the lead of economic theory on this issue. In the discipline of economics, the assumption is made that the goal of the organization is that of its owners, which entails wealth, profit, or share-price maximization. Under assumptions about the operation of competitive and efficient product and financial markets, these objectives are analytically equivalent. As long as enterprises were relatively small, there was not a lot of economic activity organized through the public sector, and most people worked in small enterprises, the issue of ownership as distinguished from control was not important. Ownership interests were dominant in the direction of the enterprises because owners were involved in their management and the enterprises were small enough so that problems of control loss and diffusion of responsibility were minimal (R. Edwards, 1979).

In the 1930s, Berle and Means (1932) posed a major theoretical challenge to the theories of economic capitalism that had (and still do) dominated thinking about the nature of the firm. These authors argued that there were fundamental changes occurring in the economic system that made the issue of whose goals the firm served increasingly problematic. Such changes involved the growth of large enterprises characterized by increasingly dispersed and diverse share ownership. Berle and Means asserted that in many such firms a self-perpetuating group of managers assumed power. These managers were not really responsible to the owners of the firm because the owners were so small and so diffuse that they could not effectively control the firm in their interests any longer. Thus, owner capitalism was replaced by managerial capitalism, and the question was posed as to what goals these managers, largely freed from ownership control, would pursue.

The ownership-control issue is fundamentally related to both economic theory and sociological theories emphasizing the importance of class. As Zeitlin (1974) noted:

> The prevailing view is that the diffusion of ownership in the large corporation among numerous stock owners has resulted in the separation of ownership and control, and, by severing the connection between the family and private property in the means of production, has torn up the roots of the

old class structure and political economy of capitalism . . . nonowning
corporate managers displace their capitalist predecessors . . . a class theory
of contemporary industrial society, based on the relationship between the
owners of capital and formally free wage workers, "loses its analytical
value as soon as legal ownership and factual control are separated" (Dahrendorf, 1959: 136) (1974: 1075).

Writing about economic theory, McEachern (1975) maintained:

> Economists have long expressed dissatisfaction with the neoclassical as-
> sumption concerning the hired manager's single-minded pursuit of profits,
> particularly in those situations where the manager is insulated from both
> product market and stockholder constraints. About 200 years ago Adam
> Smith discussed the consequences for efficiency of the separation of owner-
> ship from control . . . "The directors of such companies, however (are) the
> managers rather of other people's money than their own. . . . Negligence
> and profusion, therefore, must always prevail, more or less, in the manage-
> ment of the affairs of such a company" (Smith, 1937: 700) (1975: 1).

There are four elements in the control argument that are relevant to the
issue of organization-level rationality. First, there is the empirical dispute
about the extent to which the separation of ownership from control does, in
fact, exist. Second, there is the issue of the use of various kinds of financial
incentives to improve the correspondence between ownership and managerial interests in profit-making enterprises and the extent to which such
incentives appear to have been effective. Third, there is the question of the
extent to which the use of various control devices can ensure conformity to
the organization's rational objectives. The fourth issue is the extent to which
"as if" reasoning can be used in the analysis to avoid the empirical issues of
the separation of ownership and control and the extent to which there are
shared objectives and views of technology in the organization. Each of these
points will be briefly considered in turn.

The Empirical Fact of Ownership-Control Separation

The controversy concerning the extent of the separation of ownership from
control, and whether there has been any discernible trend, is, at some level,
basically not resolvable using the methods most frequently employed. What
is customarily done is to gather data on the concentration of share ownership and classify the firm accordingly. Such a procedure forces the analysts
to make several judgments. First, the decision must be made as to how large
a proportion of stock is required for "control." Clearly, anything more than

half is unambiguous, but it is also clear that with otherwise widely dispersed share ownership, a proportion of the shares well under 50 percent will suffice to ensure control. Berle and Means (1932) used 20 percent as defining effective control, while Larner (1970) used 10 percent, a proportion also used by J. Palmer (1972) and Sheehan (1967). Villajero (1962) used a 5 percent figure as sufficient for control, and McEachern (1975) used 4 percent. Obviously, one's classification of firms into the owner- or managerially controlled categories can vary as one's definition of *required stock ownership* varies.

Second, some decision must be made, given an amount of stock ownership that is critical, about how that stock must be held to constitute control. Berle and Means (1932) defined their critical amount of 20 percent to be in the hands of a single party. Most studies have aggregated stock owned by a single family. Gordon (1961: 43), reviewing the Temporary National Economic Committee's research that classified about two thirds of the largest 200 financial corporations as owner controlled, argued that in less than a third of the sample was there evidence of a "small compact group of individuals" exercising control. How is one to know what is a small, compact group? How does one know if the family's stockholdings represent a coordinated ownership pattern or whether the family is rife with factionalism and the ownership should not be aggregated? Obviously, such data can be obtained only on a case-by-case basis, and the overall figures on stock ownership do not provide unambiguous information. Sweezy (1939) argued that ownership control was masked through the use of financial intermediaries such as banks, brokerage firms, and trust departments, a position taken also by Kolko (1962). This led Villajero (1962) to include the holdings of investment companies and insurance companies in his measurement of control. Whether the aggregated holdings of investment companies, families, and trust departments constitutes a meaningful index of control, however, is very much open to question.

The third issue is what to do about stock ownership that is concentrated but that is concentrated in the hands of other institutions or organizations, such as pension funds or trust departments, or held as investments by other entities. What if the stockholdings are concentrated in the hands of a foundation, as opposed to a bank trust department?

Because of the essentially structural approach to measuring control adopted, with little effort to assess the behavioral outcomes of the control in terms of specific policies or decisions, there was and remains great controversy and confusion in the ownership and control literature. Some (Larner, 1970) maintained that the separation of ownership and control was substantial and growing; others, using the same data (Zeitlin, 1974), concluded that there was not much separation of ownership from control and that there was no discernible trend. Indeed, the fourth issue faced by this research is how large a proportion of the firms would have to experience ownership-control separation before it would become theoretically important, in any event.

The Use of Financial Incentives

One way of ensuring goal congruence and homogeneity within the organization is to use financial incentives, so that the organization's best interests become correlated with the financial interests of those who work in and manage them. Thus, one way of saving neoclassical assumptions about managerial profit maximization against the alternative perspective of managerial discretion that accompanies the separation of ownership and control is to demonstrate the financial incentives' effects on aligning managerial with ownership interests.

One arena in which this debate has been waged is the research on the determinants of managerial compensation and, particularly, the extent to which such compensation is determined by firm profitability as contrasted with size. Presumably, the ownership interests are those of profits, whereas managerialist theories have occasionally stressed the value of growth (Baumol, 1959; Marris, 1967), largely because of the association of size and managerial compensation (Roberts, 1959). Other reasons managers might favor growth and size could be power, prestige, and increased stability for the firm. Reid (1968), in attempting to explain why, in spite of no difference in profitability between merger-active and less active firms, many firms still pursued mergers, mustered the argument that managers in such firms were pursuing a strategy of growth without regard for profits, because of the beneficent effects of increased size on their salaries and other perquisites such as status.

Again, empirical and theoretical problems prevail. Roberts (1959) and McGuire, Chiu, and Elbing (1962) found an effect of sales but not of profits on *compensation*, defined as salary plus bonus. Baker (1969) found an effect of both sales and profits. Ciscel (1974) argued that sales and profits were so highly correlated with each other that it was virtually impossible to assess the relative contribution of these two determinants of managerial compensation empirically. Lewellen and Huntsman (1970) and Masson (1971), employing statistical techniques designed to overcome some of the specification and collinearity problems that have plagued this research, found that executive compensation was strongly related to profits and was not significantly related to firm size, as measured by sales.

Besides the correlation between sales and profits, there is the issue of what should be included in the measure of the dependent variable — managerial compensation. Increasingly, there are deferred compensation and incentive payments, often paid after the individual has left the company, but, in any event, with some lag structure so that compensation as reported in any single year is not a perfectly reliable measure. More important, many, if not most, companies compensate executives through the use of stock options, such that most executives own some of the shares of their companies. One could argue that dividend and capital gain income from these shares is also a form of compensation, and this ownership-type income should be considered in assessing the incentives confronting high-level corporate managers. Lewellen (1968, 1971), investigating the components of managerial compensation, found that ownership components (changes in stock price, capital gains, and dividends) were larger than the salary components and that, furthermore, this difference was increasing over time. Thus, Lewellen concluded that there were financial incentives for high-level managers to make decisions based on considerations of organizational rationality.

Two other questions remain in considering the connection between incentives and performance. First, there is the question of whether firms in the various owner versus managerial control categories use somewhat different compensation practices. The evidence from Larner (1970) is that they do not, but McEachern (1975), using a refined categorization of firms into three rather than two categories, did find an effect of control type on compensation structure, with there being more payoff for returns to owners in the owner-dominated (externally controlled) as contrasted with manager-dominated firms. The second question is whether the differences in compensation actually cause differences in firm performance. Masson (1971) provided the only evidence on this point, which indicated that there was a relationship between the size of the ownership component in managerial income and the firm's rate of return to stockholders. However, as McEachern (1975) pointed out, that result may simply derive from the managers' possessing inside information. If they know that a firm's profits and performance will increase, they may avail themselves of the opportunity to increase their ownership, thereby increasing the share of ownership income to the total and providing a spurious relationship between the compensation system and subsequent firm performance. Most of the studies have related ownership to performance but not to the compensation system directly. The finding that owner-controlled firms appear to outperform managerially controlled firms leads to an apparent paradox:

> . . . on the one hand the findings suggest that managers are paid to perform in the stockholders' interests, but on the other hand there is a dif-

ference in performance based on control type. If managers in general are paid for increases in profit and market value, then why the difference in performance (McEachern, 1975: 111)?

The financial incentives literature, one of the larger literatures, unfortunately does not provide a clear answer to resolving either the incentives or control question. Of course, the literature deals almost exclusively with profit-making firms (but, see Sandver, 1978; Sandver and Heneman, 1980), thereby excluding the larger sector of the economy in the public and not-for-profit domain. But even within the domain of profit-seeking firms, the evidence is ambiguous concerning the extent to which compensation systems based on returns to owners are actually effective in motivating managerial behavior that is in closer correspondence with ownership interests.

Organizational Rationality through Control

The submerging of individual interests for the purpose of achieving organizationally rational action is a theme that has dominated the organizations literature since the time of Max Weber. Weber's (1947) description of bureaucracy represents a treatment of how organizational rationality was to be achieved. Rules and procedures would be developed to ensure the equal and fair treatment of all who came in contact with the organization, while promotion opportunities within the firm would build loyalty to the organization and a willingness to comply with the rules and procedures. Weber was particularly interested in the importance of substituting universalistic criteria of hiring, promotion, and decision making for ascriptive criteria — standards based on social relationships and extraorganizational influences. Thus, for Weber and his successors, organizational rationality became embodied in a system of rules and procedures that would tend to ensure that employees worked for and in the interests of their employing organization. As Perrow (1972) has noted, common complaints about organizations often involve them not being bureaucratic enough, in the sense of applying rules and standards fairly and universally across all customers, employees, and clients.

Organization-level rational action was to be obtained through the measurement and evaluation of persons according to how well their actions conformed to the organization's expectations (Dornbusch and Scott, 1975). Blau (1955) detailed the powerful effect of measurement on the behavior of workers in both an employment service agency and a government law enforcement bureau. In both instances, although it would be hard to argue that promotions, salary, or job security depended on performance, the publication of various performance measures profoundly affected the behavior of workers in the two bureaus. As noted in Chapter 2 in the discussion on the effects of feedback, information on performance does get attended to, even if there are no obvious consequences arising from the behavior. Competition emerged among workers in Blau's bureaucracies, and it was a competition for status. Measurement and control systems focus attention and cause persons in the organization to orient their efforts to succeeding on the measured dimensions. Indeed, as Ridgway (1956) has reviewed, this profound effect of measurement means that special concern must be taken with what is measured. Quotas of shoes may result in only the same small size of shoes being produced, and quotas for tons of nails may lead to the production of fewer but heavier nails.

Blau and Scott (1962) focused on these management systems as well as other impersonal control devices in producing individual conformity to organization-level objectives. The very information and decision premises built into the organization's operations may affect how people come to think about and perform their tasks. And, as noted in the last chapter, control may become internalized through processes of socialization. The point is simply that there are a number of control strategies, including direct supervision, that may enforce conformity with the organization's goals and beliefs about technology. To the extent that these control strategies work effectively, it may be possible to speak of organization-level rationality with some validity, even with the varieties of backgrounds, interests, and perspectives represented in the work force.

The "As If" Argument

The empirical issues of the extent of ownership-control separation, the use and effectiveness of financial incentives to produce a correspondence of interests among organizational participants, and the use of various control strategies to produce unified, consistent, organizationally rational action may all be irrelevant if one adopts the "as if" argument. This position, borrowed from economic theory, maintains that organization-level theories of rational action are useful regardless of the empirical validity of their assumptions as long as they generate interesting and empirically valid predictions — in other words, as long as organizations behave "as if" they were operating in a rational fashion. How or if organizationwide shared beliefs and preferences are developed is irrelevant from this point of view. The key question is whether assumptions of organization-level rational action generate useful and empirically valid theory.

In economics, the controversy over the use of "as if" reasoning revolves around assumptions of profit or utility maximization. The position stated there has been adopted, implicitly or explicitly, by many of the theories of organization-level rationality:

> The question is not whether the firms of the real world *really* maximize money profits, or whether they even *strive* to maximize their money profits, but rather whether the *assumption* that this is the objective in the theoretical firms in the artificial world of our construction will lead to conclusions — "inferred outcomes" very different from those derived from admittedly more realistic assumptions (Machlup, 1967: 14-15).

Machlup argues that the unrealistic assumptions are all right as long as they lead to similar predictions made by a more realistic view of the firm. Friedman's (1953) position was that the proof of the assumptions was in their results:

> . . . unless the behavior of businessmen in some way or other approximated behavior consistent with the maximization of returns, it seems unlikely that they would remain in business for long. Let the apparent immediate determinant of business behavior be anything at all. . . . Whenever this determinant happens to lead to behavior consistent with the rational and informed maximization of returns, the business will prosper and acquire resources with which to expand; whenever it does not, the business will tend to lose resources and can be kept in existence only by the addition of resources from outside. The process of "natural selection" thus helps to validate the . . . hypothesis — or rather, given natural selection, acceptance of the hypothesis can be based largely on the judgment that it summarizes appropriately the conditions for survival (1953: 35).

Friedman's position assumes the existence of competitive market pressures. Since firms behave "as if" they were acting rationally, organization-level models of firm rationality are useful for describing that behavior even if not realistic in all of their assumptions. The argument of "as if" reasoning suggests that the behavioral issues of the effects of various incentives or other control devices as well as the extent of convergence and homogeneity of preferences and beliefs about technology within the firm are largely irrelevant for understanding organizational behavior at this level of analysis.

The philosophy of science underlying the use of "as if" reasoning has been attacked by E. Nagel (1963). Winter (1975) also has critiqued this form of theorizing. One of his objections is illustrated in the context of the identification problem in econometrics:

> . . . it is helpful to consider "as if" theorizing in relation to the identification problem of econometrics. In that context, the "as if" principle can be regarded as saying that optimization assumptions are an acceptable foundation for the theory of the firm because the theory leads to useful reduced form equations, and because the "true" explanation leads (or may well lead) to those same reduced form equations. Thus, the principle discounts entirely the advantages of structural estimation, and hence also the contributions of correct theory to structural estimation . . . the central advantage is the ability to generate accurate predictions when the structure changes in specified ways (1975: 93-94).

To get the right answer for the wrong reason may make the theoretical model useless, or worse, when conditions change that affect some of the underlying structural parameters in a more comprehensive and accurate representation but that would not affect the parameters in the reduced form system.

The controversy over the use of "as if" reasoning is a basic and fundamental one, striking at philosophy of science issues as well as at the utility of various approximation schemes (Winter, 1975), or the question of how good an approximation is good enough. Not resolved yet in economics, it is not about to be resolved in organization theory. The purpose in raising it is to sensitize the reader to its often subtle and implicit use buttressing theories of organization-level rationality. "As if" reasoning is one defense for the use of theories of organization-level rationality, but even this defense must confront the extent to which the predictions are consistent with the data. Interestingly, organization theory, which has taken economics to task for the unreasonableness of its behavioral assumptions and for the preference for the formal structure of theories over their empirical realism, is just as guilty at times in employing the "as if" defense to assume, rather than empirically verify, the reasonableness of assumptions of organization-level rationality.

Theories of organization-level rational action face a demanding burden. Such an approach must confront not only many of the issues faced by theories of individual-level rationality, as enumerated in Chapter 2, but also the problem of how individual-level action becomes aggregated to achieve organization-level rationality. It is clear that theories of organization-level rationality are inconsistent with the view of organizations as coalitions (Cyert and March, 1963; March, 1962) or as fundamentally political entities (Allison, 1971; Pfeffer, 1981a). To consider the production of organization-level rational action would seem to require confronting the question of the extent to which incentives, socialization, measurement systems, and other control devices produce a social system outcome usefully or reasonably approximated by models of organization-level rationality and, even more important, the conditions under which such approximations are more or less likely to hold. Following Friedman's (1953) line of reasoning, the existence of selection or competitive pressures should be one important condition. But, as we will see in the next chapter, such strong environmental constraints make it possible to account for organizational behavior without ever needing the assumptions and apparatus of organization-level rationality. It is also likely that theories of organization-level rationality are less applicable to public sector or nonmarket organizations, at least in the absence of strong socialization effects. What is notable about the theories to be reviewed is that, except in a few instances in the case of Marxist analysis, almost no attention has been paid to this issue of the production of social system homogeneity and organization-level rationality. Rather, the assumption of the unit properties of organizations is taken for granted, and analysis then proceeds without ever considering the stability of the foundation on which such analysis rests.

A MARKET FAILURES APPROACH

Coming from a foundation in institutional economics, the market failures or transactions cost approach (Williamson, 1975) adopts an efficiency-seeking view of organization-level rationality to address three issues: (1) Why are there organizations at all, as contrasted with having transactions, conducted solely through markets, and given that there are organizations, which transactions are more efficiently organized through markets as contrasted with hierarchies? This is sometimes called the efficient boundary question (Williamson, 1981). (2) Given the fact of organizations, how can such entities be structured to economize on transaction costs within the firm? This is the question of the efficient form. (3) What is the most efficient way of organizing and managing human assets in the firm, in the sense of structuring the exchange relations and incentives between the firm and its workers? Because of the efficiency orientation, "transaction cost reasoning probably has greater relevance for studying commercial than noncommercial enterprise — since natural selection forces operate with greater assurance in the former" (Williamson, 1981: 35). Carrying that argument one step further, the transactions cost approach probably is most applicable in the more competitive sectors of the economy.

Williamson (1975) argued that traditional economic theory had emphasized production cost efficiency but neglected to consider the issue of transaction cost efficiency in evaluating the advantages of market as contrasted with organizational arrangements. Transaction costs arise because of the occurrence of the following conditions in exchange relations: small numbers or noncompetitive markets; opportunism, which is self-interest seeking with guile; uncertainty concerning the future state of the environment and what will be required to cope with that world; and bounded rationality, or cognitive limits on information processing. Uncertainty coupled with bounded rationality means that it is not possible to write complete, contingent claims contracts specifying every possible future eventuality and what the obligations of each party would be under those future conditions. The inability to write complete contingent claims contracts, coupled with opportunism and small numbers problems, can lead to haggling among the transaction participants concerning how future contingencies are to be resolved. Such haggling and the transaction costs of compliance and monitoring are reduced by organizing such exchanges through organizations rather than through markets.

There are several important elements in understanding the market failures perspective and how it has been used in organizational analysis. First, as proposed, all four conditions must be present for there to be significant transaction cost problems. Without bounded rationality, it would be possible to take into account all future states of the world and to provide for every possible future contingency. Thus, contracting through markets would be possible. Without opportunism, which includes the strategic misrepresentation of information, one might rely on the goodwill and good faith of the partners in the exchange to deal with the various contingencies as they arise. Without uncertainty concerning future contingencies or states of the world, all possible eventualities would be known, and again, complete contingent contracts could be written. And finally, without small numbers, there would be no long-term incentive for behaving opportunistically, because presumably competitive pressure would drive business away from those who behaved with guile and toward those who were honest. Thus, in the absence of small numbers, competitive pressure would operate to regulate behavior.

Second, although there are four conditions specified in the theory, most of the argumentation as developed by Williamson really revolves around and involves one condition, small numbers. Opportunism is considered to be constant across individuals—the presumption is that anyone will behave opportunistically if he or she thinks it can be accomplished without discovery or cost. Also, bounded rationality is taken as a constant—all actors are subject to bounded rationality, and all are presumably just about equally hampered by this factor. Uncertainty is also viewed as being ubiquitous. Thus, most of the Williamsonian analysis deals with those conditions that make transactions more or less susceptible to small numbers problems.

The neglect of the possibility of the other factors varying significantly is potentially a problem with the analysis. This is because there is evidence of variation in the other factors producing transaction cost problems. Light (1972) has studied Chinese-American Hui and Japanese-American Tanomoshi, revolving-credit lending societies that provide capital for new businesses. And Light has contrasted the organization of these cultures with others. His research indicates that the social control of ethnic communities varies across ethnic groups, with consequent differences for opportunistic and unethical behavior. In turn, these behavioral differences have had implications for the development of ethnic enterprises. Thus opportunism is seen to vary across cultures and subcultures with implications for both the organization of economic exchange and its effectiveness. Similarly, virtually all of conventional organization theory treats uncertainty as varying (e.g., J. R. Galbraith, 1973), with implications for the organization of work. Consequently, Williamson's assumption of the ubiquity of uncertainty is probably neither warranted nor likely to lead to correct conclusions.

Williamson argues that small numbers occur not only because market conditions such as monopoly or oligopoly exist, but also because in an exchange relationship, transaction-specific investments in both knowledge and equipment may be built up (Williamson, 1979). Thus, a market may be competitive initially in that there are many potential suppliers for a particular part or service. But, once a firm chooses a specific supplier for that part or service, the supplier may develop specialized expertise in the performance of the task, invest in specialized equipment, and develop idiosyncratic knowledge about the production process and the exchange relationship. These transaction-specific investments can give the supplier advantages in any subsequent competition with other potential suppliers. Consider, for instance, the choice of a legal firm by an organization to represent it in labor relations matters. Initially, the organization might conceivably choose among all the firms that engage in labor practice. But once a transaction is begun, the law firm develops knowledge about the firm, its policies, and its legal problems and specialized competency in dealing with various individuals within the firm. The organization, to change law firms in the face of increasing fees, would have to lose this exchange-specific knowledge and, furthermore, would face the prospect of having to pay some other law firm to relearn what was already known by the firm that was already representing it.

Williamson saw the advantages of an organization over a market as deriving from the particular kinds of authority and command relations that occur in organizations but not in markets. In particular, the exercise of control through reporting systems and through supervision is an accepted and expected part of organizations. Such surveillance would, according to

Williamson, reduce the potential for opportunistic behavior. Sophisticated accounting and control systems could overcome many of the problems of information impactedness that adversely affected the ability to conduct transactions through market mechanisms. Furthermore, the very nature of the employment relationship, as a nonspecific exchange of some generalized labor for a wage, meant that the parties to the exchange did not have to foresee all the future contingencies perfectly or be able to write complete contingent claims contracts.

Of course, there may be ways to maintain some of the advantages of market exchanges while guarding against the development of small numbers conditions. Some firms, such as IBM, make it a practice to never sole-source a significant component. Recently, recommendations for holding down legal fees have also focused on using multiple law firms for similar kinds of legal work. The point in both cases is that the contracting organization may bear one kind of cost involved in maintaining multiple exchange partners to avoid being subject to the costs that arise later from the dependence on a single source of outside supply.

The Issue of Efficient Boundaries

The market failures perspective has been used to analyze the employment relation (Williamson, Wachter, and Harris, 1975), and the efficient boundary question can be clearly seen in that instance. One way of obtaining labor power is to contract for it, much as one might contract with a painter to paint some rooms. A specified price or wage per hour is set, and specified obligations for performance are offered in return. Such an arrangement will work, however, only to the extent that the unit purchasing the labor power can specify precisely the task to be accomplished, that there is some competition among potential labor suppliers, and that the technology of the production process is reasonably well understood. If the task is somewhat more complex and unpredictable than painting, the purchaser may not be able to specify completely what labor services will be desired or when. Furthermore, the laborer may learn in the course of doing the job, developing idiosyncratic knowledge of the task and enhanced skill. It may be difficult to write complete contracts specifying all eventualities in terms of the kind and amount of labor desired, and it may be difficult to specify a price deemed to be fair to both parties that reflects the potential idiosyncratic investments in the exchange that both may acquire. In such a circumstance, the employment relation offers an alternative. Labor of an unspecified kind, subject only to the constraints of the acceptance of the authority relation, is purchased. The future need not be foreseen perfectly; as contingencies arise, the tasks can be adjusted accordingly. And, to a large degree, the enhanced skill and the benefits therefrom are captured by the employing organization.

The fact that both parties to an exchange may develop idiosyncratic capital unique to that exchange relationship makes it in the interests of both to organize transactions on a more permanent basis. In the employment context, Wachter and Williamson (1978: 556) have noted, "When workers acquire imperfectly transferable skills, the firm and the worker have an interest in devising a governance structure to assure a continuing, cooperative relation between them."

In exchanges among firms, a similar issue can arise that leads to an efficiency reason for vertical integration. Williamson (1975: 104) hypothesized, "Vertical integration is favored in circumstances where small numbers bargaining would otherwise obtain — whether this prevails from the very outset or because once the initial contract is let, the parties to the transaction are effectively 'locked in' at the recontracting interval." Monteverde and Teece (1980: 10) argued that in the vehicle manufacturing industry "the creation of a first mover advantage and attendant switching costs appears to be principally associated with development activities." To avoid being locked in to an exchange relationship with a particular supplier, and the advantages that gives the supplier in extracting economic rents, Monteverde and Teece suggested that the vehicle assembler would integrate backward in the production process to acquire those parts of the operation where the development component was particularly significant.

Using a list of 133 automotive components, the amount of vertical integration by General Motors (GM) and Ford for U.S. production in 1976 was obtained. The variable was whether the particular component was produced internally or purchased on the market. A measure of relative engineering effort was the explanatory variable indexing the extent of firm-specific knowledge and, thus, the incentive to integrate for transaction costs reasons. Estimating a model using Probit analysis, Monteverde and Teece (1980: 25) found that the development effort associated with a given component was positively related to the likelihood of its being integrated in production. The test of their argument is, however, not without problems. First, the data on each part as to whether it was made internally or purchased were treated statistically as independent observations. This treatment would be suspect in general since decisions on integration are nested within a company over the items purchased by that company. In the particular case in question, since the largest amount of variation was accounted for by which company the part was for — there were large differences in the amount of integration between the two firms — treating each observation as independent is even more problematic. This effect is probably only likely to impact the statistical significance of the results but not their substance. Of 133 components, there was only one instance in which the less integrated company, Ford, produced a part that was not also produced internally by GM. Thus, there is a consistent pattern of what is produced internally versus what is contracted out across the two firms, and the amount of development effort helps to explain this pattern. Second, the fact of important differences between the firms was a result clearly not predicted by the theory. There is no reason in the formulation to explain why it is any more efficient for GM to produce internally more parts than it is for Ford. And third, the amount of explained variance, about 20 percent, means that the analysis of make-or-buy decisions could potentially depend on a number of other factors outside the scope of the theory.

The Monteverde and Teece analysis is important because it is the first direct test of the central proposition of Williamson's (1975) argument — the conditions under which markets are used rather than internal organization. There are, clearly, numerous other contexts in which this analysis could be carried out, including variation in the integration of retailing organizations backward to incorporate the source of supply (for instance, the purchase of dairies by grocery store chains) and the integration of various manufacturers (such as computers, other vehicles such as aircraft and farm equipment, and so forth) backward to incorporate various component manufacturing tasks. There are alternatives to the market failures perspective that can also potentially explain integration and its consequences. The explanation offered by resource dependence theory is considered in the next chapter. At the time this theory is introduced, the predictions made as contrasted with the market failures predictions will be detailed.

The M-Form Hypothesis

Williamson (1975) recognized the value of organizations as alternate planning and control mechanisms, substituting for the price mechanism of allocation in markets. However, he also recognized the limitations of organizations for efficiently accomplishing production. Williamson argued that many of the problems of internal organization had to do with persistence and commitment to unsuccessful operations:

> Among the more severe goal distortions of internal organizations are the biases which it experiences that are favorable to the maintenance or extension of internal operations. Biases of three types are discussed: internal procurement, internal expansion, and program persistence. Communication distortion supports all three (1975: 118–119).

Because managers were reluctant to abolish their own jobs, and because of the possible link between size and managerial compensation, there was a tendency for firms to maintain and use internal sources of supply regardless of their efficiency characteristics. Furthermore, there were pressures for internal expansion, again related to compensation incentives. Williamson was also concerned about the tendency for activities to persist in organizations regardless of their rationality:

> . . . existing activities embody sunk costs of both organizational and tangible types while new projects require initial investments of both kinds. The sunk costs in programs and facilities of ongoing projects thus insulate existing projects from displacement by alternatives which, were the current program not already in place, might otherwise be preferred (1975: 121).

Thus, it was not enough for there to be efficient boundaries; activities needed to be organized efficiently within the organization's boundaries. Williamson argued that the M-form or multidivisional form (Chandler, 1966) offered a number of advantages in efficient internal organization. In particular, the separation of strategic capital allocation from operating decisions presumably would overcome some of the persistence and internal procurement tendencies just mentioned. Moreover, the multidivisional organization could implement internal financial reporting and capital allocation procedures that, because of their increased surveillance, could be even more efficient than the external capital market. Williamson, thus, hypothesized an efficiency advantage accruing to firms that were structured in an M-form or multidivisional structure.

Armour and Teece (1978) examined the effect of the M-form structure on profitability for a sample of firms in the petroleum industry. Controlling for other factors such as size, they found that the M-form had a significant positive impact on performance, but only until the innovation had been widely adopted within the industry. Once almost all the firms had the same structure, structure per se no longer provided a competitive advantage. Teece (in press) extended the test of the M-form argument to consider a set of matched firms in 20 industries. The matching procedure was employed to control for interindustry differences. The first firm to adopt the M-form was compared with a comparable firm in terms of both product line and size. The test involved the following comparison:

> . . . the approach involves examining differences in performance within pairs over two time periods: a "before" time period in which the lead firm was M-form while the control was not, and an "after" period when both firms had the M-form structure. The differential performance before and after the innovation was adopted by the control firm is calculated. If

the lead firm in the "before" period was the superior performer, support for the . . . hypothesis would require the differential to narrow in the "after" period; conversely, if the lead firm was not the superior performer in the "before" period, support for the M-form hypothesis would require the differential to widen in the "after" period (Teece, in press: 11).

Using the sign test and Wilcoxon matched pairs signed ranks test, Teece found support for the M-form hypothesis.

The multidivisional form represents an administrative innovation with presumably enhanced operating characteristics. Teece (1980) demonstrated that a model of the diffusion of innovations, often used to study the spread of technological innovations, fit the data on the diffusion of this administrative innovation nicely. This suggested that "other insights from the study of the economics of technological innovation may be fruitfully applied to the domain of administrative and organizational innovation" (Teece, 1980: 470).

S. Allen (1978) has argued that there are a number of possible differences in firms that are ostensibly all multidivisional in form, having to do primarily with which of the various staff support services are centralized as contrasted with which are left in the divisions, as well as how budgeting and control occurs. Given these variations, the support Teece has found for the M-form hypothesis is surprisingly strong. Of course, the estimated models were relatively simple, and it is possible that something else distinguished the firms besides their structure, such as their strategy, innovativeness, or managerial competence. Thus, research on the effects of structure on performance is far from conclusive. The contribution of Teece has been to bring this issue into empirical focus.

Organizing the Employment Relation

Williamson (1981: 20) has noted, "Merely to assign a transaction to an internal governance structure does not . . . by itself assure that the efficiency purposes of transaction cost analysis will be realized." This means that both structural arrangements and arrangements for the management of human assets are important. In particular, "use of a complex structure to govern simple transactions is to incur unneeded costs, while to use a simple structure to govern a complex transaction invites strain" (Williamson, 1981: 20). Williamson argued that internal employee governance structures depended on two variables: the extent to which human assets were firm specific (if the skills and knowledge were useful primarily within the firm or if they were generally useful across many firms) and the ease with which productivity could be assessed (or the extent of labor service observability) (Alchian and Demsetz, 1972). These two dimensions could be used to define the matching of governance structures to human asset characteristics as shown in Figure 4-1.

When human assets were general and monitoring of performance was easy, an internal spot market was predicted to be the governance structure employed. When monitoring was more difficult, a primitive team was used; when monitoring was easy but assets were firm specific, an obligational market was the governance structure employed, and various ways of tying individuals to firms as through pension plans and other rewards to maintain persons in the system (Katz and Kahn, 1978) would be used; finally, when monitoring was difficult and the assets were specific, a relational team, which Williamson (1981) argued was equivalent to Ouchi's clan organization, was the governance system employed.

The internal governance issues are not nearly as well developed as some other aspects of the theory. There are two extensions to Williamson's argument that are worth discussing, as they add some detail to this line of reasoning. First, Ouchi (1980) has argued that just as markets fail, leading to the development of hierarchies, hierarchy as a system of organization fails also, which leads to the introduction of clan forms of control. Clans rely more on the internalization of values and preferences as contrasted with bureaucratic control mechanisms.

Ouchi and Jaeger (1978: 308) distinguished organizations according to the following dimensions: (1) length of employment (short-term versus

Figure 4-1. THE RELATIONSHIP OF LABOR SERVICE OBSERVABILITY AND FIRM-SPECIFIC HUMAN CAPITAL TO THE ORGANIZATION OF THE EMPLOYMENT RELATIONSHIP

| | | Specificity of Human Capital | |
		Nonspecific	Very Specific
Labor Service Observability	Easily Monitored	Spot market	Obligational market
	Monitored with Difficulty	Primitive team	Relational team

SOURCE: From Williamson (1981).

lifetime); (2) specialization of career paths within the organization, or the number of different functions in which a typical high-level manager will have worked; (3) the speed of evaluation and advancement in the organization; (4) the explicitness of the evaluation system, in qualitative and implicit to quantitative and explicit terms; (5) whether decision making is individual or consensual, accomplished more through the use of groups; (6) whether responsibility for performance is shared or assigned largely to individuals; and (7) the extent to which the individual's whole life is of concern to the organization and his or her manager, or whether it is only performance at work that is of interest. A "Type Z" organization, employing a clan form of control, is characterized by long-term employment, relatively slow advancement and evaluation, less specialized career paths, implicit, qualitative evaluation, wholistic concern for the employee, consensual decision making, but still largely individual responsibility.

Ouchi and Jaeger argued that the Type Z, or clanlike, organization is a response to increasing social anomie caused by the disintegration or diminished effectiveness of many institutions of social bonding such as the church, marriage, the family structure, and the community. Based on the possibility of achieving social integration through institutions outside of the work organization, or through the work organization as a quasi or substitute family, Ouchi and Jaeger (1978) developed predictions concerning the conditions under which the typical bureaucratic versus the clan type of organization would be more or less appropriate, which are shown in Figure 4–2. The contingent relationship between the external social structure and the appropriate type of governance for the firm is less evident in subsequent

Figure 4-2. RELATIONSHIP BETWEEN SOCIETAL AND ORGANIZATIONAL AFFILIATIONS AND WELL-BEING

		Affiliation in Society	
		High	Low
Affiliation in the Organization	High	Overloaded	Integrated
	Low	Integrated	Underloaded

SOURCE: From Ouchi and Jaeger (1978: 312).

writing (Ouchi, 1981), in which the superiority of the clan organization is presented in a much less contingent fashion.

What the clan offers is a way of overcoming many of the control and monitoring problems that make hierarchical, bureaucratic organizations difficult to operate. Ouchi (1979: 833) has noted that "markets deal with the control problem through their ability to precisely measure and reward individual contributions; bureaucracies rely instead upon a mixture of close evaluation with a socialized acceptance of common objectives; and clans rely upon a relatively complete socialization process which effectively eliminates goal incongruence between individuals." Ouchi (1979: 838) has argued that the clan has much higher social requirements than either markets or bureaucracies but also much lower informational requirements. Thus, under those conditions in which bureaucratic control mechanisms are no longer adequate because of very high surveillance costs, the internalization of control in clanlike organizations affords efficiency advantages because of the reduced need for hierarchical control and coordination and surveillance. Goal congruence, produced through socialization, substitutes for bureaucratic surveillance (Ouchi, 1980).

Following the efficiency rationale that underlies the market failures perspective, there would be expected to be an association between socialization as a form of control and economic performance, particularly in those circumstances where surveillance and bureaucratic control were not possible because of the high level of uncertainty in the organization accompanied by firm-specific knowledge, technology, and human capital. Thus, the model specified in Figure 4-3A would be presumed. However, as noted in Figure 4-3B, an alternative causal mechanism may be operating. Market power may produce the use of socialization as a control strategy as well as, of course, high economic performance. The association between market power and socialization for control occurs because of the criticality of long-term employment in the process. Without long-term employment, implicit evaluation is not possible because people are not around long enough to get to know them well and nonspecialized career paths do not make sense. But, to ensure long-term employment, it is helpful if the firm has enough market power to be able to either avoid or readily ride out fluctuations in economic demand. Furthermore, socialization and long-term employment are facilitated by firms with enough market power to pay above-market wages and to offer prestige and status to the employees. Thus, the alternative formulation does provide a reasonable competing explanation for the expected association between socialization as the form of control and economic performance. Of course, market power could be measured and the two models comparatively evaluated.

The second extension of Williamson's ideas is Goldberg's (1980) argu-

Figure 4-3. Two Possible Models of the Relationship between Socialization and Organizational Performance

A. Socialization and Inculturation producing High Performance

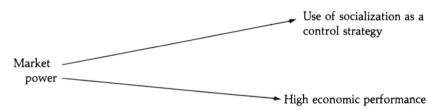

Use of socialization
as a control strategy ——————————————→ High economic
performance

B. Socialization and Inculturation as a Spurious Correlate of Performance

Market
power

→ Use of socialization as a
control strategy

→ High economic performance

ments concerning the use of deferred compensation as a way of binding workers who have developed firm-specific human capital to the firm. Goldberg noted that making exit more costly for workers not only enabled the firm to capture some of the benefits of the specialized training and skill development but also enhanced the general control of the firm over its workers:

> To direct workers to perform certain tasks and to discourage behavior that impairs performance, the firm requires devices which impose costs on the worker for non-compliance. The ability to impose costs is enhanced by making quitting expensive for the worker. If the worker could simply walk away without cost, any particular punishment . . . could be ignored; if, however, quitting imposed a substantial loss on the worker, he would be vulnerable to the threat of punishment. . . . Further, a high exit cost can be a powerful deterent in its own right. The firm can use the threat of termination to influence the worker's behavior (1980: 263).

Goldberg argued that there were a number of devices that could bind the worker to the firm. One was the payment of premium wages. However, to bind the worker to the firm, the payment had to be deferred, to be contingent on the worker's continuing satisfactory performance and maintenance of the employment relationship. Other devices include "pensions, health insurance, company-provided housing, and so forth" (Goldberg,

1980: 264). Using the ideas of the need for obligational markets to bind the worker and the firm together to capture the efficiencies from specialized human capital, it should be possible to predict the conditions under which deferred compensation will be more or less used.

Goldberg (1980) has noted that deferred compensation gives an incentive for the employer to cheat — by not paying off on the promised future rewards. Such incentives for cheating are reduced, of course, to the extent that reneging would make it more difficult, if not impossible, to use such forms of compensation in the future. However, this constraint of the needs of future recruitment is not present if the firm goes out of existence. Thus, in a merger the acquiring firm may not be constrained to honor the deferred compensation promises of the acquired organization. As Goldberg (1980: 267) noted, "If some of the 'economies' arising from merger are simply transfers to the newcomers resulting from 'confiscating' the deferred compensation of the old management, then it is easy to refrain from enthusiasm." This example is only one illustration of how profits may be increased through efficiency-oriented strategies that have little to do with "efficiency" as conceived in some public good or public policy sense.

As Goldberg has noted:

> A general theory of the employment relationship would explain why the structure varies over time, place, industry, and so forth. It would also develop the relationship between these structures and outcomes (which might range from predictions of quit rates to propositions about job satisfaction or demands for codetermination) (1980: 254).

The development of this extensive a theory has not yet been accomplished, either in the market failures framework or, for that matter, in any of the alternative radical frameworks to be considered later in this chapter.

Conceptual and Empirical Issues

The market failures perspective has a number of conceptual and empirical issues associated with it that require resolution for the theory to be evaluated fully. First and foremost is the imprecision of many (if not most) of its concepts. The critical concept of transaction costs illustrates the problem. Williamson (1979: 233) himself recognized the problem when he wrote, "There are too many degrees of freedom; the concept wants for definition." March (1981: personal communication) has commented on the tendency in the social sciences to assume that labeling or naming is the same as explanation. The problem is particularly perverse when what is being labeled is otherwise unexplained or error variance. Thus, *transactions costs* may be just one term for unexplained or error variance. To demonstrate that such is not the case, at least some of the procedures of construct validation (e.g., Bagozzi, 1980) need to be employed.

This task of measurement has been avoided thus far by avoiding the task of empirically demonstrating the validity of the various hypotheses addressed. With the notable exception of the work of Teece (e.g., Teece, Armour, and Saloner, 1980), the dominant line of argument used in the market failures research has been proof by assertion. The comparative testing of markets and hierarchies arguments against alternative theories that will involve sharpening the arguments and developing measures and metrics remains a critical task.

It should also be clear that in proceeding from the usual economic paradigm in terms of the primacy of efficiency demands and the use of "as if" reasoning, the market failures perspective uses primarily equilibrium as contrasted with dynamic analysis and provides arguments for explaining the status quo. If integration — or the movement from market-based transactions to hierarchies, or the form of the employment relationship, or anything else — occurs for efficiency reasons (an argument that is almost never tested but rather that is stated as an underlying truth), then efficiency provides both an explanation and justification for present arrangements. This line of argument can be seen most dramatically in Teece's (1976) study of diversification and integration in the petroleum industry in which efficiency arguments from the market failures perspective are mustered, ad hoc, to account for the characteristics of the domestic oil companies and to provide arguments as to why those characteristics should be preserved for the general social welfare.

STRUCTURAL CONTINGENCY THEORY

The M-form hypothesis advanced by Williamson (1975) and tested by Armour and Teece (1978) is noncontingent in the sense that the M-form is argued to enhance efficiency and, therefore, to be preferred under all conditions. The only possible contingency factor considered by Williamson (1975) was organizational size, as the arguments concerning the advantages of the M-form proceeded from the premise of the need to overcome the loss of control that can accompany increasing organizational size. The dominant approach to explaining organizational structures in the sociological and business school literatures has been structural contingency theory, which has an emphasis on efficiency, in common with the market failures approach, but also argues that the design of the organization depends on various contextual factors.

J. R. Galbraith (1973) has briefly and aptly summarized the premises of structural contingency theory:

1. There is no one best way to organize.
2. Any way of organizing is not equally effective (1973: 2).

Thus, structural contingency theory explicitly rejects the one-best-way approach to administration, arguing that the appropriate design depends on the organization's context. Many versions of the theory have some variant of the consonance hypothesis embedded in them. The consonance hypothesis states that those organizations that have structures that more closely match the requirements of the context are more effective than those that do not. Although not all tests of structural contingency theory have tested the consonance hypothesis, the basic structure of the theory has implicit in it the premise that there is an effectiveness or efficiency-seeking orientation on the part of organizational managers that acts to tend to produce congruence between organizational designs and the contextual factors that affect the appropriateness of those designs. A representative statement is that made by Perrow (1970b: 80): "We must assume here that, in the interest of efficiency, organizations wittingly or unwittingly attempt to maximize the congruence between their technology and their structure."

Structural contingency theory specifies an overall perspective of managerial adaptation to environmental constraints, but the specific structural dimensions so adapted, as well as the specific elements of context that affect structural choices, are left unspecified. In the research literature, the three elements of context most frequently investigated have been size, technology, and the organization's environment. The structural variables presumably affected by these context variables are those emerging from a Weberian (1947) conception of organizational structure: the size of the administrative component, the degree of centralization and formalization of the structure, and the amount of differentiation, or the extent of task specialization and vertical elaboration. An overview of structural contingency theory is shown in Table 4-1.

Size

Size is one of the most prominent characteristics of organizations, and the effects of size have been investigated in numerous studies (Kimberly, 1976). Weber's (1947) initial analysis argued that the elements of bureaucracy would emerge only in larger organizations, and Pugh, Hickson, and Hinings (1969) found size to be the most powerful predictor of a factor that mea-

Table 4-1. An Overview of Structural Contingency Theory

Elements of the Organization's Structure	Are Contingent on	Aspects of the Organization's Context
Formalization		Size
Differentiation		Technology
Vertical (number of levels)		Production
Horizontal (number of departments,		Information
divisions, subunits)		Environment
Size of the administrative component		Uncertainty
Centralization		Resource munificence
Complexity		Degree of competition
Span of control		
Specialization		

sured specialization, use of procedures, and reliance on paperwork. Blau (1970) has been one of the principal contributors to the size literature, arguing that size generates structural differentiation within organizations but that the differentiation increases at a decreasing rate as size increases. There are two causal arguments associated with the effects of size. One suggests that increasing size provides the opportunity to benefit from increased division of labor. This increased division of labor will be associated with the development of more subunits and also will require greater coordination by the managers because of the increasing division of labor and the coordination required by the interdependence created by that task specialization. The second argument proceeds by noting that with increasing numbers of employees personal control over the work process becomes increasingly difficult. Instead of personal, centralized control, impersonal mechanisms of control emerge, and these require a larger administrative component to operate. Thus, the basic arguments from the size literature are that size leads to increasing structural differentiation, that size is negatively related to centralization, that size is positively related to formalization, and that size is related to the size of the administrative component, though whether there are decreasing or increasing administrative economies of scale is unclear.

Blau and Schoenherr (1971) found support for these hypotheses in a study of state employment service organizations, and Meyer (1972b) found support in a study of state and municipal finance departments. Meyer's analysis was longitudinal, adding support to the idea that it was size that caused structural differentiation rather than the other way around. However, as Meyer (1971) himself noted, if one assumes reasonably constant spans of control, the relationship between size and differentiation is mathematically true by definition. Thus, there is some concern that the effects of size on differentiation are not of great theoretical interest or importance. Meyer (1972a) also reported support for the effects of size on formalization and centralization, support that has been found in other studies as well (Blau, 1973; Hall, Haas, and Johnson, 1967). The argument about size and centralization implies a trade-off between centralization and formalization as mechanisms of control. Child (1972b) has called specialization and standardization of activities the bureaucratic strategy of control and has argued (Child, 1972b, 1973a, 1973b) that specialization, the standardization and formalization of role activities, and centralization of decision making are all related, the first two positively and both negatively to the degree of centralization. Child (1973a) as well as Meyer (1972a) found that size was one of the principal factors causing variations in organizational control strategies.

The effect of size on the size of the administrative component is less clear, in large measure because of definitional dependency issues (Freeman and Kronenfeld, 1974) plaguing the research. Most studies in this genre (Anderson and Warkov, 1961; Raphael, 1967; Tosi and Platt, 1967) have correlated the proportion of administrative personnel $(A/[A + P])$ with the total organizational employment $(A + P)$, where A is the number of administrators and P is the number of production or nonadministrative employees. It is clear that the term $(A + P)$ appears on both sides of the equation; thus, the fact that there are statistically significant associations should not be surprising. Moreover, the research has tended to focus on the size of the administrative component in relationship to total size without worrying too much about the fact that the organizations being studied have varied from public organizations of different types to private firms.

Another issue in the organizational size-size of the administrative component question is the fact that the administrative component itself has been conceptualized and measured differently in different studies and is probably not a homogeneous category. Rushing (1966) argued that a wide range of occupations has been included as administrative personnel but that, in fact, the various categories of administrative personnel may be affected differently by size. If this were the case and different organizations had different mixes of the personnel, that could account for the inconsistent results across studies. Using industry-level data (which may have problems because of aggregation bias), Rushing (1966) examined the intercorrelations among six administrative/production personnel ratios as well as the relationship of these ratios to size. He found that there were moderately high correlations among the ratios but that the correlations of the ratios with size were inconsistent. He concluded that the low overall correlation of the total administrative personnel ratio to firm size was the result of "firm size having negative effects on managerial and sales personnel, positive effects on professional and clerical personnel, and a weak and inconsistent effect on service personnel" (Rushing, 1966: 106). A similar conclusion on the heterogeneity of the administrative personnel component emerged from a study by Kasarda (1974) of school districts in Colorado. He found that although the managerial component of administration declined with the size of the district, secretarial and clerical personnel and the professional component consisting of librarians, guidance counselors, and so forth increased with size.

A further problem with this literature is that almost all of the studies have been cross-sectional in nature. Freeman and Hannan (1975), studying school districts in California, have found that the size of the administrative component and its relationship to total personnel depend on whether the school district is growing or declining. Using an essentially political argument, Freeman and Hannan maintained that in times of growth all the various personnel components (teachers, administrators, other support personnel) would grow about proportionately with enrollment. However, because of their protected political position, when enrollment declined, administrative personnel would be cut more slowly. Their data (J. Freeman, 1979; Freeman and Hannan, 1975) provided support for this position. What this means for the other literature is that it is impossible to estimate the organization size-size of administrative component effect without taking into account whether the organization is growing or shrinking, which requires analysis over time.

Technology

Although there are alternative ways of measuring organizational size (Kimberly, 1976), size is nevertheless more straightforward to assess than technology, another element of the organization's context that has been related to structure. Reviewing the attempts to conceptualize and measure technology, Scott (1981) noted:

> An examination of the many recent attempts to define and measure technology indicates that the concept has been viewed very broadly to include (1) the characteristics of the *inputs* utilized by the organization; (2) the characteristics of the *transformation processes* employed by the organization; and (3) the characteristics of the *outputs* produced by the organization. Alongside this view of technologies varying by stage of processing . . . approaches to technology vary by whether analysts emphasize (1) the nature of the *materials* on which work is performed; (2) the char-

acteristics of the *operations* or techniques used to perform the work; or (3) the state of *knowledge* that underlies the transformation process (1981: 209).

In Table 4-2, Scott's (1981: 210) categorization of technology measures by stage of processing and facets of technology is reproduced. It is clear that there are a large number of ways of conceptualizing the technology construct; this has led to inconsistency in the research results. Woodward (1965, 1970) conceptualized technology in terms of the time period in which the technology was introduced and the length of the production process, with the technical scale ranging from prototype production through small batch, large batch, and process production. She was one of the first to focus on the importance of technology, and her study and measure is one of the more important in terms of the amount of research conducted on it. Woodward found that for many structural variables there was a curvilinear relationship, with batch and process production being more similar to each other than to mass assembly-line production. She also found support for the consonance hypothesis, with firms having arrangements matching their technologies being more effective than those that did not. Hickson, Pugh, and Pheysey (1969), however, failed to replicate Woodward's results for the importance of technology. They argued that one reason might be that technology impacted structure only for those units most immediately associated with the work flow. In larger organizations with a smaller proportion of the firm devoted to the actual production tasks, the effects of technology might be less observable. Mohr (1971), studying public health organizations, found little support for Woodward's central predictions and no support at all for the consonance hypothesis. Of course, given that he was studying public organizations, whether the consonance hypothesis would be expected to hold is unclear, since the performance pressures on such organizations might be reduced. Zwerman (1970), using Woodward's exact procedures and methods on a sample of U.S. firms, did replicate her results.

Most conceptualizations of technology have focused less on the operations or production technology and instead have conceptualized technology in terms of its complexity, analyzability, or routineness. Hage and Aiken (1969), for instance, found that organizations characterized by routine technology were more centralized and more formalized. Perrow (1967) argued that the extent to which procedures were analyzable and there were few or many variations in the input worked on by the organization were critical dimensions affecting the organization of work. Throughout much of the technology literature, there is an often implicit argument that runs something like this: technology, in terms of its routineness, analyzability, or complexity, affects the skills and discretion of the work force and, thus, the

Table 4-2. Classification of Technology Measures

FACETS OF TECHNOLOGY	STAGE OF PROCESSING			
	Inputs	Throughputs	Outputs	
Materials	Uniformity of inputs (Litwak, 1961) Hardness of materials (Rushing, 1968) Variability of stimuli (Perrow, 1970b)	Number of exceptions (Perrow, 1970b) Interchangeability of components (Rackham and Woodward, 1970)	Major project changes (Harvey, 1968) Homogenizing versus individuating settings (Wheeler, 1966) Multiplicity of outputs (Pugh, Hickson, and Hinings, 1969) Customization of outputs (Pugh, Hickson, and Hinings, 1969)	
Operations	Preprocessing, coding, smoothing of inputs (Thompson, 1967)	Complexity of technical processes (Udy, 1959; Woodward, 1965) Work flow integration (Pugh, Hickson, and Hinings, 1969) Routineness of work (Hage and Aiken, 1969) Automaticity of machinery (Amber and Amber, 1962) Interdependence of work units (Thompson, 1967)	Control of outputs through stockpiling, rationing (Thompson, 1967) Value added in manufacture	
Knowledge	Predictability (Dornbush and Scott, 1975) Anticipation of fluctuations in supplies (Thompson, 1967)	Knowledge of cause-effect relations (Thompson, 1967) Analyzability of search processes (Perrow, 1970b) Information required to perform task compared with information possessed (J. R. Galbraith, 1973)	Time span of definitive feedback (Lawrence and Lorsch, 1967) Anticipation of fluctuations in demand (Thompson, 1967)	

SOURCE: From Scott (1981: 210).

153

control that must be employed; different structural arrangements (centralization, formalization) imply different types of control structures and procedures; and, therefore, technology is linked to structure through its requirements for procedures to control work, which varies in its characteristics. Woodward (1970) made this argument most explicitly.

It is clear that this argument is couched largely in terms of the impact of technology on control at the level of the individual worker or work group. Routine technologies permit rules and formal procedures to be developed and implemented because how to do the job is well understood and the job is repetitive enough to justify the investment in systems, procedures, and forms. Unanalyzable tasks require control systems and structural arrangements permitting more discretion, and so forth. Scott (1981) has noted that most of the technology-structure studies have used the entire organization as the unit. Thus, the failure to find results may be, in part, the result of conducting the studies at an incorrect level of analysis.

In addition to the confusion concerning the definition and measurement of *technology* (Lynch, 1974; Meissner, 1969; Rushing, 1968), there are also problems associated with the measurement of organizational structure that affect the technology-structure literature and the other portions of the structural contingency literature as well. Pennings (1973) noted that measures of structure derived from single informants or company records did not correlate with measures of structure developed from aggregating the questionnaire or interview responses of people working in the organization. This discrepancy may occur for several reasons. In the first place, there may be differences in structural perceptions that reflect individual differences, much as there are differences in the amount of uncertainty perceived across individuals. Second, the perception of technology, particularly the routineness or the analyzability, may vary between those doing the job and those observing the task from the outside (Dornbusch and Scott, 1975). People come to terms with their tasks in a variety of ways, including developing rules of thumb and standard operating procedures that make job complexity manageable within the structural arrangements in which they work. Third, there may be variation between the level at which the objective indicators are measured and at which the individual responses are gathered. Typically, the objective measures are of technology defined for the organization as a whole; clearly, the questionnaires or interviews will measure technology at the level of the individual or the work group. And thus, fourth, to the extent there is a great deal of variation in technology or structure, or both, within the organization, the aggregate measure is meaningless and so is the procedure of combining responses from individuals across work units that have very different structural properties.

The Environment

The definitional and measurement disagreements that have plagued the technology literature, and also the levels and units of analysis problems, recur again in the literature considering the effects of the environment on organizational structure. The basic argument is that "different environmental conditions and different types of relationship with outside parties will . . . require different types of organizational structural accommodation for a high level of performance to be achieved" (Child, 1972a: 3). The environmental dimension most often considered is uncertainty, sometimes measured merely as change, sometimes including a component of complexity. Burns and Stalker (1961) were among the first to notice that different environmental conditions made different organizational structures more or less appropriate. They found that a mechanistic, or bureaucratic organizational, structure was appropriate for more stable and certain environments, while an organic, less formalized and centralized structure was found more frequently and was more successful in rapidly changing environments.

Even agreement on variability or uncertainty as an important environmental characteristic did not solve the issue of measurement and conceptualization. Duncan (1972), for instance, argued that environmental uncertainty was the result of two dimensions—complexity, or the number of elements dealt with, and variability, or the extent to which these elements changed over time. Duncan's scaling and methodological procedures, however, are open to a great deal of criticism (Downey, Hellriegel, and Slocum, 1975). In addition to the issue of how best to capture the dimensions of the environment, a second debate has centered on whether it is the objective characteristics of the environment or those characteristics as perceived by organizational decision makers that should be incorporated into studies of structure. Several studies have shown that the two are not the same thing (Downey, Hellriegel, and Slocum, 1975; Tosi, Aldag, and Storey, 1973). This has led to further work to see whether perceptions of environmental uncertainty are more characteristic of the perceiver than of the environment (Downey and Slocum, 1975). The argument has been made, on the one hand, that the organizational structure is determined by decision makers who must ultimately base their decisions on their perceptions of the context in which they are operating. However, as Abell (1975) has noted, there are problems of tautology in arguing from the position that it is managerial perceptions that determine structural results, as well, it could be added, as problems of causality. In the latter case, the argument could be made that the degree of uncertainty and differentiation in the structure conditions the extent to which a variable and complex environment is registered by the organization (Huber, O'Connell, and Cummings, 1975). In the former case, the argument that managerial beliefs or perceptions govern the structure of the organization is a hypothesis only to the extent that the converse — managerial perceptions and beliefs are not related to the structure — is plausible. Given the implausibility of this position, the relationship is more true by definition than as a scientific theory to be investigated.

Lawrence and Lorsch (1967) made a slightly different and more sophisticated argument concerning the relationship between structure and environment. They argued that different organizational units faced different subenvironments and that, for instance, the environment of a production department was very different from that faced by marketing or research and development. These authors then argued that each subunit would develop a structure matching its own subenvironment, therefore leading to a higher degree of differentiation within the organization. This higher degree of differentiation — in goal orientation, structures, and time horizons — would impose a more difficult task of integrating or coordinating the entire system. Lawrence and Lorsch argued and found, in a study of ten firms, that the more effective organizations were those that had the requisite level of internal differentiation for the different types of environments faced but that also were able to integrate the diverse departments effectively.

This study is one of the few that has avoided the problem of overaggregation to the total organization level of analysis. In addition, it introduced the concept of internal differentiation and integration. The basic environmental predictor of subunit structure was, however, again the concept of environmental uncertainty. As in the case of Duncan's research, the Lawrence and Lorsch empirical measures and procedures have been subjected to criticism (Tosi, Aldag, and Storey, 1973).

Although environmental uncertainty has been the primary variable employed in the environment-structure research, the extent of competition in the environment and the degree of resource munificence have also been considered. Pfeffer and Leblebici (1973a) argued that competition caused increased demands for control, producing direct effects for a more structured organization as well as causing product differentiation to lead to less decentralization and less structural elaboration than might otherwise be expected. Khandwalla (1973), in a study of 96 manufacturing firms, found that overall competition was associated with the use of management controls and selectivity in the use of controls. Of the three forms of competition investigated — price, marketing, and product competition — product competition had the greatest impact on top management control structure. Staw and Szwajkowski (1975) found that firms facing less munificent environments committed a larger number of illegal acts, at least as reported by the Federal

Trade Commission. One final environmental dimension that has been described as being important is the degree of interconnectedness of the system of organizations (Aldrich, 1979). Again, however, there is little empirical work investigating this dimension in terms of its effects on structure (Mindlin and Aldrich, 1975).

Pfeffer and Salancik (1978: chapter 4) argued that the three basic dimensions of the environment were the degree of concentration of resources, the scarcity or munificence of the resources, and the degree of interconnectedness of the organizations. In Figure 4-4, their diagram indicating the causal relationships among the elements of the environment, the relationships among social actors, and uncertainty is reproduced. They viewed uncertainty as the result of relationships among social actors, which in turn were governed by the conditions of the environment in which these actors operated. One implication of this argument is that uncertainty may be too global a concept to use in explaining structure and that the more fundamental dimensions of either the environment itself or relationships among the social actors should be used as the independent variables.

The Relationship between Strategy and Structure

In addition to the contingencies of size, the environment, and technology, another contingency affecting organizational structure is the organization's strategy. Chandler (1966) noted that as organizations expanded and diversified their product lines, they tended to develop multidivisional as con-

Figure 4-4. Relationships among Dimensions of Organizational Environments

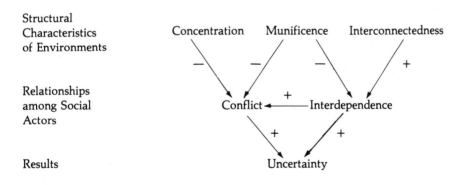

SOURCE: From Pfeffer and Salancik (1978: 68).

trasted with unitary or functional structures. Chandler's observations were systematically investigated by Rumelt (1974). In a study using data spanning three decades, Rumelt observed: (1) the proportion of diversified firms had increased significantly since the 1940s; few firms in the early 1970s continued to operate in a narrow set of product markets; (2) the proportion of multidivisionally organized firms had increased substantially since the 1940s, with a corresponding decrease in the number of firms organized functionally; whereas in the 1940s the functional form of organization had been dominant, by the 1970s the multidivisional structure was the form of organization characterizing more than 70 percent of the firms in Rumelt's large-firm sample; and (3) there was a very strong relationship between product market diversification and organizational structure; in all three periods examined, narrow productline firms tended to be organized functionally, while diversified firms had multidivisional structures. Rumelt (1974) and Chandler (1966) both argued that there was a connection between strategy, particularly product market strategy, and firm structure. Firms that pursued a strategy of diversification and market extension tended to adopt multidivisional structures, whereas more narrowly focused firms had functional organizations.

The link between strategy and structure has been further developed by Miles and Snow (1978). Miles and his colleagues identified four distinct strategic types:

1. *Domain Defenders,* organizations whose top managers perceive little or no change and uncertainty in the environment and who have little inclination to make anything other than minor adjustments in organizational structure and processes;
2. *Reluctant Reactors,* organizations where top managers perceive some change and uncertainty . . . but who are not likely to make any substantial . . . adjustments until forced to do so by environmental pressures;
3. *Anxious Analyzers,* organizations where top managers perceive a good deal of change and uncertainty . . . but who wait until competing organizations develop a viable response and then quickly adopt it; and
4. *Enthusiastic Prospectors,* organizations whose top managers continually perceive (almost create) change and uncertainty . . . and who regularly experiment with potential responses to new environmental trends (Miles, Snow, and Pfeffer, 1974: 257).

In studies of college textbook publishers, hospitals, and business firms, Miles and Snow found that various strategic types tended to coexist in the sense that one could find a mix of strategic postures within the same industry, and even within the same local environment within that industry.

This finding is relevant to the strategic choice issue to be discussed below. Miles and Snow also found that strategic type, structure, managerial processes, and managerial philosophies tended to covary. For instance, domain defenders were more likely to employ mass production rather than unit technologies and to have mechanistic, bureaucratic as contrasted with organic, flexible structures (Miles, Snow, and Pfeffer, 1974). Thus, there was evidence that strategy and structure tended to adapt to each other; firms with structures that provided flexibility and innovation tended also to pursue strategies relying on these management attributes; firms with structures that facilitated tight control and production efficiency adopted corresponding strategies. Whether strategy preceded structure or vice versa was not critical, and in fact, reciprocal relationships probably occurred. The point was that the choice of the structure fit (and needed to fit) the organization's general strategy, and vice versa.

The strategy-structure linkage has brought portions of organizational research into contact with the business policy area. In one form, strategy is viewed as yet another contingency to be taken into account in designing the organization's structure. In other versions, external influences have been argued to affect the choice of both strategy and structure within organizations.

Strategic Choice

Child (1972a) criticized all the structural contingency theories for neglecting the importance of strategic choice. Child argued that organizations were not as tightly coupled to environments as implied by most versions of structural contingency theory and, furthermore, that profits and effectiveness were not the only outcomes of interest to those in the dominant coalition who determined the structure. The first point raised the issue of there not only being one best way to organize, but the possibility that there was not just one best way to organize *given* the organization's context. The second point was that the basic managerialist, profit-seeking underpinning to structural contingency theory might be incorrect in that managers sought other things, such as power, autonomy, or stability, that were not considered in the theory.

Miles, Snow, and Pfeffer (1974) argued that organizations enacted their environments, both through perceptual processes of attention and through the choice of domain:

> In enacting its environment, the organization has, in part, defined its domain. An organization's domain consists of those activities it intends to pursue, and, in choosing a domain of activity, the organization simultane-

ously determines its pattern of interdependence with elements of the environment (1974: 250).

Thus, Miles and coworkers argued that to some extent organizations could choose the environments in which they were to operate. This is one element of strategic choice. But even within the same environment, there may be multiple responses (or equifinality, in systems terminology) that produce the same basic outcome of successful operation:

> . . . in the college textbook publishing study, two organizations whose top management perceived a great deal of change and uncertainty in their environments nevertheless made substantially different adjustments to this environmental turbulence. One firm went through a major effort to restructure the organization while simultaneously creating a program to financially underwrite a small number of free-lance professionals who were to experiment with new publishing techniques. The other organization . . . retained its current overall organization structure but set up several cross-functional project teams to develop publishing programs to deal with changing environmental demands (1974: 258).

One can employ centralization and personal control or impersonal mechanisms of control (Meyer, 1972a); one can use surveillance or develop goal congruence (Ouchi, 1980); one can use output control or behavior control (Ouchi and Maguire, 1975). Although each of these may not be equally likely or equally efficient, depending on other circumstances, there are clearly a range of structural responses available to cope with coordination and control issues faced by organizational managers. This is the point made by J. R. Galbraith (1973) in his description of the range of information processing mechanisms available in organization design.

Child (1972a) also noted that given imperfections in the market, managers had discretion to pursue other aims besides maximum efficiency or profits. Thus, the level of performance sought and the trade-offs between performance and other managerial objectives were both elements of strategic choice. Pfeffer (1978) maintained that the basic issue in organizations was governance or control, or, put in other terms, the acquisition and maintenance of the power to control and benefit from the resources at the disposal of the organization. In this struggle, profits and effectiveness were as much arguing points as actual objectives. Thus, according to the strategic choice argument, not only could organizations choose their domains, and choose responses within those domains to produce equal levels of performance, but they could even, within some broad limits, choose the target level of performance.

Finally, Child argued that the effects of the environments were mediated through the filter of managerial perceptions. Child (1972a: 4-5) argued for the need to distinguish between "variability and an experience of uncertainty, between complexity and an experience of cognitive profusion, between illiberality and an experience of stress." Similarly, Miles, Snow, and Pfeffer (1974: 264) "heavily emphasized managerial perceptions as a key variable . . . in the adjustment process." Thus, the linkage between environments and organizations was diminished through the operation of perceptual mechanisms and the various biasing effects that occur in such perceptions.

Aldrich (1979) has argued that although the strategic choice critique of contingency theory makes some good points, there are limits to the opportunity to exercise strategic choice that make managerial discretion a potentially less powerful explanation than it might appear. Aldrich argued that in terms of the choice of a domain there were various barriers to entry, including economy of scale, absolute cost, and product differentiation barriers. We might add that in regulated markets there may be the requirement for obtaining regulatory approval. Thompson (1967) also noted that an organization could not unilaterally choose its domain.

> There must be some degree of consensus among those with whom the organization comes into contact — either resource providers or critics of the organization's proposed activities — regarding the desired arena of activity, and this process of attaining domain consensus frequently constrains what activities the organization undertakes (Miles, Snow, and Pfeffer, 1974: 250).

As to the other elements of strategic choice, the existence of managerial discretion and the possibility that various structural outcomes may produce the same result, the evidence is largely missing. The issue of managerial discretion was treated as part of the ownership-control and managerial goals debate reviewed at the beginning of this chapter. The extent of product market or capital market competition is both a subject open to dispute and something that changes over time in the context of legal and regulatory changes and managerial adaptations to delimit competition. And it is certainly the case that none of the structural contingency theories have been particularly successful in explaining either structural outcomes or performance, although the pervasive units of analysis and measurement problems make it impossible to determine if this is a failure of the theory or how it has been tested thus far.

Theoretical Issues

In spite of the fact that structural contingency theory is widely accepted in the organizations literature, we have seen it has several problems. Most fundamentally,

> . . . contingency theory is not a theory at all, in the conventional sense of theory as a well-developed set of interrelated propositions. It is more an orienting strategy or metatheory, suggesting ways in which a phenomenon ought to be conceptualized or an approach to the phenomenon ought to be explained. . . . Although the overall strategy is reasonably clear, the substance of the theory is not clear (Schoonhoven, 1981: 350).

Thus, statements that there is not one best way to organize and that all ways are not equally effective want for specificity. "Contingency theory currently requires greater precision than is provided by these richly suggestive but ambiguous statements" (Schoonhoven, 1981: 351). Indeed, stated in this form, it is not clear that structural contingency theory is falsifiable. Thus, it suffers from many of the same problems of ambiguity and tautology that plague markets and hierarchies approaches.

In addition, the "lack of clarity by contingency theorists blurs the fact that an empirical interaction is being predicted" (Schoonhoven, 1981: 351). In its prediction of organizational performance or effectiveness resulting from the congruence between elements of the organization's context and its structure, an interaction is being specified. This interaction has seldom been tested, and even when tested, as Schoonhoven (1981) has pointed out, the precise form of the interaction has been ignored.

What would seem to be needed is much more precisely stated and potentially falsifiable hypotheses. These might include more attention to which of the various elements of organizational context — size, technology, or environment — was important for understanding which elements of structure, under what conditions. And, as noted in the research of Pennings (1973), Tosi, Aldag, and Storey (1973), and Scott (1981), the testing of contingency theory requires a lot more attention to the details of the measurement and operationalization of the concepts. Many of the problems confronting the transaction cost approach in terms of conceptual ambiguity and measurement also face structural contingency theory, in spite of the apparently greater understanding and acceptance of this latter approach.

MARXIST ANALYSES OF ORGANIZATIONS

If the market failures approach of Williamson anchors one end of the scale with its emphasis on efficiency, then Marxist approaches to organizational analysis anchor the other end with their focus on power. Structural contingency theory falls in the middle with its focus on effectiveness and efficiency as underlying pressures on organizational design, on the one hand, but with its recognition of strategic choice and managerial preferences, on the other. Like the other two approaches, Marxist analysis blends environmental determinism with rational, strategic choice. After all, Marx argued that the evolution of economic systems was inevitable and, in his analysis of social forces, saw the presence of certain inexorable historical trends. The decision to include Marxist approaches in this chapter is based on the judgment that, for the most part, Marxist analyses relevant to understanding organizations have proceeded from the premise of conscious, rational, strategic action taken on the part of the capitalist class and organizations controlled by that class. In this sense, it is an analysis quite consistent with other approaches presuming conscious, foresightful behavior. As Goldman (1980: 12) has noted, "The Marxian position sees a high degree of managerial consciousness and intentionality even omnipotence not only in technical decisions but also in ostensibly benign programs such as the welfare work in the early Twentieth Century or the democratization experiments of the 1970's."

Marxist perspectives are relevant to examining two issues in organizational analysis: the organization of work and the nature of the employment relationship, and the relationship among organizations and, particularly, business organizations and capitalists and political organizations. We will consider each of these subject domains in turn.

The Employment Relationship and the Organization of Work

The Marxist approach proceeds from the basic assumption that capitalists are interested in maximizing their accumulation of wealth and power in the society. Consequently, in the context of the employment relationship and the organization of work: (1) employers seek a labor force that is relatively inexpensive and powerless; and (2) employers seek a labor force that can be controlled, so that it will work in concert with ownership interests. To accomplish these two things, (3) means of production (technologies) are selected that have the effect of deskilling the workers and ensuring social control over them; and (4) the employment relationship is structured so that the power of capitalists over labor is largely hidden and control over the workers and managers is achieved. However, these efforts have consequences, some of them unintended. In particular, (5) attempts to deskill and control the work force have within them forces that produce resistance on the part of the labor force, including lack of motivation and effort as well as absenteeism, turnover, and collective action taken through labor unions;

therefore, (6) a cycle of conflict and change is engendered by the struggle between capital and labor (Goldman, 1980). Within this argument, three substantive areas have drawn significant research attention: the nature of the employment relationship and the organization of work, the choice of technology and the resultant skill requirements of the labor force, and the extent to which there is, in fact, evidence for the kind of alienation on the part of workers predicted by this analysis.

Considering first the nature of the employment relationship, Marxist theorists have argued that the development of internal labor markets was an attempt to control the work force better. R. Edwards (1975) has presented an argument that has some interesting parallels with the resource dependence perspective to be described in the next chapter:

> As the monopoly capitalist firms have grown larger and become more powerful, they have consistently drawn more and more of their environments under their control—that is, each has "internalized" forces which potentially threatened its existence. Thus they were initially formed out of previously competing firms, as a means of bringing competition within their control. Big firms have vertically integrated their operations, to ensure proper supplies of raw materials. . . . When possible, they have generated investment funds from retained earnings rather than depend on uncertain bank finance. And they have created internal labor markets (1975: 5).

Thus, the internalization of labor was seen as a process similar to internalizing the sources of raw materials and attempting to generate funds internally. All of these actions provided more power and discretion to the firm and gave it better control over factors affecting its survival.

R. Edwards (1975: 6) argued that there were three features of large firms that made the internalization of the work force both feasible and even more desirable. First, because of the monopoly power enjoyed by large firms, they faced a stable demand for labor. "Stable employment was particularly true for that growing body of workers performing administrative, sales, legal, research and development, and other tasks not directly related to production" (Edwards, 1975: 6). This led to less reliance on the external labor market because they had to hire and fire less frequently. But, not mentioned by Edwards, it also gave the firms a bargaining chip with the workers. In contrast, for instance, to a contracting arrangement in which demand mght fluctuate widely, the firms could offer stability of employment. Since there is usually some trade-off between risk and return, one could assume that workers were, to at least some extent, willing to trade off somewhat higher wages or the higher returns they might receive from operating as independent contractors for the stability of the returns they would earn as employees, particularly in large firms. Second, the mere fact of the size of the firms and their growth made the filling of higher-level jobs through internal promotions more feasible. There were more candidates and more people who could be developed for promotion. As R. Edwards (1975: 6) noted, "In an industry where there are many small firms, most of the job allocations will necessarily occur between firms; assuming no increase in job turnover, workers will necessarily move less frequently among firms where there are but one or a few large firms." And third, the increasing bureaucratization of large firms produced an abundance of job categories and hierarchical levels, thus increasing the possibility of job movement within the firm. The fact of the opportunity for internal mobility, of course, could increase the worker's commitment to the firm and his reluctance to leave. Internal mobility tied the worker more closely to the firm in which this mobility occurred, as contrasted with the larger labor market.

Both Williamson (1975) and R. Edwards (1975) noted the evolution toward internal labor markets and the incorporation of workers in the firm, organized hierarchically rather than coordinated through market mechanisms such as contracting. However, while Williamson saw this as a response to efficiency pressures, Edwards viewed the change less benignly:

> Internal labor markets, then, go hand in hand with big corporations. Big corporations exist to earn profits. But to earn profits, the corporation must maintain its hegemony over its workforce. The organizational structure of the firm—the incentives, demarcated areas of responsibility, distribution of power, and so on—represent a system in large part contrived and consciously designed to perpetuate the capitalist's control over the firm's workforce (1975: 6-7).

Bureaucratic control, or the development of rules, procedures, and formal roles, was also seen in the context of the maintenance of control over the work force. Edwards argued that as large firms grew, there were ever more levels and more people between the capitalist owners and the work force; this increasing size made personal control, as exercised through a simple hierarchy, impossible. Thus, in an argument parallel with that made by the structural contingency literature on the effects of size, Edwards argued that the growth of the firm, as well as changes in labor laws, social norms, and the growth of unions that made arbitrary power less tolerable, resulted in the development of bureaucratized control systems. This "institutionalization of hierarchical power" (R. Edwards, 1975: 9) had the beneficial side effect of making the control relationship less obtrusive and more legitimate. This legitimation of control made the organized resistance of the work force less likely and less socially acceptable when it did occur. The legitimation of managerial authority meant that labor unions could bargain over the economic terms of the exchange but that control over the workplace remained in the hands of management.

As Goldberg (1980) has noted, there are a number of parallels between the analyses of Edwards and Williamson, and in many respects it is not easy to distinguish them. R. Edwards (1976) did present data indicating that compliant behaviors, consistent with a control perspective, accounted for both supervisory ratings and earnings even when human capital variables were statistically controlled. Edwards distinguished three types of bureaucratically controlled behavior: rule compliance, habits of predictability and dependability, and the internalization of the firm's goals and values. Measures of behavior traits corresponding to each of these compliance modes were obtained for a sample of 455 workers in the Boston area. The behavior measures accounted for some 38 percent of the variation in supervisor's ratings and about 20 percent of the variation in earnings (R. Edwards, 1976). Furthermore, Edwards found that rules orientation was most important for lower-level jobs, dependability and predictability most important for middle-level jobs, and internalization of goals and values most important for higher-level jobs. The fact that these behaviors can account for salary and ratings outcomes when human capital and background factors such as IQ, educational attainment, and family background are controlled indicates the emphasis on behavioral compliance in the workplace. Collins (1979) has made a similar argument in his study of the use of educational credentials. For managerial positions, particularly, Collins argued that such credentials indicated socialization into and compliance with middle-class norms.

R. Edwards (1975) argued that the dual nature of production relations — between those large firms in the monopoly capital sector and the smaller firms in the competitive sector — would be reproduced by a dualism in labor markets. There has been extensive research in the dual economy tradition (Beck, Horan, and Tolbert, 1978; Bibb and Form, 1977; Tolbert, Horan, and Beck, 1980). This work argues that there are two sectors in the economy, a core sector characterized by capital-intensive, profitable firms with substantial market power and a periphery sector characterized by firms with low profits, usually small size and limited market power. Employment in the core is more stable and higher paid, with greater rewards being earned for individual characteristics and human capital. Following Edwards's reasoning, there should be particularly larger returns for length of employment in the firm. Career ladders exist in the core because of the existence of internal labor markets. Employment in the periphery is unstable and lower paid. There is presumably little mobility between the core and the periphery (because of the unstable work habits of workers in the periphery); furthermore, blacks and women were argued to be concentrated disproportionately in the periphery sector. Thus, there was a structural basis for the lower returns earned by these individuals (Featherman and Hauser, 1976; Welch, 1973).

The evidence for the dual economy perspective is mixed (e.g., Baron and Bielby, 1980). In particular, there are problems with sectoral definitions (Zucker and Rosenstein, 1981), which profoundly affect the results obtained. Although there are main effects differences between workers in the core and the periphery, there is seldom the predicted difference in the effects of human capital factors on attainment (e.g., Pfeffer and Ross, 1981). Also, interestingly enough, the dual economy perspective posits a division in both the capitalist class and the work force. Given the description of the sectors, a reasonable supposition is that there would be cleavage between those in the periphery—both capital and labor—and those who enjoyed the higher profits, higher wages, and more stable employment in the core sector.

Thus far, we have considered primarily issues of worker control and the nature of the employment relationship. Marxist analyses also, however, consider how the labor market operates to reduce the wages of those employed by firms. Reich (1971) has argued that employers' profits were enhanced by reducing the wages paid and that the mechanism used to reduce wages was to segment the labor market and therefore prevent the development of solidarity within the working class. Presumably, by differentiating and splitting the labor market into segments—for instance, along racial or sexual lines—the development of powerful collective organizations such as unions that could pose a threat to the power of employers would be hindered. The thesis is one of divide and conquer.

Bonacich (1972, 1976) has critiqued the divide and conquer argument. She maintained that ethnic antagonism resulted from differentials in the price paid for labor identified along ethnic lines but that such differentials were the result of resources and motives within the groups themselves, not of the actions taken by capitalists. "Business . . . supports a liberal or laissez-faire ideology that would permit all workers to compete freely in an open market. Such open competition would displace higher paid labor" (Bonacich, 1972: 557). Thus, Bonacich saw the conflict as having three sides, with business and the two labor groups, one higher paid, and with business seeking to displace the higher paid with the cheaper labor. She argued that, for instance, business was not able to benefit substantially from black unemployment. Rather, "large capitalists are unable to take advantage of ghetto labor and abandon it to marginal enterprises" (Bonacich, 1976: 49).

In addition to using various forms of labor market segmentation and exclusion to maintain powerlessness and reduce wages of the labor force, Marxist analyses place great emphasis on the role of technology in the struggle between labor and capital. Bonacich (1976: 35) has argued that "technology should be seen as a resource which parties can use in a variety of ways to further their interests, or which they may choose not to use if their interests are harmed by its introduction." R. Edwards (1979) argued that the choice of technology might be based on considerations of profitability but that profitability included more than just technical efficiency. In particular, Edwards included considerations of the leverage the technology provided the managers to transform labor power into work actually done. Edwards argued that with the growth of larger enterprises the issue of control became more important. The solution was to embed the control process in the structure of work, either through technical control or through bureaucratic control. The assembly line and the consequent deskilling of work provided interchangeability of workers and meant that a reserve army of unemployed could, in fact, be readily substituted for the firm's present employees. This lack of development of person-specific human capital maintained the power of the capitalists over the employees.

Thus, for Marxist analysis, deskilling of the work is an important part of the struggle between labor and capital, as it renders labor less powerful because it makes workers easier to replace as well as less necessary to the extent that production processes become even more automated. Noble (1978) has argued that the invention and expansion in the use of numerically controlled machine tools was motivated by the desire to reduce the power (and hence the wages) of the skilled and largely unionized machinists. The deskilling of labor is a theme also pursued by Braverman (1974) in his analysis of the evolution of jobs over time. Braverman argued that the transformation of jobs and the introduction of machine technologies have been undertaken not only for purposes of technical efficiency but also for the purpose of separating the working class into skilled and unskilled segments, thereby hindering the development of solidarity. Kraft (1977) has made similar arguments with respect to the introduction of computers and the work of programming and operating computers. Again, a deskilling process is evident in which attempts are being made to routinize the work to reduce the wages and increase the substitutability of the computer personnel.

Marxist analysis introduces an element into the strategic choice of technology that provides an alternative to economic theories based on efficiency considerations concerning why certain technologies and arrangements for production are chosen. In contrast to many organizational theories of strategic choice, tastes for technology are not exogenous but are specified as deriving from the conflict between capital and labor. As Goldberg (1980: 268) has noted, "An efficient institution is one that survives in a particular context. The efficacy of a particular arrangement will depend upon the ability of the parties to exert legal or extra-legal power."

Whether this deskilling has been effectively accomplished is a matter of some empirical dispute. Spenner (1979) has noted that there are two components to the deskilling process: the actual change in the content of jobs and the distribution of the number of workers in jobs over time. Thus, deskilling could proceed either by reducing the skill content somewhat in most jobs or through changing the structure of work so that the distribution between skilled and unskilled jobs changes. Spenner argued that in terms of the distribution of jobs since 1900 there is evidence for some downgrading in average skill requirements. Using the *Dictionary of Occupational Titles* as a data source, he argued that in the recent past there have been few changes in skill requirements over all and that there has been some upgrading in skill requirements in several sectors of the labor force. If deskilling has occurred, it has not been a significant social process, according to Spenner.

Since the average educational level attained by the population may reflect the skills needed to live generally in the society, on the one hand, as well as be the result of a credentialing process (Collins, 1979) that is largely unrelated to the actual jobs being done, on the other, evidence on educational levels or requirements is not very informative in examining the skill content of jobs and its change over time. Moreover, Braverman (1974) has cautioned about using average skill levels, even when measured correctly, to make statements about the deskilling process, because in the course of the change in work there will be an increase in the use of engineers and others to redesign the jobs and the production process so that the production work force can do the tasks that are now simpler and require less skill. He argued:

> . . . with the development of technology and the application to it of the fundamental sciences, the labor processes of society have come to embody a greater amount of scientific knowledge, clearly the "average" scientific, technical, and in that sense "skill" content of these labor processes is much greater than in the past. . . . The question is whether the scientific and "educated" content of labor tends toward *averaging*, or, on the contrary, toward *polarization*. . . . The mass of workers gain nothing from the fact that the decline in their comand over the labor process is more than compensated for by the increasing command on the part of managers and engineers. On the contrary, not only does their skill fall in an absolute sense . . . but it falls even more in a *relative* sense (Braverman, 1974: 425).

Thus, the issues of deskilling are complex both conceptually and empirically. Moreover, the arguments about the reasons for the change in jobs would need to be distinguished from efficiency considerations. This would be difficult to do in general, since profits might be increased either by organizing production more efficiently or by diminishing the power of the work force so that the wage bill could be reduced.

The Marxist argument notes that attempts at deskilling and control over the work force are ultimately counterproductive. By making workers more or less interchangeable, common fate is created that facilitates the development of class consciousness and fosters collective action. Furthermore, the deskilling of work produces worker alienation, leading to strikes, absenteeism, turnover, and even vandalism. At this point, Marxist perspectives are similar to the more traditional job and task design literature in terms of the prediction of the effects of task characteristics on worker responses.

There is some controversy over the extent to which worker alienation from the capitalist system and alienation from work is increasing. Thus, the *Work in America* (Special Task Force to the Secretary of Health, Education, and Welfare, 1973) report was just one of a series of studies and reports that presumably provided evidence for the growing "blue-collar blues" phenomenon, in which workers were increasingly dissatisfied with their jobs. However, Strauss (1974) has noted that the review of comprehensive survey data over time indicates little evidence for increasing job dissatisfaction, and Seeman (1975) has noted that there is little evidence for increasing alienation more generally. In an insightful study using fairly aggregated data, Flanagan, Strauss, and Ulman (1974) found that when factors such as general economic conditions were statistically controlled, there was no association between levels of job attitudes and work behavior such as quit rates (turnover) or strikes. This study indicated that even if job attitudes had changed (declined) over time, it would be suspect to blame the various industrial behaviors such as turnover, strikes, and low productivity on such attitudes without considering alternative explanations in a more sophisticated analysis of the problem.

Marxist theory seems to predict that in the struggle between labor and capital workers will fight rather than exit (Hirschman, 1970) or accommodate psychologically to the realities of their work situation (Salancik, 1977; Salancik and Pfeffer, 1978a). Although there is evidence consistent with the difference in attitudes indexing alienation across workers in jobs with different technological characteristics (Blauner, 1964), survey data in general do not indicate increasing alienation over time, nor are there close relationships between measures of alienation and various types of conflict behavior. Seeman (1975: 100) has argued that it is unlikely that "alienation alone, or alienation in the grand manner, can explain complex, collective, and historically situated events" such as strikes and other types of collective action and violence.

Interorganizational Behavior

Marxist analysis focuses not only on the organization of work but also on the patterns of cooperation that develop among members of the capitalist class and the relationship of that class and its business interests to other social organizations in the society. The argument is that to maintain wealth and transmit that wealth intergenerationally, and to defend itself from attempts by workers to redistribute income and to seize power, cooperation and organized activity are necessary to preserve class interests and class position. This has led to the development of a Marxist approach to analyzing interorganizational relations. The fundamental argument of this approach is: there is not a separation of ownership and control to any great degree, and class interests in economic activity, as contrasted with managerial or technocratic interests, are still dominant; various kinds of social organizations, including business firms and their boards of directors, provide an arena in which class interests can be developed and articulated; rather than seeing people as linking interdependent organizations, organizations are viewed as contexts in which class relations can be renewed and developed; and the resultant patterns of organizational and interorganizational linkage activity can be understood on the basis of class relations and class interests.

The coordination of action across parochial interests to pursue overall class interests and the development and implementation of those interests in the society have not received as much empirical attention as the organization of work and the employment relationship. Two important issues are: To what extent are there coordinated and consistent interests defined along class lines, and how is such coordination achieved? and To what extent and through what mechanisms are class interests maintained and transmitted through the various social institutions in society? There has been some study of both issues.

There is accumulating evidence that capitalists can organize themselves and use a variety of social institutions to provide the linking and socialization necessary for such organization. Whitt (1980) has distinguished between economic competition and political competition, arguing that although there is clearly economic competition within the capitalist class, there is not much political competition. Studying five referenda in California having to do with transportation issues, Whitt (1980: 106) noted that even though there might have been reasons for some companies to favor and others to oppose the issue, "the money in every case in virtually *all on one side or the other of the issue.*" Indeed, examining the campaign for the proposal to construct the Bay Area Rapid Transit System, Whitt (1979) observed a correlation of virtually 1.0 between corporate size and the amount of contribution to the campaign. He concluded that this evidenced a high degree of coordination on political issues among the business interests. Coordination of interests is achieved through association in social clubs (Domhoff, 1974), having common educational backgrounds (Mills, 1956), through the development and use of policy groups (Shoup, 1975), and coordination of interests within families is accomplished through the development of a family office (Dunn, 1980). Dunn's (1980) analysis of the Weyerhaeuser family office indicates how issues ranging from economic investments to political and charitable contributions were centrally coordinated.

Moore (1979) focused on the extent to which there was evidence for elite integration at the national level. Using interview data from a survey of 545 key position holders in a variety of important institutions in American society, Moore examined

> . . . the structure of an elite interaction network, with particular interest in whether or not it contains many distinct groups individually formed around narrow issue concerns, or, rather, a few large and inclusive groups . . . the members of this central circle are compared with others in similar top-level positions to see if circle members are more influential in ways other than circle membership . . . the relationship between social origins and current affiliations and membership in the central circle is examined to see if high status origins or influential current affiliations (beyond primary institutional position) are advantageous in achieving connections to this group (1979: 675).

Using network analysis, Moore (1979: 681) found that "of the 32 circles and cliques identified in the network, all but four are unified around concern with a common issue or through common sector membership." Moore identified primarily small cliques tightly connected and one larger group consisting of almost one third of the sample that was broad and inclusive. Moore (1979: 689) found that members of this central circle did have more policy influence but that "high status social origins are at most a very small advantage to those in elite positions in becoming connected to a central leadership circle. Similarly, affiliations with elite private sector organizations are generally unrelated to central circle membership. However, it should be noted that Domhoff and Baltzell are right in contending that social club membership is important for business leaders."

Based on her analysis, Moore concluded:

> No fragmentation of elites in different institutions or issue areas was found. On the contrary, the evidence examined here indicates that considerable integration exists among elites in all major sectors of American society. The existence of a central elite circle facilitates communication and interaction both within that large, diverse group and between its members and those in more specialized elite circles and cliques (1979: 689).

Useem (1979), using data on directorships, also found some distinction between an inner group heavily involved in the governance of other institutions and an outer group somewhat less connected. Useem noted that one of the differences between the inner group and the outer group in the business elite was that the inner group, defined as persons who had multiple directorships and tended to be more prominently represented on the boards of other organizations as well, had a political perspective that took a broader, less parochial and strictly economic self-interest perspective. Thus, this inner group was seen as being able to defend and promote the more general interests of the class, rather than merely using their positions to argue for more proximate advantage to themselves or their firms. Ratcliff (1980) has presented data on loans made by banks in St. Louis indicating that banks more tightly connected into the capitalist structure through both economic and social positions tended to make a higher proportion of their loans to businesses, whereas banks less integrated into the capitalist class through the associations of their directors allocated a somewhat higher proportion of their loans for mortgages. These data are consistent with Useem's (1979) arguments concerning the differentiation of the capitalist class into a central and less central group and demonstrate the consequences of this differentiation for behavior.

SUMMARY

In Table 4–3 we present some of the dimensions along which the three theories considered in this chapter can be compared and what the specifics of the comparison are. This overview is useful in understanding the extent to which the theories can be subjected to a comparative test as well as seeing how the theories deal with some of the issues that affect all organization-level rational perspectives on action.

If we consider first the issue of the motivational basis for organizational action, we see that there are fairly clear distinctions among the theories. The market failures perspective presumes an efficiency orientation; indeed, Williamson (1981) has argued that this orientation is one of the distinctive aspects of this approach, though that comment badly misrepresents or overlooks structural contingency theory. The Marxist perspective argues from primarily a power (both economic and social) point of view, and structural contingency theory has incorporated, at times, both an efficiency orientation as well as a focus on the strategic choice of critical organizational actors, presumably members of the dominant coalition (Thompson, 1967).

The three theories have tended to focus on somewhat different dependent variables. Market failures has attended to where the boundaries are drawn, or the extent of vertical integration, the form of the organization,

Table 4-3. An Overview of the Three Theoretical Perspectives

DIMENSIONS

THEORIES	Motivational Assumptions	Dependent Variables	Attention to Processes	Attention to History	Units of Analysis	Deals with Production of Unified, Rational Issue
Market Failures	Efficiency	Boundaries and integration Form Organization of employment relation	None	Virtually none	Total organization literature	Some, in the form of control literature
Marxist Approaches	Power, accumulation, intergenerational transmission	Organization of employment relation Accumulation and allocation Patterns of association Choice of technology	Some	Important	Organization, class, society, families	Yes, in considering coordination across separate units
Structural Contingency Theory	Efficiency and strategic choice	Form and structural dimensions	Almost none	None	Organization and its sub-units	No treatment

and the structuring of the employment relationship. Marxist approaches have emphasized the employment relationship in more detail, while also focusing on patterns of association across organizations, the choice of technology (which tends to be treated exogenously in each of the other approaches), and the patterns of accumulation and resource allocation. Structural contingency theory has the most narrow focus, attempting to explain organizational form or structural dimensions.

The theories also differ in terms of their emphasis on understanding or at least postulating processes that produce the presumed outcomes. Structural contingency theory has paid almost no attention to process, except in some instances, in the strategic choice versions. Basically, organizations are presumed to adjust or adapt their structures to the requirements of their technologies, environment, or size. There has been some attention to how the environment is perceived or registered in the perceived environmental uncertainty literature but almost no attention to how and with what lags such contingencies are used to guide the design of actual organizational structures. Market failures approaches have even less concern with process. Coming from the economics literature, they replicate that literature in terms of offering what is essentially a static, equilibrium analysis. The processes by which such equilibria are reached are of little interest. Indeed, Williamson and Ouchi (1981) make that neglect of process a virtue in their disdaining the use of power or politics as explanatory mechanisms, arguing that over time (the figure used is ten years) such considerations are eliminated by competitive or efficiency pressures. Of course, there are other processes in organizations besides political ones, but these, too, are neglected in the focus on long-run equilibrium positions. Marxist approaches, at least in some versions, do pay attention to process. Thus, there is concern with how coordination is achieved, how deskilling is accomplished, how firms are created through merger, how technology gets both chosen and implemented, and so forth.

The concern with process manifests itself again in an attention to the effects of history or historical context on organizations. Again, the market failures approach and the structural contingency model pay no attention to the effect of history, either organizational or social, on how things are done. Presumably, the effect of a given level of environmental uncertainty, technology, or pattern of transaction costs has the same implications for how the organization should be structured regardless of either the organization's own history and how it has developed, or the particular conditions prevailing in the larger social environment, to the extent such conditions are not already reflected in environmental uncertainty, technology, or transaction costs. By contrast, Marxist approaches have paid excellent attention to history and the relationship between societal context and the development of various management practices. It clearly does not require a radical orientation to pay attention to history or process, but at this time these important explanatory domains have been left primarily to Marxist theorists and researchers.

There is also some difference across the theories in terms of their units of analysis. The market failures or transaction costs approach is focused almost solely at the organization level of analysis, while Marxist theories take in social class and other interorganizational units, and structural contingency approaches are almost forced to consider variations across subunits of organizations. Finally, we can ask the extent to which each of these theories makes an effort to address the question of how coordinated, organization-level (or class-level) rationality gets produced. Structural contingency theory pays virtually no attention to this question. Indeed, the tendency to overaggregation by this approach (Scott, 1981) has already been noted. The market failures approach does pay some attention to this, if Ouchi's work on socialization versus other control mechanisms is included, as it should be. With its concern with the form of control and with issues of control loss, there is at least some attention to the problematic nature of organization-level rationality. Again, the Marxist research has been the most sensitive to this issue, in part because of the problematic nature of the concept of class. Thus, Whitt (1980) investigated the coordination of action across organizations with respect to political campaign activity, and Dunn (1980) wrote about the operation of the family office as a coordinating device. Although much work remains to be done, there is more sensitivity to the question of whether macrolevel rational action is a reasonable concept in the Marxist approach as contrasted with the others.

It may be that because of its more threatening ideological tone, Marxist theory has been forced to come to grips both in theorizing and in research with a variety of issues that the other approaches have been allowed to let slide. It is clearly the case that theories of organization-level rationality that speak to the presumed overriding goals of efficiency serve important functions of social legitimation for the large organizations ostensibly being described. This legitimation function can be seen quite clearly in the work on clanlike organizations. In this instance, the virtually complete loss of individual identity and autonomy as the organization's goals and perspectives are adopted is portrayed as a virtue contributing to the enhancement of organizational effectiveness and overall economic system competitive efficiency. Thus, control over the labor process and the work force, always both problematic and contested, is legitimated because such control is exercised by a rational organization striving to increase efficiency and thereby providing better levels of economic performance.

All of the theories considered in this chapter, but particularly the structural contingency and market failures approaches, would benefit greatly from more distancing between ideology and social science. This separation of ideology would more clearly indicate the need to confront, both theoretically and empirically, the multitude of assumptions and assertions that require both conceptual and empirical treatment.

5

THE EXTERNAL CONTROL OF ORGANIZATIONAL BEHAVIOR

Just as at the individual level of analysis, so, too, at the organizational level of analysis there is a debate concerning the extent to which behavior is externally controlled and constrained or the extent to which outcomes are the results of planned, intendedly rational actions. One implication of this debate is whether one must attend to various choice and decision processes in understanding organizational behavior or, alternatively, if attention to the system of environmental constraints and conditions is sufficient to enable the explanation and prediction of behavior.

At the organizational level of analysis, adoption of the external control perspective solves one of the two problems confronted by prospectively rational perspectives, as discussed in the last chapter. That is, if one adopts the external constraint approach, the problem of how individual preferences and beliefs get aggregated and become controlled in the service of organization-level rationality disappears. By obviating the need for attention to internal decision mechanisms and processes — because behavior is to be explained by the conditions and constraints of the environment — the external control perspective finesses the issue of how, or if, organization-level rational choice or decision making gets produced. There is a parallel here with the individual level of analysis. To adopt a rational actor approach at the individual level, one must be concerned with (largely unobservable) cognitive, intrapsychic processes of preference formation and intraindividual decision making. A focus on the effects of external constraints as determinants of behavior means that explanation for action is to be sought (and presumably found) in the conditions of the social environment; hence, the investigation or postulation of internal decision-making mechanisms is rendered unnecessary. In a similar fashion, a focus on explanation of behavior in the conditions and constraints of the environment saves the analyst from the often intractable task of exploring internal decision-making processes and, in particular, of trying to build a theory of organizational action premised on rational, decision-making theory when there is clear evidence that the production of organization-level rationality is quite problematic and can certainly not be assumed.

There are, then, three issues involved in the debate among perspectives. One is an issue of theoretical taste. It should be noted that those who are unwilling to treat the organization as a black box, using conditions of the context to account for behavior, inevitably shoulder the burden of developing theories that indicate how microbehaviors within organizations get aggregated to produce organization-level rational or quasi-rational decisions. This is an obligation that almost no theories operating at this level have thus far shown much willingness to address, with the exception of the process-oriented theories to be discussed later. A second issue is an empirical one, asking the extent to which variance can be explained by attending to environmental characteristics and ignoring microlevel processes or whether attention to such processes of decision and action are necessary and useful in accounting for behavior. And, the third issue involves which dependent variables are being examined, what about organizations the theories are trying to explain. An explanation of mortality or births and deaths might well use a different perspective than one seeking to account for the structure of boards of directors.

Within the external control of organizations perspective, there are currently two principal variants. These correspond, approximately, to the differences between behaviorism and social information processing seen at the individual level of analysis. The first, population ecology, tends to treat the organization more as a black box, focusing attention on birth and death processes as these are impacted by environmental conditions. The second, resource dependence, is concerned more with internal adaptations and the politics that occur inside organizations. This distinction is not a very strong one and, furthermore, is in part the result of differences in the level at which the analysis occurs. In the first place, population ecology theorists do evidence interest in internal politics and in processes that cause persistance or resistance to change, while at the same time some resource dependence work treats the effects of environments on organizational actions, such as merger, with little concern for the process by which the linkage between the environmental conditions and the organizational responses occurs. In the second place, *population ecology* deals, as its very name implies, with the study of *populations* of organizations; it is concerned with population characteristics and with variables defined on a population level of analysis. Resource dependence has tended to adopt much more a focal organization perspective and, thus, deals with issues theoretically and empirically from the perspective of individual organizations rather than of populations of organizations. As we will see, J. Freeman (1982) has suggested that the two perspectives are thus not in conflict but are fundamentally complementary, with resource dependence being encapsulated in the population ecology framework, providing the mechanisms and the local decision making and politics through which the population dynamics occur.

POPULATION ECOLOGY

Most treatments of organizations have emphasized change occurring through processes of learning and adaptation; by contrast, population ecology argues that change in populations of organizations occurs, in part, because of the operation of selection processes working on those organizations (Hannan and Freeman, 1977). The importance of selection derives from the fact that there are both internal and external constraints on the adaptability of organizations. Hannan and Freeman (1977: 931) noted, "Inertial pressures arise from both internal structural arrangements and environmental constraints." As internal constraints, they listed the organization's investment in plant and equipment or in sunk costs; the reduced and constrained information received by decision makers because of present activities and structures; internal political constraints, which make the redistribution of resources difficult; and the constraints emanating from history and tradition. External pressures toward inertia include legal and financial barriers to market entry and exit; external constraints on the availability of information; legitimacy considerations, which delimit the organization's flexibility in changing form or activities; and the problem of collective rationality, or the fact that even if there is some optimal strategy for an individual buyer or seller, it is not clear that a stable equilibrium emerges once each organization acts on this strategy. Thus, "we should not presume that a course of action that is adaptive for a single organization facing some changing environment will be adaptive for many competing organizations adopting a similar strategy" (Hannan and Freeman, 1977: 932).

If adaptation is constrained, selection processes are important mechanisms through which the characteristics of populations of organizations evolve over time. It is this focus, on the variety and evolution of organizational forms, that constitutes the core subject matter for the ecological perspective:

> . . . we suggest that a population ecology of organizations must seek to understand the distributions of organizations across environmental conditions and the limitations on organizational structures in different environments, and more generally seek to answer the question, Why are there so many kinds of organizations? (Hannan and Freeman, 1977: 936).

With its focus on form, the identification of distinct organizational forms is a critical issue. Hannan and Freeman (1977: 935) maintained that "an organizational form is a blueprint for organizational action, for transforming inputs into outputs." They went on to note that such a blueprint might be inferred from the organization's structure, the patterns of activity within the organization, or the normative order that characterized the particular organization. Aldrich (1979: 28) defined *organizational forms* as "specific configurations of goals, boundaries, and activities." As it has been used empirically, *form* has been defined with respect to the particular subject population being investigated and has tended to focus on structural attributes of the organization. One of the more critical distinctions among organizational forms is the difference between specialists and generalists. A specialist organization is one that does a smaller number of things more intensively compared with a generalist. Thus, for instance, some universities specialize more by focusing on a narrower range of subject matter (engineering and science only, liberal arts only) and on the education of people of a single sex. By contrast, others offer a wide range of academic programs to persons of all sexes and ages. In business organizations, one way of thinking about specialization is that it is the opposite of diversification. Specialist organizations serve a narrower range of product markets, but often because of this specialization, they know these markets and can serve them more efficiently.

Niche, another term borrowed from biological ecology, is an important concept in the population ecology of organizations. Hannan and Freeman (1977: 947) defined *niche* as "that area in constraint space (the space whose dimensions are levels of resources, etc.) in which the population outcompetes all other local populations. The niche, then, consists of all those combinations of resource levels at which the population can survive and reproduce itself." Aldrich (1979: 28) defined *environmental niches* as "distinct combinations of resources and other constraints that are sufficient to support an organization form." The empirical assessment of niches and niche widths is just beginning, but the intuitive meaning of the concept is clear.

The relationship between niche characteristics and specialism and generalism constitutes one of the more fundamental and important predictions from population ecology. Specialist organizations maximize their exploitation of the environment over a relatively narrow range of environmental conditions and have little slack or excess capacity. Generalist organizations can survive over a wider range of environmental conditions but are not optimally suited to any single condition. The trade-off is between security or risk reduction and efficiency or the exploitation of the particular environment in greater depth (Hannan and Freeman, 1977).

Environments, in ecological theory, are dimensionalized according to three criteria (Brittain and Freeman, 1980): the uncertainty of the environment; the compatibility of the different resource states, or whether changes between environmental states are large or small; and the grain of the environment, which is the frequency of changes in environmental states over time. A fine-grained environment is one in which there are many changes in environment over time; a coarse-grained environment is one in which there are relatively few (but sometimes larger) changes in environmental condition.

Hannan and Freeman (1977) argued that specialist organizations were likely to dominate when uncertainty was low. They also argued that specialist organizations would dominate when uncertainty was high and the environment was fine grained with large differences between environmental conditions. "When the environment changes rapidly among quite different states, the cost of generalism is high . . . since the environment changes rapidly, the organizations will spend most of their time and energies adjusting structure. It is apparently better under such conditions to adopt a specialized structure and 'ride out' the adverse environment" (Hannan and Freeman, 1977: 953).

The optimal adaptation in the face of uncertainty when the environment is coarse-grained is generalism. Generalism, however, has its own costs in terms of slack or excess resources. Another possibility, then, is the development of polymorphism. Polymorphism is the development of population heterogeneity, some forms of which are adapted to one environmental state and others to the other possible environmental conditions.

"With such a combination at least a portion of the population will always flourish when the environment changes state" (Hannan and Freeman, 1977: 953). Organizational equivalents of polymorphism are holding companies or confederations of organizations of different forms.

In one of the first (if not the first) empirical studies of the relationship between environmental characteristics and the relative survival of specialist versus generalist forms, Hannan and Freeman (1981) studied restaurants in 18 cities in California. Uncertainty was assessed by "regressing total restaurant sales in a given quarter on sales for the same quarter in the preceding year. We used the coefficient of alienation, $1 - R^2$, from these regressions as a measure of certainty of environmental variations" (Hannan and Freeman, 1981: 10). They argued that cities with large seasonal variations in restaurant sales had a coarse-grained environment, and, thus, the proportion of variation in sales that was quarter specific was taken as the measure of the grain of the environment. *Specialism* and *generalism* were defined from the characteristics of the menu, considering the number of different dishes, the range of selection, and hours of operation (a restaurant that served all three meals was more generalist than one serving only dinner). Studying failure rates over a three-year period, Hannan and Freeman (1981) tended to find support for their predictions. Generalists had lower death rates only when environmental variations were both large and coarse-grained. Specialist organizations were favored in all the other environmental conditions.

As developed by D. Campbell (1969), the natural selection model has three stages: variation, selection, and retention. Although J. Freeman (1981) has noted that the three processes occur simultaneously, for exposition purposes we follow Aldrich (1979) and Aldrich and Pfeffer (1976) in describing the ecological process as if it occurred in stages.

Variation

For the environment to select differentially among organizational forms, there must be some variation in the forms. The traditional managerial literature has assumed that change and innovation in organizations are planned activities, consciously directed. "The population ecology model, however, is indifferent to the ultimate source of variation, as planned and unplanned variations both provide raw material from which selection can be made" (Aldrich, 1979: 28). As Aldrich (1979) has noted, there are two types of variation: variation among organizations (as in differences between functionally and divisionally organized firms, between organic and mechanistic structures, and so forth) and variation in form within organizations, as in the variation in structure across divisions and variation in managerial practices that naturally occur in large, differentiated structures.

Variation within organizations can arise as a consequence of failures of organizational control in the sense that the reason why practices and structures may vary within a single organization is the incomplete diffusion and incorporation of the organization's policies and practices in all parts of the organization. Variation within organizations can also be planned (e.g., Lawrence and Lorsch, 1967). There is more likely to be more local variation in organizations that are loosely coupled (Weick, 1976). Glassman (1973), Weick (1976), and Aldrich (1979) have all considered the advantages and the disadvantages of loose coupling for organizational survival in contexts in which the population ecology model is assumed to be valid. Clearly, loosely coupled organizations are more likely to have more internal variation of both planned and unplanned types. This allows "portions of the organization to persist and evolve independently of other parts" (Aldrich, 1979: 83). This means that there is a greater chance that a form that fits the environment will emerge somewhere in the organization. In a centralized, tightly controlled structure, one (or a very few) solution and form will exist at any time; consequently, the chances are higher that a more appropriate form or set of activities will not have emerged as contrasted with situations in which there is more variety. Local adaptation is permitted. Also, as Aldrich (1979: 83) has argued, loose coupling permits problems or breakdowns to be localized. "A loosely coupled system with some degree of duplication and overlap is relatively immune to the failure of one component (Landau, 1969)" (Aldrich, 1979: 83). Overall, the variation and flexibility permitted by loose coupling leads to the prediction that "most organizational forms are loosely coupled" (Aldrich, 1979: 84) and also that loosely coupled forms have survival advantages over forms that are more tightly linked. Testing this argument requires developing more precise measurements of the concept of loose coupling. However, one advantage of the multidivisional form may be that it is, in general, more loosely coupled than the functional form of organization. Decentralization of operating decisions may be another way of saying that the organization is loosely coupled and that local variation is permitted within the structure.

Variation across organizations comes about primarily at the time organizations are founded. Stinchcombe (1965) has made the argument most strongly that organizational structures persist over time. Different organizations founded at different times match the context of the time of their founding. But this initial context "imprints" the organizations, so that at some later point in time, rather than seeing organizations that are essentially similar because they have adapted to the current conditions, the initial differences will remain. Thus, Stinchcombe noted that fraternities founded in various periods were essentially similar to each other and different from other fraternities founded in different periods, even to the present time. The nonsecret fraternities were all founded in a relatively short span of time and remained nonsecret, while the secret fraternities remained secret. Kimberly (1975) has traced the effect of the time of founding on differences in sheltered workshops. Stinchcombe (1965) also noted the differences in the structure, in terms of the use of unpaid family labor versus professional management, in industries that arose in the United States in different time periods. Again, the differences that were present at the time of founding tended to persist to the present.

Variations spread through the population of organizations through a diffusion process (Katz, Levin, and Hamilton, 1963). One important way in which forms and management practices diffuse is through the movement of personnel, and particularly the movement of personnel from established firms to newly created organizations. Brittain and Freeman (1980), examining the development of the semiconductor industry, have noted how the movement of personnel from one organization to another, frequently a new organization, carries organizational form and structures, albeit with some variation. Thus, for instance, semiconductor firms founded by persons from larger and older companies who came out of manufacturing have tended to have a production efficiency style of operation and structure, while those founded by persons from engineering and research and development are organized somewhat more organically and have a product strategy emphasizing technical innovation. Clearly, personnel movement across organizations is one important way in which variations in structure and decision-making procedures diffuse (Baty, Evan, and Rothermel, 1971; Pfeffer and Leblebici, 1973b). This effect can be seen in academia, in which academic program innovations and styles of operating departments are carried by faculty as they move across institutions. Thus, for example, the University of Virginia business school, populated largely by people either trained at Harvard or formerly on the Harvard faculty, is similar to Harvard with its emphasis on the case method and on teaching. Business schools staffed with persons from Carnegie-Mellon, Chicago, and Massachusetts Institute of Technology have a more theoretical, research orientation as would be expected given their backgrounds.

Variations are also diffused through a process of vicarious learning, in which others read or see demonstrated a variation that they then take back to their own organization. This diffusion of technical and administrative innovations is facilitated by professional conferences and professional publications and journals, as well as through the training provided by colleges, universities, and various professional organizations. Thus, for instance, today most students of management will be exposed to a variety of different

possible organizational structures in the course of their management education. Consequently, one does not have to develop a multidivisional structure accidentally, nor hire someone who has worked in such a structure;
rather, the learning of various organizational designs, such as the multidivisional form, can occur in schools or in other training sessions and then
be taken directly into an organization.

Selection

Once variation has occurred, for either planned or unplanned reasons, these
various organizational forms are selected according to how well they fit
their environment. This suggests that there are as many kinds of organizational forms as there are kinds of organizational environments (Hawley,
1968). It is important to note that in this selection process "it is the environment which optimizes" (Hannan and Freeman, 1977: 939). It is the environment that selects those combinations of organizational forms that are suited
to the resource base of that environment. Selection occurs principally
through the competition among forms (Hannan and Freeman, 1977). At this
point, population ecology comes to look somewhat like microeconomics
(Winter, 1975) in that both stress a tight linkage between organizations and
their environments and both emphasize the role of competition in determining what the population of organizations comes to look like.

There are two issues involving selection that are important for the population ecology perspective. The first is the extent to which selection processes operate. Just as J. K. Galbraith (1967) has argued that economic
competition has diminished and thus is not an important force for understanding firms, so has the criticism been raised that there is relatively little
selection pressure for large segments of the organizational population.
Kaufman (1976), for instance, has documented how rare an event the disappearance of a public bureaucracy is. And within the business sector of the
organizational population, the population is divided into segments that are
differentially vulnerable to failure (Aldrich, 1979). Failure of large organizations is often so politically and economically unpalatable that various
interventions are taken to keep the organizations afloat. Examples include
(but are not limited to) the government guaranteed loans made to Lock-
heed, government guaranteed loans made directly to Chrysler, and government intervention in the financial sector to salvage failing banks and savings
and loans, most often by arranging mergers or sales of the assets rather than
permitting liquidation to occur. As Stigler (1971) has documented, governments have given direct cash subsidies to firms and industries, as in ship-
building and the smaller regional airlines, and in a variety of other ways

have intervened (as in regulation, restriction on entry of competitors, and so forth) to reduce competition and provide benefits that tend to ensure the survival of organizations, particularly large organizations, already in existence.

Although it is clearly true that most organizations are small organizations (Hannan and Freeman, 1981), it is also the case that these small organizations constitute a relatively small portion of the total economic activity. As Aldrich (1979) has noted:

> Most corporations have less than $100,000 in assets, but they account for less than 2 percent of all corporate assets . . . at the very top of the corporate pinnacle, 0.1 percent have $250,000,000 or more in assets. This one-tenth of one percent of all corporations with a quarter-billion dollars or more in assets accounted in 1972 for 60.8 percent of *all* corporate assets (1979: 42).

Employment is similarly concentrated in the very largest corporations. Aldrich (1979: 43) maintained, "Clearly, businesses with millions of dollars in assets are substantially protected from the threat of direct elimination by failure." Thus, the issue is that since failure tends to be concentrated in certain economic sectors and particularly among organizations that are relatively new and relatively small, is population ecology a theory of general applicability, or is it confined primarily to those sectors in which failure is frequent and pervasive?

J. Freeman (1981) has argued that population ecology is equally applicable to large and small organizations but that the issue has been confused by the choice of an inappropriate time frame:

> . . . more important is the fact that one choses a time frame and therefore the rate of failure among big organizations relative to little ones may be irrelevant. If one is doing field research, one trades off number of organizations observed against failure rate with respect to time. During any given period, fewer elephants than fruit flies die, but no biologist would argue that natural selection processes do not affect elephants or that such a theoretical perspective should be excluded from the analysis of their evolution (1981: 1448).

If Aldrich (1979) is correct and big organizations and government bureaus do disappear less frequently, then the implication is that population ecology is still a useful framework but that the time period considered and the sample size must both be considerably expanded over what they might be in studying, for instance, restaurants.

The second issue concerns how disappearance or failure is to be measured. Unfortunately, organizations do not die quite as neatly as humans, with death certificates specifying both the time and the presumptive cause of death. Although the lists of the largest 500 firms do change over time substantially, and firms do disappear, particularly through merger, the issue of whether the firm has, in fact, disappeared is not straightforward. First, the acquiring firm may, on occasion, pay enormous premiums for the acquisition. Thus, disappearance clearly need not mean "failure"; indeed, in some industries firms are started with the intention of becoming enough of a competitive nuisance to stimulate a merger or take-over offer, so that the owners can sell out and retire. That need not present too much of a problem, for Hannan and Freeman (1977) do not attach any moral or evolutionary significance to what disappears and what remains. But what about those instances in which the firm is acquired by another organization that operates essentially as a holding company (Williamson, 1975)? The acquired firm may be operated by the same management (and frequently is), using the same internal structure, the same compensation practices, the same technology, and so forth as before. Has the firm really disappeared? It clearly has not disappeared from the point of view of its competitors, employees, suppliers, or customers. In fact, it is largely unchanged from their point of view. Selection, in such an instance, is somewhat harder to capture precisely.

A related issue is how to handle firms that change form. Frogs do not become pigs, but functionally organized firms do change to multidivisional structures. One could, of course, define *failure* or *selection* in terms of the relative numbers of the form, rather than the individual firms. One position on selection might argue that selection requires the failure of organizations to be operating. If the environment has shifted so that multidivisional firms are more suited than functionally organized firms, then one would expect to see more failures of firms that are organized functionally (also, one would expect to see fewer of such firms being started). Alternatively, firms may transform themselves from one structure to another (Chandler, 1966). In that case, although the functional form of the organization may be selected against and diminish in relative number, the individual organizations themselves may continue to exist, having changed their form. Since Hannan and Freeman (1977) base their arguments for the importance of selection processes largely on considerations of organizational inertia, transformations of form without individual organizational failure would appear to be inconsistent with the spirit, if not the formalism, of population ecology. Thus, although firms of all size classes do disappear, the form of competition implied in ecological reasoning does seem to occur more strongly with smaller firms in a set of highly competitive sectors of the economy.

The definition of *organizational disappearance* also seems easier to operationalize with respect to small firms. Restaurants indeed do fail; they move out of their premises, and their equipment and supplies are sold off. Their employees go to work for other organizations, perhaps in other industries or in other towns. Failure and disappearance are often more problematic concepts in the case of larger organizations. Take the case of the Penn Central. It was formed initially through the merger of the Pennsylvania Railroad and the New York Central. The difficulty in merging the systems, management, and facilities of these two organizations was argued by some to be one important cause of this organization's subsequent economic difficulties. Thus, the first question is, How do we treat what happened to the New York Central and Pennsylvania railroads? Did they disappear or not? Subsequently, the Penn Central bought firms in a variety of other businesses. Then, the organization went through a long and protracted bankruptcy. Because of the national interest in providing rail transportation in the Northeast, the government established the Conrail Corporation, funded from the Treasury, which bought the right of way and much of the equipment of several bankrupt railroads, including the Penn Central. With these funds plus the disposition of other assets, particularly real estate, the Penn Central Corporation reemerged from bankruptcy and since has been quite profitable, with enough cash to make a substantial tender offer for Colt Industries. From the point of view of the legal entity, the Penn Central Corporation still exists. From the point of view of what constituted the major business of the old Penn Central company, that is now largely what constitutes Conrail. The point of the difficulty in assessing organizational disappearance should be clear. Corporations are legal entities but also collections of equipment, personnel, and expertise. The legal entity can disappear but not the operations of the business, or vice versa. How to count each of those eventualities is not immediately clear.

Retention

Retention involves the maintenance of the organizational form into the future. Many of the mechanisms that Hannan and Freeman (1977) listed as impediments to adaptation are, at the same time, mechanisms of retention. As Weick (1969) has noted, variation and retention are counterposed in organizations. Those aspects of organizations that make variation and change more likely work against retention of organizational properties; by the same token, those forces that work to create the persistence of structures and practices also tend to limit the amount of variation and change in organizations.

A complete review of all the mechanisms of retention would be like re-reviewing the literature on organizations, for as Aldrich (1979: 197) has noted, "most studies of organization structure focus on internal retention mechanisms — the forces that perpetuate a particular organization's structure and activities — even though investigators themselves do not frame their analyses in these terms." Standard operating procedures (Cyert and March, 1963) which may become codified and formalized in forms, job descriptions, and manuals of operation, serve as a form of organization memory maintaining continuity in organizational operations. Socialization (Dornbusch, 1955; Feldman, 1976), in which new organizational members learn how things are done in the organization, also serves to maintain practices, structures, and ways of decision making. Many of the elements of bureaucracy facilitate retention and stability. Indeed, bureaucratization is one way of ensuring that individual variations in backgrounds, knowledge, and goals will not unduly affect the organization's operations. Idiosyncratic behavior is what bureaucracy is designed to guard against and preclude. Thus, the elements of bureaucracy noted by many authors (e.g., Blau and Meyer, 1971) are all elements that contribute to the retention of organizational structures and practices.

Retention is also facilitated by commitment processes (Salancik, 1977; Staw, 1976). People in organizations become committed to and identified with ways of doing things and ways of organizing work. These commitments bind individuals to these behaviors and make them resist change, even when confronted with instances of failure or problems. Thus, psychological commitment, discussed in more detail in Chapter 3, acts along with the structural forms of bureaucracy to ensure a high degree of retention of activities and persistence in most organizations.

Population Ecology Compared with Other Theories

Population ecology as applied to organizational analysis is in its infancy; its utility, validity, and ease of operationalization are all issues that remain to be resolved through empirical research. It is important, however, to recognize where population ecology fits in the various perspectives on organizational analysis.

It is, first and foremost, a theory of external, environmental effects couched at a relatively more macrosociological level of analysis. As Freeman has noted:

> . . . natural selection presumes a population logic. Although selection always involves things which happen to individuals, the effort is directed

> toward understanding the range of variation in morphological charac-
> teristics as displayed in some population . . . Just as biological ecologists
> do not often concern themselves with the behavior of individual organ-
> isms . . . organizational ecologists do not concern themselves with indi-
> vidual firms (1982: 3).

There is little room in population ecology for elements of rational choice
and for the operation of goals, preferences, wants, or ambitions. Freeman (1982: 23) has noted, "Natural selection approaches to the study of
organizations (focusing as they do on populations of organizations) seem to
leave no role for individual choice." In this sense, population ecology does
differ from the other perspective reviewed in this chapter; resource dependence operates more at the level of the focal organization and has
more elements of rational action embedded in the theory.

Several times in the discussion of ecological reasoning we have noted
similarities to economics — in the presumption of tight coupling between
organizations and environments, in the stress on competition, and in the use
of formal models of the competitive process. "Just as the market is viewed as
optimizing social utilities by economists, organizational ecologists view
competitive processes as optimizing fitness" (Freeman, 1982: 23). However,
there are some fundamental and substantial differences between microeconomics and population ecology, and this includes differences between
population ecology and the Williamsonian (1975) adaptation of micro-
economic logic.

Freeman has described some of the differences:

> Most fundamentally, the two approaches differ because economists do not
> usually focus on population phenomena. Their unit is most often the indi-
> vidual firm (Blau and Scott, 1962: 215). The subject . . . is the behavior of
> that firm as it varies the level of its production in response to variations in
> price. . . . Economists usually attribute *rational* behavior to firms in addi-
> tion to profit motives. Organizational ecologists make no such attribu-
> tions. Organizations may compete successfully without maximizing any
> observable utility, unless the term "utility" is tautologically defined to mean
> any consequence of organizational action (1982: 23-24).

Freeman also noted that ecological theory makes none of the assumptions of
the economists' model of perfect competition. It might be added that the
ecological model makes none of the assumptions of the market failures approach either. Thus, population ecology differs from economics in its focus
on populations rather than individual firms, in its assumptions, and in its
relaxation of rational, boundedly rational, or utility maximizing behavioral
assumptions. Economics has, for the most part, been concerned with equili-

brium conditions. Williamson and Ouchi (1981), for instance, in arguing against the consideration of power and politics as explanations, maintained that eventually (by their terms, in ten years or less) efficiency considerations would predominate. This concern with an equilibrium analysis, with where things will come out in the long run (and ten years is long) if things were allowed to reach equilibrium, contrasts sharply with the population ecologists' use of dynamic models and with their explicit concerns not only for equilibria positions, but also for their time path and length of time required to approach those equilibria. Freeman has noted:

> . . . natural selection theories . . . are dynamic. One explains the pattern of variation observable at one point in time through reference to a theory which considers the time path of some set of variables. . . . The dynamic quality of natural selection theories focuses attention on the speed with which various processes occur and the lag structures which result (1982: 3).

Because of its more general nature, population ecology has an easier time dealing with nonbusiness organizations. Selection processes and the competition among forms are general, not just mediated by market mechanisms but mediated by political mechanisms, social legitimacy, and so forth. All these forms of competition can be modeled in the population ecology framework, whereas they are largely outside the scope of economics.

Population ecology considers the net mortality of organizational forms. As such, it is concerned with birth as well as with death processes, although organizational founding has not yet been subject to the same amount of empirical research. With its concern with the birth and death of organizations, population ecology speaks to many of the issues addressed in other intellectual domains such as studies of entrepreneurship and the business policy literature. Population ecology offers models, methods, and a theoretical perspective relating generalism-specialism to environmental characteristics that provide theoretical foundations for these other fields.

RESOURCE DEPENDENCE

Resource dependence theory (Pfeffer and Salancik, 1978) also argues that organizations are externally constrained but "argues for greater attention to internal organizational political decision-making processes and also for the perspective that organizations seek to manage or strategically adapt to their environments" (Aldrich and Pfeffer, 1976: 79). Because organizations are not internally self-sufficient, they require resources from the environment and, thus, become interdependent with those elements of the environment with which they transact. This interdependence can lead to the development of interorganizational influence attempts. The imposition of external constraints can occur in a fashion analogous to that detailed by Kahn et al. (1964) for individuals — organizations are subject to a set of pressures from those with whom they are interdependent just as individuals in an organization are subject to pressures from those role occupants with whom they are connected. Indeed, Evan (1966) used the term *organization set* to describe the set of organizations with which a given focal organization transacted and argued that role pressures occurred in an organization set.

Thus, resource dependence theory suggests that organizational behavior becomes externally influenced because the focal organization must attend to the demands of those in its environment that provide resources necessary and important for its continued survival. As Pfeffer and Salancik (1978: 39) summarized, "the underlying premise of the external perspective on organizations is that organizational activities and outcomes are accounted for by the context in which the organization is embedded."

There are two elements in the resource dependence argument. The first speaks to the issue of external constraint and argues that organizations will (and should) respond more to the demands of those organizations or groups in the environment that control critical resources. In other words, resource dependence theory describes the development of interorganizational power and argues that this power affects the activities of organizations. The second element argues that, for a variety of reasons, managers and administrators attempt to manage their external dependencies, both to ensure the survival of the organization and to acquire, if possible, more autonomy and freedom from external constraint. Thus, this second part of resource dependence theory traces the various strategies of organizations and their managers to cope with external constraints resulting from resource interdependence. We will consider each of these elements of the theory in turn.

External Constraint from Resource Dependence

Pfeffer and Salancik (1978: 41) distinguished between outcome interdependence and behavior interdependence. In outcome interdependence, the outcomes, or results, achieved by one social actor are interdependent with those of another actor. In behavior interdependence, the activities themselves are dependent on the actions of another social actor; playing poker, for example, requires finding someone else who is also willing to engage in that behavior. Within outcome interdependence, they further distinguished between competitive interdependence and symbiotic interdependence (Hawley, 1950). While in a situation of symbiosis, the output or actions of one actor are the input for the other; in a competitive relationship, the two parties are in a zero-sum situation, living off the same resource pool, if you will, so that what one receives is precluded to the other. Interdependence is important because it affects the organization's ability to achieve things that it wants, including survival. The maintenance of symbiotic exchanges may be necessary for the organization to continue to operate, while if competition becomes too severe or too potent, the organization's survival may again be threatened.

Pfeffer and Salancik (1978: 44) argued that the external control of organizations resulted from the interdependence that was a corollary of the open-systems nature of organizations. And, "it is the fact of the organization's dependence on the environment that makes the external constraint and control of organizational behavior both possible and almost inevitable" (Pfeffer and Salancik, 1978: 44). They listed ten conditions that affected the extent to which a given organization would comply with external demands:

1. The focal organization is aware of the demands.
2. The focal organization obtains some resources from the social actor making the demands.
3. The resource is a critical or important part of the focal organization's operation.
4. The social actor controls the allocation, access, or use of the resource; alternative sources for the resource are not available to the focal organization.
5. The focal organization does not control the allocation, access, or use of other resources critical to the social actor's operation and survival.
6. The actions or outputs of the focal organization are visible and can be assessed by the social actor to judge whether the actions comply with its demands.
7. The focal organization's satisfaction of the social actor's requests are not in conflict with the satisfaction of demands from other components of the environment with which it is interdependent.
8. The focal organization does not control the determination, formulation, or expression of the social actor's demands.
9. The focal organization is capable of developing actions or outcomes that will satisfy the external demands.
10. The focal organization desires to survive (Pfeffer and Salancik, 1978: 45).

These conditions are similar, in some elements, with other treatments of interorganizational power (Jacobs, 1974; Thompson, 1967), though they are somewhat more comprehensive.

Pfeffer and Salancik (1978) suggested that most organizations are confronted with numerous demands from a variety of social actors, and many of these demands are incompatible. They argued:

> An organization's attempts to satisfy the demands of a given group are a function of its dependence on that group relative to other groups and the extent to which the demands of one group conflict with the demands of another. Three factors are critical in determining the dependence of one organization on another. First, there is the importance of the resource, the extent to which the organization requires it for continued . . . survival. The second is the extent to which the interest group has discretion over resource allocation and use. And, third, the extent to which there are few alternatives, or the extent of control over the resource by the interest group, is an important factor determining the dependence of the organization (1978: 45–46).

There have been no studies that have examined the entire set of conditions predicted to explain compliance to some external demands, and in fact, the empirical work on this part of resource dependence theory has been fairly limited. Randall (1973) studied the response of branch offices of the Wisconsin employment service to a change in orientation from being a free employment agency to focusing on human resource development, with concomitant efforts to provide more assistance and attention to harder-to-place clients. Although most studies of the implementation of a policy change focused on issues and conditions internal to the organization, such as control mechanisms and the processes of implementation, Randall examined how the constraints facing the individual branch offices might explain their orientation. Although the legislature and headquarters had changed the presumed orientation of the agency, they still focused extensively on the number of placements accomplished. Thus, job orders were the critical resource for the branch offices. Some offices faced an environment of primarily large employers. Large employers had the resources either to do the hiring directly or to use private employment agencies. Other offices faced primarily smaller employers. Smaller employers had fewer alternatives to the free state service. Thus, the power position of the branch was different depending on the size distribution of its potential clients. In addition, some branches were located in places that had community action programs and agencies. These organizations could presumably compete for the human resource development funds if the branch was remiss in its duties. Other offices faced no such competition. Randall (1973) found that these two conditions, the degree of interorganizational power with respect to the suppliers of a critical resource and the presence or absence of competition, did significantly affect the extent to which the various branch offices changed their orientation in the desired human resource development direction.

Pfeffer (1972a), using interview data collected by Aharoni of 141 plant managers in Israel, investigated the extent to which their dependence on the government affected their articulated willingness to pursue policies favored by the government. Three sources of possible governmental interdependence were identified. First, there was the percentage of the firm's sales made to the government. Of course, this number by itself does not say anything about the government's dependence on the firm. Firms that made and sold defense equipment were presumably in a stronger position than those that sold to the government commissary. Second, there was the firm's financial condition. The Israeli government intervenes frequently in the economy, and government-guaranteed loans, as well as direct loans, are reasonably common. Firms in worse financial position presumably would need the government more as a banker of last resort and would thus be more dependent. Finally, the percentage of foreign ownership might affect the legitimacy of the firm in the country. Firms that were largely foreign owned would be less legitimate and less accepted than Israeli-owned firms and, thus, might be more dependent on government approval and favor for both legitimacy and specific operating help, such as the ability to get earnings and currency out of the country.

Firm managers were asked about the perceived influence of various groups, about their willingness to invest in development areas if the returns would be less than could be earned elsewhere, and about their willingness to export (a favored policy) if returns were lower. The evidence indicated that there were relationships between the firm's dependence on the government and the manager's expressed willingness to pursue activities consonant with the government's interests and policies. The correlations were relatively low, and, of course, only reported willingness to comply was assessed.

Salancik (1979b) used the context of affirmative action to investigate the relationship between transactions dependence and compliance with external control. Through a series of presidential orders, enforced by several federal agencies, government contractors were required to implement affirmative action programs to increase their utilization of minority and female employees. Salancik sent a letter to the executive vice-president in each of the top 100 defense contractors inquiring about their plans for hiring women M.B.A. graduates in June. Careful records were kept of replies, including weighing the response and noting how long it took to arrive. Some firms did not reply; others sent a simple letter saying they were not hiring; others sent long letters from their affirmative action directors with recruiting material on the firm. Each organization was rated according to its responsiveness to this request, and this measure was taken as an indicator of their seriousness about affirmative action.

Some firms were dropped from the sample because they were only holding firms, or they were engineering firms and never hired persons with only an M.B.A. degree, or there was no publicly available data on their sales. The resulting sample was 78. Note that in this study design a firm that did not reply at all was still included in the final sample, coded as being less responsive to affirmative action pressure. For each of the firms in the sample, data were gathered on their total sales volume, sales to the government, and the proportion of the total defense department purchases each furnished. From this information, it was possible to compute the firm's percentage of its sales to the government, a measure of its dependence on the government for disposal of its output; the public visibility of the firm, taken as the total volume of nongovernmental sales; and the government's dependence on the firm, measured as the proportion of the total defense procurement budget that went to a particular firm.

Salancik (1979b) found that for large visible firms who did not control the production of items needed for defense, there was the expected positive correlation between the firm's sales to the government and its responsiveness to affirmative action pressure. Large visible firms with control of the supply of items needed in defense were less strongly affected by sales interdependence ($r = .46$; $p < .05$ for the latter compared with $r = .84$; $p < .01$ for the former firms). This was as predicted; these latter firms had a stronger power position with respect to the government because of their control of the supply of items needed by the government; therefore, they were less affected by their dependence on the government. For smaller, less visible firms not controlling the production of items needed in defense, there was essentially no relationship between sales interdependence and response to the requests about hiring women. And, for smaller firms with control over the production of items needed in defense, there was actually a significant negative correlation between sales interdependence and response to government affirmative action pressure. Salancik (1979b) argued that resource dependence (sales dependence) was an important factor predicting a firm's compliance to government demands but that this factor interacted with the visibility of the firm, making it more or less a focus of compliance pressure, and with the government's dependence on the firm.

Attempts to Manage Resource Dependence

According to the resource dependence perspective, firms do not merely respond to external constraint and control through compliance to environmental demands. Rather, a variety of strategies may be undertaken to somehow alter the situation confronting the organization to make compliance less necessary. The argument is that the managements of organizations seek to maintain discretion over the organization's activities, in part to maintain their own power and discretion, and in part to permit adaptation subsequently as new contingencies arise. An organization already tightly constrained by its environment has limited degrees of freedom left if and when new demands arise. Thus, departing somewhat from the population ecology perspective, the resource dependence view argues that organizations are constrained by their environment but also undertake actions that alter those environments.

Aldrich (1979) and J. Freeman (1982) have implied that the potential to alter the environment to manage external dependence is a capacity possessed primarily by large organizations and, thus, that resource dependence is a theory applicable primarily to only relatively larger organizations. This view would probably be true only if organizations exerted influence in solo. However, there are numerous examples of small organizations banding together in associations and achieving substantial control over their environments. For instance, small retailers were able to obtain passage of resale price maintenance legislation in the 1930s, which forestalled price competition from larger competitors and enabled them to maintain a larger share of the retail distribution market. Small farmers (until recently, most farming organizations were relatively small) were able to obtain government intervention in the commodities markets to maintain prices in times of excess supply. The formation of sales cooperatives and, less frequently, purchasing cooperatives by groups of (often agricultural) firms represents efforts, often quite successful, to control either sales or purchase interdependence. Other examples could be cited, but it is quite clear that the effects of firms on their environments so as to manage transactions interdependence is not a phenomenon confined only to very large firms.

The empirical research conducted to date has examined a number of organizational strategies for either establishing a negotiated environment or altering the pattern of interdependence confronting the organization. In general, two types of interdependence and their effects on organizational strategies have been considered: (1) competitive or commensalistic interdependence and (2) symbiotic interdependence, such as that found between buyers and sellers of some product or service. With regard to competitive interdependence, Pfeffer and Salancik (1978) argued that the amount of interorganizational linkage activity would follow an inverted U-shaped relationship with industry concentration, being largest when concentration was intermediate and being smallest when concentration was either very low or very high. They argued:

> When there are many firms in an industry and concentration is relatively low, the actions of any firm represents only a small proportion of the total

industry; thus, any firm has few consequential effects on most of the other firms. As concentration increases, an oligopolistic market structure is reached, in which firms have increasing impact on each other. As concentration increases even more, uncertainty begins to decrease. With only a few very large firms operating, tacit coordination becomes possible, and each develops stable expectations concerning the others' behavior . . . The inverted U-shaped relationship between concentration and uncertainty, then, derives from two factors. As concentration increases, the impact of any one firm's activities on the others increases. Similarly, as concentration increases, the ability to coordinate interfirm activity increases even in the absence of interorganizational structures or interfirm linkages. The greatest uncertainty arises when there are enough large firms to have major impact on each other but too many separate organizations to be tacitly coordinated (1978: 124-125).

The empirical evidence is consistent with this prediction. Studying the patterns of merger activity in the 20 two-digit Standard Industrial Classification (SIC) manufacturing industries, Pfeffer (1972b) found that the proportion of mergers undertaken within the same industry was negatively related to the difference in concentration from the median value. Studying 166 joint ventures that took place between 1960 and 1971, Pfeffer and Nowak (1976) reported a similar finding for this form of interorganizational linkage, with the proportion of joint ventures made between firms in the same industry being lowest at both high and low levels of concentration and being largest when industrial concentration was intermediate. Finally, Pfeffer and Salancik (1978: 166) reported that the number of officer and director interlocks among competing firms (firms operating in the same five-digit SIC industry) was a function of the level of concentration (positive) and the difference in concentration from an intermediate value (negative). Thus, the evidence for three forms of interorganizational linkage activity — mergers, joint ventures, and officer and director interlocks — is consistent with the hypothesis that activity to manage competitive interdependence occurs relatively more at intermediate levels of concentration, where competitive uncertainty is the highest.

Interfirm coordination can also be accomplished through the movement of executives across competitive firms within the same industry. The movement of personnel is an important mechanism for tying parts of a single organization together through the development of shared experiences (Edstrom and Galbraith, 1977). In an analogous fashion, the movement of personnel within an industry can tie organizations together by the transmission of a common culture and set of understandings about the industry. Pfeffer and Leblebici (1973b), pursuing this argument, analyzed patterns of executive recruitment and succession in 20 four-digit manufacturing industries. Consistent with the results reported for mergers, joint ventures, and board of director interlocks, they found that executives in firms facing a competitive environment of intermediate concentration spent more years outside the company and had a larger number of job changes, spending correspondingly fewer years inside the company. Thus, firms facing competitive uncertainty tended to recruit executives who had spent less time in the company and more time in other organizations within the *same* industry. Again, there is evidence that competitive uncertainty is associated in a predictable fashion with organizational efforts to manage that uncertainty.

With respect to symbiotic or buyer-seller interdependence, resource dependence theory suggests that interorganizational linkage activities will be undertaken to manage such interdependence. Pfeffer and Salancik (1978) argued:

> One of the problems faced by organizations interdependent with other organizations is that exchanges required for maintaining operations are uncertain and potentially unstable. Coping with organizational environments requires stabilizing them somehow. . . . When the conditions of the environment are mediated by social actors . . . uncertainty derives not only from the vagaries of nature but from the actions taken by others. In such cases, the uncertainty resulting from the unpredictable actions of others is reduced by coordinating these actors (1978: 114).

This general perspective leads to the more specific prediction that the higher the level of transactions (purchase or sales) interdependence across economic sectors, the greater the extent of interorganizational linkage activity across those sectors. Pfeffer (1972b) found that large firm mergers conformed to this pattern of results, and Pfeffer and Nowak (1976) found that joint venture linkages across sectors could also be predicted from measures of transactions interdependence. Pfeffer (1972c) found that the firm's capital structure, specifically its debt/equity ratio, an indicator of financial dependence, predicted the proportion of bankers or others from financial institutions on its board. In a study of the composition of electric utility boards of directors, Pfeffer (1974) found that representation of various economic interests (agriculture, manufacturing, and so forth) on the board was correlated with the representation of these sectors in the state's economy. In this case, the dependence involved political support and legitimacy, which was obtained through the cooptation of important economic sectors in the state in which the utility was regulated. In a study of hospital boards of directors, Pfeffer (1973) examined the function of the board, its size, composition, and the impact of the board on organizational effectiveness, defined as the ability to grow and add new services. Explanatory variables included the hospital's ownership, the type of area it served (manufacturing, agricultural, and the like), its operating and capital budget structure, and the sources for its operating funds (private payments, government, insurers). The use of the board for administration or linkage to the environment — its function — could be explained by its context including its source of funding. In turn, the size and composition of the board could be explained by the function of the board and the environmental context of the hospital. Finally, Pfeffer (1973) reported that hospitals that had boards that more closely matched their contextual requirements were better able to obtain additional resources and grow.

Burt (1980) used network analysis to develop measures of relative autonomy of industrial sectors. Burt identified two aspects of autonomy in relational (transactional) networks:

> . . . one aspect of autonomy concerns the relations among actors jointly occupying a status in a system. . . . The actors . . . will be able to escape the constraints of supply and demand imposed by actors in other positions and, accordingly, will be "autonomous" within their system, to the extent that among persons, or corporate actors, occupying the position there exists an oligopoly . . . or, in the extreme of centralization, a monopoly (1980: 895-896).

> . . . a second aspect of autonomy concerns the manner in which actors jointly occupying a status are related to actors occupying other statuses in their system. . . . Actors . . . will be able to balance demands from other actors and, accordingly, will be "autonomous" within their system, to the extent that the pattern of relations defining position J ensures high competition among those actors who interact with the occupants of position J . . . a measure of autonomy via group-affiliation must consider two things: the extent to which actors occupying a status have diversified relations with other statuses, and the extent to which they have relations only with statuses that are too poorly organized to make collective demands (1980: 899).

Burt argued that autonomy considerations should help to explain both variations in industry profitability and in the pattern of cooptive relations. He found support for autonomy explaining profitability and for explaining patterns of merger activity. Burt, Christman, and Kilburn (1980) found evidence that the structure of the transactional market could predict the use of interlocking directorates as well.

The evidence on the ability of resource dependence considerations to predict patterns of interfirm linkage and coordination tends to support the theory, but there is also some inconsistent evidence. M. Allen (1974), in a study of manufacturing firms, failed to replicate Pfeffer's (1972c) findings, derived from a broader sample, of the relationship between firm financial structure and the proportion of persons from financial institutions on the board. Pennings (1980) found no evidence for the effects of board interlocking on firms' performance, although this result, in and of itself, may not be completely inconsistent with the theory. And D. Palmer (1980) has reported that only a small fraction of corporate interlocks that are accidentally broken (as through the death or retirement of the person maintaining the interlock) are renewed. Palmer argued that this called into question the importance of interfirm coordination as an explanation for board of director interlocking. If director interlocks maintained important cooptive relationships, they should be renewed more frequently when broken.

A Mechanism for Environmental Effects on Organizational Actions

Although largely couched in terms of the relationship between environmental conditions (e.g., market structure) and firm responses, resource dependence theory has paid some attention to the issue of how environmental conditions might impact the decisions and strategies adopted by firms. This attention to the mechanisms by which environments affect organizations is important:

> A perspective which merely posits some relationship between the environment and the organization does not provide theoretical understanding. There is an important distinction between a theory and the empirical predictions derived from the theory. . . . A focus on the "how" of change leads one to consider who brings change about and who resists it . . . If change is a consequence of decisions, who is empowered to take actions which alter the organization become critical. One is inevitably led to consider who controls the organization and how such power and influence distributions arise (Pfeffer and Salancik, 1978: 227).

Pfeffer and Salancik (1978) argued that the environment affected the organization through the impact of environmental contingencies on the distribution of power within the organization. This power distribution, in turn, affected who succeeded to administrative positions and what point of view came to characterize the organization's decision making. These factors, in turn, affected the actions and structures of the organization. If the process worked relatively smoothly and without much lag, these actions and structures would be appropriate for the environmental contingencies and constraints. This model of organizational change is shown in Figure 5-1.

Figure 5-1. A MODEL OF ORGANIZATIONAL ADAPTATION TO ENVIRONMENTAL
CONSTRAINTS

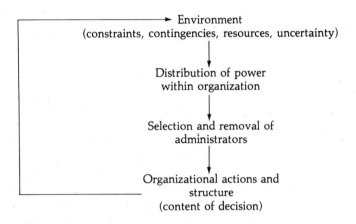

SOURCE: Adapted from Pfeffer and Salancik (1978: 229).

There is, of course, some empirical support for the various links in the model. The strategic contingencies view of intraorganizational power (e.g., Hickson et al., 1971) reviewed in Chapter 2 speaks to the first link, between the environmental context and the distribution of power. Pfeffer (1981a) has reviewed evidence on the effects of power on the selection and removal of executives. The literatures on commitment, selective attention and perception, and socialization all speak to the effect of point of view and background on the information gathered and used and the types of decisions made.

Thus, the resource dependence perspective links environmental effects with internal political processes in organizations. But because politics is also a process operating somewhat independently of environmental factors, the resource dependence view implies a looser coupling between organizations and their environments than that implied by economics or population ecology:

> The model indicates that organizational actions result from political processes within organizations, a view compatible with the political economy framework proposed by Zald (1970a; 1970b) . . . the model is inconsistent with theoretical positions that maintain that organizational actions and structures are inevitably constrained by environmental requirements. . . . Organizations are only loosely coupled with their environments, and . . . power is one important variable intervening between environments and organizations (Pfeffer and Salancik, 1978: 229-230).

Resource dependence theory, then, not only posits one mechanism for linking organizations to environments but further develops the argument that because of other factors operating in the linkage, understanding the process and its various component steps is important in understanding organizational behavior. While organizations are linked and constrained to and by the environment, processes such as internal politics are highlighted in the resource dependence view.

Resource Dependence and Other Theories

Resource dependence is most comparable to population ecology in that both theories emphasize the effects of environments on organizations and take a somewhat less rationalistic approach than the theories reviewed in the last chapter. Resource dependence is also similar in terms of some of the dependent variables considered in the market failures approach, as both deal with mergers and vertical integration, and to Marxist approaches to organizations, since both theories in that case consider issues of interfirm linkages.

Both population ecology and resource dependence emphasize the importance of examining environmental characteristics and constraints in understanding forms and interorganizational behavior. However, there are a number of differences between them (Scott, 1981). First, there is a level of analysis difference. As J. Freeman (1982) has noted, natural selection presumes a population logic. Resource dependence is more concerned with the adaptations and actions of single organizations; the focus is on a focal organization or the organization set rather than on a population of organizations. Freeman has suggested that political economy approaches such as that represented by resource dependence theory, focused at the individual organization level of analysis, can provide insights on the functioning of single organizations that link studies of organizational populations to those of single organizations, thereby providing a more complete picture of organizational life cycles. The implication of Freeman's argument is that rather than being, in some sense, competing theories, by operating at different levels of analysis the two perspectives are complementary. Resource dependence provides some specific mechanisms by which ecological processes operating at the population level may occur. Whether the theories are competing or complementary would require examining the predictions of each for some specific aspects of organizations to see if the predictions are similar or different.

Second, there is a difference in time frame between the two perspectives, in part related to the level of analysis distinction. Population ecology takes a longer perspective than resource dependence.

Third, there are some differences in the conceptualization of the environment in the two perspectives, although there are also strong similarities. Both perspectives emphasize the critical importance of the environmental dimension of scarcity — munificence and both also emphasize the importance of change and uncertainty. However, the ecological perspective tends to view the environment as strictly exogenous, although it can certainly change over time. In the resource dependence approach, not only does the environment change, but there is a presumption that the environment itself changes and reflects the actions taken by organizations to manage problems of interdependence.

Fourth, population ecology is, with its population orientation, concerned with birth and death processes, which are largely outside the scope of the theoretical and certainly the empirical purview of resource dependence theory.

Fifth, and perhaps most fundamentally, there are some differences in terms of how much rationality is presumed to be operating. Population ecology is less normative in its orientation than resource dependence and contrasts with that approach in terms of its emphasis on randomness as opposed to deliberate action. Resource dependence, although arguing from the perspective of the external control of organizations, and incorporating a coalition model of organizations (Cyert and March, 1963), has more elements of rational action and rational choice embedded within it than does population ecology. The image of the manager as a responder to environmental demands and constraints, while simultaneously attempting to mitigate those constraints, evinces more deliberate action and choice than is emphasized in population ecology. Part of this distinction is, however, again related to the level of analysis issue. Population ecology looks less inside the organization to see what is going on and more at overall population effects.

The comparison with markets and hierarchies indicates that both theories are operating largely at the level of the individual firm. Furthermore, both theories incorporate some fairly similar concepts. The market failure perspective considers the small numbers problem, or the number of potential transaction partners, to be a critical element explaining vertical integration. Resource dependence, with its emphasis on the concentration of resource control, also speaks to the issue of the number of potential transaction partners. In addition, resource dependence emphasizes the importance of the resource (the proportion of purchases or sales) as a predictor of integration; this variable is not considered in the market failures predictions. Note, for instance, that in the Monteverde and Teece (1980) study of integration in the automobile industry, the components are assessed only in terms of their engineering time (presumably related to the small numbers issue), not in terms of the amount of the car (in value) they constitute. The primary difference, however, between the two approaches is in the assumptions about the motivation for vertical integration. The market failures approach, with its economics heritage, argues from an efficiency point of view. Vertical integration, the choice of structural form, and the choice of the form of the employment relationship are all presumed to be governed by efficiency concerns. There is a presumption of competitive pressure to force efficiency on organizations. The resource dependence perspective, on the other hand, argues that the principal concern motivating integration is the attempt to reduce uncertainty and that this uncertainty reduction will be pursued even at the expense of profits, albeit subject at some level to a profit constraint when mergers among business firms are considered. Concerned more with issues of power and politics both within the firm and between firms, resource dependence essentially argues, as seen in Burt's analyses, from the perspective of power maintenance and power acquisition. Structural autonomy, or freedom from external constraint, and the ability to constrain or affect other firms motivate the various cooptive strategies used by firms. Power may have profit outcomes (e.g., Burt, 1980), but profit or efficiency is not the sole or perhaps even the dominant motivating force.

It is always difficult to distinguish between theories that differ only in their presumed motivational bases. Fortunately, resource dependence and markets and hierarchies emphasize somewhat different explanatory variables for understanding vertical integration. This makes it possible to distinguish between them empirically; however, such research has yet to be accomplished.

Finally, there are some important differences between the Marxist approach and resource dependence theory that emerge as one examines how they treat the issue of interlocking directorates. Fundamentally, resource dependence sees such interfirm linkages as linking firms together to manage various kinds of interdependence, including transactions interdependence and financial interdependence. Marxist approaches view firms less as separate actors and more as instruments of the capitalist class. As noted in the last chapter, then, interlocking is seen not as individuals linking firms but, rather, as firms linking individuals with economic interests together. D. Palmer's (1980) study of broken ties provides a potential mechanism for studying this issue. Palmer argued that the fact that ties between firms were not renewed frequently when they were broken indicated that such ties were not important. Turning this argument on its side, one might examine the extent to which ties among elements in the capitalist class were renewed when they were broken. Such an analysis would require defining elements of the class (such as families) to examine linkages among them. If one takes the position that there are no such relevant subdivisions, and that the class is a whole, then the analysis would not be theoretically meaningful. However, it still might be possible to look at the number of linkages over time and try to explain this change in interlocking by either variables from resource dependence theory (the degree of concentration of the environment, the degree of resource munificence, the extent of organizational interconnectedness) or from the Marxist perspective.

Clearly, the differences and similarities among these various perspectives on interorganizational behavior have only begun to be developed, and the empirical evidence is sparse. Yet, it is just this kind of conceptual comparison and comparative empirical testing that is necessary to help sharpen the arguments advanced by each perspective, as well as to gain insight into their relative validity.

6

SOCIAL
CONSTRUCTIONIST
VIEWS OF
INDIVIDUAL
BEHAVIOR

Both the perspectives on action considered thus far — rational and external control — are, in a sense, stimulus-response (S-R) theories (Tuggle, 1978). That is, both take some conditions initially defined (such as preferences and expectancies) and alternative behaviors, or external constraints and interdependencies, and predict the individual's or organization's action from these conditions. In each instance, there is some (internal or external) stimulus that elicits some (organizational or individual) response. In both cases, the structure of the theories can be displayed in terms of causal models — of diagrams of connections between exogenous variables and the endogenous results of those factors.

By contrast, the theories to be considered in this and the next chapter differ in several respects. First, they tend to be more focused on process, on how action and interaction unfold in organizations over time, how meaning and interpretations are constructed around such events. Second, the theories tend to be more interactive in their approach to explanation, emphasizing reciprocal causation and multiple determination of outcomes. Thus, in many instances, they are less easily representable in terms of conventional causal diagrams. As a consequence, it is often difficult to discern precisely what is being explained—what are the dependent and independent variables. Third, with some notable exceptions, these theories have tended to rely more on qualitative methodologies for their investigation. This is in contrast to the use of more quantitative comparative data employed more often in examining the other perspectives on action.

And the theories in this chapter, focusing on the individual level of analysis, differ somewhat from those in the next chapter, in which a more organizational level of analysis is employed. Although all of the theories are essentially cognitive and social definitionist in nature, particularly as developed in the general sociological literature, there are at least two important subgroups within the social constructionist perspective. Although not yet as sharply defined with respect to organizational analysis, the cleavages are still in place and happen to follow fairly closely level of analysis differences, as well as the relative emphasis placed on internal versus external control of behavior. The two perspectives are (1) an interactionist approach, growing out of either the symbolic interactionist (Blumer, 1962; Mead, 1938) or ethnomethodological tradition (Cicourel, 1964, 1974; Garfinkel, 1967; Schutz, 1967); and (2) a structuralist approach (Berger and Luckmann, 1966; Goffmann, 1961, 1974; Holtzner and Marx, 1979). As Zucker (1980c) has noted, the interactionist approach focuses on the emergent properties of the interaction, and on the processes by which individuals create and attribute meanings to the events of the action and interaction occuring around them. The structural approach begins with the socially given "facts," the result of the consensus and social definition of the situation, and then treats how these social facts are imported and used in given social interactions (Gonos, 1977). In other words, the interactionists see all action as emergent and situationally defined and specific. The structuralists see patterns of meaning shaped by roles and shared paradigms that structure and constrain the interpretations that are given to interaction patterns. The interactionist position tends toward extreme relativism, as each event is knowable only in the frame of the person experiencing the event. Structuralists, by contrast, see more shared understandings and social definitions in situations, even though these shared definitions are themselves the consequences of processes of meaning creation.

There is, then, a duality in the social constructionist view (Giddens, 1976, 1977), reflecting the fact that social structures are both human creations and, at the same time, constraints on the process of meaning creation. Pettigrew (1979: 572) can at once note that man is "a *creator* and *manager* of *meaning*" but can also note the constraining effects of culture on interaction within that culture. Thus, "man creates culture and culture creates man" (Pettigrew, 1979: 577). But, it is the duality of this process that is maintained by this perspective on action:

> . . . causal relations which theoretical generalizations express do not refer to mechanical connections established in nature, but to the outcomes of human doings. . . . As such (social structures) are the reproduced unintended consequences of intended acts and are malleable in light of the development of human knowledge (Giddens, 1976: 154).

The focus of the theories reviewed in this chapter, operating at the individual level of analysis, has tended to be on the individual as the creator of meaning, on the subjective nature of reality. In the next chapter, at the organizational level of analysis, the focus tends to become more one of the constraining effects of social definitions of reality on behavior. What is important to keep in mind in reviewing this work, of course, is both sides of the picture.

The kinds of analysis to be described have been, thus far, largely focused on various kinds of public organizations. However, as Pettigrew (1979: 580) has argued, the perspective probably has broader applicability. That, of course, raises the question of the social context of this perspective and how this context has tended to produce a focus on public rather than private organizations. There are a number of possible explanations, but one plausible one goes as follows. The idea that meaning and reality are socially constructed implies that there is no necessary or natural order to social arrangements. Such arrangements, as well as their meaning, are products of human action and cognition. This means that institutionalization and legitimation are themselves processes open to study, debate, and contest. Consequently, all social arrangements are problematic rather than inevitable, and this point of view evokes the critical inspection of social arrangements.

Indeed, the phenomenological approach is an important part of a perspective called critical theory (Bernstein, 1976; Connerton, 1976). Thus, just as Braverman (1974) has argued that work arrangements are not the inevitable result of technological advance or economic progress, so this perspective argues that no social arrangement or social institution is predetermined but, rather, is in part the result of human action taken within a shared cultural context. Just as Braverman's treatment of the organization of work opens questions concerning the legitimacy of how work is organized and managed, so this perspective, with its emphasis on the relativistic nature of the world, invites inspection and reflection on the social order. This reflection and analysis itself calls into question the taken-for-granted nature of that order and, thereby, threatens its stability. It is thus not surprising that while the rational, proactive approach is the one most commonly found in professional schools, the social constructionist approach is a perspective less likely to be found.

Even considering only theories operating primarily at the individual level of analysis, some differences are apparent in the perspectives to be reviewed in this chapter. As Sproull (1981) has noted:

> Some theorists view every situation as a unique combination of actions and roles . . . These theorists are interested in how people make sense of puzzling situations. A striking characteristic of their work is that no matter how bizarre the situations, people express beliefs that the situations are understandable and construct plausible interpretations of them. . . . Other theorists look for ways in which people construct beliefs about recurring situations. . . . A major premise of the . . . theories is that people use socially determined typifications to make sense of the situations in which they find themselves (1981: 207-208).

One dimension, then, is the extent to which situations are considered unique or whether the theories strive for explanations of sense making that generalize across contexts. Another dimension is the amount and kind of cognitive processing involved. Although many of the theories are heavily cognitive in orientation, there are emerging some alternatives that deemphasize the role of cognitive processes in understanding interaction processes. A third dimension distinguishing among the theories is the extent to which they focus on cultural elements such as myths, symbols, settings, and vocabulary, as contrasted with more of an emphasis on quasi-rational causal cognitive work as the process by which explanations for situations are derived. None of these distinctions are necessarily clean and precise, but the differences in the theories along the various dimensions should be clear as they are described.

THE ETHNOMETHODOLOGICAL PERSPECTIVE

The ethnomethodological approach is characterized by its relative emphasis on a situation-specific frame of reference and its emphasis on cognitive sense making. Although social processes and social situations are emphasized.

there is less attention to the elements of culture, broadly defined (Pettigrew, 1979) to include symbols, myths, ritual, ideology, belief, and language, and more emphasis on the development of accounts for events by individuals using their own cognitive processes within a social context. Thus, as an example, Garfinkel (1967) noted:

> . . . *recognizable* sense, or fact, or methodic character, or impersonality, or objectivity of accounts are not independent of the socially organized occasions of their use. Their rational features *consist* of what members do with, what they "make of" the accounts in the socially organized actual occasions of their use (1967: 3-4).

Van Maanen (1979c) has enumerated the various assumptions taken by this approach, as well as by several of the other cognitive perspectives on human interaction found in this chapter, as follows:

> At the outset, it is vital to recognize that the objects, facts, events, and relationships seemingly present in the everyday world have no meaning apart from what an observer chooses to give them. . . . From this view of the world as potentially devoid of meaning . . . come several key assumptions . . . *First*, all human behavior or action is based upon some sort of belief, accurate or faulty, about what is going on in the immediate situation, as well as what it is one wants to accomplish by some given action within that situation. . . . human behavior is both interpretive and purposeful. . . . *Second*, events, objects, persons, facts, relationships, and so forth exist for us only insofar as they are conceived in our minds. . . . *Third*, the interpretations we build of our experiences and the purposes we give to our actions are social in origin . . . it is only through the continuous interaction with others that we can construct certain meanings for things in the world toward which we can then gear our behavior (1979c: 18–19).

Note the primacy of cognition and also the imputation of intentionality and purpose to human activity even in this more interactional approach. Indeed, one might argue that its difference from expectancy theory is primarily in its emphasis on the *social* nature of interaction and its emphasis on the process by which such meanings and preferences get worked out and accounted for.

One example of the application of the ethnomethodological approach to organizational analysis is to be seen in Gephart's (1978) study of his own succession in a graduate student association. Gephart argued that most traditional succession studies (e.g., Grusky, 1961, 1963; Helmich, 1974, 1977; Helmich and Brown, 1972) paid little attention to the departure of the predecessor and, more important, neglected the process by which members negotiated a common scheme that both facilitated the succession process and made sense of it in a way shared by those in the social system. Using his own forced replacement as an officer in a graduate student organization as the case under study, Gephart used Goffman-like (1959) terminology to note how the need for replacement was socially constructed and then how various gambits were employed to provide an opportunity for the succession issue to surface and for dissatisfaction of the members with his role to be articulated and used to force succession in a process of status degradation.

Gephart (1978: 578) concluded that succession through a process of status degradation occurred when an enforceable scheme is developed for interpreting the reality of organizational members; the behavior of the person being replaced becomes defined as problematic because it violates important organizational rules, it evidences poor style or poor taste, and it is harmful to the integrity of the organization; and those who identify the problem specify the solution as the replacement of the position occupant. Gephart (1978: 578) further argued that when succession occurred through a process of status degradation, the replacement would be "an actor whose words and deeds are 'the embodiment' (explicitly consistent with) the organizational scheme enforced in the accomplishment of the degradation." Gephart argued that the dramaturgy associated with forced replacement is probably different from the meanings and schemes associated with other types of succession, such as retirement, voluntary resignation, promotion or transfer, and death of the position incumbent. He argued for the development of similar ethnomethodological cases for these other types of succession events to see if the cognitive processes and rituals differed, and how, among the different forms.

Another example of the ethnomethodological approach applied to organizational analysis is Garfinkel's (1967) inquiry into why there are "bad" clinic records. The inquiry grew out of a research attempt to understand the flow of patients through the Outpatient Psychiatric Clinic at the UCLA Medical Center. Unfortunately, there was very little useful data, even demographic data or background material, in the files. Thus, the study evolved:

> When, after the first year's experience, we reviewed our troubles in collecting information from the files, we came to think that these troubles were the result of our seeking information that we or anyone else, whether they were insiders or outsiders to the clinic, could probably not have, because any self-reporting system had to be reconciled with the routine ways in which the clinic operated. We came to tie the unavailable information to

the theme of "good" organizational reasons for "bad" records. It is this theme to which our remarks are addressed (Garfinkel, 1967: 187).

Garfinkel argued that the presence of bad records was more than just an instance of lax control or the fact that the information to be collected was of limited immediate utility, as it was oriented more toward future research use, which meant that there were few incentives for its collection. Rather, the source of the record-keeping practices was to be sought in how the clinic operated, what it was about:

> . . . clinic records, such as they are, are not something clinic person-
> nel get away with, but . . . the records *consist of procedures and conse-*
> *quences of clinical activities as a medico-legal enterprise.* . . . *the contents*
> *of clinic folders are assembled with regard for the possibility that the rela-*
> *tionship may have to be portrayed as having been in accord with expecta-*
> *tions of sanctionable performances by clinicians and patients* (1967: 198–199).

Thus, clinic records could be seen, on the one hand, as a form of actuarial record; on the other, they could be read as a *"record of a therapeutic contract* between the clinic . . . and the patient" (Garfinkel, 1967: 198). The fact that the clinic records were kept more to facilitate the organization's relationships with the university, medical specialties, governmental organizations, the public at large, and the legal system reflected the primacy of the need to publicize and justify the organization (Garfinkel, 1967: 206-207). Thus, the clinic records could be understood as accounts — and the type of accounts that were required by the organization's relationship to its environment. Practices, procedures, and records particularly take on the form expected by the environmental context in which the organization operates and are to be understood only in relationship to that context.

In the case of Gephart's incidence of status degradation and Garfinkel's analysis of clinic records, there are two common themes that deserve emphasis. First, things happen for reasons. As Van Maanen (1979c) suggested, action is purposeful and goal directed in some social context. Second, the reasons are presumed to be functional for the organization, even if not necessarily functional for the researcher trying to use the clinic records or the person being demoted. It is noteworthy that even in the social constructionist mode of analysis there is the presence of both of the concepts of intent or purposeful activity and the serving or organizational needs or purposes through such activity. This argument of functionality distinguishes many of these analyses from critical theory, and the argument of intent distinguishes these analyses from other perspectives to be described later in the chapter that deemphasize the role of cognition and intent.

COGNITIVE THEORIES OF ORGANIZATIONS

Weick (1979: 42) has argued that "an organization is a body of thought thought by thinking thinkers." Under this view, the job of the manager is to manage myths, images, and symbols. "Because managers traffic so often in images, the appropriate role for the manager may be evangelist rather than accountant" (Weick, 1979: 42). Weick specifically rejected the conceptualization of organizations as being dominated by routines, standard operating procedures, and uncertainty-reducing mechanisms, with a corresponding deemphasis on thought and cognition. For him, organizations are at once bodies of thought, or causal schemata, and also embody specific types of thinking practices, or algorithms. Weick suggested that under this conceptualization of organizations important issues for investigation were: What are such causal schemata and how do they change in organizations? What are some algorithms and what are their functions and dysfunctions? and What is the relationship between thinking and action in organizations, particularly, what happens when action precedes thinking?

There are two dimensions that might be used to characterize cognitive maps or causal schemata: how differentiated or complex they are and the specific relationships embodied in the causal structure. P. Goodman (1968) measured the organizational maps of managers in two departments of an insurance firm through interviews and then coded the interviews to measure the degree of differentiation in the cognitive maps. As Goodman noted, there were two possible ways of assessing the degree of differentiation:

> Two types of differentiation can be noted. First, there is differentiation of regions . . . within organization . . . space. That is, an individual may have only one or many different regions (e.g., his job activity, reward structure, sociometric structure, goal structure, etc.) within this map. Second, there is differentiation within regions. For example, an individual's perception of the authority structure (one region) may vary from a limited vertical picture to a complex horizontal and vertical representation. (1968: 247-248).

P. Goodman (1968: 248) defined and measured differentiation for his analysis by the amount of differentiation within regions. P. Goodman (1968: 249) investigated five regions: "the individual's perception of the salary structure, promotional structure, financial structure, authority structure, and major organization problems." He related the amount of differentiation both to demographic factors such as the number of different jobs held, the level in the organization's hierarchy, and the length of service in the organization and to individual personality variables such as the degree of cognitive complexity, the level of aspiration, and the level of job involvement.

Goodman's measure of differentiation, in fact, taps how much knowledge and how refined is that knowledge that an individual possesses. For instance, questions about the financial region "focused on the respondent's knowledge of the company's sales, market position, and the general financial picture" (P. Goodman, 1968: 254). Interestingly, there were not particularly strong relationships between the individual demographic factors and the amount of measured differentiation of the cognitive maps. This was because although long service, higher level, and more jobs individuals had almost without exception differentiated maps, others sometimes had differentiated and sometimes less differentiated organization maps:

> . . . high differentiators were found in low-level and high-level jobs; . . . few low differentiators are found in high-level jobs . . . low differentiators were not long-service employees, nor had they experienced frequent job changes . . . high differentiators . . . were found in both short and long job-service categories and in few and many job-change categories (P. Goodman, 1968: 257).

It would be interesting to have done a longitudinal analysis to see for those just beginning their organizational careers if the degree of organization map differentiation predicted subsequent promotion. Those individuals who expected further advancement (Goodman's measure of aspiration level) did seem to have more differentiated organization maps. There was, however, no relationship between job involvement and the differentiation of the organization map, nor were there many significant associations with cognitive complexity.

While P. Goodman (1968) made an initial effort to measure and study the degree of differentiation of the cognitive maps held by organizational members, Bougon, Weick, and Binkhorst (1977) attempted to study the causal structure of an organization map empirically. The methodology they used was to get jazz orchestra members to enumerate a long list of activities and outcomes. Then, each member was given the job of constructing a causal map for the variables. Thus, some activities might lead to other activities, and still other activities might lead to various kinds of outcomes. For each member, then, a causal map can be created linking the variables to each other, to the extent that relationships are perceived. Using techniques for measuring the similarity of matrices, it is possible to assess the extent to which members of an organization — in this case, a jazz orchestra — share causal schemata, as well as to discover those relationships for which causal perceptions vary. These causal schemata, in turn, reflect the members' understanding of the organization and represent the organization and its organizing process. It might be presumed that such causal schemata affect how members react to various situations and provide a guide to action in the organizational context.

In Bougon and coworker's (1977) analysis of cognitive maps, they distinguished between factors that are originators of activity and ones that are terminators. They found that musicians believed they had more control over terminating factors, such as the quality of the performance, than over originating factors, such as the quality of the arrangement. Furthermore, the musicians seemed to feel they had more control over factors that were highly influenced by numerous other factors than ones that were not. The authors' interpretation for this result was that multiple paths leading to some factor permit more direct and indirect influences on that factor to operate, thereby providing the feeling of more control because there are more avenues or opportunities for control.

In addition to understanding the causal structures that underlie organizations, there are two uses for the causal maps derived from organizational members. The first is as a diagnostic to improve decision making in the organization. Axelrod (1976), for instance, has used archival sources for constructing causal maps of foreign policy decisions. Axelrod indicated that such maps could be used to predict further decisions. Also, by laying bare the underlying causal logic, such representations could be used to improve decision making by having decision makers — in this case, foreign policy makers — confront the reasonableness and validity of their formerly implicit causal assumptions.

Second, causal maps can permit the diagnosis of organizational problems arising from disagreements about organizational operations. Simon (1953) has argued that organizing involved the process of individuals coming to share the same image or belief system about what the new organization should look like. Thus, disagreements about what the organization's structure should be or what its activities should be can indicate that the organizing process is not yet completed and that taking action in such a context can be difficult. Dunbar and Dutton (1981) have examined Grayson's attempts to change the Southern Methodist University business school using this analytical approach. They argued that one problem was that Grayson and some others had a model of how the school operated that made sense of what they wanted to do but that was inconsistent with the causal structure held by long-time members of the faculty. And, the causal structure held by these long-time faculty members implied negative outcomes arising from many of the things Grayson was attempting. Consequently, the resistance to change could be understood by an analysis of the causal structures, and the bases and sources of such resistance could be predicted. The implication of the analysis is that if such causal maps had been developed prior to the change effort, resistance could have been foretold and steps taken, by operating on the variables as represented in the causal structure, to mitigate at least some of this resistance. Alternatively, effort could have been made to develop a consistent set of representations of the organization across its membership.

These studies are important because they illustrate that cognitive maps of organizations can be systematically collected, compared, and analyzed. They also, however, illustrate the difficulty of accomplishing that process, particularly on a large scale. Yet, these studies demonstrate that the presumed association between methodology and core assumptions about human behavior (Burrell and Morgan, 1979; Morgan and Smircich, 1980) may not be completely valid and that cognitive approaches to understanding social systems need not rely solely on case studies or other qualitative methodologies.

LANGUAGE IN ORGANIZATIONS

Sproull (1981: 204) noted, "Because cognitive processing uses category systems that are molded by languages, languages strongly influence beliefs." Thus, the emphasis on the social construction of meaning and the development of accounts leads naturally to a focus on language and its development and use in organizations. In his exposition of the development and effects of organizational culture, Pettigrew (1979) also emphasized the critical role of language:

> Another aspect of organizational culture is the system of vocal signs we call language. . . . language can typify and stabilize experience and integrate those experiences into a meaningful whole . . . language is not just outside us and given to us as part of our cultural and historical heritage, it is also within us, we create it, and it impels us. Language is also a vehicle for achieving practical effects. . . . Socially built and maintained, language embodies implicit exhortations and social evaluations. By acquiring the categories of a language, we acquire the structured "ways" of a group, and along with the language, the value implications of those ways. . . . The study of organizational vocabularies is long overdue (1979: 575).

Pondy (1978) argued that because language is one of the key tools of social influence, and organizations are contexts in which social influence is exercised, language is important in understanding organizations and how they are managed. Analyzing leadership from the perspective of language, Pondy (1978: 89) maintained that "to practice, say, democratic leadership is to understand the set of meanings (values?) to be conveyed, to give them primitive expression, to translate them into stylistic representations, and ultimately, to choose sounds and actions that manifest them." Pondy's argument would suggest that linguistic and dramaturgical skills should be predictive of leadership success. If language is important in the exercise of influence, and leaders exercise influence, then effective leadership may require a large vocabulary, or at least a very evocative and affect-producing vocabulary.

Because organizations can be viewed as language systems, the amount of overlap and common understanding of language becomes an important variable describing organizations. Pondy (1978: 92), for instance, has hypothesized that to the extent the language of the leader overlaps the language of his or her subordinates, the leader will be more effective. It might also be argued that cohesiveness within the organization or organizational subunit will be a function of the degree of language overlap among the participants. Thus, one of the tasks of administration or management can be viewed as the creation of shared language or a shared vocabulary within the organization. One can see this activity clearly in the various professions, in which the specialized jargon of the technical task of the profession serves to bind members of the profession to each other and to differentiate them from other professions and the general environment. Following Pondy's logic, one might predict that the more specialized the professional vocabulary, the greater the cohesiveness within the profession.

Pondy defined leader or managerial effectiveness in terms of language, also. He argued:

> . . . the effectiveness of a leader lies in his ability to make activity meaningful for those in his role set — not to change behavior but to give others a sense of understanding what they are doing and especially to articulate it so they can communicate about the meaning of their behavior (1978: 94).

Thus, leadership occurred through the development of evocative language, widely shared in the organization, that assisted people in making sense of their activities using symbols that were meaningful to all or most of the participants.

Pondy (1977) illustrated his point about the importance of language in his critique of the strategic contingencies' and resource dependence perspectives on power. He argued that what were the organization's most critical contingencies, or what resources were most necessary for survival, were not predetermined but rather emerged through a process of social influence and social definition of the organization, its paradigm, and its mission. To understand power, Pondy maintained, one needed to understand how such definitions of critical problems or contingencies were created, and this was a process involving language and the social construction of reality. Thus, Pondy (1977, 1978) argued that language could fundamentally affect the decisions made in organizations.

Elaborating the distinction between the approach taken by Pondy and others in the phenomenological tradition to the understanding of power and influence and the approach taken by a strategic contingencies' (Hickson et al., 1971) or resource dependence (Salancik and Pfeffer, 1974) approach is useful in helping to understand the fundamental assumptions of the social constructionist approach to organizational analysis. The strategic contingencies' or resource dependence approaches tend to proceed from the material conditions of the organization and its exchanges with its environment. Thus, power accrues to those who can obtain important resources or who can cope with critical uncertainties. These resources, or uncertainties, presumably have some material concrete reality in the pattern of transactions or in the pattern of operations of the organization. By contrast, Pondy's (1977) argument proceeds as follows: (1) reality is socially constructed, and reality is fundamentally a cognitive (rather than a material) outcome; (2) therefore, strategic contingency perceptions, or perceptions concerning what are resources and what resources are important, are the result of a process by which reality gets defined and created; (3) language is critically important in the process of reality construction; (4) therefore, what comes to be defined as a critical contingency or an important resource is the result of the development and use of a shared language that produces a socially constructed world view within the organization. Rather than looking to material conditions for the understanding of behavior, this perspective looks to the patterns of social interaction through which definitions of the situation become defined.

Although Pondy (1978) has tended to emphasize the cognitive, meaning component of language and is thus tied very much to the phenomenological tradition, Edelman (1964) saw language as important for its emotional, affect-producing properties. Edelman argued that effective political language beclouded analysis and permitted the result to emerge in which one side obtained the rhetoric and the other the reality. Because of its ability to arouse support and quiet opposition, language is an important political tool (Edelman, 1964). The importance of Edelman's analysis is to note that language may be important because of its effect on emotions, not because of its effects on causal maps or perceptions of reality. Edelman has implicitly argued an important point: that our hearts and our heads may be relatively loosely coupled, and that it is possible to affect sentiments independently of substantive actions, and vice versa. This point has also been developed by Pfeffer (1981a: chapter 6).

AFFECT-BASED PROCESSES

Edelman's argument concerning the distinction between rhetoric and reality, or the loose coupling between substantive action and outcome, and the sentiments and beliefs around such phenomena raises the issue of the extent to which the emphasis on cognitive processes that is characteristic of the theories reviewed thus far is either necessary or useful. Recall, for example, in Chapter 3 when the social information processing approach was described in the context of the discussion of the effects of environment on behavior, the argument was made that behavior resulted from processes other than cognitive evaluation and sense making. There are direct influences of the social context on behavior, and many of these influences are emotional rather than cognitive in origin. Thus, for instance, it might be argued that the reaction to the threat of group rejection if one does not conform is not just mediated by a process in which the group's importance to the individual (for whatever set of reasons) is compared with the importance of the behavior or attitude along which conformity is being demanded. Rather, rejection and expulsion have emotional components and effects that are in large measure independent of the group's objective or material value to the individual. Thus, the issue is raised as to the extent to which the theories considered in this chapter, because of their emphasis on cognitive processes as part of the reality construction process, are either comprehensive in terms of understanding behavior or valid.

The argument that behavior may be largely noncognitive arises from several sources. Interestingly, cognitive psychologists have begun to question the role of cognition as they have come to recognize the importance of scripts (Abelson, 1976) or sequences of activities that occur largely automatically once the sequence is started or triggered. Langer (1978) has argued the point as follows:

> . . . people are pictured primarily as information processors who continually and consciously ask what and why questions and then behave in ways that correspond to their answers. . . . perhaps the more general issue that needs to be considered is how much time is actually spent in *any* kind of thoughtful action. Much . . . research relies on a theoretical model that depicts the individual as one who is cognitively aware most of the time, and who consciously, constantly, and systematically applies "rules" to incoming information about the environment in order to formulate interpretations and courses of action (1978: 35).

Langer reviewed a large body of literature that indicated that action was dictated as much by habit as by thought (Solomons and Stein, 1896), that the more one is involved in an event, the more one enjoys it, but that this involvement is facilitated by not paying attention to the particulars of the situation. Thus, the research on social cognition increasingly indicates how little cognitive activity there often is occurring.

The criticism of the emphasis on cognition has also appeared in the sociological literature treating interaction. Collins (1981) has argued that most of the time things are taken for granted and there is relatively little cognitive work done in social structures. He has noted:

> Both neorationalist self-criticisms and microsociological evidence agree that complex contingencies cannot be calculated rationally, and hence that actors must rely largely on tacit assumptions and organizational routine. But the actual structures of the social world . . . involve continuous monitoring by individuals of each other's group loyalties . . . negotiations are carried out implicitly, on a different level than the use of consciously manipulated verbal symbols (1981: 994).

Collins has proposed that the mechanism linking people together and forming social structures is emotional rather than cognitive.

The argument advanced by Collins is interesting and important because he starts at the same point as Weick (1969, 1979) but winds up in a very different place. He, for instance, has defined social structure as "people's repeated behavior in particular places, using particular physical objects, and communicating by using many of the same symbolic expressions repeatedly with certain other people" (Collins, 1981: 994). This is certainly similar to Weick's description of organizing as interlocked cycles of behavior. Collins, too, sees interlocked cycles of behavior. The difference comes in how each views the cycles as being maintained. For Weick, the cognitive understanding of the structure, the causal schemata, are critical. For Collins, the basis is certainly not cognitive:

> The most easily identifiable part of this repetition, moreover, is physical: the most enduring repetitions are those around particular places and objects . . . there is also symbolic communication that goes on among these people . . . the repetitiveness is not to be explained primarily by the *content* of this symbolic communication. The social structure is not a set of meanings that people carry in their heads . . . The structure is in the repeated *actions* of communicating, not in the contents of what is said; those contents are frequently ambiguous or erroneous, not always mutually understood or fully explicated (1981: 995).

The question arises, What, if not cognition, maintains the repetiveness of behavior, maintains the interlocked cycles of interaction? As noted above, for Collins, this glue holding social structures together is affect or emotion. He argued: "People follow routines because they feel natural or appropriate. . . . The underlying emotional dynamics . . . centers on feelings of membership in coalitions" (Collins, 1981: 997). Collins has argued that organizations, and other social structures, are markets in which cultural and emotional resources are the media of exchange.

Byrne (1969) has argued that similarity is one of the more important and pervasive bases of attraction. One can assume that interpersonal attraction is a fundamental mechanism mediating feelings of inclusion and belongingness. Thus, similarity, and the emotional affect it produces, is a critical factor binding people together in social structures. The oft-noted tendency for similarity to affect decisions such as promotion and hiring (e.g., Kanter, 1977; Salancik and Pfeffer, 1978b) may have a basis in the importance of emotion and affect, in part generated by similarity, in producing stable social structures. Collins's argument, then, provides yet another way of understanding the role of interpersonal similarity in social life. The argument leads to somewhat different predictions than those previously advanced. Salancik and Pfeffer (1978b) and Kanter (1977) have implied that similarity is valued for its uncertainty-reducing properties. Collins, however, suggests that the importance of similarity may be in its link to interpersonal attractiveness and feelings of inclusion and acceptance and the resultant assurance of interlocked and maintained cycles of interaction. Uncertainty, per se, would not produce increased tendencies toward producing and choosing similarity; rather, it would be the extent to which the uncertainty was related to the maintenance of the social structure in its current form.

The implications of Collin's argument for organizational analysis have yet to be worked out in detail. The argument would seem to be quite consistent with the importance of rituals and ceremonies that create feelings of belongingness and positive affect and with an emphasis on understanding the emotional as well as the cognitive side of organizational life. Indeed, taken to its logical conclusion, the argument would suggest that if activities could be found that led to different emotional and rational outcomes (for instance, obtaining a rationally valued objective in a way that led to a negative affect), the emotional component of the activity would be more important than its rational outcropping. Although the importance of emotion and affect reinforces the significance of feelings and attitudes, the basis of the affect is not so much in the relationship of persons to their environment, including tasks and task attributes, but in their relationship to each other. Thus, it may be the affiliative implications of task and organizational design that have fundamental consequences for the organization's operations, rather than other components.

The mindlessness and affect and emotion perspectives offer an alternative to the cognitive, quasi-rationalistic perspectives that have come to dominate the social constructionist approaches to organizational analysis just as they have been so strongly represented in the dominant, individual rationality approaches.

SUMMARY

In this chapter, we have examined those theories that have tended to focus more on the individual level of analysis and to emphasize the production and creation of meanings and beliefs in taking an emergent, process-oriented approach to organizational analysis. Several things should be evident from this admittedly brief overview of these perspectives. First, in some important respects they share elements with the rational, individualistic approach to organizational analysis. For the most part, they emphasize the role of intention and purpose, albeit often also recognizing the duality of structure as being both a product of human interaction and a constraint on that interaction. And they also emphasize the importance of cognition in organizational analysis. Weick (1979) even goes so far as to define organizations as cognitive entities, which is a departure from his earlier emphasis on interstructured activities (action) rather than cognition as the essential organizational element (Weick, 1969).

We have seen that this emphasis on cognition and purpose can give these theories the same problems that occur in the case of theories of individual, rational action. Several challenges are posed. One of the most important is the extent to which action is mediated by cognition, either prospectively or retrospectively or, rather, is mindless, perhaps governed more by affect and emotion. The growing overwhelming emphasis on cognitive processes does not seem warranted in the context of a cognitive psychology literature that itself has increasingly questioned the role of cognition in accounting for behavior. In any event, theories emphasizing the importance of cognitively constructed reality will need to confront the extent to which there is this much cognitive work occurring in social systems, including organizations.

Another set of challenges emerges from the position taken often implicitly and occasionally explicitly that action is meaningful (things have reasons) and that such activity is usually functional in the sense of serving some organizational or subunit (including individual) interest. It is somewhat surprising to see functionalism appear in a literature stressing emergent process, but it is there, nevertheless. Both of these assumptions — that things have reasons and that the reasons are functional — need to be closely examined. One might wonder if they are good foundations on which to build an explanation of human behavior, given the criticisms of the individual, rationalistic approach to explaining actions noted in Chapter 2.

Second, it is clear that a variety of methodological approaches are consistent with the social constructionist view of organizations. Quantitative analysis of causal maps is one research strategy, as is the kind of ethnomethodological qualitative research that is more often thought of with this approach.

Third, it is clear that in some of its versions the approach departs the most radically from the materialist assumptions that underlie the external control approach and, to a somewhat lesser degree, the rational perspective on organizational analysis. This departure is one of the more distinctive aspects of these theories but, of course, also another domain in which the assumptions underlying the approach are open to question.

This departure from the materialistic position is inherent in the argument that reality is socially constructed. By inference, this means that the social world is almost infinitely malleable, as long as language and cultural systems can be developed that produce social consensus on what the world is and how it is to be accounted for. In contrast, the external control perspective particularly emphasizes the effect of external constraints that impose themselves without regard to the cognitive mechanisms or personal characteristics of those operating in the system. By implication, then, this external constraint approach argues for a material, objective reality that is, at least in some measure, independent of the particular individual traits or cognitive processes through which the reality is filtered.

Of course, the two perspectives may appear to be more different than they are in part because they tend to take different time frames and different points of departure. Ultimately, the external constraint perspective would have to answer where the norms, values, and social pressures come from and, at that point, would begin to look more like the social construction of reality position. However, it tends to see more stability and structure in the world and starts the explanation of behavior from that structure rather than asking how the structure got there in the first place. By contrast, particularly those versions of the social constructionist argument reviewed in this chapter have emphasized the idiosyncratic, emergent property of social life.

There is another position that argues for the importance of emergent process but also recognizes the fact that in most instances action, meanings, and norms are taken for granted and exist in a system of beliefs and culture that tends to change rather slowly and therefore conditions the processes by which action gets created and interpreted. It is this version of the social constructionist view that is examined in the next chapter.

7

ORGANIZATIONS AS PARADIGMS AND PROCESSES

As discussed in the last chapter, one can adopt an emergent, process-oriented focus on organizations incorporating elements of the social construction perspective without confining the analytical framework to the individual level and without relying as heavily on assumptions of cognition and intentional action. Rather, organizations can be conceived as paradigms and processes, and the explanation and prediction of behavior can proceed by incorporating to a much greater extent structural and contextual effects while still retaining some of the developmental perspective and the theme of the social construction of reality. The three streams of research reviewed in this chapter — organizations as paradigms, the decision process approach to organizational analysis, and institutionalization theory — all illustrate this combination of an emphasis on the effects of structure and context in the framework of theories emphasizing process and the importance of social reality creation processes. By incorporating both aspects of structural effects and social reality construction, it might be argued that these perspectives offer some advantages by overcoming several of the problems enumerated in the last chapter.

Recall that the theories covered in the last chapter emphasized the development of belief and meaning as emerging from a social interaction process as well. What is different is in the emphasis — on whether situations are generally viewed as unique or typical and whether the attention tends to be focused more on the process of meaning creation or on what happens once meaning systems are created. Since stability is at least as much a phenomenon observed in organizations as change, it is important to understand some of the sources of this stability. This is the emphasis of the theories to be described in this chapter — how the socially constructed sets of meanings that emerge affect and constrain behavior, even as they, at one point, emerged from behavior themselves.

Sproull (1981) has explained clearly how shared understandings develop and come to take on a life of their own, constraining subsequent action and the development of meaning:

> People who talk together come to share the same verbal categories and explanations. This has a convincing effect that results from two processes. One is the sharing of taken-for-granted assumptions, a consistency process. The second is the accumulating of meaning within and across conversations, a continuity process. People cannot constantly interrupt each other to ask, What do you mean by that? They must assume they share the same meanings for at least some of the words they use. As these assumptions persist from conversation to conversation, meanings become socially objectified (1981: 207).

These socially objectified, typified meanings and action patterns then serve to constrain subsequent behavior.

ORGANIZATIONS AS PARADIGMS

Brown (1978) has conceptualized organizations in terms of the concept of paradigm. As used in science (Kuhn, 1970), paradigm refers to the shared understanding and, as important, the shared exemplars that emerge in scientific disciplines to guide research and instruction in the discipline. A paradigm is a way of doing things, a way of looking at the world. Lodahl and Gordon (1972) equated the level of a discipline's paradigm development with the certainty of technology, and the connection between paradigms and technologies is an apt one. A paradigm is a technology, including the beliefs about cause-effect relations and standards of practice and behavior, as well as specific examples of these, that constitute how an organization goes about doing things. Brown (1978) maintained that the development of shared paradigms is what occurs in formal organizations.

Pfeffer (1981a: chapter 6) argued that one of the critical administrative tasks involves the articulation of the organization's paradigm. He noted that one of the reasons the School of Criminology at Berkeley could not defend itself against attack and eventual dismemberment was that it lacked any shared, readily articulated view of what it was about. Selznick (1957) had earlier noted that a critical leadership task was to provide myths and beliefs that infused day-to-day activity with meaning and purpose.

There are several implications of the view of organizations as paradigms. First, Kuhn (1970) has argued that in science paradigms seldom evolve over time; rather, old paradigms are replaced virtually in toto by new paradigms in a fashion that is more revolutionary than evolutionary. This is because an organizational paradigm, once in place, tends to turn the organization into a closed system. A paradigm, recall, is not just a view of the world; it embodies procedures for inquiring about the world and categories into which these observations are collected. Thus, paradigms have within them an internal consistency that makes evolutionary change or adaptation nearly impossible. The only way to displace an internally consistent, fairly tightly coupled system is with an alternative system; changing the parts of the first system is almost impossible. This point has been noted by Golding (1980):

> The process of abstraction and simplification enables "a world" to be constructed and given meaning, but in a way which tends to result in a viewing of the construction as the only possible world. The whole transaction has a tendency to become self-fulfilling. . . . The particular is made general and becomes accepted to the extent that the access to the totality of the larger world, in the shape of possible alternative views, is blocked. Perspectives tend to become ossified (1980: 763).

Sheldon (1980) has used the imagery of paradigm revolutions to describe problems organizations have in changing in some fundamental dimensions. He used the idea of paradigm as a diagnostic, to help forecast when change would be relatively easy (when fundamental parts of the paradigm were not at issue) and when change would be more difficult and would need to be more comprehensive (when the basic paradigm was the object of change). Thus, if paradigms are the glue binding the organization together and differentiating it from its environment and other organizations, paradigm shifts are traumatic and fundamental organizational events. Jonsson and Lundin (1977) studied Swedish Investment Development Companies (IDCs) and found evidence supporting the paradigm revolution view. They argued that there were cycles of enthusiasm and depression that occurred around leading ideas or myths. "The prevailing myth is the one that presently guides the behavior of individuals at the same time that it justifies their behavior to themselves" (Jonsson and Lundin, 1977: 163). The existing paradigm or myth tends to try to incorporate any and all new information coming into the organization; information tends to be distorted to be seen as consistent with the prevailing view. It is, according to these authors, only when sufficient anomalies build up that cynicism and depression arise around the old myths. Then a new myth is created, and with enthusiasm, action takes place again in the new organizing framework.

There is a cycle, then, of stability and change, in part because fundamental change is so traumatic and unsettling. This self-protective nature of paradigms, and the trauma associated with their change, naturally leads to the question of the conditions under which paradigms change, or as Rounds (1981: 1) puts it: why the defense mechanisms that normally protect organizations against fundamental change sometimes fail. Rounds has noted that there are two mechanisms of change that have been proposed. One holds that change comes through the acquisition of information that indicates that the present technology is not working. This approach holds that information, and particularly technical information, is critical in the change process. Describing the application of this perspective to changes in the California state hospital system dealing with the mentally retarded, Rounds (1981) noted:

> . . . the process of change . . . has been a confrontation between those acting rationally on the basis of reliable, valid information, and those acting from personal motives, in defiance of the negative information concerning the hospital system, to preserve the traditional structures. . . . change begins with rejection (by some individual or small group) of the most fundamental assumptions of the closed system (1981: 8).

The alternative view of change is that paradigms do not change all at once in a profound way, at least initially.

> The process begins at the periphery, with information indicating failure to meet some acknowledged, limited goal of the system. This is interpreted as indicating some specific flaw in design or implementation has retarded the success of an otherwise viable system. . . . The action taken is not radical, but is rather a conservative attempt to preserve the system with the least possible increment of change. The corrective measures . . . have the unanticipated consequence of raising some new ambiguity about the system . . .

> Another flaw is perceived, and further corrective action is taken . . . An elaborate feedback loop develops, which results in stripping away the layers . . . one by one. . . . in this model the ground is prepared for a radical reconceptualization of the field through a transitional process in which conservative attempts to protect the system have the unanticipated consequence of undermining it (Rounds, 1981: 10).

Rounds has presented two illustrations of the different perspectives on change and the role of information in the change process. One dealt with change in the paradigms of prisons (Rounds, 1979); the other with the change in the system of treating the severely mentally retarded in California (Rounds, 1981). Rounds has argued that paradigms die because the underlying social theory and values shift, not because one sees changes in technology or knowledge that produce failure in a technical or technological sense. Thus, Rounds (1979) suggested that shifts from incarceration-punishment orientation to a therapy-rehabilitation paradigm in prisons occurred not because of an increase in crime, recidivism, or new knowledge about how to change criminal behavior; rather, the change in paradigm occurred because the dominant social values and social theory in the society at large had changed. Rounds also argued that investment in ritual activities reaffirming the paradigm would increase as the paradigm was in crisis; reaffirmation of the faith, as it were, is most necessary when the faith is called into question.

The process of paradigm change can be examined well in Rounds's description of the change in the California hospital system that dealt with the mentally retarded. In particular, he was interested in explaining the development and growing power of a deinstitutionalization movement, whose goal was the closing of all the state hospitals and placing the retarded in community-based and -oriented treatment facilities. Rounds noted that in 1960 almost all retarded persons receiving state services in California were congregated in five state hospitals. During the next 20 years, the population of these hospitals declined from 13,000 to 8,200, and "more than 60,000 developmentally disabled citizens were receiving 'community-based' services through 21 regional centers located throughout the state" (Rounds, 1981: 11). Two events seemed to initiate the change process. First, in 1963 the federal government began to provide funds for state-level planning for mental retardation. Because there was a retarded person in the Kennedy family, the Kennedy administration had shown increased interest in the treatment and care of retardation. Second, at about the same time, it became clear to state planners that there was no financially feasible way to solve the problem of growing waiting lists and demands for admission to state hospitals. The recognition of the financial bind coupled with the legitimation of an external authority, the President's panel, for the use of previously underexploited community-based services caused a reorientation in the system.

However, the fundamental paradigm was not challenged at this point. Under existing California law, the access to state financial help in caring for the retarded was through hospitalization.

> A simple diagnosis was available which posed no challenge at all to the value of hospitalization for the severely retarded: a good system had gone awry because of an administrative flaw that encouraged violation of the principles of the technology, causing persons to be hospitalized who should have remained in the community. What was rejected in the 1960s was not the hospital technology, but the assumption that the system could continue expanding at a faster rate than the state population — a problem which was declared to have been the result only of "inappropriate hospitalizations" (Rounds, 1981: 32–34).

Rounds provided data indicating that the paradigm of institutionalization itself was not under attack. Even as the community-based facilities were being put into place, there was continued expansion of the hospital system. Moreover, there were very few articles or research reports cited by any of the committees working on the problem in the legislature or the executive branch that raised fundamental criticisms concerning the appropriateness of institutionalization in general.

But, the change to community-based facilities changed the process of governance and access to the system in ways that made the destruction of the paradigm proceed. New professionals were recruited into the system to work in the community-based facilities; many of these were not doctors, and thus the physician-dominated perspective on mental retardation began to be eroded. The release of the less retarded back into the community left the hospitals short of free janitorial labor, and faced with economic necessity, they began to use Down's syndrome patients. Suddenly, they learned that persons who were previously considered to be virtually incapable of doing anything could do some useful work. This called into question the entire technology of diagnosis. The very fact that alternative treatment modalities were now permitted increased the technical ambiguity. The new regional centers "stimulated a frenzy of professional organizing. The flow of . . . funds into new forms of service not dominated by the psychiatrists who controlled the hospitals afforded opportunities for less powerful professions to stake out claims" (Rounds, 1981: 41). This further increased the technological ambiguity, by importing into the system persons with ever more diverse backgrounds and paradigms. Thus, what started as an initial, conservative change became transformed over time to a questioning of the fundamental technical assumptions that had so long been taken for granted. It is doubtful that any of this progression of events was foreseen at the time the initial changes were made in the middle 1960s. Finally, Rounds argued that the advent of the civil rights movement prepared the ideological ground for undercutting the assumption that people who are different should be segregated. Thus, "fundamental organizational change is likely only in times of ferment in the broader society" (Rounds, 1981: 50).

A current setting in which to test the idea that paradigms change because of values and changes in social theory, not because of technical failures, would be the movement to embrace quality-of-working-life concepts more fully, as in Ouchi's (1981) "Theory Z" management and the incorporation of quality circles and giving workers more responsibility and autonomy in the workplace. One argument is that such change in a management paradigm is caused by some technical failure of the old paradigm — in this case, declining productivity and increased competition from abroad that could be traced to old management practices. The alternative argument would be that there are not significant differences in productivity change or competitive position that differ substantially in this period than in the past; rather, what differ are the espoused social theory and the values of democracy and individual freedom (or, depending on one's view, paternalism and authoritarianism) that are associated with the new management paradigms. Rounds would argue that shifts in organizational paradigm are not so much related to performance problems, objectively defined and measured, as to shifts in power, as paradigms rationalize political deals. In this sense, although power may shift as a result of organizational contingencies and problems, and then lead to shifts in the organization's paradigm, the link between paradigm and objective technical reality is, at best, indirect.

Paradigms come to be embodied in stories, sagas (Clark, 1972), myths, and technologies for doing work that are accepted as articles of faith. Clark (1972) examined the sagas told at three private liberal arts colleges. He noted that these sagas provided both a sense of collective identity and a justification for future actions and efforts. Martin (forthcoming) has noted the pervasiveness of stories in organizations that are controlled strongly through inculturation and socialization. These stories, some of which may be true, and some of which may not be, are important because they provide vivid and explicit exemplars of the paradigm in action. Similarly, how work is done, the procedures for producing the product or service, represents the organization's paradigm. Thus, to affect and control behavior, the paradigm must be made real and concrete. This occurs through the telling of explicit stories and through the actual procedures of operation in the organization.

Two points from the organizations as paradigms perspective deserve emphasis. First, the perspective emphasizes the relatively closed-system, nonadaptive nature of organizations. It provides another perspective on why selection processes, as described in Chapter 5, rather than adaptation, may be critical to understanding organizational change. The system gets closed because bounded rationality requires a simplification of the informational environment in which the organization makes decisions. Furthermore, because "the closed system is a summation of the experience of many persons, it is in principle impossible for any individual to understand fully why all of the programs are the way they are, or the basis for each of the multitude of past decisions that fixed them in their present form. At any time the validity of the bulk of the closed system must simply be taken for granted" (Rounds, 1981: 2-3). Second, the perspective emphasizes the unfolding, processual nature of change. Meanings are not questioned and overthrown all at once. Rather, actions are taken, often within the dominant paradigm, to solve some small problem, which in turn lead to other problems, other actions, and finally, the unraveling of the old system of meaning and its replacement with an alternative paradigm. The role of information in this process is more to serve as an arguing point and to provide data around small problems. There is little indication that the paradigm itself is suddenly overthrown through the appearance of new, important and relevant facts.

DECISION PROCESS THEORIES AND ADMINISTRATIVE RATIONALITY

At several points in the preceding discussion and in the last chapter, we have noted that much organizational activity is relatively mindless, in the sense that a practice or pattern of doing things is instituted and gets used over time without much new evaluation of how sensible it is. Paradigms and the practices embedded in those paradigms are relatively stable and seldom questioned. This suggests that it might be possible to analyze organizations and predict their behavior from an understanding of their programs for gettings things done.

Performance programs develop as a way of economizing on information (March and Simon, 1958). Suppose, for instance, that a pricing decision must be made. To make the economically rational decision of equating marginal revenue with marginal cost, the firm will have to estimate the demand curve for the product it is selling, or how many units it can expect to sell at various possible prices. Such information may be difficult to obtain and, furthermore, uncertain. In addition, the firm will need to know the marginal cost of supplying various quantities of the product, which requires knowing fixed and variable cost components over a range of sales quantities. This information is also costly and problematic. Consequently, the firm may adopt a simple rule of thumb such as following the pattern set by some competitive store or product or pricing on the basis of some markup over readily attainable cost figures. Once instituted, this particular pricing rule is likely to remain in existence for a long time, in part because as Rounds (1981) has suggested, no individual knows enough about all the organization's operations really to question the fundamental premises underlying the decision rule.

March and Olsen (1976: 12) have argued that these administrative decision processes are used and are important for understanding what goes on in organizations because there is ambiguity present in many choice situations. They identified four types of ambiguity: the ambiguity of intention, or organizations that are characterized by inconsistent or ill-defined preferences; the ambiguity of understanding, which refers to the fact that technologies may be uncertain and that feedback from the environment may be misinterpreted; the ambiguity of history, which refers to the fact that what happened and why may be difficult to understand; and the ambiguity of organization, which refers to the varying degrees of involvement and participation of various organizational actors in choice situations. March and Olsen (1976) argued:

> . . . individuals find themselves in a more complex, less stable, and less understood world than that described by standard theories of organizational choice . . . Intention does not control behavior precisely. Participation is not a stable consequence of properties of the choice situation or individual preferences. Outcomes are not a direct consequence of process. Environmental response is not always attributable to organizational action. Belief is not always a result of experience (1976: 21).

Because of the problematic and ambiguous nature of preferences (March, 1978), the rational model of choice is inapplicable. How can one choose to maximize (or even satisfice) one's goals or preferences when these are either unknown, ambiguous, or internally contradictory? Furthermore, because feedback from the environment is often delayed and then may be misperceived because of its ambiguity, and in any event may be only loosely coupled to what the organization did (because of the operation of chance factors), models emphasizing the external control of organizations as explanations of organizational behavior are also incorrect. If the environment only imperfectly reflects what the organization did and information from the environment is itself ambiguous, how can behavior be oriented toward satisfying environmental demands and constraints? Thus, decision process models argue that the administratively rational thing to do, and what organizations, in fact, do, is to develop performance programs, standard operating procedures, rules of thumb, and so forth, and use these in making decisions. To understand a given organization, then, it is necessary and largely sufficient to understand these performance programs or procedures.

Empirically examining decision process models is a nontrivial task. One approach has been to rely on computer simulations that embody the presumed operating rules and procedures of the firm. Thus, Cyert and March (1963) showed how the use of a series of standard operating procedures oriented around subgoal satisficing concerning pricing and output levels produced certain joint results under conditions of duopoly, while Gerwin (1969) and Crecine (1967) examined process approaches to understanding school district and municipal budgeting, respectively. Clarkson (1962) used simulations employing simple information processing rules to replicate the behavior of trust officers. And, more recently, Cohen, March, and Olsen (1972) used a series of decision process routines to represent decision making in organized anarchies, a model that they aptly refer to as a "garbage can model of organizational choice."

Cohen, March, and Olsen (1972) conceptualized organizations as contexts (or garbage cans) into which there poured problems, solutions, participants, and choice opportunities. The key structural variable considered was the right to participate in choice opportunities. Several different decision structures were specified. In the unsegmented decision structure, diagrammatically represented in Figure 7-1A, every actor has the right to participate in every decision. In the specialized decision structure, shown in Figure 7-1B, the right to participate in certain decisions or classes of decisions is limited to specific individuals or groups who are presumed to have some unique competence or expertise for this type of decision. In a hierarchical decision structure, shown in Figure 7-1C, the structure is segmented in that not everyone can participate in all decisions. However, it is also different from the specialized decision structure in that rank has its privileges. Those of the highest rank can participate in all decisions, with persons of lower rank having the right to participate in successively fewer decisions or types of decisions.

In their simulation of decision making, Cohen and coworkers concluded that problems were seldom resolved, the process was quite sensitive to variations in decision load, decision makers and problems tended to follow each other through choice situations, important problems were more likely to be resolved than unimportant ones, and important choices were somewhat less likely actually to resolve problems than were unimportant choices.

Because simulation of decision processes has been a frequently used

Figure 7.1 REPRESENTATION OF ALTERNATIVE DECISION STRUCTURES

A *Unsegmented Decision Structure*

	Decision Opportunities						
	1	2	3	4	5	6	7
A	X	X	X	X	X	X	X
B	X	X	X	X	X	X	X
C	X	X	X	X	X	X	X
D	X	X	X	X	X	X	X
E	X	X	X	X	X	X	X
F	X	X	X	X	X	X	X

Organizational Participants or Groups

B *Specialized Decision Structure*

	Decision Opportunities						
	1	2	3	4	5	6	7
A	X	0	0	0	0	0	0
B	0	X	0	0	0	0	0
C	0	0	X	0	0	0	0
D	0	0	0	X	0	0	0
E	0	0	0	0	X	0	0

Organizational Participants or Groups

C *Hierarchical Decision Structure*

	Decision Opportunities						
	1	2	3	4	5	6	7
A	X	X	X	X	X	X	X
B	0	X	X	X	X	X	X
C	0	0	X	X	X	X	X
D	0	0	0	X	X	X	X
E	0	0	0	0	X	X	X

Organizational Participants or Groups

X = Can participate in decision

0 = Cannot participate in decision

analytical technique, it is important to consider what can and cannot be learned from simulations (Cohen and Cyert, 1965). Some mathematical models (such as differential equations and linear programs) can be solved for unique or at least bounded solution sets. However, frequently the social process being modeled will be complex enough so that there are no mathematical procedures that enable one to diagnose what happens to the system under study. In such circumstances, the use of computer simulations can enable the researcher to observe what happens as the various decision processes interact and play themselves out over time. Thus, simulations enable the analysis of what will happen in the social system under study if the processes in question are operating over some time period. The fact that the simulation outcomes approximate what is empirically observed in the organization or other social system does not necessarily validate the input assumptions, nor is the converse the case. Rather, the use of simulation methodology permits the inference of nonintuitive results from sets of complex processes interacting over time. Whether such processes actually occur in organizations is another matter, and the issue of simulation validation is one that is both perplexing and controversial (Cohen and Cyert, 1961).

Decision process models have also been examined by case study methodology. Here, the effort is made to investigate the extent to which various processes or performance programs appear to be operating by observing the organization in action. In chapters in the March and Olsen (1976) volume, for instance, the garbage can model of choice was investigated using case study methodologies. The decisions studied included the selection of a dean (Olsen, 1976a), reorganization (Olsen, 1976b), the location of Norwegian university campuses (Stava, 1976), and the policies developed to deal with desegregation in San Francisco public schools (Weiner, 1976). In each case, the garbage can framework was employed to make sense of the choice process, and in turn, elements of the choice process were used to illustrate the features of the garbage can model. Cohen and March (1974) have argued that the garbage can, or organized anarchy, model is descriptive of many universities.

Of course, case studies have their own issues of validity and reliability. In particular, it is often difficult to know whether the explanation derived to account for what is going on in the situation is, in fact, the correct one, or whether there are alternative explanations, from other theoretical approaches or perhaps representing other decision processes, that might also account for the data. In some instances (e.g., Stava, 1976), there is attention to alternative explanations, but this is not usually found in case studies.

Finally, decision processes can, in some instances, be investigated using conventional comparative designs and data analysis. Even here, however, the process is difficult. For instance, one commonly hypothesized decision

process is that of incrementalism (Padgett, 1980). Incrementalism economizes on information processing and decision time by taking last year's
allocation pattern as a base and making marginal adjustments from that
base. Incrementalism has been most frequently studied in the context of
budgetary decisions. The typical finding has been that last year's budget is
the best predictor of this year's, and this finding has been observed in governmental organizations (Davis, Dempster, and Wildavsky, 1966) as well as
in universities (Pfeffer and Moore, 1980).

But, can one really infer the decision process from that data? The
answer, unfortunately, is no. Williamson (1966) has shown, in the case of
allocations, how the observation of stable patterns of allocation over time
may be quite consistent with an optimizing, rational choice model. For instance, what if the first allocations are approximately the right ones, and
nothing changes? Then, subsequent allocations would be expected to be
quite similar to the first, which will appear as incrementalism. Power might
also account for the results. After all, power distributions are probably fairly stable in most organizations most of the time, particularly on a year-to-
year basis. Thus, the fact that one year's allocations predict the next may
mean nothing more than both are being accounted for by the distribution of
power and influence. Thus, in this case, and in others, one cannot necessarily make inferences about the processes that are operating by observing only
the outcomes produced by those processes. Of the methods, a more clinical
approach getting directly at the process would seem to be preferable. In any
event, the demonstration of the operation of decision processes in accounting for organizational behavior is not simple.

The decision process approach, as exemplified by March and Olsen
(1976), does incorporate elements of the social constructionist perspective.
They argued that "most of what we believe we know about events within
organizational choice situations as well as the events themselves, reflects an
interpretation of events by organizational actors and observers" (March and
Olsen, 1976: 19). Indeed, it is because of the interpretation process that
some of the ambiguity noted previously gets introduced. What the decision
process or administrative rationality approach has not done, as often, is to
ask where the various decision rules or performance programs come from.
In the case of incrementalism, there has been some discussion of this issue,
with the argument being that it is forced on the organization by computational limitations. Indeed, bounded rationality is often asserted to be the
underlying reason behind simplified decision procedures. However, it
should be noted that there may be a variety of simplified decision rules,
each of which is consistent with information processing limitations. Thus, it
is important also to ask the question of why some rules and processes are
adopted and not others. It is in this domain that the organization as
paradigm approach offers some insight and some advantages.

INSTITUTIONALIZATION THEORY

To speak of practices or procedures that are continued and transmitted without question, to speak of meanings that become typified and transmitted to newcomers in the organization and shared without thought or evaluation, is to speak of the process of institutionalization. Thus, it is useful and appropriate to conclude our discussion of the social constructionist perspective by considering institutionalization theory, a perspective that addresses the issue of how and why meanings and forms and procedures come to be taken for granted and what the consequences of this institutionalization are.

The idea of organizations as institutions has a history extending back to Selznick's (1948) reference to the pressures of the institutional environment and his treatment (Selznick, 1957) of organizations as institutions. For Selznick (1957), the idea of institutionalization implied imparting a permanence to the organization that would extend its life beyond the requirements of the task at hand. Organizations, instrumentally conceived, could be allowed to disappear if their purpose was fulfilled or if other organizations emerged that could do the task better. Organizations conceived as institutions, on the other hand, could not be allowed to disappear. Thus, Selznick saw the quest for institutionalization as a quest for organizational immortality and protection against the vagaries of competition, broadly defined to include competition among organizational forms as well as competition for particular sets of resources. There is an underlying theme that this attempt at institutionalization represents, in part, a departure from the organization's real goals and functions and the adoption of new forms, practices, and activities simply to survive and grow (Perrow, 1972).

There is, however, another approach to understanding institutionalization. As defined by Meyer and Rowan (1977: 341), "institutionalization involves the processes by which social processes, obligations, or actualities come to take on a rulelike status in social thought and action." Institutionalization deals with the persistence and perpetuation of activity. As we have seen in earlier chapters, action can be perpetuated because it is rational — that is, it is tied to the achievement of some goal or preferred state of the world. Or, action can be perpetuated because it is reinforced, in that it leads to positive outcomes for those performing the action, after the fact. Or, action can be perpetuated because it is demanded by those in the social unit's environment who have the power (or at least some power) to enforce those demands. Institutionalization theory argues that none of these bases are necessarily required for action to be undertaken and to persist:

> . . . internalization, self-reward, or other intervening processes need not be present to ensure cultural persistence because social knowledge once

institutionalized exists as a fact, as part of objective reality, and can be transmitted directly on that basis. For highly institutionalized acts, it is sufficient for one person simply to tell another that this is how things are done. Each individual is motivated to comply because otherwise his actions and those of others in the system cannot be understood (Zucker, 1977: 726).

In other words, institutionalized acts are done for no reason other than that is how things are done. "Other acts are meaningless, even unthinkable" (Zucker, 1977: 728).

Zucker (1981b) goes on to note:

> . . . institutionalization is rooted in conformity . . . rooted in the taken-for-granted aspects of everyday life . . . Within an organization, institutionalization operates to produce common understandings about what is appropriate and, fundamentally, meaningful behavior. . . . Institutionalization, when external to an organization, leads to adoption of common practices: "purposes, positions, policies, and procedural rules that characterize formal organizations" (Meyer and Rowan, 1977: 346) (1981b: 6-7).

Zucker (1977) and Meyer and Rowan (1977) both saw institutionalization as a variable. This insight permits the integration of the various perspectives on action. For institutionalized acts or institutionalized structures, there is a stable structure of interaction and definition of the situation, which is not necessarily based on rational or instrumental considerations. For acts that are not institutionalized, there are more likely to be incentives or a rational calculus involved in understanding them, and the idea of emergent structure in the context of not yet consensually shared definitions and situational meanings is more relevant and applicable. Thus, the degree of institutionalization determines the extent to which rational versus emotional and nonrational bases of action predominate; it also determines the extent to which action is structurally determined and comparatively stable or emergent and subject to new and reinterpretations. As Zucker (1980c) has argued:

> . . . interpretation of social interaction is expected to be more specific to the particular interaction when institutionalization is low, similar to the interactionist predictions. However, when institutionalization is high, interpretation of social interaction is expected to be placed in the context of the wider social structure, similar to the structuralist prediction (1980c: 5).

There are, then, two aspects to understanding institutionalization theory. First, since institutionalization is a variable, it is necessary to under-

stand what determines the extent to which some action or structure is institutionalized. Then, it is important to understand the consequences of an action
or structure being institutionalized for analyzing organizational behavior.
The effects of institutionalization have been examined in a number of
contexts; before examining them, we consider the determinants of institutionalization.

Some Determinants of Institutionalization

Zucker (1977) argued that one determinant of the extent to which an action
or activity would be seen as institutionalized was the context in which it occurred. Some contexts, such as organizations, have associated with them
the idea that activities are undertaken, repeated, and performed without
question. Roles within organizations are settings that are even more prone
to lead to expectations of institutionalization. Zucker argued:

> Settings can vary in the degree to which acts in them are institutionalized.
> By being embedded in broader contexts where acts are viewed as institu-
> tionalized, acts in specific situations come to be viewed as institutionalized.
> Indicating that a situation is structured like situations in an organization
> makes the actors assume that the actions required of them by other
> actors . . . will be those typical of more formal and less personal interac-
> tion. This assumption leads the actors to believe that acts will be more
> regularized and that the interaction will be more definitely patterned than if
> the situation were not embedded in an organizational context. Any act per-
> formed by the occupant of an office is seen as highly objectified and exte-
> rior. When an actor occupies an office, acts are seen as nonpersonal and as
> continuing over time . . . in contrast to office, personal influence is de-
> pendent on the particular unique actor. There is no rationale under which
> such an actor can be replaced without changing many of the expectations
> for behavior (1977: 728-729).

In a replication of the Jacobs and Campbell (1961) experiment, Zucker
reproduced their findings of a decay in the laboratory microculture relatively rapidly over trials. Jacobs and Campbell used a modification of Sherif's
(1935) autokinetic experiment to study transmission of culture. Jacobs and
Campbell established an artificial laboratory microculture concerning the
distance a point of light appeared to move by using confederates and one
naïve subject and then watched the decay of this microculture over trials as
confederates were gradually replaced by naïve subjects over successive generations. Zucker replicated this condition and added two more. In the organization condition, subjects were led to believe they were joining an ex-

perimental but still ongoing organization. In the office condition, the organization instructions were supplemented by giving the person who had been in the organization the longest the title (role) of Chief Light Operator. The basic transmission experiment was followed by a maintenance experiment in which one subject returned the following week and worked alone on the distance estimation task for 30 trials. There was also a resistance-to-change experiment, in which after the maintenance experiment was completed, a confederate was brought in and identified as another subject, and then he attempted to establish a lower baseline response by responding first with smaller distance estimates. Zucker's (1977) results were consistent across the three experiments. Subjects in the office condition demonstrated less decay in the distance estimates over time, evidenced greater maintenance, and were more resistant to change. Subjects in the organization condition were next, and subjects in the personal influence condition, with no organization or position instructions, demonstrated the least resistance, the least maintenance, and the smallest transmission of the distance estimates over trials.

Zucker's experimental results are a powerful demonstration of the effects on behavior of occupying positions in organizations. Her results indicate that in such settings there is a tendency to take knowledge and belief as transmitted by others as real and to accept it without question and without much overt social influence. Culture is accepted and transmitted because of its institutionalized character. The greater degree of institutionalization, the more action is maintained without direct social control (Zucker, 1977: 741).

Zucker's earlier experimental findings on the determinants of institutionalization were subsequently extended in another series of experiments. Zucker (1980c) argued:

> The degree of institutionalization varies depending on the degree to which acts are both: (1) Exterior, such that subjective understandings are reconstructed as intersubjective, so that acts are seen as part of the external world; and (2) Objective, such that acts are potentially repeatable by other actors without changing the meaning of the act (nonpersonal) (1980c: 3).

Zucker argued that to the extent that acts were typified, or were readily categorized and explained, they would be seen as more institutionalized.

In one experiment, Zucker (1980c) had subjects watch ten videotapes of a brief interaction sequence. Facial expressions were not particularly visible on the videotape, and there was no verbal interaction between the two actors. Subjects were asked to describe the interaction they had witnessed. Also, subjects were asked to describe as briefly as possible an interaction they had observed during the past week between two people who were not very well acquainted with each other or the subject. This was done to control for a verbosity factor, or how much people tended to write in describing interactions. For the dependent measure, Zucker used the ratio of the number of words used to describe each of the videotaped interactions to the number of words used to describe the other interaction previously observed. Zucker noted that Brown and Lenneberg (1954) had found that when subjects were shown 24 colors, the briefer the description of the color given, the shorter the response time, the higher the agreement among subjects, and the greater the ability to remember the particular colors seen from a larger set of colors. Thus, by analogy, Zucker argued that the length of the description indexed the typification of the interaction. The more typical and readily categorized the interaction, the shorter the description.

In the first experiment, Zucker observed the predicted association between the typification of the interaction and the extent to which the subjects reported the action as being institutionalized. For readily categorized and understood interactions, the response time for writing the description was shorter, and the certainty and perceived intersubjectivity was also greater. In a second experiment, Zucker varied the extent to which setting and role information was present. The experimental setting was the same, except only three videotaped sequences were shown. Providing information on the setting increased the degree of typification, but providing information on the role of the two individuals increased it even more strongly. Thus, consistent with Zucker's (1977) earlier results, there was evidence that institutionalization was affected by information about the setting and the role that made the interaction sequence more readily categorized and understood. In the third experiment, Zucker demonstrated that inconsistency in the elements of information decreased both typification and institutionalization. She concluded:

> . . . action is typified to varying degrees . . . the extent of typification is strongly related to the degree of institutionalization, and . . . setting and role information increase both typification and institutionalization. Responses to inconsistency among types of information indicate that making accounts is a fundamental response to such incongruent cues (1980c: 16).

Thus, in addition to role and context information, institutionalization is determined by the extent to which actions are seen as typical and the extent to which information about the action or interaction pattern is congruent.

Meyer and Rowan (1977) developed arguments about the presence or absence of many institutionalized rules and roles in larger social structures such as societies. Again treating the degree of institutionalization as a variable, they argued that the degree of societal modernization affected the prevalence of rationalized institutional elements. The same modernization process that produces the development of bureaucratic organizations produces institutionalized rules of conduct and action that govern the operation of these organizations. Meyer and Rowan also suggested that the degree of institutionalization and the number of institutionalized rules and practices would be higher the more elaborate relational networks among organizations were and the greater the collective organization of the environment. Elaborate networks and collective organization both produce roles, and as noted by Zucker (1977), roles increase the extent to which rules and practices as well as actions are viewed as institutionalized.

Institutionalization and Organizational Structure

One of the first contexts in which institutionalization theory was developed — and, indeed, the setting that may have sparked its development — was the study of the organizational structure of schools and school districts. As summarized by Meyer et al. (1978), there was very little evidence for the organizational properties of school districts. There was little evidence that there was agreement on policies and practices between school district superintendents and their principals, between principals in the same district, between teachers and principals, and between teachers in the same school. Thus, there was little evidence in school organizations of vertical coordination across levels or even for a common culture of technology that unified the organization at either the school or the district level of analysis. Although there was little evidence for control and coordination of teaching activities, administrative apparatus did exist, and in many respects, school districts were quite bureaucratized. Teachers could only be hired if they were credentialed, and there was a very formal evaluation process used in the hiring decision. The district and the school kept detailed records on student attendance and files on student performance in class; of course, detailed financial records were kept covering the expenditure of resources on various personnel and supplies necessary to operate the schools. There was, then, detailed financial accounting and reporting and detailed files on students and, in some instances, on teachers. All the trappings of bureaucracy were in place, without the coordination and control of work usually assumed to be produced in formal, bureaucratized organizations.

Meyer and Rowan (1977) argued that there are two bases for observing formal structure in organizations. "In conventional theories, rational formal structure is assumed to be the most effective way to coordinate and control the complex relational networks involved in modern technical or work activities" (1977: 342). However, these theories of rational structure and control assume that such technical considerations are fundamentally important for organizational success and survival. Meyer and Rowan argued that in some cases this was true and that there were technical, rational bases for organizational structures. However, in other cases, the organizations were essentially free from many of the technical, rational constraints because the technology of the organization was not understood, or the organization was not closely evaluated, or it was located in a sector (such as the public sector) in which market mechanisms of control and technical efficiency or effectiveness concerns did not operate as strongly, if at all. In such circumstances, the organization's structure was to be understood not from considerations of technical rationality but in terms of matching or fulfilling the expectations of the environment for what such an organization should look like:

> . . . organizations are driven to incorporate the practices and procedures defined by prevailing rationalized concepts of organizational work and institutionalized in society . . . To maintain ceremonial conformity, organizations that reflect institutional rules tend to buffer their formal structures from the uncertainties of technical activities by becoming loosely coupled, building gaps between their formal structures and actual work activities (Meyer and Rowan, 1977: 340–341).

Thus, Meyer and Rowan argued that organizations are, indeed, linked to their environments, but not in the way specified by either resource dependence theory or population ecology. Because there are shared, institutionalized views in the environment about what organizations should look like and how organizational work should get performed, to maintain their legitimacy (Dowling and Pfeffer, 1975), organizations import the form, if not the substance, of these rules and incorporate them in their structure, rules, and reporting requirements. However, since such rules and structures may have little to do with how the work can or should get performed, in fact there is little impact on task performance and the behavior of those organizational members who actually do the work. This decoupling, Meyer and Rowan argued, is actually useful to the organization. It permits the work to get done according to the localized judgments of those doing the work, while presenting to the outside world the appearance of legitimated, rational organization of work.

The internally decoupled nature of organizations is, it should be evident, the result of there being no shared, well-defined technology for doing the work. In the presence of institutionalized social norms about organizations but in the absence of the knowledge that would facilitate doing the work, institutionalized organizations develop in which ceremonies and symbols are used to ensure continued support and legitimacy from the social environment, while not actually impacting the organization's operations. Meyer and Rowan (1977) argued that schools resist evaluation because in the absence of a known technology of instruction, all that evaluation could do would be to call into question their legitimacy and the legitimacy of the structures and procedures in place. The view of institutionalized organizations described by Meyer and Rowan is a form of confidence game in which neither the organization nor those it is fooling have any incentive to examine more closely what is going on.

The Diffusion of Innovations

Structures can be considered administrative innovations (Teece, 1980), and thus the Meyer and Rowan argument can be generalized to consider the effects of institutionalization on the innovation process. The argument is fairly straightforward. Once an innovation is institutionalized, it is adopted and accepted not because it has rational or technical properties but because social expectations are that good, well-managed organizations will do so. This line of reasoning suggests that prior to its institutionalization the adoption of some innovation or administrative practice could be predicted from rational or technical considerations but that after the innovation has been institutionalized, such factors account for less (if any) of the variance in adoption and acceptance.

Zucker and Tolbert (1981), studying the diffusion of civil service reform, provided data that bear directly on this argument. They examined the factors predicting the adoption of civil service reforms of personnel practices during the period between 1880 and 1930. In 1900, 17 percent of the cities had adopted civil service reforms; by 1930, about two thirds of the cities had adopted such reforms. Zucker and Tolbert found that in the case of the early adopters characteristics of the city could be used to distinguish between adopters and nonadopters. "As predicted, early adopters tended to be 'middle class' cities (i.e., to have an educated, white collar population) with narrower governmental scope" (1981: 22). By 1930, civil service reforms were institutionalized; they were accepted practices of good government. At that point, specific city characteristics explained less the distinction between those cities that had adopted and those that had not. Also, Zucker and Tolbert distinguished between cities in states in which laws were passed mandating civil service reform and those that had no such laws. The passage of such a law, they argued, institutionalized the personnel practices and, again, had the effect of making specific city characteristics less important in understanding the time of adoption or whether adoption had occurred. Rather than specific city characteristics related to either the need or the demand for civil service reform, for institutionalized practices the key explanatory variable was more likely to be the degree of the city's integration in the social network that provided the social basis for institutionalization. Summarizing their results, Zucker and Tolbert noted:

> Prior to institutionalization, adoption was largely an individual process, rooted in the rational need for efficient/effective city administration. Later, however, . . . transmission became less problematic . . . and specific city characteristics became generally less important as determinants of adoption (1981: 23).

Meyer and Rowan (1977: 344-345) argued that there were many administrative practices that could be analzyed as institutionalized forms adopted for, perhaps, little or no reason other than their general acceptance as ways of doing things:

> . . . technologies are institutionalized and become myths binding on organizations. Technical procedures of production, accounting, personnel selection, or data processing become taken-for-granted means to accomplish organizational ends. Quite apart from their possible efficiency, such institutionalized techniques establish an organization as appropriate, rational, and modern. Their use displays responsibility and avoids claims of negligence (1977: 344).

It would be possible to study a variety of administrative practices and structural forms using the perspective developed by Meyer and Rowan and illustrated in the Tolbert and Zucker study of civil service reform. Two other completed studies of this type should be noted.

Rowan (1980) examined the diffusion of innovations during the 1930-70 period in California school districts. The innovations were new personnel positions. In the case of the innovations studied, the state and federal governments instituted requirements for local school districts. What Rowan was interested in explaining is why some of these innovations diffused much more rapidly and why some tended to persist. Rowan found that as requirements became more generally accepted as defining "good" schools, they diffused much more rapidly. Persistence patterns varied depending on whether the new position became institutionalized. Rowan (1980: 8) found that institutionalization was achieved and maintained more readily "where technical procedures are highly certain and standards of evaluation are easy to formulate." Thus, although 80 percent of the schools maintained positions in health that survived over ten years, only 62 percent retained positions in psychology, and only 41 percent in curriculum and instruction. In part because of the ethos of local control of school activities, it was easier to institutionalize a health position requirement (an issue of general safety and public welfare) than one dealing with curriculum or instruction, presumably more in the purview of the local authorities. Rowan's study illustrates that the presence of legislative requirements can facilitate but certainly does not ensure the institutionalization of new activities. Institutionalization is affected by the prevailing social values as well as by the technical certainty of the new activity. To the extent that social values are consistent and technical certainty, which makes evaluation easier, is present, innovations will tend to be institutionalized, which will be reflected in more rapid diffusion and in persistence over time.

Zucker (1981a) examined the presence and role of evaluation units in schools. She argued:

> . . . while all schools exist in an institutional environment . . . the degree of institutionalization does vary as a function of the differences in the amount of federal funds and regulations (depending on size, location, and minority/poor enrollment) and as a function of state differences in funding and control over local public schools (1981a: 20).

She reported that in contexts in which there was high state involvement in regulation and funding, 45 percent of the districts had evaluation units; by contrast, where there was low state involvement, only 16.2 percent had evaluation units.

Zucker (1981a: 20) noted that evaluation units essentially served as signals of compliance to external directives and interests, and thus, it was not surprising that there was little use of evaluation information internally. Furthermore, "as external use of the evaluation information increases in importance relative to internal use, the unit becomes increasingly loosely coupled to the rest of the organization, with organizational characteristics becoming less important in predicting how effective the evaluation unit perceives itself to be in affecting use of its results" (Zucker, 1981a: 21). Evaluation units can be seen as structural signals (Meyer, 1980), providing tangible evidence of apparent compliance to some important activity demanded by the environment. In this case, the increased flow of federal and state funds to local schools was followed by demands for accountability as to the use and worth of these expenditures. Since direct federal or state control was difficult because of the organizational and often geographic distances involved, the requirement was for internal evaluation units to be created to signal a concern with the evaluation activity. Zucker's (1981a) findings indicate that such units were created to the extent demanded by the institutional environment but were loosely coupled to the rest of the organization, serving primarily the function of external legitimation.

There is an important implication of these analyses for studies of the diffusion of innovation. Depending on when in the process the analysis is conducted, the results will differ. If the factors predicting early adoption are to be understood, it is important the process be examined before the innovation becomes institutionalized. At the same time, once the innovation is institutionalized, different factors come into play to determine the subsequent course of diffusion. As in many other aspects of the study of organizations, time and longitudinal analysis are important, given the effects of institutionalization on diffusion.

Additional Topic Domains

The general concept and insights of institutionalization theory are quite broad in their substantive applications. This, in fact, is one of the theory's strengths. Zucker (1980b), for instance, has examined issues of occupational mobility using the perspective of institutionalization theory. Zucker argued that newly emerging occupations were less institutionalized than occupations that had existed for some time. Consequently, one would expect to find more rapid occupational mobility and more openness and less credentialism in new, noninstitutionalized occupational specialties. New occupational specialties are more likely to be found in new organizations, and new organizations are, in any event, likely to be less institutionalized because of their shorter history.

Zucker argued that the institutionalized nature of most occupations explained the stability of the occupational status and the "rule-like allocation of individuals to occupations" (Zucker, 1980b: 5). This meant, however, that in noninstitutionalized occupations there would be more mobility and more open allocation of occupational status. Zucker tested these notions by examining the change in occupational status of both the staff and clients in new social agencies conducting job-training programs. Zucker found that the staff, working in relatively new organizations and in certainly newer occupational specialties (for example, job developer), experienced more net increase in mobility as a consequence of the program than did the clients. This was, she argued, because the clients were being trained for more institutionalized roles, whereas the staff benefited from the lack of institutionalization associated with their occupations.

Institutionalization concepts have also been used to analyze social psychological experiments. Zucker (1980a) has argued that just as in other social situations interaction in experimental situations varies in the extent to which it is determined by preexisting, structural elements or emergent from the social reality that becomes defined in the situation. Meaning is situated in the experimental context (Alexander and Knight, 1971; Alexander, Zucker, and Brody, 1970) and can be used to predict the responses of subjects to the experiment. The argument is that the subjects are responding to meanings rather than to the experimental manipulations themselves.

The Alexander and Knight (1971) study illustrates this phenomenon. It is worth considering in some detail because of its implications for the use of social psychological experiments and their results in developing theories of behavior. Alexander and Knight argued that responses in experimental situations were affected by the implications of the response for the "situated identity" of the subject.

> The term "situated identity" . . . designates the dispositional imputations about an individual that are conveyed by his actions in a particular social context. When a person acts, he communicates information about the kind of person he presumes to be and obliges others to regard him as being that kind of person (1971: 65-66).

They hypothesized that subjects would be interested in portraying the most favorable situated identities and would choose responses to experimental manipulations with such considerations in mind. Of course, such effects will not be present in all conditions. Rather, they will be present only to the extent that experimental conditions are socially defined and institutionalized with respect to their implications for the perceptions of the individuals involved:

> For situations to be socially defined there must be relative consensus about the meaning of actions. . . . it is necessary that there be some agreement about the dispositional *dimensions* that are relevant to describe an individual's conduct, and about how a particular action is to be *evaluated* along those dimensions. When these conditions are met, then we can say that a situation has consensual meaning or social reality (Alexander and Knight, 1971: 66).

The specific theory examined using these concepts was cognitive dissonance. Festinger and Carlsmith (1959) had found that subjects who had performed a dull, boring task and then lied about its interest in a face-to-face interaction with another person reported liking the task more when they received $1 than when they received $20 — the insufficient justification prediction. Presumably, the subjects who received $20 could say they lied because they received the money; this was less plausible in the $1 condition, and thus the only way to explain their behavior was to revalue their interest in the task. Unfortunately, Carlsmith, Collins, and Helmreich (1966) were able to replicate these original results only in the case of the face-to-face interaction situation. When subjects were to write a counterattitudinal essay, task liking increased with the amount of incentive offered. Alexander and

Knight (1971: 68) replicated the Carlsmith, et al. (1966) study using an interpersonal simulation (Bem, 1967) and found that "response alternatives of the task-liking question are associated with differentially evaluated situated identity attributions and that subjects chose the most favorable one in each condition."

The implications of these results for the data produced by social psychological experiments are striking:

> At present, we can only wonder how many studies in the experimental literature of social psychology have achieved their results because of the situated identities at stake. . . . The situated identity approach provides a means for detecting these influences in experimental situations. Prior simulations of intended experiments could determine the influence of situated identities in the various conditions and gathering this kind of data as part of the experimental procedure would yield valuable information about subjects' definitions of the situation (1971: 80).

Unfortunately, this theme has been largely ignored in the subsequent experimental literature. Zucker (1980a) has demonstrated that by bringing in normative elements that challenge the experimenter's authority, demand characteristics results (Orne, 1962) can be altered. Zucker's experimental results demonstrate, again, the importance of institutionalized, normative control in understanding social interaction, including when such interaction is part of a psychological experiment.

Ideas from the institutionalization perspective can even help to explain individual reactions to work environment characteristics. Lincoln, Hanada, and Olson (1981) studied the reactions of Japanese, Japanese-American, and American employees in 28 organizations in southern California that were owned by Japanese parent firms. Lincoln and his colleagues found that employees of Japanese origin tended to favor more paternalistic work practices but exhibited lower levels of job satisfaction. They also observed that vertical differentiation had a positive effect on the work attitudes of Japanese and Japanese-Americans but no effect on the American workers, while horizontal differentiation had a negative effect on the extent of personal ties and job satisfaction for those workers of Japanese origins and for Japanese-Americans but no effect on the non-Japanese-Americans. Thus, there was evidence for cultural differences in the reactions to organizational arrangements.

From the perspective of institutionalization theory, there are certain employment practices and organizational arrangements that come to be culturally accepted and defined as good. These expectations for practices and arrangements condition the responses of individuals to the particular work context encountered. Furthermore, these organizational properties need not have any close connection to efficiency or technical rationality. Thus, in a fashion analogous to that of Meyer and Rowan (1977), Lincoln and colleagues (1981) argued that it was important for organizations to match their cultural context — but for purposes of conforming to institutionalized norms and requirements, not for purposes of technical efficiency. They argued:

> . . . organizational phenomena are shaped by the cultural values and beliefs, as well as the institutional arrangements, of the populations in which they are embedded . . . Organizational structures may indeed be loosely coupled to formal goals, but they are closely tied to the cultural and social orientations of the people involved with them (1981: 114).

This link between organizations and cultural norms and values, created by institutionalized expectations, is a prediction that is quite consistent with institutionalization theory.

The research on institutionalization theory illustrates how social definitionist and social construction of organizational reality concepts can be investigated using both experimental methods and quantitative field data. And, ideas from institutionalization theory have applicability to topics as diverse as occupational mobility and understanding the diffusion of various administrative practices.

SUMMARY

The theories reviewed in this chapter illustrate how a social constructionist view can be adopted that is nevertheless consistent with an emphasis on the effects of structure on behavior. In the case of the focus on organizational paradigms, it was seen that the paradigm, once in place, constrains how new information is interpreted and, indeed, whether new information is sought. Policies and procedures are taken for granted, with there being little questioning or even thinking about the underlying rationale. Changes in paradigm evolve, then, not from the sudden discovery of discrepant information, which indicates the failure of the paradigm in some technical sense, but rather from a series of localized, initially conservative actions taken in the context of the paradigm to solve what are perceived to be fairly small problems. The decision process theories, derived from considerations of administrative rationality in information processing constrained situations, also are founded on the premise of taken-for-granted procedures. These procedures emerge and are maintained because of the ambiguity inherent in taking organizational action and making decisions. And finally, in the case of institutionalization theory, the processes by which elements become taken for granted, as well as some of the consequences of institutionalization for structures, are explored.

As noted at several points, these theories permit the incorporation of processes emanating from social interaction and social reality construction but do so without as much recourse to assumption of intention or to reliance on hypothetical individual cognitive processes. It is suggested that these features make these perspectives advantageous as frameworks for understanding and explaining action.

8

DEVELOPING
ORGANIZATION
THEORY

There has recently been a great deal of reflection and introspection concerning the state of organization theory — its conditions, paradigms, and prospects. For instance, a conference reviewing several major programs of organizational research was held with the intent of reflecting on where research should next proceed (Van de Ven and Joyce, 1981). Recently, at least one paper (and associated commentary) explicitly focused on the direction of the field in the coming decade was published (Cummings, 1981; Van de Ven and Astley, 1981). Attention has been paid to explicating the various paradigms of organizational analysis and their political and methodological connections (Burrell and Morgan, 1979). And there has been attention to the issue of the methodologies used in organizational research, with explicit concern about broadening these to include qualitative analysis (Daft and Wiginton, 1979; Van Maanen, 1979b). The appearance, in a two-year period, of this much commentary, reflection, and introspection is striking because previously there has not been this much self-conscious examination of the state of organization theory in print.

A review of this literature indicates a growing sense of ambiguity. Certainly, no consensus emerges from these reviews and overviews. The recommendations have ranged from studying the interaction of micro- and macroprocesses in the context of understanding change (Van de Ven and Astley, 1981) to tightening up the measurement and validation of concepts used in research (Cummings, 1981). In considering the methodological questions, the recommendations have ranged from getting closer to the organization one is studying, in essence, becoming a participant observer (Van Maanen, 1979a), to stimulating the organizations being investigated at a distance and watching their response (Salancik, 1979a).

One is tempted to argue that this growing review and reflection coupled with ambiguity is indicative of a paradigm crisis in organization theory. If so, it is long overdue. As we have noted at several points, the dominant perspective on action that has characterized organizational research has been the rational model of choice; moreover, for the most part, the vast majority of the research has focused on the individual level of analysis. The review of the individually rational approach in Chapter 2 makes clear the numerous problems and issues with this approach, and as Chapter 4 argued, except for the Marxist or intraclass (D. Palmer, 1980) perspective, theories of organization-level rationality have not fared very well either. Structural contingency approaches have yielded mixed empirical results, and the market failures perspective has yet to be seriously empirically examined. The underlying theoretical premise of the rational perspective — that social actors do things because they want to (Mayhew, 1980, 1981) — has grown increasingly troublesome because of its inherent circularity. And, the temporary diversion into individual-level phenomenology and ethnomethodology has proved or will soon prove to be no solution at all. That is because this approach actually moves even further into the explanation of behavior in terms of hypothetical constructs — namely, the unobserved processes of cognition and meaning creation that go on inside people's heads — and furthermore has imbedded within it the same fundamental assumptions of purposeful, goal-directed action. Thus, for instance, Van Maanen (1979c: 15) argued that "we behave selectively within this perceived world" and that "human behavior is both interpretive and purposeful" (1979c: 19). Selective, purposeful behavior is rational or quasi-rational behavior, and such an explanation for action almost inevitably reduces to a theory of choice that resembles the rational, individual model.

As Mirvis (1981: 2) has so perceptively noted, we have moved far away from studying organizations as what we know them to be: "social entities characterized by demographic, relational, and physical (material?) structures." We have lost sight of the ground for all the figures we have drawn on it (1981: 9). In some sense, what resource dependence and population ecology at the organizational level of analysis, the theories reviewed in Chapter 3 at the individual level of analysis, and even institutionalization theory from a more social constructionist point of view have tried to do is to introduce more concrete, material, externally based explanations for behavior. Hopefully, such explanations could obviate the need to assume what needs to be studied (for example, the motivation and basis of action) and, furthermore, by focusing explanation on the concrete and more material and objective aspects of social reality, develop theories of behavior that were at once more comprehensible and empirically falsifiable.

To return to the metaphor of the garden, many of the plants have been found to be in bad condition, and it is time to plant some new crops. Thus, this concluding chapter has two purposes. First, it briefly reviews some of the ground covered in our more detailed coverage of the various perspectives in the previous chapters. Second, it offers three alternative sets of approaches to analyzing organizations that are more consistent with the relational, demographic, and physical realities of organizations. These three perspectives are organizational demography, network analysis, and the analysis of physical settings and space in organizations. They are examples of the kinds of analytical approaches that, along with theories like population ecology and other approaches reviewed in Chapters 3, 5, and 7, hold promise for advancing our understanding of organizations. This promise is largely unfulfilled because for the most part we have, indeed, conceived of organizations as bodies of thought thought by thinking thinkers (Weick, 1979). What I hope the reader has grasped from our review of the approaches that emanate from such a perspective is how difficult that approach is to operationalize in a way that leads to falsifiable, parsimonious, and readily comprehensible explanations for behavior. It may fit some cognitive biases we share, but it has yet to demonstrate the ability to advance organizational analysis efficiently or effectively. The current state of the field provides evidence of this problem.

AN OVERVIEW

It should be explicitly noted that although we have given one chapter to each of the perspectives and levels of analysis, the existing literature in no way reflects such an even distribution. Rather, the rational perspective on action greatly dominates the other two, with the external constraint perspective probably coming in a close third behind the phenomenological approaches. And, the individual level of analysis has dominated the research on organizations, particularly as that research has been conducted in schools of administration.

For the most part, then, the literature on organizations appears to be fascinated with cognitive processes. Such processes take the form of rational or quasi-rational decision making, as in expectancy theory in which actions are chosen to maximize the likelihood of attaining instrumentally valued outcomes; retrospective rationality as in the various self-perception and commitment approaches, in which sense is inferred and goals constructed to make meaningful behavior that has already occurred; and social construction of reality, in which accounts are produced that come to be shared and condition actors' perceptions of, and actions in, the world. In each of these approaches, there is reliance on unobservable hypothetical processes that occur inside people's heads and that, furthermore, make most sense when discussed and described at the individual level of analysis. Thus, the fascination with thinking and cognition, regardless of the particular perspective on thinking taken, tends to force attention to the individual level of analysis. And it is only a short shift to move from the content of thought, what is being believed and socially constructed, to emphasize how people feel or their attitudes about the world around them.

Consequently, what might begin as a study of organizational behavior comes, in many instances, to look like a study of individual attitudes. The two are not the same thing. Attitudes are not necessarily tightly linked to behavior, or even connected at all (Salancik, 1975). And certainly there is no simple and straightforward mechanism for moving from individual-level behavior to the actions of large aggregates, or, for that matter, vice versa. As Alba (1981: 764) has noted, "There are . . . dangers in viewing large structures as merely aggregates of smaller ones." We certainly have no quarrel with those who think it important to try to understand individual thought processes and the development of affective responses to the environment. However, it should be clear that the connections between such studies and theories and the analysis of organizations, macrostructural entities, requires demonstration, if that is possible, and cannot be assumed. Organizations need to be studied on their own terms as relational, demographic, and physical entities. Whether or how the analysis of individual cognition and affect can help in this analysis remains to be demonstrated. We have seen, in reviewing the various theories in Chapter 2, that this approach faces a large number of conceptual and empirical problems.

This fascination with cognition, and its tendency to focus attention on the individual level of analysis and to slide into a concern with affective responses, can be seen, we have argued, as being consistent with some important social values, such as beliefs in rationality and personal control. More important, such an orientation serves very well to direct organizational inquiry in a fashion that produces a focus on practice that is of use to those who control organizations and that is quite compatible with the power structure of the society. This occurs in the following way. First, almost no attention is focused on the determination of organizational features themselves, and when such attention is given, the argument emerges that such features are the inevitable consequence of technical requirements motivated by efficiency concerns. Thus, for theories of individual-rational choice, the organizational context is taken as a given, and the focus is on the adaptation or blending of individual interests with organizational structural and technical requirements. For theories of organizationally rational choice, the focus is on how requirements for efficiency (with the exception of the Marxist analyses) dictate certain structural outcomes. Thus, structures are seen to be produced by efficiency and technical considerations. In turn, these structures necessitate various strategies for recruiting individuals into them and controlling their behavior once in place. These two themes — of a technical or efficiency-based determinism, and the resultant focus on the process of adapting and controlling workers — were noted by Braverman (1974):

> . . . this conclusion had already been sufficiently encouraged by the tendency of modern social science to accept all that is *real* as *necessary*, all that exists as inevitable, and thus the present mode of production as eternal. In its most complete form, this view appears as a veritable technological determinism: the attributes of modern society are seen as issuing directly from smokestacks, machine tools, and computers. We are, as a result, presented with the theory of a *societas ex machina*, not only a "determinism" but a *despotism* of the machine (1974: 16).

> In this line of reasoning we see the cognition on the part of sociology that modern labor processes are indeed degraded; the sociologist shares this foreknowledge with management, with whom he also shares the conviction that this organization of the labor process is "necessary" and "inevitable." This leaves to sociology the function, which it shares with personnel administration, of assaying not the nature of the work but the degree of adjustment of the workers. Clearly, . . . the problem does not appear with the degradation of work, but only with overt signs of dissatisfaction on the part of the worker. From this point of view, the only important matter, the only thing worth studying, is not work itself but the reaction of the worker to it (1974: 29).

The choices among levels of analysis and perspectives on action are themselves governed by the same type of context effects we would use to analyze any organizational system. Thus, levels of analysis are governed, in part, by disciplinary boundaries but also by the focus taken on the organizational analysis. A focus seeking to be "practical," by which my colleagues seem to mean serving the interests of those managers who hire them and pay

the bills, would almost inevitably tend to focus on individual-level rationality. For rational action is the preferred metaphor or image of managers, and
the individual level is where managerial action and potency is at least
conceivable. One cannot think readily about changing social systems, economic systems, or larger social structures. Thus, to be "practical," or "implementable," or "actionable," the analysis must invariably come down to the
individual or at most the group level, where action is feasible. A focus, on
the other hand, seeking to understand rather than to manage, might con-
centrate on that same level of analysis and take the same perspective on action, but it need not. Particularly if one accepts the view that social actors at
all levels are adaptive, at least within constraints, the analyst is led to look
at the context to which adaptation is occurring for the explanation of behavior. Almost paradoxically, the very adaptation and proaction assumed
by the rational perspective virtually dictates understanding action in terms
of the context, including the history, in which it occurs.

It seems clear that many of the theories of organizations developed and
empirically examined have not paid attention to the fundamental criteria
for evaluating theory outlined in Chapter 1. Strict application of the criteria
of parsimony, logical coherence, falsifiability, clarity, and consistency with
empirical data would shorten considerably the multitude of approaches and
perspectives current in this field. Second, in many instances assumptions
have been confused with facts, assertions confused with empirical proof,
questions confused with answers, and hypotheses confused with the demonstration of empirical reality. Thus, the assumption of cognitive work going
on or the assumption of rational decision making has in many instances
been confused with whether these assumptions have any factual basis. The
assertion of the primacy of efficiency (Williamson, 1981) has been confused
and taken as empirical proof. Assertions are not proof, they are assertions.
The question of what is the most productive level and perspective to take
for analyzing organizations has been confused with an answer—the individual level and the rational or quasi-rational approach. And, hypotheses,
concerning the motivational bases of action, the predictors of organizational structures, and the determinants of the organization of the employment relationship, have often been confused with the demonstration or
empirical examination of these hypotheses.

The literature in this field, as a whole, has tended to move too far from
the data and findings. Or, put another way, there is too much ideology and
assertion and not enough attention to the results (or lack thereof) of the various empirical investigations that have been undertaken. And the literature
has moved too far from the basic properties of organizations. Organizations
are material entities with physical characteristics, characterized by social
relationships and demographic processes. We can take each of these char-

acteristics, in turn, and develop some new approaches for enriching and expanding organizational analysis.

ORGANIZATIONS AS PHYSICAL STRUCTURES

Organizations are, in many instances, physical entities. They have offices, buildings, factories, furniture, and some degree of physical dispersion or concentration. They come to define spatial as well as social distances between individuals and subunits. They vary not only in terms of their organizational design, the formal network of relationships among roles, tasks, and activities, but also in their physical arrangements. As Collins (1981) has noted, the physical characteristics of organizations are among their more enduring, and activities come to be associated with certain places (for example, meetings in specific conference rooms at prescribed times, informal interactions in other locations, and so forth). In spite of this physical reality of organizations, there has been relatively little systematic work on linking the physical aspects of organizations into organization theory more generally (see Becker, 1981, for an attempt to begin such an analysis). Perhaps it is because the physical effects are almost too obvious to be of interest — after all, people do not walk through partitions or shout through walls, so one might say that the effects of partitions and walls are clear. Perhaps it is also because, as Becker (1981) has argued, the work of designing structures has been placed in the hands of architects and interior designers — and thus outside the purview of organizational analysis. Nevertheless, the effects of physical design are both important and pervasive. What limited literature does exist is strongly suggestive that the physical aspects of organizations are critical in affecting numerous aspects of their functioning. Furthermore, these physical characteristics place constraints on and constitute the context in which social interaction occurs. Thus, the analysis of organizations would seem to begin profitably by considering the physical reality of organizations as social entities.

Measures and Dimensions

To incorporate physical design characteristics into organizational analysis, it is first necessary to have some metrics or dimensions for describing the physical characteristics of organizations. There are some of these currently available in the literature, but it is clear that research is needed to expand and refine this list. The dimensions presented are all those that would seem to have some effects on behavior in organizations, but the list is far from exhaustive.

Physical arrangements can be first of all characterized by their size. Are the buildings or offices in the buildings large or small? Many firms have implicit and, on occasion, explicit standards assigning so many square feet of space to different departments or to employees of different ranks. Interestingly, this space assignment is most often hierarchically based, which means that the actual requirements of the work are not taken into account to any great degree; rather, status in the organizational hierarchy is the most important determinant of space. Size is an important dimension of the environment because of the symbolic and expressive effects of large size. As Becker (1981: 9) has noted, "Our physical surroundings serve symbolic and expressive purposes as well as instrumental ones." The competition for building height becomes a competition for status and prominence among organizations, as the competition for office space becomes a competition for status among individuals and subunits within the organization. Thus, business schools covet their own buildings, and if the buildings are large, that is all the better. A colleague in sociology was persuaded from taking an offer at another university in part by the promise to set up a research institute for him, with its own distinct building. The fact of the building provided symbolic assurance as to the importance of the endeavor, particularly on a campus in which space was the most critical and scarce resource. Similar events are commonplace in the medical school at the same university, in which the rewards offered for remaining are frequently in the form of more laboratory space and even, on occasion, separate buildings and facilities. Thus, size is the first dimension to be considered in assessing the physical nature of organizations.

Related to size, but distinct from it, is the quality of the physical space. Is it spartan or richly decorated? If size is assessed in square feet per employee or square feet per division or office, then quality might be assessed as the dollars spent per square foot on decoration and finish. Again, hierarchy is an important determinant of the quality of the space. At a major San Francisco law firm, when the firm moved into new quarters, each employee was given a budget to be spent in decorating his or her office, with furniture, paintings, and the like. The amount of the budget differed between the lawyers and the paraprofessionals; within the ranks of the lawyers, between the partners and the associates; and within the ranks of the partners, by length of service with the firm. Thus, one can tell a great deal about the individual one is visiting just by the characteristics of the decor of the office.

Size and quality are important symbolic aspects of physical space, but they also have effects on work quantity and quality. Another important symbolic dimension of space, which also has implications for performance, is the flexibility of the space. At the building or system level, this reflects whether walls and partitions are readily movable, so that new arrangements can be designed. At the office or subsystem level, this reflects things such as the availability of electrical outlets and walls and furniture configurations that permit rearrangement. Flexibility also is evident in varying degrees in clasroom layouts. Most readers will be familiar with the two extremes — on the one hand, fixed desks and chairs, as found in amphitheater-type classrooms, in which no rearrangement is possible; on the other hand, separate desk-chair assemblies that are not fixed to the floor and that can be rearranged in any configuration without difficulty. Classrooms are also more flexible to the extent they have blackboards on several walls (providing more opportunity for changing what is the "front" of the room) and multiple doors. Flexibility permits the design of space to fit the people and the tasks currently occupying the space. A poignant illustration of lack of flexibility and its consequences comes to mind. I once taught at a university in a classroom in which there were wooden desk-seat assemblies that were linked together by a board running through the legs. One might presume this was done to make it more difficult to steal the chairs and their associated desk tops. In any event, the seats were attached too close for easy comfort if people occupied every chair. One student, finally tiring of having to sit uncomfortably close to his neighbors, brought a saw to class and separated his desk from the others, reintroducing flexibility in seating arrangements in a way not quite anticipated by the designers of the furniture.

A fourth important dimension of physical space is arrangement. Arrangement has several aspects, one of the more important being the distance between people or facilities. Thus, we can ask, How far is it from the personnel department to the controller's office? That question can be answered in terms of the adjacency in vertical space (what is on the same floor) as well as horizontal space, in terms of how many feet it is from one office or one department to another. Within offices, arrangement consists of how the furniture is oriented. Is the desk between the door and the office occupant, for instance, or is the desk against one of the side or back walls, which would produce a different physical orientation between the office occupant and a visitor to the office? In classrooms, one might ask if the furniture was arranged in a circle, or if the desks were all oriented toward the front of the room. Arrangement has both symbolic, evocative effects on persons as well as consequences for the amount and type of social interaction that occurs. One is, other things being equal, more likely to interact with those who are physically close or adjacent.

A fifth, related dimension, is that of privacy. Privacy is in part a function of the amount of space per person and the arrangement of that space. But, it is also a function of the use of walls, partitions, solid versus glass doors, and so forth, as well as the degree of sound- or noise-proofing designed into the construction. Privacy, as with many of the other dimensions, has symbolic as well as substantive importance. The symbolic importance comes from the fact that privacy often indicates hierarchical rank. A private rather than a shared office may be reserved for professionals rather than clerical workers and for those more senior in the chain of command. The substantive impact can occur because of the effects of the presence of others, or the social facilitation effect (Zajonc, 1965), on task performance.

Location is the sixth dimension that is important in understanding the physical dimension of organizations. By location we mean where, in terms of quality of the neighborhood, type of neighborhood, the organization is set, that is, the placement of the organization and its various facilities. For example, Safeway, a retail grocery store chain with annual sales of well over $10 billion, has its corporate headquarters in an older, three- or four-story building located in the produce market and industrial warehouse section of Oakland, California. There are no other corporate headquarters nearby. By contrast, Fidelity Financial, the parent company of Fidelity Savings and Loan, a $2 billion California savings and loan, built a new headquarters building near Kaiser Center in Oakland, a multistory building near Lake Merritt and numerous other high-rises. This was done even as Fidelity incurred substantial financial difficulties. In further contrast, other companies are willing to pay premium prices to have their headquarters in San Francisco. Thus, Shaklee, the food supplement concern, left a headquarters building in Emeryville, on the bay with a view of San Francisco, to build its own building in San Francisco at substantially increased occupancy expense. Similarly, one can inquire about satellite facilities to see where they are placed, in what kind of setting, and near what other buildings. Location also has symbolic and substantive consequences. The substantive consequences include the fact that location may impact the labor market in which the organization recruits, as well as its ease or difficulty of attracting employees.

These six aspects of physical space — size, quality, flexibility, arrangement, privacy, and location — are only a beginning in terms of the types of dimensions one might use to describe the physical aspects of organizations. Moreover, it should be clear that the measurement and dimensionalization of these variables remains as an important task. Nevertheless, they do represent one set of important aspects that can be studied. They have been selected because all have at least some literature associated with them treating their consequences. But, first, it is necessary to understand the determinants of these dimensions of the physical manifestation of organizations.

Some Causes of Particular Physical Dimensions

Interestingly, although there has been some limited research investigating the consequences of some of these physical dimensions of organizations, there is almost no work exploring how and why organizations come to be physically located and structured the way they are. The two sets of factors that have been considered are the requirements for space necessitated by the technology and the work flow, and the effects of power and influence on design.

The effects of technology on design appear most strongly in the layout of machine shops, assembly lines, and process production facilities. But even here, the technical requirements are scarcely as binding as one might think. After all, automobiles can be assembled as they roll down an assembly line, or, as in some Volvo plants, they can be assembled by groups of workers operating in a more circular, as contrasted with linear, spatial arrangement. Moreover, there are numerous instances of design failures from a technical point of view, as in a hospital in Berkeley, California, in which the X-ray facilities were located quite far away from surgery, and this in a newly designed facility. Thus, technical considerations have some effect on the design of organizations in terms of setting space requirements and arrangement, but they are far from the most important factor in most circumstances. As Braverman (1974) has argued, there are typically a variety of technical arrangements that can be used to accomplish some work. Thus, technical determinism is inadequate as a basis for understanding organizational physical structures.

More important are considerations of power, influence, and social control. As Becker (1981) has argued:

> . . . a major function of the physical setting of organizations can be seen as an attempt to visually and physically reduce the ambiguity of social position and power within the organization by marking distinctions among job classifications with clear signs of spatial privilege (size of office, quality of furnishings) and by minimizing distinctions within job classifications by rendering all environmental support identical (1981: 25–26).

One determinant of design is the job classification system of the organization. Presumably, more elaborate and differentiated job hierarchies are matched with more elaborate and differentiated gradations of physical space. Another determinant of design is the attempt to achieve control through the use of physical constraints on behavior. Becker (1981: 25) argued, "Social control, in terms of the maintenance of established patterns of influence among persons occupying different positions in the organizational hierarchy . . . becomes a critical attribute and major form determinant of the environmental-support system." He goes on to note:

> . . . the goal of design becomes one of removing as many options as possible from the workers so that discretionary activities are difficult or impossible. . . . If individual differences cannot be stamped out, and attempts to do so are counterproductive, why do they continue? The answer seems to lie in a view of control as a value in its own right, irrespective of its effect on efficiency. The absence of control is equated with an inherent tendency toward disorder and dissolution in the organization. It is also seen as undermining a necessary social order (1981: 68–69).

One might speculate, then, that the technical deskilling noted by Braverman (1974) and the shift in the form of control hypothesized by R. Edwards (1979) should be manifest not only in terms of changing technical conditions of work and in changing forms of control but also in changing physical arrangements and structures associated with organizations. As a simple example, the shift from personal, hierarchical control to technical and bureaucratic control would clearly permit more geographic dispersion and more physical separation between the supervisors and those being supervised. The shift toward technical control would seem to place greater importance on the design of physical facilities from the point of view of achieving control over behavior. This might be seen in reduced flexibility in aspects of the design of work settings as well as more separation among workers accomplished through noise levels or physical arrangements.

Power and influence are at once symbolically represented by physical arrangements and produced by those very arrangements. Thus, it seems reasonable to argue that "decisions about the nature and use of space and equipment in organizations are political ones (e.g., they concern allocation of scarce resources on the basis of values)" (Becker, 1981: 58). Consequently, it would seem to be reasonable to search for the causes of physical arrangements in those factors of power and influence that have been used to account for the allocation of other resources in organizations as well as to account for the changing patterns of control and the organization of work across organizations.

Some Consequences of Physical Design

There have been more studies of the consequences of physical arrangements, particularly the use of open-space office arrangements, than of the causes of variation in physical designs. However, even in this instance, the research is fairly sparse and much remains to be done. In general, three types of dependent variables have been treated as effects of physical arrangements: the amount of interaction that occurs in a social system, the affective reaction to the job and the organization, and the affective reaction and orientation to those with whom one interacts.

If we consider first the quantity of interaction, the typical supposition underlying the literature has been that more interaction is better than less. Interaction often leads to interpersonal attraction (Newcomb, 1956; Thibaut and Kelley, 1959; Zajonc, 1968). This may be because interaction has the effect of increasing attitudinal similarity (Newcomb, 1956), an important basis for interpersonal liking (Byrne, 1969). Interpersonal attraction is an important component of effective interpersonal communication, which is necessary for coordination, and also provides rewards for staying in the social system and thereby supplies an important source of social system maintenance.

Interaction, in terms of both quantity and pattern, is profoundly affected by variables such as distance and layout of physical space. Festinger, Schacter, and Back (1950), studying friendship patterns in a student housing complex, found that interaction tended to follow a distance relationship, with those who were in closer physical proximity interacting more and being more likely to be friends. They also found that the design of the buildings in terms of features like having only one stairway (forcing more contact on the single stairway) and having doors that opened to a central hallway, so that people were more likely to run into each other, increased interaction. Studying interaction among people in different seating arrangements around tables, Sommer (1959: 257) noted, "the trend in all the data is that people sitting in neighboring chairs . . . will be more likely to interact than people sitting in distant chairs." Although side-by-side seating in fact produced less interaction than some other (corner, for instance) arrangements, in general, the relationship between distance and the amount of interaction was again found. Vertical distance, as in being on separate floors of a building, is much more disruptive to interaction than horizontal distance. Thus, other things being equal, one would expect to observe more interaction in an organization located on fewer, larger floors than one located in a building having more and smaller floors.

The effect of open-space or open-plan offices on the amount of interaction has also been investigated. In many instances, perceptions or attitudes rather than actual data on interactions have been collected. This leads to reports on what people expect to result from such arrangements rather than what does, in fact, occur. Brookes and Kaplan (1972) observed an increase in reported group sociability after a change to an open-plan office, while Ives and Ferdinands (1974) reported that most employees who moved to an open office believed that communication had increased after the move. However, contrary findings have been more frequently reported, particularly when better data are collected. Oldham and Brass (1979) found that reported interaction did not increase after the change to an open office arrangement. Oldham and Brass argued that for important and meaningful interaction to occur, some degree of privacy was necessary. This privacy is lacking in open office arrangements, and thus these arrangements hinder the interpersonal communication process. Clearwater (1980) found that the landscaped, open office was less adequate on several dimensions of communication behavior, including interoffice communication, communication with different divisions, interaction with supervisors, and the development of friendships with coworkers, than conventional office designs. The rhetoric of enhanced communication may mask the real reasons for moving to open office arrangements. Canty (1977) reported that open office arrangements typically had 50 percent of the square footage per employee of conventional arrangements, which results in a substantial savings of money. And, Becker (1981: 59) suggested that "a major reason for moving to the new form of office environment is to create the impression of increased efficiency through the adoption of the latest in office design." Cost reduction and symbolic affirmation of modern management may outweigh the actual effects on interaction of the open office arrangement.

The effect of physical arrangements on interaction has also been investigated in classroom settings. Sommer (1969), summarizing these studies, reported that interest and involvement in the class, as well as performance, can be predicted from where in the lecture hall the individual happens to be sitting. Persons sitting in more distant locations perform less well and interact less often in class. Ironically, even the Western Electric studies, which are so often cited as evidence of the potency of social factors over the physical environment, provide evidence for the power of physical arrangements to shape interaction patterns and the resulting social consequences.

> The men were working in a room of a certain shape, with fixtures such as benches oriented in a certain way. They were working on materials with certain tools. These things formed the physical and technical environment in which the human relationships within the room developed, and they made these relationships more likely to develop in some ways than in others. For instance, the sheer geographical position of the men within the room had something to do with the organization of work and even with the appearance of cliques (Homans, 1950: 80–81).

The effect of physical arrangements on reactions to the job and the organization have also been investigated. Of course, one such effect can be mediated through the extent to which social interaction leads to the development of friendship ties, and we have just seen that this interaction is itself affected by the physical arrangements. There are direct effects as well. Becker (1981) noted:

> As a direct support system for work activities, the physical setting was identified in a national Harris poll of office workers, in 1977, as a major impediment to efficiency. Major problems found were unsuitable office furniture and inadequate office tools, equipment, and materials. Distractions and the lack of privacy were the most negative attributes of offices because these prevented adequate concentration. These kinds of problems influence one's ability to carry out work effectively, as well as acting as "hygienic" factors . . . that influence the total work experience (1981: 55).

Oldham and Brass (1979) reported that the move to the open space office location reduced job satisfaction. Sloan (1972) found that providing individuals with flexibility to arrange and structure their own space led to more positive attitudes toward the job and the work organization. It clearly makes sense that an attractive office or setting that provides both privacy and flexibility for the individual and encourages significant interpersonal interactions will result in more favorable affective responses to work.

Physical arrangements also impact how individuals orient and relate to others. Several studies, for instance, have investigated how physical conditions and the physical setting impact interpersonal perception. Maslow and Mintz (1956) investigated the effects of a beautiful, average, or ugly room on the judgment of energy and well-being in photographs of faces. Subjects rated energy and well-being as higher in the beautiful than in the average or ugly room. In a follow-up study, Mintz (1956) had two examiners test others in a beautiful and an ugly room, alternating rooms between sessions. Mintz found that scores on the rating task were higher in the beautiful room; moreover, in 27 out of 32 instances, the examiner in the ugly room finished before the one working in the attractive room. Sauser, Arauz, and Chambers (1978) had subjects make salary recommendations for simulated candidates in a noisy and a quiet setting. Salaries were significantly higher in the quiet room. Griffitt (1970) found that interpersonal attraction responses were more negative under high and uncomfortable temperature conditions than under conditions of moderate temperature. These studies taken together all indicate that physical arrangements and conditions do impact people's responses to others. Affect is reduced and harsh judgments are increased when the individuals making the judgments are physically uncomfortable because of noise, crowding, temperature, or the quality of the setting.

The effect of office arrangements on affective responses to others has also been investigated. One critical issue in office layout involves the placement of the desk and whether in the interaction one party sits behind the desk — in a position of power — or whether a more collegial, side-by-side arrangement is used. Zweigenhaft (1976) studied faculty office arrangements and the effect of desk location on student interactions and perceptions. He found, in a survey of students, that faculty who placed their desks between themselves and the students were rated less positively on student-faculty interaction than those who used alternative designs (for example, the desk against one wall). Joiner (1971), studying office arrangements in a sample of English organizations, reported that higher-status occupants tended to place the desk between themselves and the door more often and that faculty members as contrasted with businessmen tended to use that kind of arrangement less. D. E. Campbell (1979) found that office furniture arrangement had little effect on student ratings of faculty, although plants and wall posters led to positive ratings and clutter led to negative ratings. Campbell employed an experimental design in which photographs of office arrangements were rated by students. This research avoids confounding variables that might affect the other studies — for instance, that persons who use office arrangements to maintain power relationships are also more distant in other ways as well. Using a similar type of experimental design involving the rating of photographs, Morrow and McElroy (1981) had 100 student subjects rate slides of faculty offices that varied in terms of their tidiness, desk arrangement, and presence of status symbols. Morrow and McElroy (1981: 648) found that desk arrangement did significantly affect subjects' feelings of visitor comfort and visitor welcomeness. They noted that "it is apparent that office occupants do convey nonverbal messages to their visitors through office design" (1981: 650).

Sommer (1969) reported that different seating arrangements are used in situations of casual conversation, competition, or coaction (working together). He has argued that the very setting, because of its association with these different interaction patterns, may help to produce a different type of interaction depending on the seating arrangement. Thus, putting groups across a table from each other may tend to produce more competitive or adversarial interactions, other things being equal, because of the association of this seating arrangement with competitive interactions in the past.

Of course, settings do much to convey authority and leadership. Lecuyer (1976) reported that when groups with leaders were seated at circular tables, the leader was forced to ease group tension arising from the articulation of conflicting points of view. Leaders of groups seated at rectangular tables (at the head) found their ability to direct the group enhanced because of their position. In a second set of studies, Lecuyer found that positions voluntarily chosen at a rectangular table reflected the social relations that had developed previously in discussions around a circular table. Sommer (1969) has also noted the tendency for leaders to assume positions at the head of the table, and, conversely, for those in such physical positions to be treated with more deference and respect, as though they were the leaders. Thus, spatial arrangements affect power and influence perceptions and, as a consequence, achieved influence in group settings.

Steele (1973) has noted how physical settings can assist in organizational development processes. Taking physical space considerations into account can be productive in terms of both affective reaction of employees and productivity. At the Santa Teresa Laboratories of IBM, the particular requirements of computer programmers in terms of working space, furniture design, and conference room and computer terminal access were taken into account in the physical design of the facility. McCue (1978) reported that the results were very positive.

In Figure 8-1, we summarize the preceding discussion by presenting the determinants of design, the design dimensions, and the outcomes of physical design we have briefly summarized. This is far from a complete model or explication of the effects of physical space. Rather, the intent is to show the importance of physical aspects of organizations and to indicate how research on such aspects might be focused.

It is important to note that the emphasis on organizations as physical, material entities is quite consistent with the perspective on understanding behavior by examining its context, a theme that we have tried to develop throughout this book. Becker (1981) has summarized this argument well:

Figure 8-1. PHYSICAL DESIGN AND ORGANIZATIONAL BEHAVIOR

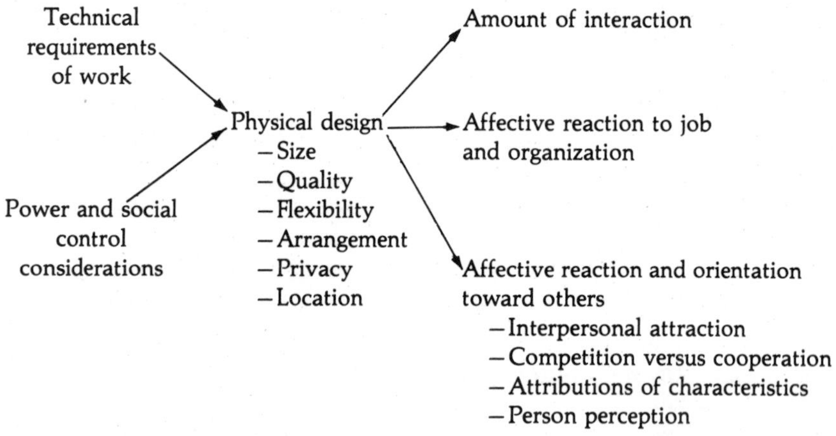

Technical requirements of work

Amount of interaction

Physical design
- Size
- Quality
- Flexibility
- Arrangement
- Privacy
- Location

Power and social control considerations

Affective reaction to job and organization

Affective reaction and orientation toward others
- Interpersonal attraction
- Competition versus cooperation
- Attributions of characteristics
- Person perception

> Ecological psychology was originally developed by Roger Barker (1968) as an alternative to a stimulus-response-oriented model of human behavior. . . . Their most striking conclusion was that the behaviors of children could be predicted more accurately from knowing the situations the children were in than from knowing individual characteristics of the children. This was a major departure from the belief that individuals have stable personality traits that they carry from situation to situation and that, in each situation, guide their behavior in similar ways (1981: 125).

Organizations are, indeed, physical structures that have consequences for interaction. Understanding how such structures emerge and get to look the way they do, as well as understanding their consequences, would seem to be an important place to begin to enrich the analysis of organizations. If settings matter, then we need to pay much more attention to the determinants and consequences of these settings in physical, material terms.

ORGANIZATIONS AS RELATIONAL NETWORKS

In addition to their physical properties, organizations consist of patterned, repeated interactions among social actors (Weick, 1969). Weick defined organizing as the process of developing stable patterns of interaction and noted that such patterned interaction served to remove some of the equivocality from the interaction process. This increased certainty and stability was necessary for coordinated action to occur. To speak of patterned interaction is to speak of a structure of social intercourse. It is possible to represent the patterns of interaction in a network framework. Thus, social structure can be represented "in terms of relationships (ties) between social objects (e.g., groups and people)" (Tichy and Fombrun, 1979: 924). Then, "network analysis deals with the types and patterns of relationships and the causes and consequences of these patterns" (Tichy and Fombrun, 1979: 924). In turn, a social network has been defined as "a specific set of linkages among a defined set of persons, with the additional property that the characteristics of these linkages as a whole may be used to interpret the social behavior of the persons involved" (J. Mitchell, 1969: 2).

Some of the earliest work in organization theory used the network paradigm and social network analysis (Bavelas, 1950; Guetzkow and Simon, 1955; Leavitt, 1951; Mulder, 1960; Roby and Lanzetta, 1956). All of these studies used small experimental groups. Network analysis in field settings imposes, as we will see, much greater data collection and analysis requirements; thus, this initial work using social network concepts has been largely ignored until recently. It was much easier to collect data on a single form in a brief time span on persons' attitudes and perceptions of their work environment than it was to attempt to assess the network of interactions occurring in the organization. This difference in measurement ease may be another case of getting what you pay for — the readily collectible perceptual data at the individual level may be less able to facilitate analysis of organizations as organizations, which includes their relational network properties.

Measurement and Dimensions

Again, before exploring the causes and consequences of network properties, it is necessary to consider how networks in organizations may be measured and dimensionalized. Tichy, Tushman, and Fombrun (1979) have noted that there are four basic data collection procedures for assessing the relational structure of organizations: using positional analysis, using a reputational or attributional method, undertaking a decision analysis, or relying on interactional methods. Positional analysis involves using formal organizational charts and other formal data that indicate the prescribed reporting and communication patterns. This method is good for getting a picture of how things are intended to work, but it obviously fails to provide any information on the actual pattern of interactions and relationships in the organization. The reputational or attributional method involves asking presumably informed sources about network properties, such as who are the most influential or most central actors in some social network (Tichy, Tushman, and Fombrun, 1979: 511). It is analogous to the reputational method as used in community power research (Hunter, 1953). It also economizes on data collection but suffers from the problem of providing shared perceptions of network properties rather than the network properties as they occur.

The decision analysis procedure attempts to overcome the problems of the reputational method by examining actual decisions. The method involves finding out who was actually involved, how much, and at what points, in various parts of numerous decision processes. From this analysis, one can get a picture of the network of interaction around specific decision issues. In the interactional method, "the flow of interactions (or influences) and their feedback is the central focus, and power is taken to be a constraint guiding these flows" (Tichy, Tushman, and Fombrun, 1979: 511). The interactional method relies on reported contacts among participants provided in a summary fashion (as in, How frequently do you have contact with person X?); on the use of diary methods in which actual interactions are reported over some time period, often at randomly selected times of the day; or on observational methods, in which actual patterns of interaction are observed by the researcher. The interactional method produces the most comprehensive data on actual relationships but also involves the most expense in terms of data collection and analysis.

Tichy, Tushman, and Fombrun (1979: 508) have noted that networks can be characterized along several dimensions. First, there is the transactional content of the network. These authors "distinguish four basic flows in the organizational context: (1) exchange of goods; (2) affect and liking (expressive); (3) information and ideas (cognitive); and (4) influence and power" (Tichy and Fombrun, 1979: 927). Second, the authors distinguish the nature of the links themselves in terms of their intensity, reciprocity, multiplexity, and clarity of expectations. Third, various structural measures and characteristics of networks are defined. These fundamental structural properties include: (1) the size of the network; (2) the centrality of the network; (3) the density or connectedness of the structure; (4) the degree of clustering; (5) the degree of network stability over time; (6) reachability, or the average number of links between any two individuals in the network; (7) the openness of the network, defined as the number of links between the network in question and other networks, sometimes expressed as a proportion of such possible links; and (8) characteristics of individual actors in the network defined in terms of their structural position, including the identification of stars, liaisons, bridges, gatekeepers, and isolates. These network dimensions and their definitions are presented in Table 8-1.

The network analysis framework is important because it demonstrates how structure can be described as a distinct concept. Thus, for instance, Mackenzie (1966) developed a measure of network centrality that reflected actual patterns of communication channel use and was sensitive to the differences in network structure. Such measures of structure take individual behavior—interactions and transactions—as their fundamental building blocks but are able to get beyond these individual-level behaviors and properties to describe organizations, or parts of organizations, in terms of their relational characteristics. Relational structures can be analyzed as dependent variables and used as independent variables in their own right. This analytical process is not reification but rather the definition and measurement of organizations in terms of a fundamental property, their interaction structure.

Some Determinants of Network Characteristics

As in the case of physical structures, the research on network characteristics has tended to focus more on effects than on the determinants of network properties. This research emphasis possibly emerges from the tendency to

Table 8.1 DIMENSIONS AND PROPERTIES OF NETWORKS

Property	Definition
A. Transactional content	Type of exchange in network: expression of affect, influence, exchange of information, exchange of resources or goods and services
B. Nature of the links	
1. Intensity	Strength of the relation
2. Reciprocity	Degree to which relation is commonly perceived by all parties to the relation
3. Clarity of expectations	Degree of clearly defined expectations
4. Multiplexity	Degree to which individuals are linked by multiple relations
C. Structural dimensions	
1. Size	Number of people in network
2. Density or connectedness	Number of actual links in network as a proportion of total possible links
3. Clustering	Number of dense regions or groupings in network
4. Centrality	Degree of hierarchy and restriction on communication in network
5. Stability	Degree to which network pattern changes over time
6. Reachability	Average number of links between any two individuals in network
7. Openness	Number of actual external links as a proportion of total possible external links
8. Star	Individual with highest number of nominations
9. Bridge	Individual who is a member of multiple clusters in a network
10. Gatekeeper	A star who also links the network to external networks
11. Isolate	An individual with few (or no) links to others in the network

SOURCE: Adapted from Tichy, Tushman, and Fombrun (1979: 508).

focus on individuals and individual-level outcomes. This leads to an emphasis on the effects of structural or contextual factors, such as relational structures, on individuals. Nevertheless, it is clearly important to understand how and why network structures come to be the way they are.

Network properties have been most often studied as a consequence of the nature of the task or technology confronting the social entity. Faucheux and Mackenzie (1966) investigated the structure of groups facing two types of tasks; one task was a simple one, involving identifying the common symbol, color, word, or number from among those on lists possessed by each of the group members; the second task was more complex, involving performing a network decomposition, again using information shared among the participants. Faucheux and Mackenzie found that groups facing the simple task requiring only information sharing and compilation tended to operate in a centralized, star structure. When confronted with the more complex task requiring more information processing, a more open, all-channel structure tended to emerge. Thus, at the level of individual interaction, the connection between technological routineness and centralization (e.g., Hage and Aiken, 1969) was observed.

Tichy and Fombrun (1979) reexamined Payne and Pheysey's (1973) data on managers in three organizations in England, originally part of the organizations studied by Pugh and his associates (Pugh et al., 1968). Within each of the companies, two networks were assessed: an interaction network and a network of attributed influence. Two of the organizations were mechanistic in structure, and one was more organic. Tichy and Fombrun sought to illustrate how the differences in organizational style and control would manifest themselves in measures of the network properties of the three firms. Tichy (1981) has suggested:

> The more organic a configuration is: (a) the more interaction should occur, (b) the more equal should be the interaction levels of individual participants, (c) the rarer should be interaction isolates, (d) the more interconnected should be each interaction cluster, and (e) the more bridge roles should appear in the interaction network (1981: 238).

Tichy and Fombrun (1979) found general support for these propositions except for the one about bridge roles. Thus, for instance, interaction patterns in the two mechanistic organizations were more differentiated than in the organic firm. In that firm, Brum, there was only one all-encompassing cluster, while there were four and five clusters in the other two firms. These analyses suggest that the type of organizational structure adopted does have effects at the level of network structures among persons within the structure. By extension, this suggests that those conditions associated with mechanistic rather than organic structures, such as the level of technical routineness and environmental certainty, should have effects on the structure of relations within organizations.

Consequences of Network Structures

Several consequences of network structure have been investigated. The earliest network analyses investigated the effects of structure on both the performance of groups and the satisfaction of various group members. Not surprisingly, those who occupied the most central positions in more centralized structures enjoyed the task more and reported more satisfaction with their position. In all-channel, less centralized structures, there was less differentiation in attitudes toward the task and the network. Performance tended to be higher in centralized structures (Leavitt, 1951), but as Faucheux and Mackenzie (1966) later demonstrated, this was because of the particular task chosen. Thus, the indication from these early studies is that performance is affected by the network structure in a way predicted by structural contingency theory: network structures that match the task requirements in terms of sharing of information and expertise tend to be associated with more effective group performance, when that performance is measured either as time to solve the problem or number of errors made.

Pettigrew (1972, 1973), although not using formal network analysis, has illustrated how the structure of communication patterns can affect power in organizations. This result was also observed in the earliest small group experiments, in which the person put in the central role was seen as most powerful and exercised most influence on the group. In Pettigrew's research, power accrued to the individual who served in a gatekeeper or bridging role, and the individual was thereby able to filter information passing between the organization and its board of directors concerning the choice of a new computer. It makes sense that to the extent information and the control over uncertainty provides power (e.g., Hickson et al., 1971) network properties would tend to be associated with the distribution of power and influence within social structures.

Tushman (1977, 1978) has investigated the importance of various individual communication roles in networks, such as boundary spanners and gatekeepers, on the operation of research and development teams. Tushman found that depending on whether the project involved basic research, development, or more technical engineering, the linkage with other project groups and with the cosmopolitan research community outside the laboratory differed in both amount and how it was accomplished. Tushman also found that there was a relationship between the development of appropriate communication roles in research and development groups and the effectiveness of these groups.

At the moment, social network analysis is more of a paradigm and framework than a theory, and more promise than fulfilled potential. Although the difficulties of data collection remain, many of the computational problems have been overcome with new generations of computers and with the availability of sophisticated network analysis programs (e.g., Alba and Gutmann, 1974; Roberts and O'Reilly, 1974). Network concepts link easily with the idea of roles and role analysis. Network measures have been used in the study of larger organizational structures (Mackenzie, 1978). What is required is to move beyond the algorithmic and dimensionalization stage to develop predictors of network dimensions and further analyses of the consequences of these dimensions both for individual-level attributes and for organization-level outcomes.

The importance of the findings of the network studies performed to date and the fundamentally structural nature of network characteristics argues for the additional development of theories and research on organizations using network properties both in hypotheses describing and explaining the development of networks and in relating network characteristics to other organizational properties. Organizations are, in important respects, relational networks and need to be addressed and analyzed as such.

DEMOGRAPHIC PROCESSES IN ORGANIZATIONS

The third compelling empirical reality of organizations is that they are demographic entities characterized by demographic processes.* Demography refers to the composition, in terms of basic attributes such as age, sex, educational level, length of service or residence, race, and so forth, of the social entity under study. Demographic processes are those processes such as recruitment, growth, and turnover that alter the composition of the organization. Demographic factors have been used to account for variables such as the form of city government (Kessel, 1962; Schnore and Alford, 1963), the operation of interest group politics (Cutler, 1977), and attitudes (e.g., Glenn, 1969). Demographic measures can be defined in organizations, and the causes and consequences of these demographic variations can be examined as a way of analyzing organizations.

Such compositional effects may be important. Kanter (1977) has argued that proportions—and, specifically, the proportions of men and women in organizations—can have important effects on group processes and on what happens to those in minority status. In an empirical examination of this idea, Spangler, Gordon, and Pipkin (1978) investigated differences between women students in two law schools, one in which they made up about a third of the class and one in which they comprised only about 20 percent. In the law school in which women were more in the minority, the women

---

*This section draws heavily on Pfeffer (forthcoming).

students were more likely to go into "feminine" or public law specialties, were less likely to press for clarification of points in or outside of class, and did less well academically than in the school in which they constituted about a third of the class. Compositional effects and cohort size are important features of organizations, thus far largely neglected in organizational analysis. Thus, demographic analyses offer some additional analytical levers that may be useful in developing organization theory.

Dimensions and Measurement

Of particular interest is the distribution of the organization's work force by length of employment or tenure in the organization. Length of employment is one of the key characteristics differentiating U.S. from Japanese firms, and also between U.S. firms using bureaucratic as contrasted with socialization and acculturation strategies of control (e.g., Ouchi and Jaeger, 1978). Time in the organization has been found to be related to a number of variables assessed at the individual level, such as commitment evidenced either by willingness to do more or by intentions to quit or actual quitting behavior (Mobley, Horner, and Hollingsworth, 1978; Porter and Steers, 1973) and job satisfaction (Locke, 1976). And, as will be developed in detail below, organizations with different demographic distributions in terms of length of service of their work forces may be different in a number of respects. Thus, for our purposes, we will speak of organizational demography in terms of the length of service distribution of the organization. However, this should not preclude the effort to examine the effects of other components of demography on aspects of organizational behavior subsequently; rather, this choice reflects the singular importance of organizational tenure distributions on a number of organizational processes and outcomes.

It is the distributional properties of the demography of the organization, not merely single descriptive statistics such as the mean or median years of service, that are often critical in understanding demographic effects in organizations. Therefore, it is important to employ methodologies that enable the researcher to capture the properties of the distribution, and such methods are not as yet well developed.

McNeil and Thompson (1971) have proposed the regeneration index, based on the idea of the half-life as borrowed from the physical sciences, as an indicator of demographic properties. These authors defined the regeneration index as the amount of time that elapses before the ratio of new members to old reaches 1:1. The regeneration index is, however, equivalent to the median years of service. At the median, half the organizational population has more than that many years of service and half has fewer — or the ratio of newcomers to old-timers is 1:1. A related measure of an organization's demography is the mean years of service, computed by taking the number of persons at each years of service level multiplied by the number of years served and then dividing the result by the total number of people in the organization. This measure also only provides one piece of information about the organization's demography. Another procedure that begins to incorporate more information about the distribution is to identify significant years of service numbers and then compute the proportion of personnel with more or less than those years of service. For instance, in most academic organizations, tenure decisions are made in the sixth or seventh year of service, so persons with less than seven years of service are, in many instances, very different in terms of status and organizational commitment from those with more than seven.

Two other measures of distributional properties have been suggested by Blau (1977). The index of heterogeneity measures the extent to which there are a number of significant groups or categories in a distribution and the dispersion of the organizational population over these categories. Blau (1977: 78) defined the index of heterogeneity as $(1 - \Sigma\ P_i^2)$ where P_i is the fraction of the organization's membership in each tenure or length or service category, given that demography was the basis being used to categorize members. The other measure of the demographic distribution is the Gini index, which represents an attempt to assess the degree of inequality (in this case, inequality in length of service) in a social system. This index was operationalized by Blau (1977: 67) as follows:

$$G = \frac{2\ \Sigma\ s_i P_i\ (P_{b_i} - P_{a_i})}{2\ \Sigma\ s_i P_i},$$

where s_i is the mean value in a category, P_i is the fraction of the population in that category, and P_{b_i} and P_{a_i} are the fractions of the population with values below and above the category in question, respectively. The Gini index is a reasonable indicator of the inequality in a status distribution.

Pfeffer (1981b) reported data from 36 academic departments on two campuses of a large state university system that indicate the extent to which the various measures provide similar or different information on the demographic distribution. The average years of service was almost perfectly correlated with the regeneration index and was also fairly highly correlated with the proportion of personnel with more than 21 years of service and less than 7 years of service. However, average years of service was not significantly correlated with the Gini index and only moderately correlated with the index of heterogeneity. An inspection of these results indicates that multiple measures are needed to reflect the information in a given demographic distribution fully.

In the discussion that follows, two demographic attributes will be of particular interest: the extent to which the organization is characterized by relatively long and short length of service distributions; and the extent to which there is a more continuous length of service distribution among personnel, or, in contrast, whether there are discontinuities that may be associated with the identification of fairly distinct cohorts.

One other issue is important in considering the measurement and dimensionalization of organizational demography. That is, the concept is distinct from the concept of turnover. Clearly, turnover can affect demographic distributions, but turnover and demography are not the same thing. Turnover measures the rate at which individuals leave the organization. Turnover rates, however, provide no information on who is leaving and, in particular, whether it is those with short, medium, or long years of service who are turning over. The turnover rate provides no information on the distributional properties of organizational membership in terms of tenure. Even though turnover is often concentrated primarily among the newer organizational members, there is enough variation to mean that one concept is not a reasonable proxy for the other. McCain, O'Reilly, and Pfeffer (1981), for instance, in a study of 32 academic departments, observed that full professors were more than twice as likely to resign as associates and almost 25 percent more likely to resign than assistants, even though full professors on average had longer length of service in the organization than the other two groups. And, there was tremendous variation across departments not only in the turnover rate but also where in the length of service distribution resignations tended to occur. Thus, organizational demography is an attribute of organizations that is distinct from the concept of turnover.

Sources of Variation in Organizational Demography

Four factors may help to account for variation in demographic distributions across organizations. These are the rate of growth in employment; the technology employed in the organization; the personnel policies in place, particularly as these relate to factors affecting layoffs, quits, and involuntary discharges; and unionization of the organization's work force, which has important effects on several of these personnel practices.

One critical factor affecting the median length of service in an organization is the growth rate, both of the organization itself and the industry in which it operates. An organization growing at a rate of 20 percent per year cannot have a long-tenured work force even if everyone who joins the organization stays. For an organization growing at this rate, half of the people in the organization will not have worked there longer than four years, even if there is no quitting, retirements, or firing. The rate of growth in an organization's industry can affect its demography regardless of its own growth rate. This is because an expanding labor market tends to be associated with recruitment from other firms within the industry. Hiring from another firm in the same industry is likely to reduce training costs and the risk of hiring persons completely new to the industry. By contrast, an organization in a slowly growing or no-growth industry is likely to have a longer-tenured work force, as there are fewer new job opportunities within the industry for its own employees to move to.

Growth has another effect that would tend to reduce the median years of service in the organization and to produce a more even, in contrast with a skewed, length of service distribution. This effect results from the fact that growth has significant impacts on mobility prospects for persons. Keyfitz (1973), using stable population theory, found that promotion is considerably faster in a growing firm than in a stable one; that growth has a greater effect on promotion than mortality; that a decrease in firm size has a greater proportional impact on promotion than a comparable increase; and that the effect of growth on promotion chances is less near the top of the hierarchy. Stewman and Konda (1982) have shown that some of Keyfitz's results were the consequence of his use of stable population demography as the analytic apparatus, but Stewman and Konda replicated Keyfitz's findings concerning the effects of growth on promotion chances.

It is reasonable to assume that promotion chances are an important incentive for persons in organizations and that promotion as an incentive is particularly important for people newer in their careers. Thus, growth will act to decrease the median years of service distribution by tending to keep the newer workers in the organization because of the greater promotion opportunities. Also, because new workers will not get discouraged by the lack of advancement and leave, there will be a more continuous length of service distribution in the firm. By contrast, in very slowly growing firms, those with long years of service are likely to stay, but those with less investment in the firm will turn over. Thus, the firm facing slow or no growth will have a more senior length of service distribution of its work force and also a more bimodal distribution, with new people coming in and then leaving as soon as their prospects for advancement become better defined.

Technology can affect the demography of organizations in several ways. In organizations confronting rapidly changing technologies, there will be some premium for hiring persons more recently graduated and for obtaining those with the most advanced and up-to-date level of training. This will mean that the organizations will pay well to attract new persons with good technical skills. Such an organization will tend to have a less-senior-years-of-service work force. Furthermore, more senior and possibly technically obsolete persons will be less in demand in other firms in the industry. Thus, not only will there be a tendency for more junior length of service distributions, but there will also be a more bimodal distribution with few people of intermediate service time. Both interindustry recruitment and recruitment from school will provide a large group of persons who have entered the organization recently. And, the reduced mobility prospects for those with longer years of service will tend to keep them in the company.

The third important factor impacting organizational demography is the firm's personnel and employment practices. Organizations differ with respect to the provision of various forms of deferred compensation, with consequent effects on the tendency of people to stay in the firm. Organizations vary in the extent to which they promote from within and engage in other practices to encourage long-term employment (Ouchi and Jaeger, 1978). Organizations differ not only in terms of the structuring of their incentives for long-term employment but also in terms of their punishment policies. Some organizations emphasize positive forms of control, while others, particularly in the past and in some sectors of the economy, emphasize punitive control, maintaining control through threats of firing or other forms of punishment (R. Edwards, 1979). Thus, short-term or long-term employment is encouraged through the structuring of incentive and control systems.

Unionization impacts a number of employment and personnel practices that, in turn, affect the length of service distribution in the relevant organizations. For a number of reasons, unionized organizations are likely to have work forces (or at least that portion covered by collective bargaining) that have longer years of service, on average. The effect of unionization on the evenness of the length of service distribution is a function of the stability in demand and employment for the organization and industry in question. Under conditions of highly variable demand, the tendency for a bimodal length of service distribution to develop will be somewhat greater in a unionized setting, though this effect is also a function of the duration of the upswings and downswings. And, the effects of variability in demand is impacted not only by unionization but by the technological nature of the work and whether the work would tend to favor, in the absence of other constraints, workers with more or fewer years of service. Such technological characteristics may include physical demands as well as the knowledge component of work.

Unions change the basis and structure of compensation, the distribution of compensation between wage and nonwage components, the tendency of workers to quit, and the incidence of layoffs as well as where in the work force such layoffs are likely to fall. Considering first the effects on compensation, the evidence from a number of studies indicates that in the union sector there is less return to individual characteristics such as education, years of experience, socioeconomic origins, and race (Bloch and Kuskin, 1978; Pfeffer and Ross, 1980). Although the effects of all factors are diminished, it has been argued (e.g., Johnson and Youmans, 1971) that the effects on skill and productivity are greater than the effects on seniority. Thus, there is a seniority advantage in the union sector, which would make staying in the organization more attractive to more senior workers and hence conducive to creation of a more senior demographic distribution.

A similar incentive for senior workers to stay in the firm would result from there being a higher nonwage component of total compensation in unionized firms. Freeman and Medoff (1979) have noted that the proportion of wages paid in fringe benefits is higher for organized blue-collar workers than for nonunionized workers. Furthermore, R. Freeman (1978) has noted that the fringes that tend to be increased are pensions, vacations, and life accident and health insurance rather than bonuses. Thus, "the greatest increases in fringes induced by unionism are for deferred compensation, which is generally favored by older, more stable employees" (Freeman and Medoff, 1979: 82).

Unions also tend to reduce quit rates, particularly at the more senior levels, because of the deferred compensation effects, but the effect on quits is visible at every point of the length of service distribution. The effect on quit rates occurs, it has been argued (Freeman and Medoff, 1979), because unions offer the opportunity for "voice" as an option to "exit" (Hirschman, 1970) for workers who are unhappy or dissatisfied with some aspect of their work environment. Freeman and Medoff (1979: 79), summarizing the results of several studies, noted that unionization increased tenure between 15 and 38 percent and decreased quits anywhere from 11 to 107 percent. The largest effects on average tenure and quits were found for those studies that used samples of older workers, but in all instances there was evidence for a significant effect of unionization to decrease quits and increase tenure in organizations.

Finally, unionization affects both the tendency for firms to use layoffs as contrasted with other adjustment mechanisms when product demand falls as well as who in the work force is likely to be laid off. Freeman and Medoff (1979: 84) have noted that in addition to layoffs swings in economic demand can be met by cuts in wage growth, reduced hours, or voluntary attrition. They reported that unionized firms were much more likely than nonunionized firms to use layoffs, in large measure because the more senior workers with more power in the unionized settings prefer the layoff alternative. Thus, in unionized settings, fluctuations in demand are likely to leave a firm with a higher length of service distribution than might otherwise exist, since in the absence of union-based protection for senior workers there will be less incentive for the firm to use layoffs and more incentive to lay off the more senior and more expensive workers, if layoffs do occur. And, to the extent that rehiring is not rapid because of a long downturn in demand, the next time hiring is done, new workers will be attracted to the firm. Over time, the work force will come to resemble a bimodal distribution, with senior workers staying with the firm through the fluctuations in demand and new workers coming in during rising demand and then leaving when demand falls and layoffs result.

In Figure 8-2, the preceding arguments concerning the sources of variation in organizational demography are summarized. Clearly, research is needed to investigate both these and other determinants of variations in demography in organizations.

Some Consequences of Organizational Demography

Demographic effects in organizations are ubiquitous. These effects have been explored in more detail elsewhere (Pfeffer, forthcoming) and are just briefly summarized here. First, demography has an impact on change, adaptation, innovativeness, and performance. Staw (1980a) has noted that jobs may have an inverted U-shaped performance curve where performance is plotted against tenure. The new employee may lack experience and skill needed to do the job but is probably enthusiastic and motivated. The more senior employee may have the experience but may now lack the motivation. Thus, performance is likely to be highest at an intermediate level of tenure,

Figure 8-2.   SOURCES OF VARIATION IN ORGANIZATIONAL DEMOGRAPHY

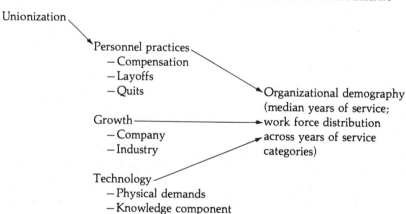

in which there is both skill and experience and still a high level of motivation for doing the work. This inverted U-shaped relationship has been observed in research and development groups, when performance is plotted against average group age. Group age is calculated as the average of the individual tenures in the research group. This finding of a curvilinear effect of group age on research and development group performance was first reported by Wells and Pelz (1966) and subsequently found by Katz (1981, 1982). Katz (1982) argued that increasing group longevity tended to produce increased behavioral stability, selective exposure to information, greater group homogeneity, and increasingly differentiated roles within the group. Thus, Katz argued, both intraproject and project-environment communication might be reduced for projects in which members had worked together longer. Furthermore, the effects of demography would depend on the nature of the project and the amount of communication required. Katz's (1982) study of 50 project groups found support for these predictions.

Organizational demography also has effects on both the rate and type of administrator succession. Succession rates and type (inside or outside) can also have impacts on organizational innovation, adaptation, and performance. For instance, Helmich (1974) provided evidence that firms in which the succession pattern was two insiders in a row underperformed firms that interspersed inside with outside succession. Carlson (1962, 1972) and Helmich and Brown (1972) both presented evidence that outside succession was associated with more organizational change.

The effects of demography on succession appear to be clear. Organizations with longer length of service distributions should tend to experience inside rather than outside succession and should experience succession less frequently. A more senior tenure distribution would provide more inside contenders for vacancies when they occurred. And, a more senior length of service distribution would mean that most of the members had worked together a long time. This long period of close association would tend to develop more stable, predictable, and shared expectations and behaviors. The maintenance of such shared expectations and behaviors would require that an insider, familiar with the culture that had developed in the organization, be chosen to fill any high-level vacancy. The shared and stable expectations would tend to make conflict less likely and less severe. People who are used to working with each other over a long period of time will have developed more consonant interaction patterns through years of association. Therefore, succession frequency would be expected to be less, as the reduced conflict and increased behavioral stability in a system of members with long tenure would make the job more pleasant for the incumbent and would be associated with fewer palace revolts or coups.

Ouchi and Jaeger (1978) have argued that organizations pursue fundamentally different strategies of control, with some firms relying on bureaucratic, explicit control and others relying on the development of shared culture through processes of socialization. It seems clear that the average tenure of organizational members is the most important factor distinguishing between firms of the two types identified by Ouchi and Jaeger (1978). This is because many of the other dimensions — such as nonspecialized career paths, slow evaluation and promotion, implicit evaluation, and a more collective orientation — are dependent on having the individual in the organization for a longer period of time. Making a similar argument, McNeil and Thompson (1971) argued that organizations with a higher proportion of new employees will expend more effort on socialization activities. An alternative argument, and the one adopted here, is that an organization with a larger number of new members will rely more on bureaucratic as contrasted with cultural control.

In addition to effects on the form of control employed, organizational demography can be expected to impact the number of personnel assigned the task of control, or the size of the administrative component. Control effected through formal bureaucratic mechanisms requires more people to design, implement, and update such mechanisms. Reduced familiarity with the organization's goals and values may require more intense hierarchical supervision and also can result in more questions and problems being referred up the hierarchy for resolution. McNeil and Thompson (1971) have made a similar point:

> If our reasoning is correct, a high rate of regeneration places important burdens on the administrative process. . . . And if the administrative load is increased, then we would expect the ratio of administrative activities to other activities to expand (1971: 634).

The length of service of organizational participants can define cohorts: "the aggregate of individuals (within some population definition) who experienced the same event within the same time interval" (Ryder, 1965: 845). The effects of cohorts on organizations can be significant. The cohort concept as an explanation for behavior is predicated partly on an imprinting notion — people are relatively more malleable at some life stages than at others, and experiences during these malleable periods exert a lasting influence on both beliefs and actions. Transitions to new occupations or new organizations often engender uncertainty associated with the assumption of new roles, and this uncertainty makes individuals particularly susceptible to informational social influence and thus to the development of distinctive frames of reference that emerge at that time.

In organizations, cohorts are associated with two important effects:

(1) potential conflict across cohort groups and (2) sponsorship, solidarity, attraction, and mutual choice within cohort groups. Gusfield's (1957) study of the Women's Christian Temperance Union (WCTU) presents a clear case of cohort conflict and its effects on organizations. Two responses to the repeal of Prohibition were in evidence in the WCTU:

> One type of response . . . emphasized the continuance of the tactics and goals of the prohibition period. . . . The second type of response we shall call "public-oriented." Those who advocated this response wished to substitute the primacy of educational and persuasional aims for those of less respectable legal and political measures to restrict the sale of liquor (1957: 323-324).

The "conviction-oriented" belief was held primarily by older members, who were also in control of the organization; the "public-oriented" beliefs were advocated by younger and newer members.

Gusfield detailed how the older members were able to keep control of the organization. As a consequence, many of the younger members left, and the recruitment of new members was made very difficult. The conflict between cohorts led to a decline in membership and a significant weakening in the organization. Gusfield argued that such conflicts across age groups in organizations were common:

> Conflicts of power and policy between age groups are a common feature of many organizational structures. Factories, churches, labor unions, and political parties often distribute power, prestige, and income along an age-grade hierarchy. . . . A depiction of the age-grade problem as one of culture conflict points to the difficulties age differences entail for organizational unity. . . . When two or more generations appear within the same organization, we may . . . anticipate factional conflict (1957: 323).

Gusfield's analysis stressed the effect of differing power positions of different cohorts on the organization's strategy and policies with resultant consequences for the organization's fortunes. McCain, O'Reilly, and Pfeffer (1981) examined not just the relative size of cohorts, but also the extent to which the distribution of personnel followed a fairly smooth or skewed distribution. In a study of 32 academic departments, these authors sought to investigate the extent to which the existence of definable cleavages or discontinuities in the entry of the organization's membership resulted in higher turnover in the department. McCain et al., examined two aspects of organizational demography as these affected turnover — the proportion of members who had entered at about the same time and the gap between the entry of persons into the subunit. For the first factor, the proportion of persons with the same time of entry, these authors noted:

> The larger the proportion of members with the same or approximately similar tenure, the greater the opportunity for similarity of outlook to develop within that group, as well as interpersonal attraction, and the more distinct that cluster will be from others in the unit (1981: 7-8).

The second source of demographic difficulty involves the size of the gaps between cohorts. The argument was made as follows:

> If an organization hires on a regular basis, the processes of integration and succession are likely to proceed in an orderly manner, with new members able to interact with slightly less similar more senior members, and through these persons, to link with even more senior members of the unit. . . . However, when there are large gaps between cohorts . . . it is likely that perceptions, values, and beliefs will differ more, and the opportunity for communication failures to occur will increase. The existence of well-differentiated cohorts increases the possibility of the development of different group norms and expectations and the likelihood for observing intragroup solidarity within the cohorts and intergroup conflict between them (1981: 8-9).

A number of forms of turnover were examined: resignations at the assistant, associate, and full professor ranks; early retirements in the case of full professors; involuntary resignations for assistant professors; and a measure that summarized total turnover for each department in the study. The authors controlled for some other predictors of turnover, such as departmental size, the level of the department's scientific paradigm, and the resource scarcity confronted by the department. The demographic variables were operationalized as follows. Faculty were arrayed by date of initial hire. The number of years between entry dates for adjacent hires was computed, and then a distribution of such gaps was produced for each department. The measure used in the analysis was the number of five-, six-, seven-, and eight-year gaps between entrants in the department that characterized each department. The other demographic measure was the proportion of the department that had entered in a given ten-year period. "This variable indexes both the clustering of the department and, more importantly, the extent to which the older, and presumably more powerful members, dominated the department on a numerical basis" (McCain, O'Reilly, and Pfeffer 1981: 13).

The authors found support for the prediction that departmental demography affected departmental turnover. The demographic distribution in

1974/75 was used to account for turnover during the 1975-79 period. Total faculty resignations were significantly associated with both demographic measures, even when size, the department's budget, and paradigm development level were controlled. Moreover, the formulation was able to account for almost 50 percent of the variation in turnover. The demographic factors tended to be associated with each of the other forms of turnover as well, with the amount of variation explained ranging from 20 to almost 50 percent. Thus, the evidence for the importance of demographic effects, defined in cohort terms, on departmental turnover from this study of university departments parallels in many respects the findings from Gusfield's case study of the WCTU.

Yet another case of intergenerational conflict and its consequences for organizations can be seen in the U.S. coal industry (Connerton, Freeman, and Medoff, 1979). Under the presidency of John L. Lewis, the coal miners' union traded increasing mechanization and a decline in the number of miners employed for increased wages, pensions, and other benefits for those who remained in the mining labor force. However, during the 1960s, the demand for coal ceased to decline and started to increase; in addition, the demand for coal shifted increasingly to a demand generated by public utilities, who tended to be more stable and reliable customers than the more cyclical manufacturing industries such as steel. Thus, in the late 1960s and into the 1970s, the mining labor force expanded; needless to say, this expansion was accomplished through the recruitment of young workers. Thus, Connerton, Freeman, and Medoff (1979: 6) noted, "United Mine Workers data reveal that the average age of active UMWA members had decreased from approximately 49 years in 1964 to 31 years in 1977." As in many unions, the mine workers' union in the late 1960s had an older leadership and an increasingly large and vocal segment of much younger workers who had much less seniority in both their companies and the industry. Differences in opinion over governance, economic issues, and other matters resulted in a union that grew increasingly restive and ungovernable, with consequent increases in labor strife and union-management conflict.

This is the argument made by Connerton and his colleagues (1979), who noted:

> Changes in the demographics of the industry's work force have contributed to the internal problems of the union. Younger, better-educated workers, who are more likely to question authority, have entered the labor market. In contrast to older miners' concerns over wages and pension benefits, younger workers possess a different set of priorities, expressing particular interest in improved working and housing conditions and better treatment on the job. With the older membership retaining a disproportionate voice in

the determination of national union policies, younger workers have shown a tendency to take their demands to management at the mine face and have been critical of the role and operation of the union (1979: 11).

These authors noted (1979: 13-14) that in the period from 1970 to 1976 there were an average of 947 stoppages per year in coal, with 1,005 stoppages per year in years in which the national coal agreement was *not* being negotiated. This contrasted with 184 stoppages per year between 1960 and 1969 and 314 in the period between 1950 and 1959. Connerton et al. (1979: 14) noted, "The recent incidence of strikes far exceeds that of the tumultuous 1943 to 1952 period, when stoppages averaged around 500 annually."

Union leadership, at both the national and local levels, has been increasingly unstable because of the intercohort conflicts. Turnover of officers has increased significantly. And, the differences of opinion between the two groups within the union have made negotiating a national contract with economic provisions acceptable to both sides increasingly difficult, as the rejection of the national contract in recent coal negotiations by the membership attests. Again, changing demography can be seen to have consequent effects on turnover, intercohort conflict, and other aspects of organizational functioning.

Cohort effects arising from organizational demography and resulting in conflict and turnover represent only one part of the story, however. The other cohort effect is the tendency to choose and associate with others from within the same general tenure group. The operations of search committees, referral networks, and patterns of resource allocation would be predicted to follow cohort demarcations to the extent cohort identification was facilitated at the time of entry into the organization. Sponsorship mobility (Turner, 1960) within age-organizational tenure groupings may be a consequence of organizational demography.

Cohorts and demography may also have effects on interorganizational relationships. As noted previously, length of service in an organization is negatively associated with the likelihood of interorganizational mobility. Such movement can not only bring new ideas and change to the organizations, but personnel movement across organizational boundaries is an important mechanism of interorganizational coordination. Investigating clusters of recruiting of business school faculty, Baty, Evan, and Rothermel (1971) argued that when individuals move, they take with them knowledge of the old organization's culture, methods of operation, and beliefs about technology. Thus, ideas diffuse and practices spread in large measure through personnel movement. Pfeffer and Leblebici (1973b) argued that the movement of personnel among business firms was one important way in which stable structures of coordinated activity emerged to manage interfirm competition. They found that patterns of executive recruitment were significantly associated with contextual variables assessing the extent of competition and the possibilities for coordinating such competition through interfirm linkages. Edstrom and Galbraith (1977) have argued that the movement of personnel across countries within a firm can bind the individuals to the company, providing them with a common point of view. In an analogous fashion, separate organizations can be bound together to the extent there is extensive personnel movement among them.

Organizational demography may be related to the extent of interorganizational personnel movement and, consequently, to the development of interorganizational structures or cultures of behavior. And, cohorts crossing organizational boundaries may affect the ease or difficulty of conducting interorganizational exchanges. Following a cohort logic, one would predict that organizations populated by or managed by individuals from similar cohorts will transact more easily than those managed by individuals from different cohorts. In other words, transaction patterns would be expected to follow cohort lines, or the costs of such transactions would presumably be lower and transactions would be easier to accomplish to the extent that the demography of the interacting organizations matched. Thus, one would expect to observe organizations such as banks not only attempting to match the formal rank of the interaction partner, as in creating many vice-presidents so that exchanges can be between people of equal title; but, also, one would expect such organizations to establish transaction partners inside the organization who matched the client company in terms of demographic cohort. To the extent this was not done, one would expect the relationship to proceed less smoothly.

Finally, cohorts and demography have profound effects on mobility and career processes in organizations. Large cohorts, entering at one time, will tend to fill up the hierarchy, leaving fewer opportunities for subsequent entrants. Large cohorts also mean that competition for advancement will be more intense within the cohort, as there will be more competitors for promotional opportunities.

Stewman and Konda (1982) found that persons in fairly small cohorts, assuming equal distributions of talent or ability across cohorts, benefited from having earlier career movement and more rapid advancement throughout their careers. Furthermore, the very fact of early promotion of some people within the cohort had the effect of further reducing competition among the remaining, not yet promoted cohort members. Career mobility prospects are psychologically and motivationally important (e.g., Halaby and Sobel, 1979; Kanter, 1977). Therefore, organizational demography can have effects on the extent of career plateauing problems and on the recruitment and retention of new, young people in the organization.

These effects are illustrated nicely in the case of the railroad industry. Morris (1973: 321) noted that the industry grew about 67 percent in number of employees between 1900 and 1910, but by 1920 the expansion of the rail system had largely stopped, and the 1930s saw increasing competition from trucking. Morris (1973: 330) noted that the average age of persons holding senior positions increased, and promotion opportunities, especially for younger people, were blocked. Many of the more educated and better skilled people left the industry as a consequence. In a process affected importantly by demography, the railroad industry was deprived of managerial talent and entrepreneurial skills.

Drucker (1979) has argued that the same factors that produced a difficult situation in the railroad industry are operating to produce career prob-

Figure 8-3. CONSEQUENCES OF ORGANIZATIONAL DEMOGRAPHY

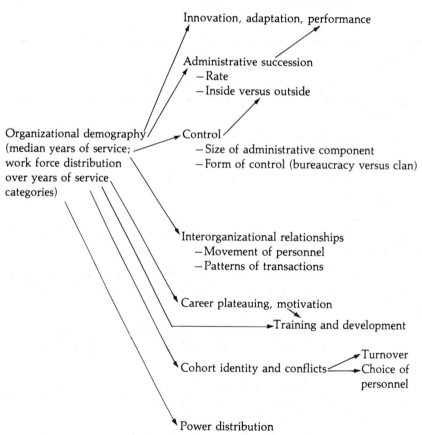

lems throughout the economy. With the early birth cohorts of the baby boom now over 30 years old and filling up many of the middle and upper-middle positions, new entrants to the job market face limited promotional opportunities, in spite of the high starting salaries being offered. Drucker noted:

> It used to take 25 years in a "respectable" bank to become assistant vice president; in the late sixties and early seventies one reached that position in three or four years. Similarly, it used to take 20 years in a major university to reach full professor. In the sixties and early seventies it often took only five or ten. . . . But the same demographics that made for fast progress in earlier years are going to slow down the ones now entering the job market. The path to rapid advancement will be blocked by people who are just as well educated but only a little older — people who will be on the job for another 25 to 35 years (1979: 18).

Demographic processes in organizations, then, are pervasive and have important effects. Career mobility and career plateauing are affected by cohort size and growth patterns, while cohort patterns also can affect conflict, turnover, and even productivity within organizations. Interorganizational relationships, particularly as these are accomplished through movement of personnel among organizations, are potentially affected by the demography of the organizations involved, as are succession patterns, the size of the administrative component, and innovativeness and adaptability. In Figure 8-3, some of the consequences of organizational demography previously discussed are displayed. It seems clear that demographic factors can substantially enrich our analysis and understanding of organizations.

CONCLUSION

A colleague of mine once described the discipline of organizational behavior as "lay preaching." The phrase is particularly apt. The gospel that has been preached has been one of individual, proactive, foresightful choice. It is, indeed, a gospel that resonates nicely with many of the gospels espoused by the nonlay (that is, the actual) preachers and with a variety of social values. As Braverman (1974), among others, has argued, it is also a gospel that works nicely to legitimate and reinforce the way things are, which is to say, the economic and political structure of power in the society. It is "lay preaching" in that most of its practitioners either do not recognize or acknowledge the extent to which values and ideals permeate their theory and empirical research — thus, it is almost unintentional, accidental, and certainly not ordained preaching.

Now, there is certainly nothing wrong with preaching as a vocation or, for that matter, as an avocation. And values, beliefs, and ideas are important elements that bind societies, much as they act to bind organizations, together. The problem, as Gergen (1978) has suggested, comes when we dress lay preaching up in scientific clothes, claiming for our theories and research an objectivity — and, hence, an unassailability — that simply belies the facts. If there is one theme that pervades this review of organization theory it is this: That the persistence and extensiveness of interest in various theories, levels of analysis, or perspectives on action has had much more to do with the social context and values of such theories than their empirical or scientific utility. Research on some topics, and using some perspectives, has been pursued with almost boundless energy, in spite of its meager results, while other perspectives, with at least the potential for offering both parsimonious and more valid analyses of organizations, have been ignored.

Perhaps, as Gergen (1978) has suggested, that is inevitable. But even if, or especially if, organization theory is to be so tightly coupled to ideology, belief, and values, then it is incumbent on research to counterpose perspective with perspective, with one set of values and beliefs with others. That is Gergen's message: in the absence of "scientific objectivity," the null hypothesis is almost useless as a test for the strength of an idea, and the only reasonable test is another competing perspective, theory, or set of values and beliefs. Preferably, such comparisons are even more useful when the theories differ not only in form but also in basic assumptions about action and its foundations and even in their suppositions about the most productive level of analysis. Thus, the range of theories and perspectives reviewed is more than a mapping of the domain of the field; it represents some of the competing perspectives that need to be taken into account as empirical research and theory development proceeds, in whatever cell of the matrix one happens to be working.

Possibly with a greater sensitivity to the range of approaches and perspectives available, greater awareness of the extent to which research and thinking about organizations has been affected by the context in which such theory was developed and the prevailing types and conditions of organizational and management problems, and some reminders about the various criteria by which social science theory is evaluated, we can collectively get back to the task of pruning the garden of unproductive theory and growing some new, more useful varieties.

REFERENCES

Abell, Peter
1975   "Organizations as Technically Constrained Bargaining and Influence Systems." In Peter Abell, Organizations as Bargaining and Influence Systems: 114–128. London: Heinemann.

Abelson, Robert P.
1976   "Script Processing in Attitude Formation and Decision Making." In J.S. Carroll and J. W. Payne (eds.), Cognition and Social Behavior. Hillsdale, NJ: Lawrence Erlbaum.

Adam, E. E., Jr.
1972   "An Analysis of Changes in Performance Quality with Operant Conditioning Procedures." Journal of Applied Psychology, 56: 480–486.

Adam, E. E., Jr.
1974   "Behavior Modification in Quality Control." Academy of Management Journal, 18: 662–678.

Adam, E. E., Jr., and W. E. Scott, Jr.
1971   "The Application of Behavioral Conditioning Procedures to the Problems of Quality Control." Academy of Management Journal, 14: 175–193.

Adams, J. S.
1965   "Inequity in Social Exchange." In L. Berkowitz (ed.), Advances in Social Psychology, Vol. 2: 267–299. New York: Academic Press.

Ajzen, I., and M. Fishbein
1969   "The Prediction of Behavioral Intentions in a Choice Situation." Journal of Experimental Social Psychology, 5: 400–416.

Alba, Richard D.
1981   "Review of Perspectives on Social Network Research Edited by
          Paul W. Holland and Samuel Leinhardt." American Journal of
          Sociology, 87: 762–764.

Alba, Richard, and Myron P. Gutmann
1974   SOCK: A Sociometric Analysis System. New York: Bureau of
          Applied Social Research, Columbia University.

Alchian, Armen A., and Harold Demsetz
1972   "Production, Information Costs, and Economic Organization."
          American Economic Review, 62: 777–795.

Alderfer, Clayton P.
1972   Human Needs in Organizational Settings. New York: Free Press
          of Glencoe.

Alderfer, Clayton P.
1977   "A Critique of Salancik and Pfeffer's Examination of Need-Satis-
          faction Theories." Administrative Science Quarterly, 22: 658–
          669.

Aldrich, Howard E.
1979   Organizations and Environments. Englewood Cliffs, NJ: Pren-
          tice-Hall.

Aldrich, Howard E., and Jeffrey Pfeffer
1976   "Environments of Organizations." In Alex Inkeles, James Cole-
          man, and Neil Smelser (eds.), Annual Review of Sociology, Vol.
          2: 79–105. Palo Alto, CA: Annual Reviews.

Alexander, C. Norman, and Gordon W. Knight
1971   "Situated Identities and Social Influence." Sociometry, 40: 225–
          233.

Alexander, C. Norman, Lynne G. Zucker, and Charles Brody
1970   "Experimental Expectations and Autokinetic Experiences: Con-
          sistency Theories and Judgmental Convergence." Sociometry,
          33: 108–122.

Allen, Michael P.
1974   "The Structure of Interorganizational Elite Cooptation: Inter-
          locking Corporate Directorates." American Sociological Review,
          39: 393–406.

Allen, Robert W., Dan L. Madison, Lyman W. Porter, Patricia A. Renwick, and Bronston T. Mayes
1979   "Organizational Politics: Tactics and Characteristics of Its Actors." California Management Review, 22: 77–83.

Allen, Stephen A.
1978   "Organizational Choices and General Management Influence Networks in Divisionalized Companies." Academy of Management Journal, 21: 341–365.

Allison, Graham T.
1971   Essence of Decision. Boston: Little, Brown.

Allport, Floyd H.
1962   "A Structuronomic Conception of Behavior: Individual and Collective." Journal of Abnormal and Social Psychology, 64: 3–30.

Amber, G. H., and P. S. Amber
1962   Anatomy of Automation. Englewood Cliffs, NJ: Prentice-Hall.

Anderson, John C., and Charles A. O'Reilly
In   "Effects of an Organizational Control System on Managerial
press   Satisfaction and Performance." Human Relations, (in press).

Anderson, Theodore R., and Seymour Warkov
1961   "Organizational Size and Functional Complexity: A Study of Differentiation in Hospitals." American Sociological Review, 26: 23–28.

Annett, J.
1969   Feedback and Human Behavior: The Effects of Knowledge of Results, Incentives and Reinforcement on Learning and Performance. Baltimore: Penguin Books.

Argyris, Chris
1957   Personality and Organization. New York: Harper & Row.

Argyris, Chris
1968   "Some Unintended Consequences of Rigorous Research." Psychological Bulletin, 70: 185–197.

Argyris, Chris
1972   The Applicability of Organizational Sociology. London: Cambridge University Press.

Armour, Henry O., and David J. Teece
1978   "Organizational Structure and Economic Performance: A Test of the Multidivisional Hypothesis." Bell Journal of Economics, 9: 106–122.

Arnold, Hugh J.
1981   "A Test of the Validity of the Multiplicative Hypothesis of Expectancy-Valence Theories of Work Motivation." Academy of Management Journal, 24: 128–141.

Aronson, Elliot
1972   The Social Animal. San Francisco: W. H. Freeman.

Arvey, R. D., H. D. Dewhirst, and J. C. Boling
1976   "Relationships between Goal Clarity, Participation in Goal Setting and Personality Characteristics on Job Satisfaction in a Scientific Organization." Journal of Applied Psychology, 61: 103–105.

"At Emery Air Freight: Positive Reinforcement Boosts Performance."
1973   Organizational Dynamics, 1 (No. 3): 41–50.

Axelrod, Robert
1976   Structure of Decision: The Cognitive Maps of Political Elites. Princeton, NJ: Princeton University Press.

Bacharach, Samuel B., and Edward J. Lawler
1980   Power and Politics in Organizations. San Francisco: Jossey-Bass.

Bagozzi, Richard P.
1980   Causal Models. New York: Wiley.

Baker, S. H.
1969   "Executive Incomes, Profits, and Revenues: A Comment on Functional Specification." Southern Economic Journal, 25: 379–383.

Baldridge, J. Victor
1971   Power and Conflict in the University. New York: Wiley.

Bandura, Albert
1969   Principles of Behavior Modification. New York: Holt, Rinehart, and Winston.

Bandura, Albert
1977   Social Learning Theory. Englewood Cliffs, NJ: Prentice-Hall.

Baritz, Joseph H.
1960 The Servants of Power. Middletown, CT: Wesleyan University Press.

Barker, Roger
1968 Ecological Psychology. Palo Alto, CA: Stanford University Press.

Barnard, Chester I.
1938 Functions of the Executive. Cambridge, MA: Harvard University Press.

Barnard, Chester I.
1948 Organization and Management. Cambridge, MA: Harvard University Press.

Baron, James N., and William T. Bielby
1980 "Bringing the Firm Back In: Stratification, Segmentation, and the Organization of Work." American Sociological Review, 45: 737–765.

Baty, Gordon, William Evan, and Terry Rothermel
1971 "Personnel Flows as Interorganizational Relations." Administrative Science Quarterly, 16: 430–443.

Baumol, William
1959 Business Behavior, Value and Growth. New York: Macmillan.

Bavelas, Alex
1950 "Communication Patterns in Task-Oriented Groups." Journal of Acoustical Society of America, 22: 725–730.

Beck, E. M., Patrick M. Horan, and Charles M. Tolbert
1978 "Stratification in a Dual Economy: A Sectoral Model of Earnings Determination." American Sociological Review, 43: 704–720.

Becker, Franklin D.
1981 Workspace: Creating Environments in Organizations. New York: Praeger.

Becker, Howard S., and Blanche Geer
1958 "The Fate of Idealism in Medical School." American Sociological Review, 23: 50–56.

Bedeian, Arthur G., and Achilles A. Armenakis
1981 "A Path-Analytic Study of the Consequences of Role Conflict and Ambiguity." Academy of Management Journal, 24: 417–424.

Bem, Daryl J.
1967   "Self-Perception: The Dependent Variable of Human Performance." Organizational Behavior and Human Performance, 2: 105–121.

Bem, Daryl J.
1970   Beliefs, Attitudes, and Human Affairs. Belmont, CA: Brooks/Cole.

Bem, Daryl J.
1972   "Self-Perception Theory." In Leonard Berkowitz (ed.), Advances in Experimental Social Psychology, Vol. 6: 1–62. New York: Academic Press.

Bem, Daryl J., and A. Allen
1974   "On Predicting Some of the People Some of the Time: The Search for Cross-Situational Consistencies in Behavior." Psychological Review, 81: 506–520.

Bem, Daryl J., and D. C. Funder
1978   "Predicting More of the People More of the Time: Assessing the Personality of Situations." Psychological Review, 85: 485–501.

Berger, Chris J., L. L. Cummings, and Herbert G. Heneman
1975   "Expectancy Theory and Operant Conditioning Predictions of Performance under Variable Ratio and Continuous Schedules of Reinforcement." Organizational Behavior and Human Performance, 14: 227–243.

Berger, Peter L., and Thomas Luckmann
1966   The Social Construction of Reality. New York: Doubleday.

Berle, Adolph, Jr., and Gardiner C. Means
1932   The Modern Corporation and Private Property. New York: Macmillan.

Berlew, David E., and Douglas T. Hall
1966   "The Socialization of Managers: Effects of Expectations on Performance." Administrative Science Quarterly, 11: 207–223.

Bernstein, Richard J.
1976   The Restructuring of Social and Political Theory. New York: Harcourt, Brace, Jovanovich.

Bibb, Robert, and William H. Form
1977   "The Effects of Industrial, Occupational, and Sex Stratification on Wages in Blue-Collar Markets." Social Forces, 55: 974–996.

Bidwell, C. E., and J. D. Kasarda
1975   "School District Organization and Student Achievement."
          American Sociological Review, 40: 55–70.
Bidwell, Charles E., and John D. Kasarda
1976   "Reply to Hannan, Freeman and Meyer, and Alexander and
          Griffin." American Sociological Review, 41: 152–160.

Blai, B., Jr.
1962   "An Occupational Study of Job Satisfaction and Need Satisfac-
          tion." Journal of Experimental Education, 32: 383–388.

Blalock, Hubert M., Jr.
1967   "Status Inconsistency, Social Mobility, Status Integration and
          Structural Effects." American Sociological Review, 32: 790–801.

Blau, Peter M.
1955   The Dynamics of Bureaucracy. Chicago: University of Chicago
          Press.

Blau, Peter M.
1960   "Structural Effects." American Sociological Review, 25: 178–193.

Blau, Peter M.
1964   Exchange and Power in Social Life. New York: Wiley.

Blau, Peter M.
1970   "A Formal Theory of Differentiation in Organizations." Ameri-
          can Sociological Review, 35: 201–218.

Blau, Peter M.
1973   The Organization of Academic Work. New York: Wiley.

Blau, Peter M.
1977   Inequality and Heterogeneity. New York: Free Press.

Blau, Peter M., and Marshall W. Meyer
1971   Bureaucracy in Modern Society. New York: Random House.

Blau, Peter M., and Richard Schoenherr
1971   The Structure of Organizations. New York: Basic Books.

Blau, Peter M., and W. Richard Scott
1962   Formal Organizations. San Francisco: Chandler.

Blauner, Robert
1964   Alienation and Freedom: The Factory Worker and His Family.
          Chicago: University of Chicago Press.

Bloch, Farrell E., and Mark S. Kuskin
1978   "Wage Determination in the Union and Nonunion Sectors." In-
          dustrial and Labor Relations Review, 31: 183–192.

Blumenfeld, W. E., and T. E. Leidy
1969   "Effectiveness of Goal Setting as a Management Device: Re-
          search Note." Psychological Reports, 24: 24.

Blumer, Herbert
1962   "Society as Social Interaction." In Arnold M. Rose (ed.), Human
          Behavior and Social Processes: An Interactionist Approach:
          179–192. Boston: Houghton Mifflin.

Bonacich, Edna
1972   "A Theory of Ethnic Antagonism: The Split Labor Market."
          American Sociological Review, 37: 547–559.

Bonacich, Edna
1976   "Advanced Capitalism and Black/White Race Relations in the
          United States: A Split Labor Market Interpretation." American
          Sociological Review, 41: 34–51.

Booker, Gene
1969   "Behavioral Aspects of Disciplinary Action." Personnel Journal,
          48: 525–529.

Bougon, Michel, Karl Weick, and Din Binkhorst
1977   "Cognition in Organizations: An Analysis of the Utrecht Jazz
          Orchestra." Administrative Science Quarterly, 22: 606–631.

Bowers, Kenneth S.
1973   "Situationism in Psychology: An Analysis and a Critique." Psy-
          chological Review, 80: 307–336.

Braverman, Harry
1974   Labor and Monopoly Capital: The Degradation of Work in the
          Twentieth Century. New York: Monthly Review.

Brayfield, A. H., and W. H. Crockett
1955   "Employee Attitudes and Employee Performance." Psychological
          Bulletin, 52: 396–424.

Brehm, J. W., and A. E. Cohen
1962   Explorations in Cognitive Dissonance. New York: John Wiley.

Brief, Arthur P., and Ramon J. Aldag
1975   "Employee Reactions to Job Characteristics: A Constructive
          Replication." Journal of Applied Psychology, 60: 182–186.

Britt, David W., and Omer Galle
1974   "Structural Antecedents of the Shape of Strikes: A Comparative Analysis." American Sociological Review, 39: 642–651.

Brittain, Jack W., and John H. Freeman
1980   "Organizational Proliferation and Density-Dependent Selection." In John Kimberly and Robert Miles (eds.), Organizational Life Cycles: 291–338. San Francisco: Jossey-Bass.

Brookes, M. J., and A. Kaplan
1972   "The Office Environment: Space Planning and Effective Behavior." Human Factors, 14: 373–391.

Brown, Richard Harvey
1978   "Bureaucracy as Praxis: Toward a Political Phenomenology of Formal Organizations." Administrative Science Quarterly, 23: 365–382.

Brown, R., and E. H. Lenneberg
1954   "A Study in Language and Cognition." Journal of Abnormal and Social Psychology, 59: 454–462.

Bucher, Rue
1970   "Social Process and Power in a Medical School." In Mayer N. Zald (ed.), Power in Organizations: 3–48. Nashville, TN: Vanderbilt University Press.

Burns, Tom, and G. M. Stalker
1961   The Management of Innovation. London: Tavistock.

Burrell, Gibson, and Gareth Morgan
1979   Sociological Paradigms and Organisational Analysis. London, England: Heinemann.

Burt, Ronald S.
1977   "Positions in Multiple Network Systems, Part One: A General Conception of Stratification and Prestige in a System of Actors Cast as a Social Topology." Social Forces, 56: 106–131.

Burt, Ronald S.
1980   "Autonomy in a Social Topology." American Journal of Sociology, 85: 892–925.

Burt, Ronald S., Kenneth P. Christman, and Harold C. Kilburn, Jr.
1980   "Testing a Structural Theory of Corporate Cooptation: Interorganizational Directorate Ties as a Strategy for Avoiding Market Constraints on Profits." American Sociological Review, 45: 821–841.

Byrne, D.
1969   "Attitudes and Attraction." In Leonard Berkowitz (ed.), Advances in Experimental Social Psychology, Vol. 4: 35–89. New York: Academic Press.

Calder, Bobby J.
1977   "An Attribution Theory of Leadership." In Barry M. Staw and Gerald R. Salancik (eds.), New Directions in Organizational Behavior: 179–204. Chicago: St. Clair Press.

Calder, Bobby J., and Michael Ross
1973   Attitudes and Behavior. Morristown, NJ: General Learning Press.

Calder, Bobby J., and Paul H. Schurr
1981   "Attitudinal Processes in Organizations." In L. L. Cummings and Barry M. Staw (eds.), Research in Organizational Behavior, Vol. 3: 283–302. Greenwich, CT: JAI Press.

Caldwell, David F., Charles A. O'Reilly, and James H. Morris
1981   "Intrinsic Motivation and Responses to an Organizational Reward: A Field Test of the Sufficiency of Justification Hypothesis." Unpublished ms., School of Business, University of Santa Clara.

Campbell, Angus, Philip E. Converse, and Willard L. Rodgers
1976   The Quality of American Life: Perceptions, Evaluations, and Satisfactions. New York: Russell Sage Foundation.

Campbell, David E.
1979   "Interior Office Design and Visitor Response." Journal of Applied Psychology, 64: 648–653.

Campbell, Donald
1969   "Variation and Selective Retention in Sociocultural Evolution." General Systems, 16: 69–85.

Campbell, John P., and Marvin D. Dunnette
1968   "Effectiveness of T-Group Experiences in Managerial Training and Development." Psychological Bulletin, 70: 73–104.

Canty, D.
1977   "Evaluation of an Open Office Landscape: Weyerhaeuser Co." American Institute of Architects Journal, 66: 40–45.

Caplan, R.
1971   Organizational Stress and Individual Strain: A Social-Psycho-
        logical Study of Risk Factors in Coronary Heart Disease among
        Administrators, Engineers, and Scientists. Unpublished Ph.D.
        dissertation. Ann Arbor: University of Michigan.

Carlsmith, J. Merrill, Barry E. Collins, and Robert L. Helmreich
1966   "Studies in Forced Compliance: I. The Effect of Pressure for
        Compliance on Attitude Change Produced by Face-to-Face Role
        Playing and Anonymous Essay Writing." Journal of Personality
        and Social Psychology, 4: 1–13.

Carlson, Richard O.
1962   Executive Succession and Organizational Change. Danville, IL:
        Interstate Printers and Publishers.

Carlson, Richard O.
1972   School Superintendents: Career and Performance. Columbus,
        OH: Charles E. Merrill.

Carroll, S. J., and H. L. Tosi
1970   "Goal Characteristics and Personality Factors in a Management
        by Objectives Program." Administrative Science Quarterly, 15:
        295–305.

Cartwright, Dorwin
1979   "Contemporary Social Psychology in Historical Perspective."
        Social Psychology Quarterly, 42: 82–93.

Chaffee, Ellen E.
1980   Decision Models in University Budgeting. Unpublished Ph.D.
        dissertation. Palo Alto, CA: Stanford University.

Chandler, Alfred D., Jr.
1966   Strategy and Structure. New York: Doubleday, Anchor Books
        Edition.

Child, John
1972a   "Organizational Structure, Environment and Performance: The
        Role of Strategic Choice." Sociology, 6: 2–22.

Child, John
1972b   "Organization Structure and Strategies of Control: A Replica-
        tion of the Aston Study." Administrative Science Quarterly, 17:
        163–177.

Child, John
1973a   "Predicting and Understanding Organization Structure." Administrative Science Quarterly, 18: 168–185.

Child, John
1973b   "Strategies of Control and Organizational Behavior." Administrative Science Quarterly, 18: 1–17.

Cicourel, Aaron V.
1964   Method and Measurement in Sociology. New York: Free Press.

Cicourel, Aaron V.
1974   Cognitive Sociology. New York: Free Press.

Ciscel, David H.
1974   "Determinants of Executive Compensation." Southern Economic Journal, 40: 613–617.

Clark, Burton R.
1972   "The Organizational Saga in Higher Education." Administrative Science Quarterly, 17: 178–184.

Clarkson, G. P. E.
1962   Portfolio Selection: A Simulation of Trust Investment. Englewood Cliffs, NJ: Prentice-Hall.

Clearwater, Y.
1980   Comparison of Effects of Open and Closed Office Designs on Job Satisfaction and Productivity. Unpublished Ph.D. dissertation. Davis: University of California-Davis.

Clegg, Stewart
1975   Power, Rule and Domination. London: Routledge and Kegan Paul.

Clegg, Stewart, and David Dunkerley
1980   Organization, Class and Control. London: Routledge and Kegan Paul.

Cohen, Kalman J., and Richard M. Cyert
1961   "Computer Models in Dynamic Economics." Quarterly Journal of Economics, 75: 112–127.

Cohen, Kalman J., and Richard M. Cyert
1965   "Simulation of Organizational Behavior." In James G. March (ed.), Handbook of Organizations: 305–354. Chicago: Rand McNally.

Cohen, Michael D., and James G. March
1974   Leadership and Ambiguity: The American College President. New York: McGraw-Hill.

Cohen, Michael D., James G. March, and Johan P. Olsen
1972   "A Garbage Can Model of Organizational Choice." Administrative Science Quarterly, 17: 1–25.

Collins, Randall
1979   The Credential Society. New York: Academic Press.

Collins, Randall
1981   "On the Microfoundations of Macrosociology." American Journal of Sociology, 86: 984–1014.

Comer, R., and J. D. Laird
1975   "Choosing to Suffer as a Consequence of Expecting to Suffer: Why Do People Do It?" Journal of Personality and Social Psychology, 32: 92–101.

Comstock, Donald E., and W. Richard Scott
1977   "Technology and the Structure of Subunits: Distinguishing Individual and Workgroup Effects." Administrative Science Quarterly, 22: 177–202.

Condry, J.
1977   "Enemies of Exploration: Self-Initiated versus Other-Initiated Learning." Journal of Personality and Social Psychology, 35: 459–477.

Connerton, M., R. B. Freeman, and J. L. Medoff
1979   "Productivity and Industrial Relations: The Case of U.S. Bituminous Coal." Unpublished ms., Harvard University.

Connerton, Paul (ed.)
1976   Critical Sociology: Selected Readings. New York: Penguin.

Copeland, R. E., R. E. Brown, and R. V. Hall
1974   "The Effects of Principal-Implemented Techniques on the Behavior of Pupils." Journal of Applied Behavioral Analysis, 7: 77–86.

Crecine, J. P.
1967   "A Computer Simulation Model of Municipal Budgeting." Management Science, 13: 786–815.

Crozier, Michel
1964   The Bureaucratic Phenomenon. Chicago: University of Chicago Press.

Cummings, Larry L.
1981   "Organizational Behavior in the 1980s." Decision Sciences, 12: 365–377.

Cummings, Larry L.
1982   "Organizational Behavior." Annual Review of Psychology, 33: 541–579.

Cutler, Neal E.
1977   "Demographic, Social-Psychological, and Political Factors in the Politics of Aging: A Foundation for Research in 'Political Gerontology.'" American Political Science Review, 71: 1011–1025.

Cyert, Richard M., and James G. March
1963   A Behavioral Theory of the Firm. Englewood Cliffs, NJ: Prentice-Hall.

Dachler, H. P., and W. H. Mobley
1973   "Construct Validation of an Instrumentality-Expectancy-Task-Goal Model of Work Motivation." Journal of Applied Psychology, 58: 397–418.

Daft, Richard L.
1980   "The Evolution of Organization Analysis in ASQ: 1959–1979." Administrative Science Quarterly, 25: 623–636.

Daft, Richard L., and John C. Wiginton
1979   "Language and Organization." Academy of Management Review, 4: 179–191.

Dahl, Robert A.
1957   "The Concept of Power." Behavioral Science, 2: 201–215.

Dahrendorf, Ralf
1959   Class and Class Conflict in Industrial Society. Stanford, CA: Stanford University Press.

Daniel, W. W.
1971   "Productivity Bargaining and Orientation to Work—A Rejoinder to Goldthorpe." Journal of Management Studies, 8: 329–335.

Davis, James A., Joe L. Spaeth, and Carolyn Huson
1961   "A Technique for Analyzing the Effects of Group Composition."
        American Sociological Review, 26: 215–225.

Davis, James H.
1969   Group Performance. Reading, MA: Addison-Wesley.

Davis, Otto A., M. A. H. Dempster, and Aaron Wildavsky
1966   "A Theory of the Budgeting Process." American Political Science
        Review, 60: 529–547.

Davis, Tim R. V., and Fred Luthans
1980   "A Social Learning Approach to Organizational Behavior."
        Academy of Management Review, 5: 281–290.

Deci, Edward L.
1971   "Effects of Externally Mediated Rewards on Intrinsic Motiva-
        tion." Journal of Personality and Social Psychology, 18: 105–
        115.

Deci, Edward L.
1972   "The Effects of Contingent and Noncontingent Rewards and
        Controls on Intrinsic Motivation." Organizational Behavior and
        Human Performance, 8: 217–229.

Delbecq, Andre L., Andrew H. Van de Ven, and David H. Gustafson
1975   Group Techniques for Program Planning. Glenview, IL: Scott,
        Foresman.

Deslauriers, Brian C., and Peter B. Everett
1977   "Effects of Intermittent and Continuous Token Reinforcement
        on Bus Ridership." Journal of Applied Psychology, 62: 369–375.

Deutsch, M., and H. Gerard
1955   "A Study of Normative and Informational Social Influences on
        Individual Judgment." Journal of Abnormal and Social Psychol-
        ogy, 51: 629–636.

Domhoff, G. William
1974   The Bohemian Grove and Other Retreats: A Study in Ruling
        Class Cohesiveness. New York: Harper & Row.

Dornbusch, Sanford M.
1955   "The Military Academy as an Assimilating Institution." Social
        Forces, 33: 316–321.

Dornbusch, Sanford M., and W. Richard Scott
1975   Evaluation and the Exercise of Authority: A Theory of Control
        Applied to Diverse Organizations. San Francisco: Jossey-Bass.

Dowling, John, and Jeffrey Pfeffer
1975   "Organizational Legitimacy: Social Values and Organizational
        Behavior." Pacific Sociological Review, 18: 122–136.

Downey, H. Kirk, Don Hellriegel, and John W. Slocum, Jr.
1975   "Environmental Uncertainty: The Construct and Its Applica-
        tion." Administrative Science Quarterly, 20: 613–629.

Downey, H. K., J. E. Sheridan, and J. W. Slocum, Jr.
1975   "Analysis of Relationships among Leader Behavior, Subordinate
        Job Performance and Satisfaction: A Path-Goal Approach."
        Academy of Management Journal, 18: 253–262.

Downey, H. Kirk, and John W. Slocum, Jr.
1975   "Uncertainty: Measures, Research, and Sources of Variation."
        Academy of Management Journal, 18: 562–578.

Drucker, Peter F.
1979   "Baby-Boom Problems." Wall Street Journal, February 5, 1979:
        18.

Dulany, D. E.
1968   "Awareness, Rules, and Propositional Control: A Confrontation
        with S-R Behavior Theory." In D. Horton and T. Dixon (eds.),
        Verbal Behavior and General Behavior Theory. Englewood
        Cliffs, NJ: Prentice-Hall.

Dunbar, Roger L. M., and John M. Dutton
1981   "Cognitive Control Processes and a Faculty Change Effort." Un-
        published ms., Graduate School of Business Administration,
        New York University.

Duncan, Robert B.
1972   "Characteristics of Organizational Environments and Perceived
        Environmental Uncertainty." Administrative Science Quarterly,
        17: 313–327.

Dunn, Marvin G.
1980   "The Family Office: Coordinating Mechanism of the Ruling
        Class." In G. William Domhoff (ed.), Power Structure Research:
        17–45. Beverly Hills, CA: Sage.

Dyer, L., and D. F. Parker
1975   "Classifying Outcomes in Work Motivation Research: An Exam-
          ination of the Intrinsic-Extrinsic Dichotomy." Journal of Applied
          Psychology, 60: 455–458.

Dyer, William G.
1977   Team Building: Issues and Alternatives. Reading, MA: Addison-
          Wesley.

Easterlin, Richard A.
1980   Birth and Fortune: The Impact of Numbers on Personal Welfare.
          New York: Basic Books.

Edelman, Murray
1964   The Symbolic Uses of Politics. Urbana: University of Illinois
          Press.

Edstrom, Anders, and Jay R. Galbraith
1977   "Transfer of Managers as a Coordination and Control Strategy
          in Multinational Organizations." Administrative Science Quar-
          terly, 22: 248–263.

Edwards, Richard C.
1975   "The Social Relations of Production in the Firm and Labor Mar-
          ket Structure." In R. C. Edwards, M. Reich, and D. M. Gordon
          (eds.), Labor Market Segmentation: 3–26. Lexington, MA:
          D. C. Heath.

Edwards, Richard C.
1976   "Worker Traits and Organizational Incentives: What Makes a
          'Good' Worker?" Journal of Human Resources, 11: 51–68.

Edwards, Richard C.
1979   Contested Terrain: The Transformation of the Workplace in the
          Twentieth Century. New York: Basic Books.

Edwards, Ward
1961   "Behavioral Decision Theory." Annual Review of Psychology,
          12: 473–498.

Edwards, Ward
1962   "Subjective Probabilities Inferred from Decisions." Psychological
          Review, 69: 109–135.

Emerson, Richard M.
1962   "Power-Dependence Relations." American Sociological Review,
          27: 31–41.

Epstein, Seymour
1979   "The Stability of Behavior: I. On Predicting Most of the People
        Much of the Time." Journal of Personality and Social Psychol-
        ogy, 37: 1097–1126.

Erez, M.
1977   "Feedback: A Necessary Condition for the Goal Setting-Perfor-
        mance Relationship." Journal of Applied Psychology, 62: 624–
        627.

Evan, William
1966   "The Organization-Set: Toward a Theory of Interorganizational
        Relations." In James D. Thompson (ed.), Approaches to Organi-
        zational Design: 175–190. Pittsburgh: University of Pittsburgh
        Press.

Evans, Martin G.
1970   "The Effects of Supervisory Behavior on the Path-Goal Relation-
        ship." Organizational Behavior and Human Performance, 5:
        277–298.

Faber, Homo
1973   "Introduction." In Special Task Force to the Secretary of Health,
        Education, and Welfare (eds.), Work in America: 1–28. Cam-
        bridge, MA: MIT Press.

Faucheux, Claude, and Kenneth D. Mackenzie
1966   "Task Dependency of Organizational Centrality: Its Behavioral
        Consequences." Journal of Experimental Social Psychology, 2:
        361–375.

Featherman, David L., and Robert M. Hauser
1976   "Sexual Inequalities and Socioeconomic Achievement in the
        U.S., 1962–1973." American Sociological Review, 41: 462–483.

Feldman, Daniel Charles
1976   "A Contingency Theory of Socialization." Administrative Sci-
        ence Quarterly, 21: 433–452.

Festinger, Leon
1954   "A Theory of Social Comparison Processes." Human Relations,
        7: 117–140.

Festinger, Leon
1964   Conflict, Decision and Dissonance. Stanford, CA: Stanford Uni-
        versity Press.

Festinger, Leon, and J. Merrill Carlsmith
1959   "Cognitive Consequences of Forced Compliance." Journal of Abnormal and Social Psychology, 58: 203–210.

Festinger, L., S. Schacter, and K. Back
1950   Social Pressures in Informal Groups. Stanford, CA: Stanford University Press.

Fishbein, M.
1967   "Attitude and the Prediction of Behavior." In M. Fishbein (ed.), Readings in Attitude Theory and Measurement. New York: John Wiley.

Flanagan, Robert J., George Strauss, and Lloyd Ulman
1974   "Worker Discontent and Work Place Behavior." Industrial Relations, 13: 101–123.

Flanders, J. P.
1968   "A Review of Research on Imitative Behavior." Psychological Bulletin, 69: 316–337.

Fleishman, E. F., and D. R. Peters
1962   "Interpersonal Values, Leadership Attitudes, and Managerial 'Success.'" Personnel Psychology, 15: 127–143.

Freeman, John Henry
1973   "Environment, Technology and the Administrative Intensity of Manufacturing Organizations." American Sociological Review, 38: 750–763.

Freeman, John Henry
1978   "The Unit of Analysis in Organizational Research." In Marshall W. Meyer and Associates (eds.), Environments and Organizations: 335–351. San Francisco: Jossey-Bass.

Freeman, John H.
1979   "Going to the Well: School District Administrative Intensity and Environmental Constraint." Administrative Science Quarterly, 24: 119–133.

Freeman, John Henry
1981   "Review of Organizations and Environments by Howard E. Aldrich." American Journal of Sociology, 86: 1447–1450.

Freeman, John
1982   "Organizational Life Cycles and Natural Selection Processes." In Barry M. Staw and L. L. Cummings (eds.), Research in Organizational Behavior, Vol. 4: 1–32. Greenwich, CT: JAI Press.

Freeman, John H., and Michael T. Hannan
1975 "Growth and Decline Processes in Organizations." American Sociological Review, 40: 215–228.

Freeman, J. H., and J. E. Kronenfeld
1974 "Problems of Definitional Dependency: The Case of Administrative Intensity." Social Forces, 52: 108–121.

Freeman, Richard B.
1978 "The Effect of Trade Unionism on Fringe Benefits." Working Paper No. 292. Cambridge, MA: National Bureau of Economic Research.

Freeman, Richard B., and James L. Medoff
1979 "The Two Faces of Unionism." Public Interest, 57: 69–93.

French, J., Jr., and B. Raven
1959 "The Bases of Social Power." In D. Cartwright (ed.), Studies in Social Power. Ann Arbor: Institute for Social Research, University of Michigan.

French, Wendell L., and Cecil H. Bell, Jr.
1973 Organization Development. Englewood Cliffs, NJ: Prentice-Hall.

Friedland, Edward I.
1974 Introduction to the Concept of Rationality in Political Science. Morristown, NJ: General Learning Press.

Friedman, Milton
1953 "The Methodology of Positive Economics." In Milton Friedman, Essays in Positive Economics. Chicago: University of Chicago Press.

Galbraith, Jay R.
1973 Designing Complex Organizations. Reading, MA: Addison-Wesley.

Galbraith, Jay, and Larry L. Cummings
1967 "An Empirical Investigation of the Motivational Determinants of Task Performance: Interactive Effects between Instrumentality-Valence and Motivation-Ability." Organizational Behavior and Human Performance, 2: 237–257.

Galbraith, John K.
1967 The New Industrial State. Cambridge, MA: Houghton Mifflin.

Ganster, Daniel C.
1980   "Individual Differences and Task Design: A Laboratory Experi-
          ment." Organizational Behavior and Human Performance, 26:
          131–148.

Garfinkel, Harold
1967   Studies in Ethnomethodology. Englewood Cliffs, NJ: Prentice-
          Hall.

Gephart, Robert P., Jr.
1978   "Status Degradation and Organizational Succession: An Ethno-
          methodological Approach." Administrative Science Quarterly,
          23: 553–581.

Gergen, Kenneth J.
1969   The Psychology of Behavior Exchange. Reading, MA: Addison-
          Wesley.

Gergen, Kenneth J.
1978   "Toward Generative Theory." Journal of Personality and Social
          Psychology, 36: 1344–1360.

Gerwin, Donald
1969   "A Process Model of Budgeting in a Public School System."
          Management Science, 15: 338–361.

Giddens, Anthony
1976   New Rules of Sociological Method. New York: Basic Books.

Giddens, Anthony
1977   Studies in Social and Political Theory. New York: Basic Books.

Glassman, Robert
1973   "Persistence and Loose Coupling." Behavioral Science, 18: 83–98.

Glenn, Norval D.
1969   "Aging, Disengagement, and Opinionation." Public Opinion
          Quarterly, 33: 17–33.

Goffman, Erving
1959   The Presentation of Self in Everyday Life. New York: Double-
          day.

Goffman, Erving
1961   Encounters: Two Studies in the Sociology of Interaction. New
          York: Bobbs-Merrill.

Goffman, Erving
1974   Frame Analysis. New York: Harper & Row.

Goldberg, Victor P.
1980   "Bridges over Contested Terrain: Exploring the Radical Account of the Employment Relationship." Journal of Economic Behavior and Organization, 1: 249–274.

Golding, David
1980   "Establishing Blissful Clarity in Organizational Life: Managers." Sociological Review, 28: 763–782.

Goldman, Paul
1980   "The Marxist Analysis of Organizations: Values, Theories, and Research." Unpublished ms., Department of Sociology, University of Oregon.

Gonos, George
1977   "'Situation' versus 'Frame': The 'Interactionist' and 'Structuralist' Analyses of Everyday Life." American Sociological Review, 42: 854–867.

Goodman, Paul S.
1968   "The Measurement of an Individual's Organization Map." Administrative Science Quarterly, 13: 246–265.

Goodman, R. A.
1968   "On the Operationality of the Maslow Need Hierarchy." British Journal of Industrial Relations, 6: 51–57.

Gordon, Michael E., Lawrence S. Kleiman, and Charles A. Hanie
1978   "Industrial-Organizational Psychology: Open Thy Ears O House of Israel." American Psychologist, 33: 893–905.

Gordon, Robert A.
1961   Business Leadership in the Large Corporation. Berkeley: University of California Press.

Gordon, Robert A., and James E. Howell
1959   Higher Education for Business. New York: Columbia University Press.

Graen, George
1969   "Instrumentality Theory of Work Motivation: Some Empirical Results and Suggested Modifications." Journal of Applied Psychology Monograph, 53: 1–25.

Granovetter, Mark
1981   "Toward a Sociological Theory of Income Differences." In Ivar
          Berg (ed.), Sociological Perspectives on Labor Markets: 11–47.
          New York: Academic Press.

Greene, D., and M. R. Lepper
1974   "Effects of Extrinsic Reward on Children's Subsequent Intrinsic
          Interest." Child Development, 45: 1141–1145.

Griffin, Ricky W.
1981   "Technological and Social Processes in Task Redesign: A Field
          Experiment." Unpublished ms., Texas A & M University.

Griffin, Ricky W., Ann Welsh, and Gregory Moorhead
1981   "Perceived Task Characteristics and Employee Performance: A
          Literature Review." Academy of Management Review, 6: 655–
          664.

Griffitt, W.
1970   "Environmental Effects on Interpersonal Affective Behavior:
          Ambient-Effective Temperature and Attraction." Journal of Per-
          sonality and Social Psychology, 15: 240–244.

Gross, N., W. S. Mason, and A. W. McEachern
1958   Explorations in Role Analysis: Studies of the School Superin-
          tendency Role. New York: John Wiley.

Grusky, Oscar
1961   "Corporate Size, Bureaucratization, and Managerial Suc-
          cession." American Journal of Sociology, 67: 261–269.

Grusky, Oscar
1963   "Managerial Succession and Organizational Effectiveness."
          American Journal of Sociology, 69: 21–31.

Guetzkow, Harold, and Herbert A. Simon
1955   "The Impact of Certain Communication Nets upon Organization
          and Performance in Task-Oriented Groups." Management Sci-
          ence, 1: 233–250.

Gulick, Luther, and L. Urwick
1937   Papers on the Science of Administration. New York: Institute of
          Public Administration, Columbia University.

Gusfield, Joseph R.
1957   "The Problem of Generations in an Organizational Structure."
          Social Forces, 35: 323–330.

Hackman, J. Richard
1978   "The Design of Work in the 1980s." Organizational Dynamics, 7
          (Summer): 3–17.

Hackman, J. Richard, and Edward E. Lawler, III
1971   "Employee Reactions to Job Characteristics." Journal of Applied
          Psychology, 55: 259–286.

Hackman, J. Richard, and Greg R. Oldham
1975   "Development of the Job Diagnostic Survey." Journal of Applied
          Psychology, 60: 159–170.

Hackman, J. Richard, and Greg R. Oldham
1976   "Motivation through the Design of Work." Organizational Be-
          havior and Human Performance, 16: 250–279.

Hackman, J. Richard, and Greg R. Oldham
1980   Work Redesign. Reading, MA: Addison-Wesley.

Hackman, J. R., G. R. Oldham, R. Janson, and K. Purdy
1975   "A New Strategy for Job Enrichment." California Management
          Review, 17: 57–71.

Hackman, J. R., J. L. Pearce, and J. C. Wolfe
1978   "Effects of Changes in Job Characteristics on Work Attitudes
          and Behaviors: A Naturally Occurring Quasi-Experiment."
          Organizational Behavior and Human Performance, 21: 289–304.

Hackman, J. Richard, and Lyman W. Porter
1968   "Expectancy Theory Predictions of Work Effectiveness." Orga-
          nizational Behavior and Human Performance, 3: 417–426.

Hage, J., and M. Aiken
1969   "Routine Technology, Social Structure and Organizational
          Goals." Administrative Science Quarterly, 14: 366–376.

Halaby, Charles N., and Michael E. Sobel
1979   "Mobility Effects in the Workplace." American Journal of So-
          ciology, 85: 385–416.

Hall, Douglas T.
1972   "A Model of Coping with Role Conflict: The Role Behavior of
          College Educated Women." Administrative Science Quarterly,
          17: 471–486.

Hall, D. T., and K. E. Nougaim
1968   "An Examination of Maslow's Need Hierarchy in an Organiza-
          tional Setting." Organizational Behavior and Human Perfor-
          mance, 3: 12–35.

Hall, Richard H., J. Eugene Haas, and Norman J. Johnson
1967   "Organizational Size, Complexity and Formalization." American
          Sociological Review, 32: 903–912.

Hamner, W. Clay, and Ellen P. Hamner
1976   "Behavior Modification on the Bottom Line." Organizational
          Dynamics, 4 (Spring): 3–21.

Hannan, Michael T.
1971   Aggregation and Disaggregation in Sociology. Lexington, MA:
          Heath-Lexington.

Hannan, Michael T., and John H. Freeman
1977   "The Population Ecology of Organizations." American Journal
          of Sociology, 82: 929–964.

Hannan, Michael T., and John Freeman
1981   "Niche Width and the Dynamics of Organizational Popula-
          tions." Technical Report #2, Organizational Studies Section, In-
          stitute for Mathematical Studies in the Social Sciences. Palo
          Alto, CA: Stanford University.

Hannan, Michael T., John H. Freeman, and John W. Meyer
1976   "Specification of Models for Organizational Effectiveness."
          American Sociological Review, 41: 136–143.

Harackiewicz, J. M.
1979   "The Effects of Reward Contingency and Performance Feedback
          on Intrinsic Motivation." Journal of Personality and Social Psy-
          chology, 37: 1352–1363.

Hargens, Lowell L.
1969   "Patterns of Mobility of New Ph.D.'s among American Aca-
          demic Institutions." Sociology of Education, 42: 18–37.

Harre, R., and P. F. Secord
1972   The Explanation of Social Behavior. Oxford: Basil Blackwell
          and Mott.

Harvey, Edward
1968   "Technology and the Structure of Organizations." American Sociological Review, 33: 247–259.

Hauser, Robert M.
1970   "Context and Consex: A Cautionary Tale." American Journal of Sociology, 75: 645–664.

Hauser, Robert M.
1971   Socioeconomic Background and Educational Performance. Washington, D.C.: Arnold and Caroline Rose Monograph Series of the American Sociological Association.

Hawley, Amos H.
1950   Human Ecology: A Theory of Community Structure. New York: Ronald Press.

Hawley, Amos H.
1968   "Human Ecology." In David L. Sills (ed.), International Encyclopedia of the Social Sciences: 328–337. New York: Macmillan.

Heizer, Jay
1976   "Transfers and Terminations as Staffing Options." Academy of Management Journal, 19: 115–120.

Helmich, Donald L.
1974   "Organizational Growth and Succession Patterns." Academy of Management Journal, 17: 771–775.

Helmich, Donald L.
1977   "Executive Succession in the Corporate Organization: A Current Integration." Academy of Management Review, 2: 252–266.

Helmich, Donald, and Warren Brown
1972   "Successor Type and Organizational Change in the Corporate Enterprise." Administrative Science Quarterly, 17: 371–381.

Herman, J. B., R. B. Dunham, and C. L. Hulin
1975   "Organizational Structure, Demographic Characteristics, and Employee Responses." Organizational Behavior and Human Performance, 13: 206–232.

Herman, Jeanne B., and Charles L. Hulin
1972   "Studying Organizational Attitudes from Individual and Organizational Frames of Reference." Organizational Behavior and Human Performance, 8: 84–108.

Herzberg, F., B. Mausner, and B. Snyderman
1959   The Motivation to Work, 2nd ed. New York: John Wiley.

Hickson, D. J., C. R. Hinings, C. A. Lee, R. E. Schneck, and J. M. Pennings
1971   "A Strategic Contingencies' Theory of Intraorganizational
            Power." Administrative Science Quarterly, 16: 216–229.

Hickson, David J., Derek S. Pugh, and Diana Pheysey
1969   "Operations Technology and Organization Structure: An Em-
            pirical Reappraisal." Administrative Science Quarterly, 14:
            378–397.

Hills, Frederick S., and Thomas A. Mahoney
1978   "University Budgets and Organizational Decision Making." Ad-
            ministrative Science Quarterly, 23: 454–465.

Hinings, C. R., D. J. Hickson, J. M. Pennings, and R. E. Schneck
1974   "Structural Conditions of Intraorganizational Power." Adminis-
            trative Science Quarterly, 19: 22–44.

Hirschman, Albert O.
1970   Exit, Voice, and Loyalty. Cambridge, MA: Harvard University
            Press.

Holtzner, B., and J. H. Marx
1979   Knowledge Application: The Knowledge System in Society.
            Boston: Allyn and Bacon.

Homans, George
1950   The Human Group. New York: Harcourt, Brace, and World.

Homans, George C.
1962   Sentiments and Activities. New York: Free Press.

House, Robert J.
1971   "A Path Goal Theory of Leadership Effectiveness." Administra-
            tive Science Quarterly, 16: 321–338.

House, Robert J., and Gary Dessler
1974   "The Path-Goal Theory of Leadership: Some Post Hoc and A
            Priori Tests." In J. G. Hunt and L. L. Larson (eds.), Contingency
            Approaches to Leadership: 29–55. Carbondale, IL: Southern Il-
            linois University Press.

Huber, George P., Michael J. O'Connell, and Larry L. Cummings
1975   "Perceived Environmental Uncertainty: Effects of Information
            and Structure." Academy of Management Journal, 18: 725–740.

Hulin, Charles L., and Milton R. Blood
1968   "Job Enlargement, Individual Differences, and Worker Responses." Psychological Bulletin, 69: 41–55.

Hunter, Floyd
1953   Community Power Structure. Chapel Hill: University of North Carolina Press.

Ivancevich, J.
1976   "Effects of Goal Setting on Performance and Job Satisfaction." Journal of Applied Psychology, 61: 605–612.

Ivancevich, J. M.
1977   "Different Goal Setting Treatments and Their Effects on Performance and Job Satisfaction." Academy of Management Journal, 20: 406–419.

Ives, R. S, and R. Ferdinands
1974   "Working in a Landscaped Office." Personnel Practice Bulletin, 30: 126–141.

Jablonsky, Stephen F., and David L. DeVries
1972   "Operant Conditioning Principles Extrapolated to the Theory of Management." Organizational Behavior and Human Performance, 7: 340–358.

Jacobs, David
1974   "Dependency and Vulnerability: An Exchange Approach to the Control of Organizations." Administrative Science Quarterly, 19: 45–59.

Jacobs, R. C., and D. T. Campbell
1961   "The Perpetuation of an Arbitrary Tradition through Successive Generations of a Laboratory Microculture." Journal of Abnormal and Social Psychology, 62: 649–658.

James, Lawrence R., and Allan P. Jones
1980   "Perceived Job Characteristics and Job Satisfaction: An Examination of Reciprocal Causation." Personnel Psychology, 33: 97–135.

Janis, Irving L.
1972   Victims of Groupthink. Boston: Houghton Mifflin.

Jenkins, W. O., and J. C. Stanley, Jr.
1950   "Partial Reinforcement: A Review and Critique." Psychological Bulletin, 47: 193–234.

Johns, Gary
1978   "Attititudinal and Nonattitudinal Predictors of Two Forms of
          Absence from Work." Organizational Behavior and Human Per-
          formance, 22: 431–444.

Johnson, George E., and Kenwood C. Youmans
1971   "Union Relative Wage Effects by Age and Education." Industrial
          and Labor Relations Review, 24: 171–180.

Joiner, D.
1971   "Office Territory." New Society, 7: 660–663.

Jones, Edward E., and Richard E. Nisbett
1971   The Actor and the Observer: Divergent Perceptions of the
          Causes of Behavior. Morristown, NJ: General Learning Press.

Jonsson, Sten A., and Rolf A. Lundin
1977   "Myths and Wishful Thinking as Management Tools." In Paul C.
          Nystrom and William H. Starbuck (eds.), Prescriptive Models of
          Organizations: 157–170. New York: Elsevier North-Holland Inc.

Kahn, Robert L., Donald M. Wolfe, Robert P. Quinn, and J. Diedrick
Snoek
1964   Organizational Stress: Studies in Role Conflict and Ambiguity.
          New York: John Wiley.

Kanfer, F. H.
1954   "The Effect of Partial Reinforcement Acquisition and Extinction
          of a Class of Verbal Responses." Journal of Experimental Psy-
          chology, 48: 424–432.

Kanter, Rosabeth Moss
1977   Men and Women of the Corporation. New York: Basic Books.

Karpik, Lucien
1978   "Organizations, Institutions and History." In Lucien Karpik
          (ed.), Organization and Environment: Theory, Issues and Real-
          ity: 15–68. Beverly Hills, CA: Sage.

Kasarda, J. D.
1974   "The Structural Implications of Social System Size: A Three-
          Level Analysis." American Sociological Review, 39: 19–28.

Katz, Daniel, and Robert L. Kahn
1978   The Social Psychology of Organizations, 2nd ed. New York:
          John Wiley.

Katz, Elihu, Martin L. Levin, and Herbert Hamilton
1963   "Traditions of Research on the Diffusion of Innovation." American Sociological Review, 28: 237–252.

Katz, Ralph
1981   "Managing Careers: The Influence of Job and Group Longevities." In Ralph Katz (ed.), Career Issues in Human Resource Management: 154–181. Englewood Cliffs, NJ: Prentice-Hall.

Katz, Ralph
1982   "The Effects of Group Longevity on Communication and Performance." Administrative Science Quarterly, 27: 81–104.

Kaufman, Herbert
1976   Are Government Organizations Immortal? Washington, D.C.: Brookings.

Kelley, Harold H.
1952   "Two Functions of Reference Groups." In G. E. Swanson, T. M. Newcomb, and E. L. Hartley (eds.), Readings in Social Psychology, 2nd ed. New York: Holt, Rinehart and Winston.

Kelley, Harold H.
1971   Attribution in Social Interaction. Morristown, NJ: General Learning Press.

Kempen, R. W., and R. V. Hall
1977   "Reduction of Industrial Absenteeism: Results of a Behavioral Approach." Journal of Organizational Behavior Management, 1: 1–21.

Kessel, John H.
1962   "Governmental Structure and Political Environment: A Statistical Note about American Cities." American Political Science Review, 56: 615–620.

Keyfitz, Nathan
1973   "Individual Mobility in a Stationary Population." Population Studies, 37: 335–352.

Khandwalla, Pradip
1973   "Effect of Competition on the Structure of Top Management Control." Academy of Management Journal, 16: 285–295.

Khandwalla, Pradip N.
1974   "Mass Output Orientation of Operations Technology and Organizational Structure." Administrative Science Quarterly, 19: 74–97.

Kiesler, Charles A.
1971   The Psychology of Commitment: Experiments Linking Behavior
          to Belief. New York: Academic Press.

Kiesler, Charles A., and Sara B. Kiesler
1969   Conformity. Reading, MA: Addison-Wesley.

Kim, J., and W. Hamner
1976   "The Effect of Performance Feedback and Goal Setting on Pro-
          ductivity and Satisfaction in an Organizational Setting." Journal
          of Applied Psychology, 61: 48–57.

Kimberly, John R.
1975   "Environmental Constraints and Organizational Structure: A
          Comparative Analysis of Rehabilitation Organizations." Ad-
          ministrative Science Quarterly, 20: 1–9.

Kimberly, John R.
1976   "Organizational Size and the Structuralist Perspective: A Re-
          view, Critique, and Proposal." Administrative Science Quar-
          terly, 21: 571–597.

King, Albert S.
1974   "Expectation Effects in Organizational Change." Administrative
          Science Quarterly, 19: 221–230.

Kipnis, David, Stuart Schmidt, and Ian Wilkinson
1980   "Interorganizational Influence Tactics: Explorations in Getting
          One's Way." Journal of Applied Psychology, 65: 440–452.

Kolko, Gabriel
1962   Wealth and Power in America. New York: Praeger.

Komaki, Judi, Kenneth D. Barwick, and Lawrence R. Scott
1978   "A Behavioral Approach to Occupational Safety: Pinpointing
          and Reinforcing Safe Performance in a Food Manufacturing
          Plant." Journal of Applied Psychology, 63: 434–445.

Kotter, John P., and Paul R. Lawrence
1974   Mayors in Action: Five Approaches to Urban Governance. New
          York: John Wiley.

Kraft, Philip
1977   Programmers and Managers: The Routinization of Computer
          Programming in the United States. New York: Heidelberg Sci-
          ence Library.

Kruglanski, A. W., I. Friedman, and G. Zeevi
1971   "The Effects of Extrinsic Incentives on Some Qualitative Aspects of Task Performance." Journal of Personality, 39: 606–617.

Kuhn, Thomas S.
1970   The Structure of Scientific Revolutions, 2nd ed. Chicago: University of Chicago Press.

Ladd, Everett Carll, and Seymour Martin Lipset
1975   The Divided Academy: Professors and Politics. New York: McGraw-Hill.

Landau, Martin
1969   "Redundancy, Rationality, and the Problem of Duplication and Overlap." Public Administration Review, 29: 346–358.

Langer, Ellen J.
1975   "The Illusion of Control." Journal of Personality and Social Psychology, 32: 311–328.

Langer, Ellen J.
1978   "Rethinking the Role of Thought in Social Interaction." In John H. Harvey, William Ickes, and Robert F. Kidd (eds.), New Directions in Attribution Research, Vol. 2: 35–58. Hillsdale, NJ: Lawrence Erlbaum Associates.

Larner, Robert J.
1970   Management Control and the Large Corporation. New York: Dunellen.

Latham, G. P., and J. J. Baldes
1975   "The Practical Significance of Locke's Theory of Goal Setting." Journal of Applied Psychology, 60: 122–124.

Latham, G. P., and S. B. Kinne, III
1974   "Improving Job Performance through Training in Goal Setting." Journal of Applied Psychology, 59: 187–191.

Latham, G. P., T. R. Mitchell, and D. L. Dossett
1978   "Importance of Participative Goal Setting and Anticipated Rewards on Goal Difficulty and Job Performance." Journal of Applied Psychology, 63: 163–171.

Latham, G. P., and G. A. Yukl
1975a   "Assigned versus Participative Goal Setting with Educated and Uneducated Woods Workers." Journal of Applied Psychology, 60: 299–302.

Latham, Gary P., and Gary A. Yukl
1975b   "A Review of Research on the Application of Goal Setting in Organizations." Academy of Management Journal, 18: 824–845.

Latham, G. P., and G. A. Yukl
1976   "Effects of Assigned and Participative Goal Setting on Performance and Job Satisfaction." Journal of Applied Psychology, 61: 166–171.

Lawler, Edward E.
1967   "Secrecy about Management Compensation: Are There Hidden Costs?" Organizational Behavior and Human Performance, 2: 182–189.

Lawler, Edward E.
1973   Motivation in Work Organizations. Monterey, CA: Brooks/ Cole.

Lawler, Edward E.
1974   "For a More Effective Organization – Match the Job to the Man." Organizational Dynamics, 3 (Summer): 19–29.

Lawler, E. E., J. R. Hackman, and S. Kaufman
1973   "Effects of Job Redesign: A Field Experiment." Journal of Applied Social Psychology, 3: 49–62.

Lawler, Edward E., and Lyman W. Porter
1967   "Antecedent Attitudes of Effective Managerial Performance." Organizational Behavior and Human Performance, 2: 122–142.

Lawrence, Paul R., and Jay W. Lorsch
1967   Organization and Environment. Boston: Graduate School of Business Administration, Harvard University.

Leavitt, Harold J.
1951   "Some Effects of Certain Communication Patterns on Group Performance." Journal of Abnormal and Social Psychology, 46: 38–50.

Leavitt, Harold J.
1954   Managerial Psychology. Chicago: University of Chicago Press.

Leavitt, Harold J.
1962   "Toward Organizational Psychology." In B. von H. Gilmer (ed.), Walter Van Dyke Bingham Lectures: 23–30. Pittsburgh, PA: Carnegie Institute of Technology.

Leavitt, Harold J.
1978   Managerial Psychology, 4th edition. Chicago: University of Chicago Press.

Lecuyer, R.
1976   "Social Organization and Spatial Organization." Human Relations, 29: 1045–1060.

Lepper, M. R., and D. Greene
1975   "Turning Play into Work: Effects of Adult Surveillance and Extrinsic Rewards on Children's Intrinsic Motivation." Journal of Personality and Social Psychology, 31: 479–486.

Lepper, M. R., and D. Greene
1978   The Hidden Costs of Reward: New Perspectives on the Psychology of Human Motivation. Hillsdale, NJ: Lawrence Erlbaum.

Lepper, M. R., D. Greene, and R. E. Nisbett
1973   "Undermining Children's Interest with Extrinsic Rewards: A Test of the 'Overjustification' Hypothesis." Journal of Personality and Social Psychology, 28: 129–137.

Levinson, Harry
1964   Executive Stress. New York: Harper & Row.

Lewellen, Wilbur G.
1968   Executive Compensation in Large Industrial Corporations. New York: National Bureau of Economic Research.

Lewellen, Wilbur G.
1971   The Ownership Income of Management. New York: National Bureau of Economic Research.

Lewellen, Wilbur G., and Blaine Huntsman
1970   "Managerial Pay and Corporate Performance." American Economic Review, 60: 710–720.

Lieberman, Seymour
1956   "The Effects of Changes in Roles on the Attitudes of Role Occupants." Human Relations, 9: 385–402.

Lieberson, Stanley, and James F. O'Connor
1972   "Leadership and Organizational Performance: A Study of Large Corporations." American Sociological Review 37: 117–130.

Light, Ivan H.
1972   Ethnic Enterprise in America. Berkeley: University of California Press.

Lincoln, James R., Mitsuyo Hanada, and Jon Olson
1981   "Cultural Orientations and Individual Reactions to Organiza-
        tions: A Study of Employees of Japanese-Owned Firms." Admin-
        istrative Science Quarterly, 26: 93–115.

Lincoln, James R., and Gerald Zeitz
1980   "Organizational Properties from Aggregate Data: Separating In-
        dividual and Structural Effects." American Sociological Review,
        45: 391–408.

Lindblom, Charles E., and David Braybrooke
1970   A Strategy of Decision. New York: Free Press.

Lipset, Seymour Martin, Martin Trow, and James Coleman
1956   Union Democracy. Glencoe, IL: Free Press.

Litwak, Eugene
1961   "Models of Bureaucracy Which Permit Conflict." American
        Journal of Sociology, 67: 177–184.

Locke, Edwin A.
1968   "Toward a Theory of Task Motivation and Incentives." Organi-
        zational Behavior and Human Performance, 3: 157–189.

Locke, Edwin A.
1976   "The Nature and Causes of Job Satisfaction." In Marvin D. Dun-
        nette (ed.), Handbook of Industrial and Organizational Psy-
        chology: 1297–1349. Chicago: Rand McNally.

Locke, Edwin A.
1977   "The Myths of Behavior Mod in Organizations." Academy of
        Management Review, 2: 543–553.

Lodahl, Janice, and Gerald Gordon
1972   "The Structure of Scientific Fields and the Functioning of Uni-
        versity Graduate Departments." American Sociological Review,
        37: 57–72.

Logan, F. A., and A. R. Wagner
1966   Reward and Punishment. Boston: Allyn and Bacon.

London, M., and G. Oldham
1976   "Effects of Varying Goal Types and Incentive Systems on Per-
        formance and Satisfaction." Academy of Management Journal,
        19: 537–546.

Louis, Meryl Reis
1980   "Surprise and Sense Making: What Newcomers Experience in Entering Unfamiliar Organizational Settings." Administrative Science Quarterly, 25: 226–251.

Luthans, Fred, and Robert Kreitner
1974   "The Management of Behavioral Contingencies." Personnel, 51 (July-August): 7–16.

Luthans, Fred, and Robert Kreitner
1975   Organizational Behavior Modification. Glenview, IL: Scott, Foresman.

Luthans, Fred, Robert Paul, and Douglas Baker
1981   "An Experimental Analysis of the Impact of Contingent Reinforcement on Salespersons' Performance Behavior." Journal of Applied Psychology, 66: 314–323.

Luthans, R., and D. White
1971   "Behavior Modification: Application to Manpower Management." Personnel Administration, 34 (July-August): 41–47.

Lynch, Beverly P.
1974   "An Empirical Assessment of Perrow's Technology Construct." Administrative Science Quarterly, 19: 338–356.

Machlup, F.
1967   "Theories of the Firm: Marginalist, Behavioral, Managerial." American Economic Review, 57: 1–33.

Mackenzie, Kenneth D.
1966   "Structural Centrality in Communications Networks." Psychometrika, 31: 17–25.

Mackenzie, Kenneth D.
1978   Organizational Structures. Arlington Heights, IL: AHM.

Mackenzie, Kenneth D., and Robert House
1978   "Paradigm Development in the Social Sciences: A Proposed Research Strategy." Academy of Management Review, 3: 7–23.

Manns, Curtis L., and James G. March
1978   "Financial Adversity, Internal Competition, and Curriculum Change in a University." Administrative Science Quarterly, 23: 541–552.

March, James G.
1962   "The Business Firm as a Political Coalition." Journal of Politics, 24: 662–678.

March, James G.
1966   "The Power of Power." In David Easton (ed.), Varieties of Political Theory: 39–70. Englewood Cliffs, NJ: Prentice-Hall.

March, James G.
1976   "The Technology of Foolishness." In James G. March and Johan P. Olsen, Ambiguity and Choice in Organizations: 69–81. Bergen, Norway: Universitetsforlaget.

March, James G.
1978   "Bounded Rationality, Ambiguity, and the Engineering of Choice." Bell Journal of Economics, 9: 587–608.

March, James G., and Johan P. Olsen
1976   Ambiguity and Choice in Organizations. Bergen, Norway: Universitetsforlaget.

March, James G., and Herbert A. Simon
1958   Organizations. New York: John Wiley.

Marris, Robin
1967   The Economic Theory of 'Managerial' Capitalism. London: Macmillan.

Martin, Joanne
1981   "Relative Deprivation: A Theory of Distributive Injustice for an Era of Shrinking Resources." In L. L. Cummings and Barry M. Staw (eds.), Research in Organizational Behavior, Vol. 3: 53–107. Greenwich, CT: JAI Press.

Martin, Joanne
Forth-   "Stories and Scripts in Organizational Settings." In A. Hastorf
coming   and A. Isen (eds.), Cognitive Social Psychology. New York: Elsevier-North Holland.

Martin, Joanne, and Alan Murray
1981   "Catalysts for Collective Violence: The Importance of a Psychological Approach." Research Paper No. 607. Palo Alto, CA: Graduate School of Business, Stanford University.

Maslow, Abraham H.
1943   "A Theory of Human Motivation." Psychological Review, 50: 370–396.

Maslow, Abraham H.
1954   Motivation and Personality. New York: Harper.

Maslow, A., and M. Mintz
1956   "Effects of Aesthetic Surroundings: I. Initial Effects of Three
          Aesthetic Conditions upon Perceiving 'Energy' and 'Well-Being'
          in Faces." Journal of Psychology, 41: 247–254.

Masson, Robert T.
1971   "Executive Motivations, Earnings, and Consequent Equity Per-
          formance." Journal of Political Economy, 79: 1278–1292.

Matsui, T., and Y. Ohtsuka
1978   "Within-Person Expectancy Theory Predictions of Supervisory
          Consideration and Structure Behavior." Journal of Applied Psy-
          chology, 63: 128–131.

Mayhew, Bruce H.
1980   "Structuralism versus Individualism: Part I, Shadowboxing in
          the Dark." Social Forces, 59: 335–375.

Mayhew, Bruce H.
1981   "Structuralism versus Individualism: Part II, Ideological and
          Other Obfuscations." Social Forces, 59: 627–648.

McCain, Bruce R., Charles O'Reilly, and Jeffrey Pfeffer
1981   "The Effects of Departmental Demography on Turnover: The
          Case of a University." Unpublished ms., University of Iowa.

McClelland, David C.
1961   The Achieving Society. Princeton, NJ: Van Nostrand.

McCue, Gerald M.
1978   "IBM's Santa Teresa Laboratory – Architectural Design for Pro-
          gram Development." IBM System Journal, 17: 4–25.

McDermott, Thomas, and Thomas Newhams
1971   "Discharge-Reinstatement: What Happens Thereafter." Indus-
          trial and Labor Relations Review, 24: 526–540.

McEachern, William A.
1975   Managerial Control and Performance. Lexington, MA: D. C.
          Heath.

McGuire, J. W., J. S. Y. Chiu, and A. O. Elbing
1962   "Executive Incomes, Sales, and Profits." American Economic
          Review, 52: 753–761.

McNeil, Kenneth, and James D. Thompson
1971   "The Regeneration of Social Organizations." American Socio-
        logical Review, 36: 624–637.

Mead, George Herbert
1938   The Philosophy of the Act. Chicago: University of Chicago
        Press.

Mechanic, David
1963   "Some Considerations in the Methodology of Organizational
        Studies." In Harold J. Leavitt (ed.), The Social Science of Orga-
        nizations. Englewood Cliffs, NJ: Prentice-Hall.

Meissner, Martin
1969   Technology and the Worker. San Francisco: Chandler.

Merton, Robert K.
1968   Social Theory and Social Structure. Glencoe, IL: Free Press.

Merton, Robert K.
1975   "Structural Analysis in Sociology." In Peter Blau (ed.), Ap-
        proaches to the Study of Social Structure: 21–52. New York:
        Free Press.

Meyer, John W., and Brian Rowan
1977   "Institutionalized Organizations: Formal Structure as Myth and
        Ceremony." American Journal of Sociology, 83: 340–363.

Meyer, John W., W. Richard Scott, Sally Cole, and Jo-Ann K. Intili
1978   "Instructional Dissensus and Institutional Consensus in Schools."
        In Marshall W. Meyer and Associates (eds.), Environments and
        Organizations: 233–263. San Francisco: Jossey-Bass.

Meyer, Marshall W.
1971   "Some Constraints in Analyzing Data on Organizational Struc-
        tures." American Sociological Review, 36: 294–297.

Meyer, Marshall W.
1972a   Bureaucratic Structure and Authority. New York: Harper and
        Row.

Meyer, Marshall W.
1972b   "Size and Structure of Organizations: A Causal Analysis."
        American Sociological Review, 37: 434–440.

Meyer, Marshall W.
1975   "Leadership and Organizational Structure." American Journal of
        Sociology, 81: 514–542.

Meyer, Marshall W.
1980   "Organizational Structure as Signaling." Pacific Sociological Review, 22: 481–500.

Miles, Raymond E., and Charles C. Snow
1978   Organizational Strategy, Structure, and Process. New York: McGraw-Hill.

Miles, Raymond E., Charles C. Snow, and Jeffrey Pfeffer
1974   "Organization-Environment: Concepts and Issues." Industrial Relations, 13: 244–264.

Mills, C. Wright
1956   The Power Elite. New York: Oxford University Press.

Mindlin, Sergio, and Howard Aldrich
1975   "Interorganizational Dependence: A Review of the Concept and a Re-Examination of the Findings of the Aston Group." Administrative Science Quarterly, 20: 382–392.

Miner, John B., and J. Frank Brewer
1976   "The Management of Ineffective Performance." In Marvin D. Dunnette (ed.), Handbook of Industrial and Organizational Psychology: 995–1029. Chicago: Rand McNally.

Mintz, M.
1956   "Effects of Aesthetic Surroundings: II. Prolonged and Repeated Experience in a 'Beautiful' and an 'Ugly' Room." Journal of Psychology, 41: 459–466.

Mintzberg, Henry
1973   The Nature of Managerial Work. New York: Harper & Row.

Mirvis, P.
1981   Personal Correspondence: Review of Organizations and Organization Theory.

Mischel, Walter
1968   Personality and Assessment. New York: John Wiley.

Mitchell, J. C.
1969   "The Concept and Use of Social Networks." In J. C. Mitchell (ed.), Social Networks in Urban Situations. Manchester, England: University of Manchester Press.

Mitchell, Terence R.
1974   "Expectancy Models of Job Satisfaction, Occupational Prefer-
        ence and Effort: A Theoretical, Methodological and Empirical
        Appraisal." Psychological Bulletin, 81: 1053–1077.

Mitchell, Terence R.
1979   "Organizational Behavior." Annual Review of Psychology, 30:
        243–281.

Mitchell, Terence R., and Anthony Biglan
1971   "Instrumentality Theories: Current Uses in Psychology." Psy-
        chological Bulletin, 76: 432–454.

Mobley, William H.
1977   "Intermediate Linkages in the Relationship between Job Satisfac-
        tion and Employee Turnover." Journal of Applied Psychology,
        62: 237–240.

Mobley, William H., Stanley O. Horner, and A. T. Hollingsworth
1978   "An Evaluation of Precursors of Hospital Employee Turnover."
        Journal of Applied Psychology, 63: 408–414.

Mohr, Lawrence
1971   "Organizational Technology and Organizational Structure." Ad-
        ministrative Science Quarterly, 16: 444–459.

Monteverde, Kirk, and David J. Teece
1980   "Supplier Switching Costs and Vertical Integration in the U.S.
        Automobile Industry." Research Paper No. 575. Palo Alto, CA:
        Graduate School of Business, Stanford University.

Moore, Gwen
1979   "The Structure of a National Elite Network." American Socio-
        logical Review, 44: 673–692.

Morgan, Gareth, and Linda Smircich
1980   "The Case for Qualitative Research." Academy of Management
        Review, 5: 491–500.

Morris, Stuart
1973   "Stalled Professionalism: The Recruitment of Railway Officials
        in the United States, 1885–1940." Business History Review, 47:
        317–334.

Morrow, Paula C., and James C. McElroy
1981   "Interior Office Design and Visitor Response: A Constructive Replication." Journal of Applied Psychology, 66: 646–650.

Mowday, Richard T.
1978   "The Exercise of Upward Influence in Organizations." Administrative Science Quarterly, 23: 137–156.

Mulder, Mark
1960   "Communication Structure, Decision Structure, Communication, and Group Performance." Sociometry, 23: 1–14.

Nadler, David A.
1977   Feedback and Organization Development: Using Data Based Methods. Reading, MA: Addison-Wesley.

Nagel, E.
1963   "Assumptions in Economic Theory." American Economic Review, 53: 211–219.

Nagel, Jack H.
1975   The Descriptive Analysis of Power. New Haven, CT: Yale University Press.

Nehrbass, Richard G.
1979   "Ideology and the Decline of Management Theory." Academy of Management Review, 4: 427–431.

Neisser, U.
1976   Cognition and Reality. San Francisco: Freeman.

Newcomb, T.
1956   "The Prediction of Interpersonal Attraction." American Psychologist, 11: 575–586.

Newman, John E.
1975   "Understanding the Organizational Structure-Job Attitude Relationship through Perceptions of the Work Environment." Organizational Behavior and Human Performance, 14: 371–397.

Nicholson, N., C. A. Brown, and J. K. Chadwick-Jones
1976   "Absence from Work and Job Satisfaction." Journal of Applied Psychology, 61: 728–737.

Noble, David F.
1978   "Social Choice in Machine Design: The Case of Automatically Controlled Machine Tools, and a Challenge for Labor." Politics and Society, 8: 313–348.

Nord, Walter
1969   "Beyond the Teaching Machine: The Neglected Area of Operant
          Conditioning in the Theory and Practice of Management." Or-
          ganizational Behavior and Human Performance, 4: 375–401.

Nord, Walter R.
1970   "Improving Attendance through Rewards." Personnel Adminis-
          tration, 33: 37–41.

Oldham, Greg R., and Daniel J. Brass
1979   "Employee Reactions to an Open-Plan Office: A Naturally Oc-
          curring Quasi-Experiment." Administrative Science Quarterly,
          24: 267–284.

Olsen, Johan P.
1976a   "Choice in an Organized Anarchy." In James G. March and
          Johan P. Olsen, Ambiguity and Choice in Organizations: 82–
          139. Bergen, Norway: Universitetsforlaget.

Olsen, Johan P.
1976b   "Reorganization as a Garbage Can." In James G. March and
          Johan P. Olsen, Ambiguity and Choice in Organizations: 314–
          337. Bergen, Norway: Universitetsforlaget.

O'Reilly, Charles A., and David Caldwell
1979   "Informational Influence as a Determinant of Perceived Task
          Characteristics and Job Satisfaction." Journal of Applied Psy-
          chology, 64: 157–165.

O'Reilly, Charles A., and David F. Caldwell
1980   "Job Choice: The Impact of Intrinsic and Extrinsic Factors on
          Subsequent Satisfaction and Commitment." Journal of Applied
          Psychology, 65: 559–565.

O'Reilly, Charles A., and David F. Caldwell
1981   "The Commitment and Job Tenure of New Employees: Some
          Evidence of Postdecisional Justification." Administrative Science
          Quarterly, 26: 597–616.

O'Reilly, C. A., G. N. Parlette, and J. R. Bloom
1980   "Perceptual Measures of Task Characteristics: The Biasing Ef-
          fects of Differing Frames of Reference and Job Attitudes." Acad-
          emy of Management Journal, 23: 118–131.

O'Reilly, Charles A., and Karlene H. Roberts
1975   "Individual Differences in Personality, Position in the Organiza-
            tion, and Job Satisfaction." Organizational Behavior and Human
            Performance, 14: 144–150.

O'Reilly, Charles A., and Barton A. Weitz
1980   "Managing Marginal Employees: The Use of Warnings and Dis-
            missals." Administrative Science Quarterly, 25: 467–484.

Orne, Martin T.
1962   "On The Social Psychology of the Psychology of the Psycholog-
            ical Experiment: With Particular Reference to Demand Char-
            acteristics and Their Implications." American Psychologist, 17:
            776–783.

Orpen, Christopher
1978   "Effects of Bonuses for Attendance on Absenteeism of Industrial
            Workers." Journal of Organizational Behavior Management, 1:
            118–124.

Orpen, Christopher
1979   "The Effects of Job Enrichment on Employees Satisfaction, Moti-
            vation, Involvement, and Performance: A Field Experiment."
            Human Relations, 32: 189–217.

Ouchi, William G.
1979   "A Conceptual Framework for the Design of Organizational
            Control Mechanisms." Management Science, 25: 833–848.

Ouchi, William G.
1980   "Markets, Bureaucracies, and Clans." Administrative Science
            Quarterly, 25: 129–141.

Ouchi, William G.
1981   Theory Z. Reading, MA: Addison-Wesley.

Ouchi, William G., and Alfred M. Jaeger
1978   "Type Z Organization: Stability in the Midst of Mobility." Acad-
            emy of Management Review, 3: 305–314.

Ouchi, William G., and Mary Ann Maguire
1975   "Organizational Control: Two Functions." Administrative Sci-
            ence Quarterly, 20: 559–569.

Padgett, John F.
1980   "Bounded Rationality in Budgetary Research." American Po-
            litical Science Review, 74: 354–372.

Pallak, M. S., S. R. Sogin, and A. Van Zante
1974 "Bad Decisions: Effects of Volition, Locus of Causality, and Negative Consequences on Attitude Change." Journal of Personality and Social Psychology, 30: 217–227.

Palmer, Donald A.
1980 "Broken Ties: Some Political and Interorganizational Determinants of Interlocking Directorates among Large American Corporations." Paper presented at the Annual Meetings of the American Sociological Association, New York.

Palmer, John
1972 "The Separation of Ownership from Control in Large U.S. Industrial Corporations." Quarterly Review of Economics and Business, 12: 55–62.

Parker, D. F., and L. Dyer
1976 "Expectancy Theory as a Within-Person Behavioral Choice Model: An Empirical Test of Some Conceptual and Methodological Refinements." Organizational Behavior and Human Performance, 17: 97–117.

Parsons, Talcott
1951 The Social System. Glencoe, IL: Free Press.

Parsons, Talcott, and Neil J. Smelser
1956 Economy and Society. New York: Free Press.

Patchen, Martin
1974 "The Locus and Basis of Influence on Organizational Decisions." Organizational Behavior and Human Performance, 11: 195–221.

Payne, Roy, and Diana Pheysey
1973 "Organization Structure and Sociometric Nominations amongst Line Managers in Three Contrasted Organizations." European Journal of Social Psychology, 1: 261–284.

Pedalino, Ed, and Victor U. Gamboa
1974 "Behavior Modification and Absenteeism: Intervention in One Industrial Setting." Journal of Applied Psychology, 59: 694–698.

Pennings, Johannes M.
1973 "Measures of Organizational Structure: A Methodological Note." American Journal of Sociology, 79: 686–704.

Pennings, Johannes M.
1975   "The Relevance of the Structural-Contingency Model for Orga-
        nizational Effectiveness." Administrative Science Quarterly, 20:
        393–410.

Pennings, Johannes M.
1980   Interlocking Directorates. San Francisco: Jossey-Bass.

Pepitone, Albert
1981   "Lessons from the History of Social Psychology." American
        Psychologist, 36: 972–985.

Perrow, Charles
1967   "A Framework for Comparative Organizational Analysis."
        American Sociological Review, 32: 194–208.

Perrow, Charles
1970a   "Departmental Power and Perspectives in Industrial Firms." In
        Mayer N. Zald (ed.), Power in Organizations: 59–89. Nashville,
        TN: Vanderbilt University Press.

Perrow, Charles
1970b   Organizational Analysis: A Sociological View. Belmont, CA:
        Wadsworth.

Perrow, Charles
1972   Complex Organizations: A Critical Essay. Glenview, IL: Scott,
        Foresman.

Peters, Lawrence H.
1977   "Cognitive Models of Motivation, Expectancy Theory and Ef-
        fort: An Analysis and Empirical Test." Organizational Behavior
        and Human Performance, 20: 129–148.

Peters, Thomas J.
1978   "Symbols, Patterns, and Settings: An Optimistic Case for Get-
        ting Things Done." Organizational Dynamics, 7: 3–23.

Pettigrew, Andrew M.
1972   "Information Control as a Power Resource." Sociology, 6: 187–
        204.

Pettigrew, Andrew M.
1973   The Politics of Organizational Decision-Making. London:
        Tavistock.

Pettigrew, Andrew M.
1979   "On Studying Organizational Cultures." Administrative Science
        Quarterly, 24: 570–581.

Pfeffer, Jeffrey
1972a   "Interorganizational Influence and Managerial Attitudes." Acad-
        emy of Management Journal, 15: 317–330.

Pfeffer, Jeffrey
1972b   "Merger as a Response to Organizational Interdependence." Ad-
        ministrative Science Quarterly, 17: 382–394.

Pfeffer, Jeffrey
1972c   "Size and Composition of Corporate Boards of Directors: The
        Organization and Its Environment." Administrative Science
        Quarterly, 17: 218–228.

Pfeffer, Jeffrey
1973   "Size, Composition and Function of Hospital Boards of Direc-
        tors: A Study of Organization-Environment Linkage." Adminis-
        trative Science Quarterly, 18: 349–364.

Pfeffer, Jeffrey
1974   "Cooptation and the Composition of Electric Utility Boards of
        Directors." Pacific Sociological Review, 17: 333–363.

Pfeffer, Jeffrey
1977   "The Ambiguity of Leadership." Academy of Management Re-
        view, 2: 104–112.

Pfeffer, Jeffrey
1978   "The Micropolitics of Organizations." In Marshall W. Meyer and
        Associates (eds.), Environments and Organizations: 29–50. San
        Francisco: Jossey-Bass.

Pfeffer, Jeffrey
1980   "A Partial Test of the Social Information Processing Model of
        Job Attitudes." Human Relations, 33: 457–476.

Pfeffer, Jeffrey
1981a   Power in Organizations. Marshfield, MA: Pitman.

Pfeffer, Jeffrey
1981b   "Some Consequences of Organizational Demography: Potential
        Impacts of an Aging Work Force on Formal Organizations." In
        S. B. Kiesler, J. N. Morgan, and V. K. Oppenheimer (eds.),
        Aging: Social Change. New York: Academic Press.

Pfeffer, Jeffrey
Forth-   "Organizational Demography." In L. L. Cummings and Barry
coming   M. Staw (eds.), Research in Organizational Behavior, Vol. 5.
            Greenwich, CT: JAI Press.

Pfeffer, Jeffrey, and John Lawler
1980   "Effects of Job Alternatives, Extrinsic Rewards, and Behavioral
            Commitment on Attitude toward the Organization: A Field Test
            of the Insufficient Justification Paradigm." Administrative Sci-
            ence Quarterly, 25: 38–56.

Pfeffer, Jeffrey, and Huseyin Leblebici
1973a   "The Effect of Competition on Some Dimensions of Organiza-
            tional Structure." Social Forces, 52: 268–279.

Pfeffer, Jeffrey, and Huseyin Leblebici
1973b   "Executive Recruitment and the Development of Interfirm Orga-
            nizations." Administrative Science Quarterly, 18: 449–461.

Pfeffer, Jeffrey, and Anthony Leong
1977   "Resource Allocations in United Funds: Examination of Power
            and Dependence." Social Forces, 55: 775–790.

Pfeffer, Jeffrey, Anthony Leong, and Katherine Strehl
1977   "Paradigm Development and Particularism: Journal Publication
            in Three Scientific Disciplines." Social Forces, 55: 938–951.

Pfeffer, Jeffrey, and William L. Moore
1980   "Power in University Budgeting: A Replication and Extension."
            Administrative Science Quarterly, 25: 637–653.

Pfeffer, Jeffrey, and Phillip Nowak
1976   "Joint Ventures and Interorganizational Interdependence." Ad-
            ministrative Science Quarterly, 21: 398–418.

Pfeffer, Jeffrey, and Jerry Ross
1980   "Union-Nonunion Effects on Wage and Status Attainment." In-
            dustrial Relations, 19: 140–151.

Pfeffer, Jeffrey, and Jerry Ross
1981   "Market Power and Sectoral Variation in Wage and Status At-
            tainment." Unpublished ms., Graduate School of Business, Stan-
            ford University.

Pfeffer, Jeffrey, and Gerald R. Salancik
1974   "Organizational Decision Making as a Political Process: The
            Case of a University Budget." Administrative Science Quarterly,
            19: 135–151.

Pfeffer, Jeffrey, and Gerald R. Salancik
1975   "Determinants of Supervisory Behavior: A Role Set Analysis."
          Human Relations, 28: 139–154.

Pfeffer, Jeffrey, and Gerald R. Salancik
1977   "Administrator Effectiveness: The Effects of Advocacy and In-
          formation on Resource Allocations." Human Relations, 30: 641–
          656.

Pfeffer, Jeffrey, and Gerald R. Salancik
1978   The External Control of Organizations: A Resource Dependence
          Perspective. New York: Harper & Row.

Pfeffer, Jeffrey, Gerald R. Salancik, and Huseyin Leblebici
1976   "The Effect of Uncertainty on the Use of Social Influence in Or-
          ganizational Decision Making." Administrative Science Quar-
          terly, 21: 227–245.

Pinder, Craig., and Larry F. Moore (eds.)
1979   "Middle Range Theory and the Study of Organizations." Leiden,
          The Netherlands: Martinus Nijhoff.

Plott, Charles R., and Michael E. Levine
1978   "A Model of Agenda Influence on Committee Decisions." Amer-
          ican Economic Review, 68: 146–160.

Polsby, Nelson W.
1960   "How to Study Community Power: The Pluralist Alternative."
          Journal of Politics, 22: 474–484.

Pondy, Louis R.
1977   "The Other Hand Clapping: An Information-Processing Ap-
          proach to Organizational Power." In Tove H. Hammer and
          Samuel B. Bacharach (eds.), Reward Systems and Power Dis-
          tribution: 56–91. Ithaca, NY: School of Industrial and Labor
          Relations, Cornell University.

Pondy, Louis R.
1978   "Leadership Is a Language Game." In Morgan W. McCall, Jr.,
          and Michael M. Lombardo (eds.), Leadership: Where Else Can
          We Go?: 87–99. Durham, NC: Duke University Press.

Porac, Joseph F., and Gerald R. Salancik
1981   "Generic Overjustification: The Interaction of Extrinsic Re-
          wards." Organizational Behavior and Human Performance, 27:
          197–212.

Porter, Lyman W., and Richard M. Steers
1973   "Organizational, Work, and Personal Factors in Employee Turn-over and Absenteeism." Psychological Bulletin, 80: 151-176.

Porter, L. W., R. M. Steers, R. T. Mowday, and P. V. Boulian
1974   "Organizational Commitment, Job Satisfaction, and Turnover among Psychiatric Technicians." Journal of Applied Psychology, 59: 603-609.

Pritchard, R. D., and M. I. Curtis
1973   "The Influence of Goal Setting and Financial Incentives on Task Performance." Organizational Behavior and Human Performance, 10: 175-183.

Pritchard, R. D., D. W. Leonard, C. W. Von Bergen, Jr., and R. J. Kirk
1976   "The Effects of Varying Schedules of Reinforcement on Human Task Performance." Organizational Behavior and Human Performance, 16: 205-230.

Pugh, Derek S.
1966   "Modern Organization Theory: A Psychological and Sociological Study." Psychological Bulletin, 66: 235-251.

Pugh, Derek, David Hickson, and Robert Hinings
1969   "The Context of Organizational Structures." Administrative Science Quarterly, 14: 91-114.

Pugh, D. S., D. J. Hickson, C. R. Hinings, and C. Turner
1968   "Dimensions of Organization Structure." Administrative Science Quarterly, 13: 65-105.

Rackham, Jeffrey, and Joan Woodward
1970   "The Measurement of Technical Variables." In Joan Woodward (ed.), Industrial Organization: Behaviour and Control: 19-36. London: Oxford University Press.

Randall, R.
1973   "Influence of Environmental Support and Policy Space on Organizational Behavior." Administrative Science Quarterly, 18: 236-247.

Raphael, Edna
1967   "The Anderson-Warkov Hypothesis in Local Unions: A Comparative Study." American Sociological Review, 32: 768-776.

Ratcliff, Richard E.
1980   "Declining Cities and Capitalist Class Structure." In G. William
          Domhoff (ed.), Power Structure Research: 115–138. Beverly
          Hills, CA: Sage.

Rauschenberger, John, Neal Schmitt, and John E. Hunter
1980   "A Test of the Need Hierarchy Concept by a Markov Model of
          Change in Need Strength." Administrative Science Quarterly,
          25: 654–670.

Regan, D., and R. Fazio
1977   "On the Consistency between Attitudes and Behavior: Look to
          the Method of Attitude Formation." Journal of Experimental
          Social Psychology, 13: 28–45.

Reibstein, David J., Stuart A. Youngblood, and Howard L. Fromkin
1975   "Number of Choices and Perceived Decision Freedom as a De-
          terminant of Satisfaction and Consumer Behavior." Journal of
          Applied Psychology, 60: 434–437.

Reich, Michael
1971   "The Economics of Racism." In David M. Gordon (ed.), Prob-
          lems in Political Economy: 107–113. Lexington, MA: D. C.
          Heath.

Reid, S. R.
1968   Mergers, Managers, and the Economy. New York: McGraw-
          Hill.

Reynolds, G. S.
1968   A Primer of Operant Conditioning. Glenview, IL: Scott, Fores-
          man.

Ridgway, V. F.
1956   "Dysfunctional Consequences of Performance Measurements."
          Administrative Science Quarterly, 1: 240–247.

Rindfuss, R. R.
1978   "Changing Patterns of Fertility in the South." Social Forces, 57:
          621–635.

Rivers, W. H. R.
1916   "Sociology and Psychology." Sociological Review, 9: 1–13.

Rizzo, John R., Robert J. House, and Sidney I. Lirtzman
1970   "Role Conflict and Ambiguity in Organizations." Administrative
          Science Quarterly, 15: 150–163.

Roberts, David R.
1959   Executive Compensation. Glencoe, IL: Free Press.

Roberts, Karlene H., and William Glick
1981   "The Job Characteristics Approach to Task Design: A Critical
          Review." Journal of Applied Psychology, 66: 193–217.

Roberts, Karlene H., Charles L. Hulin, and Denise M. Rousseau
1978   Developing an Interdisciplinary Science of Organizations. San
          Francisco: Jossey-Bass.

Roberts, Karlene, and Charles O'Reilly
1974   "Measuring Organizational Communication." Journal of Ap-
          plied Psychology, 59: 321–326.

Robinson, William S.
1950   "Ecological Correlations and the Behavior of Individuals."
          American Sociological Review, 15: 351–357.

Roby, T. B., and J. T. Lanzetta
1956   "Work Group Structure, Communication, and Group Perfor-
          mance." Sociometry, 19: 105–113.

Roethlisberger, F. J., and W. J. Dickson
1939   Management and the Worker. Cambridge, MA: Harvard Uni-
          versity Press.

Roistacher, Richard C.
1974   "A Review of Mathematical Methods in Sociometry." Socio-
          logical Methods and Research, 3: 123–171.

Ross, Lee
1977   "The Intuitive Psychologist and His Shortcomings: Distortions
          in the Attribution Process." In L. Berkowitz (ed.), Advances in
          Experimental Social Psychology, Vol. 10. New York: Academic
          Press.

Rounds, J.
1979   Social Theory, Public Policy and Social Order. Unpublished
          Ph.D. dissertation. Los Angeles: University of California.

Rounds, J.
1981   "Information and Ambiguity in Organizational Change." Paper
          presented at the Carnegie-Mellon Symposium on Information
          Processing in Organizations. Pittsburgh, PA: Carnegie-Mellon
          University.

Rowan, Brian
1980   "Organizational Structure and the Institutional Environment:
            The Case of Public Schools." Unpublished ms., Texas Christian
            University.

Rumelt, Richard
1974   Strategy, Structure, and Economic Performance. Boston: Har-
            vard Business School, Harvard University.

Rushing, William A.
1966   "Organizational Size and Administration: The Problems of
            Causal Homogeneity and a Heterogeneous Category." Pacific
            Sociological Review, 9: 100–108.

Rushing, William A.
1968   "Hardness of Material as Related to Division of Labor in Manu-
            facturing Industries." Administrative Science Quarterly, 13:
            229–245.

Ryder, Norman B.
1965   "The Cohort as a Concept in the Study of Social Change." Amer-
            ican Sociological Review, 30: 843–861.

Salancik, Gerald R.
1974   "Inference of One's Attitude from Behavior Recalled under Lin-
            guistically Manipulated Cognitive Sets." Journal of Experimental
            Social Psychology, 10: 415–427.

Salancik, Gerald R.
1975   "Notes on Loose Coupling: Linking Intentions to Actions." Un-
            published ms., Department of Business Administration, Uni-
            versity of Illinois.

Salancik, Gerald R.
1977   "Commitment and the Control of Organizational Behavior and
            Belief." In Barry M. Staw and Gerald R. Salancik (eds.), New
            Directions in Organizational Behavior: 1–54. Chicago: St. Clair
            Press.

Salancik, Gerald R.
1979a   "Field Stimulations for Organizational Behavior Research." Ad-
            ministrative Science Quarterly, 24: 638–649.

Salancik, Gerald R.
1979b   "Interorganizational Dependence and Responsiveness to Affir-
            mative Action: The Case of Women and Defense Contractors."
            Academy of Management Journal, 22: 375–394.

Salancik, Gerald R., and Mary Conway
1975   "Attitude Inferences from Salient and Relevant Cognitive Content about Behavior." Journal of Personality and Social Psychology, 32: 829–840.

Salancik, Gerald R., and Jeffrey Pfeffer
1974   "The Bases and Use of Power in Organizational Decision Making: The Case of a University." Administrative Science Quarterly, 19: 453–473.

Salancik, Gerald R., and Jeffrey Pfeffer
1977a   "An Examination of Need-Satisfaction Models of Job Attitudes." Administrative Science Quarterly, 22: 427–456.

Salancik, Gerald R., and Jeffrey Pfeffer
1977b   "Who Gets Power — And How They Hold On To It: A Strategic-Contingency Model of Power." Organizational Dynamics, 5: 3–21.

Salancik, Gerald R., and Jeffrey Pfeffer
1978a   "A Social Information Processing Approach to Job Attitudes and Task Design." Administrative Science Quarterly, 23: 224–253.

Salancik, Gerald R., and Jeffrey Pfeffer
1978b   "Uncertainty, Secrecy, and the Choice of Similar Others." Social Psychology, 41: 246–255.

Sampson, Edward E.
1981   "Cognitive Psychology as Ideology." American Psychologist, 36: 730–743.

Sandver, Marcus Hart
1978   "Determinants of Pay for Large Local Union Officers." Industrial Relations, 17: 108–111.

Sandver, Marcus Hart, and Herbert G. Heneman, III
1980   "Analysis and Prediction of Top National Union Officers' Total Compensation." Academy of Management Journal, 23: 534–543.

Sarason, Irwin G., Ronald E. Smith, and Edward Diener
1975   "Personality Research: Components of Variance Attributable to the Person and the Situation." Journal of Personality and Social Psychology, 32: 199–204.

Sauser, W., C. Arauz, and R. Chambers
1978   "Exploring the Relationship between Level of Office Noise and Salary Recommendations: A Preliminary Research Note." Journal of Management, 4: 57–63.

Schacter, S.
1951   "Deviation, Rejection and Communication." Journal of Abnormal and Social Psychology, 46: 190–207.

Schacter, Stanley
1959   The Psychology of Affiliation: Experimental Studies of the Sources of Gregariousness. Stanford, CA: Stanford University Press.

Schein, Edgar H.
1968   "Organizational Socialization and the Profession of Management." Industrial Management Review, 9: 1–16.

Schelling, Thomas C.
1978   Micromotives and Macrobehavior. New York: W. W. Norton.

Schmidt, F. L.
1973   "Implications of a Measurement Problem for Expectancy Theory Research." Organizational Behavior and Human Performance, 10: 243–251.

Schnore, Leo F., and Robert R. Alford
1963   "Forms of Government and Socioeconomic Characteristics of Suburbs." Administrative Science Quarterly, 8: 1–17.

Schoonhoven, Claudia Bird
1981   "Problems with Contingency Theory: Testing Assumptions Hidden within the Language of Contingency 'Theory.'" Administrative Science Quarterly, 26: 349–377.

Schutz, Alfred
1967   "The Phenomenology of the Social World." Evanston, IL: Northwestern University Press.

Schwab, Donald P., and Larry L. Cummings
1970   "Theories of Performance and Satisfaction: A Review." Industrial Relations, 9: 408–430.

Scott, Marvin B., and Stanford M. Lyman
1968   "Accounts." American Sociological Review, 33: 46–62.

Scott, W. Richard
1981   Organizations: Rational, Natural, and Open Systems. Engle-
          wood Cliffs, NJ: Prentice-Hall.

Seashore, Stanley E.
1954   Group Cohesiveness in the Industrial Work Group. Ann Arbor:
          Institute for Social Research, University of Michigan.

Seeman, Melvin
1975   "Alienation Studies." In Alex Inkeles, James Coleman, and Neil
          Smelser (eds.), Annual Review of Sociology, Vol. 1: 91–123.
          Palo Alto, CA: Annual Reviews.

Seligman, C., and J. Darley
1977   "Feedback as Means of Decreasing Residential Energy Consump-
          tion." Journal of Applied Psychology, 62: 363–368.

Selznick, Philip
1948   "Foundations of the Theory of Organization." American So-
          ciological Review, 13: 25–35.

Selznick, Philip
1949   TVA and the Grass Roots. Berkeley, CA: University of Cali-
          fornia Press.

Selznick, Philip
1957   Leadership in Administration. Evanston, IL: Row, Peterson.

Shearing, Clifford D.
1973   "How to Make Theories Untestable: A Guide to Theorists." The
          American Sociologist, 8: 33–37.

Sheehan, Robert
1967   "Proprietors in the World of Big Business." Fortune, 75 (June):
          178–183.

Sheldon, Alan
1980   "Organizational Paradigms: A Theory of Organizational Change."
          Organizational Dynamics, 8 (Winter): 61–80.

Sherif, M.
1935   "A Study of Some Social Factors in Perception." Archives of
          Psychology, No. 187.

Shoup, L. H.
1975   "Shaping the Postwar World: The Council on Foreign Relations
          and United States War Aims during World War Two." Insurgent
          Sociologist, 5: 9–52.

Simon, Herbert A.
1953   "Birth of an Organization: The Economic Cooperation Adminis-
         tration." Public Administration Review, 13: 227–236.

Simon, Herbert A.
1957   "A Behavioral Model of Rational Choice." In Herbert A. Simon,
         Models of Man. New York: John Wiley.

Simon, Herbert A.
1962   "The Architecture of Complexity." Proceedings of the American
         Philosophical Society, 106: 467–482.

Simon, Herbert A.
1972   "Theories of Bounded Rationality." In C. B. McGuire and Roy
         Radner (eds.), Decision and Organization. Amsterdam: Elsevier
         North-Holland.

Simon, Herbert A.
1978   "Rationality as Process and as Product of Thought." American
         Economic Review, 68: 1–16.

Sims, J. P., and A. D. Szilagyi
1976   "Job Characteristic Relationships: Individual and Structural
         Moderators." Organizational Behavior and Human Perfor-
         mance, 17: 211–230.

Skinner, B. F.
1953   Science and Human Behavior. New York: Macmillan.

Sloan, S.
1972   "Translating Psycho-Social Criteria into Design Determinants."
         In W. Mitchell (ed.), Proceedings of Environmental Design Re-
         search Association. Los Angeles: University of California.

Smith, Adam
1937   An Inquiry into the Nature and Causes of the Wealth of Nations.
         New York: Modern Library.

Smith, Peter B.
1973   Groups within Organizations. New York: Harper & Row.

Solomons, L. M., and G. Stein
1896   "Normal Motor Automatism." Psychological Review, 3: 492–
         512.

Sommer, Robert
1959   "Studies in Personal Space." Sociometry, 22: 246–260.

Sommer, Robert
1969   Personal Space: The Behavioral Basis of Design. Englewood
          Cliffs, NJ: Prentice-Hall.

Sorcher, M., and A. P. Goldstein
1972   "A Behavior Modelling Approach in Training." Personnel Ad-
          ministration, 35: 35–41.

Spangler, Eva, Marsha A. Gordon, and Ronald M. Pipkin
1978   "Token Women: An Empirical Test of Kanter's Hypothesis."
          American Journal of Sociology, 85; 160–170.

Special Task Force to the Secretary of Health, Education and Welfare
1973   Work in America. Cambridge, MA: MIT Press.

Spence, Michael A.
1975   Market Signalling. Cambridge, MA: Harvard University Press.

Spenner, Kenneth
1979   "Temporal Changes in Work Content." American Sociological
          Review, 44: 968–975.

Sproull, Lee S.
1981   "Beliefs in Organizations." In Paul C. Nystrom and William H.
          Starbuck (eds.), Handbook of Organizational Design, Vol. 2:
          203–224. New York: Oxford University Press.

Stava, Per
1976   "Constraints on the Politics of Public Choice." In James G.
          March and Johan P. Olsen, Ambiguity and Choice in Organiza-
          tions: 206–224. Bergen, Norway: Universitetsforlaget.

Staw, Barry M.
1974   "Attitudinal and Behavioral Consequences of Changing a Major
          Organizational Reward: A Natural Field Experiment." Journal of
          Personality and Social Psychology, 29: 742–751.

Staw, Barry M.
1976   "Knee-Deep in the Big Muddy: A Study of Escalating Commit-
          ment to a Chosen Course of Action." Organizational Behavior
          and Human Performance, 16: 27–44.

Staw, Barry M.
1980a   "The Consequences of Turnover." Journal of Occupational Be-
          havior, 1: 253–273.

Staw, Barry M.
1980b   "Rationality and Justification in Organizational Life." In B. M.
         Staw and L. L. Cummings (eds.), Research in Organizational
         Behavior, Vol. 2: 45–80. Greenwich, CT: JAI Press.

Staw, B. M., B. J. Calder, R. K. Hess, and L. E. Sandelands
1980   "Intrinsic Motivation and Norms about Payment." Journal of
         Personality, 48: 1–14.

Staw, Barry M., and Frederick V. Fox
1977   "Escalation: Some Determinants of Commitment to a Previously
         Chosen Course of Action." Human Relations, 30: 431–450.

Staw, Barry M., and Jerry Ross
1978   "Commitment to a Policy Decision: A Multi-Theoretical Per-
         spective." Administrative Science Quarterly, 23: 40–64.

Staw, Barry M., and Jerry Ross
1980   "Commitment in an Experimenting Society: A Study of the At-
         tribution of Leadership from Administrative Scenarios." Journal
         of Applied Psychology, 65: 249–260.

Staw, Barry M., and Eugene Szwajkowski
1975   "The Scarcity-Munificence Component of Organizational En-
         vironments and the Commission of Illegal Acts." Administrative
         Science Quarterly, 20: 345–354.

Stedry, A. C., and E. Kay
1966   "The Effects of Goal Difficulty on Performance." Behavioral
         Science, 11: 459–470.

Steele, Fred I.
1973   Physical Settings and Organization Development. Reading,
         MA: Addison-Wesley.

Steers, Richard M.
1975   "Task-Goal Attributes, Achievement, and Supervisory Perfor-
         mance." Organizational Behavior and Human Performance, 13:
         392–403.

Steers, R. M., and D. G. Spencer
1977   "The Role of Achievement Motivation in Job Design." Journal of
         Applied Psychology, 62: 472–479.

Stephens, Tedd A., and Wayne A. Burroughs
1978   "An Application of Operant Conditioning to Absenteeism in a
         Hospital Setting." Journal of Applied Psychology, 63: 518–521.

Stewman, Shelby, and Suresh L. Konda
In   "Careers and Organizational Labor Markets: Demographic
press   Models of Organizational Behavior." American Journal of So-
          ciology, (In press).

Stigler, George J.
1971   "The Theory of Economic Regulation." Bell Journal of Econom-
          ics and Management Science, 2: 3–21.

Stinchcombe, Arthur L.
1965   "Social Structure and Organizations." In James G. March (ed.),
          Handbook of Organizations: 142–193. Chicago: Rand McNally.

Stinson, J. E., and T. W. Johnson
1975   "The Path-Goal Theory of Leadership: A Partial Test and Sug-
          gested Refinement." Academy of Management Journal, 18:
          242–252.

Stogdill, Ralph M.
1974   Handbook of Leadership. New York: Free Press.

Stogdill, R. M., and A. E. Coons
1957   Leader Behavior: Its Description and Measurement. Columbus,
          OH: Bureau of Business Research, College of Commerce and
          Administration, Ohio State University.

Stone, Eugene F.
1976   "The Moderating Effect of Work-Related Values on the Job
          Scope-Job Satisfaction Relationship." Organizational Behavior
          and Human Performance, 15: 147–167.

Stone, Eugene F., Richard T. Mowday, and Lyman W. Porter
1977   "Higher Order Need Strengths as Moderators of the Job Scope-
          Job Satisfaction Relationship." Journal of Applied Psychology,
          62: 466–471.

Strauss, George
1974   "Job Satisfaction, Motivation, and Job Redesign." In G. Strauss,
          R. E. Miles, C. C. Snow, and A. S. Tannenbaum (eds.), Organi-
          zational Behavior: Research and Issues: 19–49. Belmont, CA:
          Wadsworth.

Sweezy, Paul
1939   "Interest Groups in the American Economy." The Structure of
          the American Economy, Part I. Washington, D.C.: National
          Resource Committee.

Taylor, Frederick W.
1911   The Principles of Scientific Management. New York: Harper.

Teece, David J.
1976   Vertical Integration and Vertical Divestiture in the U.S. Oil Industry. Palo Alto, CA: Stanford University Institute for Energy Studies.

Teece, David J.
1980   "The Diffusion of an Administrative Innovation." Management Science, 26: 464–470.

Teece, David J.
In   "Internal Organization and Economic Performance: An Empirical Analysis of the Profitability of Principal Firms." Journal of Industrial Economics, (In press).
press

Teece, David J., Henry Ogden Armour, and Garth Saloner
1980   "Vertical Integration and Risk Reduction." Unpublished ms., Graduate School of Business, Stanford University.

Terborg, J.
1976   "The Motivational Components of Goal Setting." Journal of Applied Psychology, 61: 613–621.

Terborg, J., and H. Miller
1978   "Motivation, Behavior and Performance: A Closer Examination of Goal Setting and Monetary Incentives." Journal of Applied Psychology, 63: 29–39.

Thibaut, J. W., and H. H. Kelley
1959   The Social Psychology of Groups. New York: John Wiley.

Thompson, James D.
1967   Organizations in Action. New York: McGraw-Hill.

Tichy, Noel M.
1981   "Networks in Organizations." In Paul C. Nystrom and William H. Starbuck (eds.), Handbook of Organizational Design, Vol. 2: 225–249. New York: Oxford University Press.

Tichy, Noel, and Charles Fombrun
1979   "Network Analysis in Organizational Settings." Human Relations, 32: 923–965.

Tichy, Noel M., Michael L. Tushman, and Charles Fombrun
1979   "Social Network Analysis for Organizations." Academy of Management Review, 4: 507–519.

Tolbert, Charles, Patrick M. Horan, and E. M. Beck
1980   "The Structure of Economic Segmentation: A Dual Economy Approach." American Journal of Sociology, 85: 1095–1116.

Tosi, Henry, Ramon Aldag, and Ronald Storey
1973   "On the Measurement of the Environment: An Assessment of the Lawrence and Lorsch Environmental Uncertainty Scale." Administrative Science Quarterly, 18: 27–36.

Tosi, Henry, and Henry Platt
1967   "Administrative Ratios and Organizational Size." Academy of Management Journal, 10: 161–168.

Tuggle, Francis D.
1978   Organizational Processes. Arlington Heights, IL: AHM.

Turner, A, N,, and P. R. Lawrence
1965   Industrial Jobs and the Worker: An Investigation of Response to Task Attributes. Boston: Harvard University.

Turner, R. H.
1960   "Sponsored and Contest Mobility and the School System." American Sociological Review, 25: 855–867.

Tushman, Michael
1977   "Communication across Organizational Boundaries: Special Boundary Roles in the Innovation Process." Administrative Science Quarterly, 22: 581–606.

Tushman, Michael
1978   "Technical Communication in Research and Development Laboratories: Impact of Project Work Characteristics." Academy of Management Journal, 21: 624–645.

Udy, Stanley H., Jr.
1959   "'Bureaucracy' and 'Rationality' in Weber's Organization Theory." American Sociological Review, 24: 791–795.

Underwood, B. J.
1966   Experimental Psychology. New York: Appleton-Century-Crofts.

Unger, R. M.
1975   Knowledge and Politics. New York: Free Press.

Urwick, Lyndall, and E. F. L. Brech
1946   The Making of Scientific Management, Vol. 2. London: Management Publications Trust.

Useem, Michael
1979   "The Social Organization of the American Business Elite and Participation of Corporation Directors in the Governance of American Institutions." American Sociological Review, 44: 553–572.

Van de Ven, Andrew H.
1979   "Review of Organizations and Environments by Howard E. Aldrich." Administrative Science Quarterly, 24: 320–326.

Van de Ven, Andrew H., and W. Graham Astley
1981   "A Commentary on Organizational Behavior in the 1980's." Decision Sciences, 12: 388–398.

Van de Ven, Andrew H., and W. Graham Astley
1981   "Mapping the Field to Create a Dynamic Perspective on Organization Design and Behavior." In A. H. Van de Ven and W. F. Joyce (eds.), Perspectives on Organization Design and Behavior: 427–468. New York: Wiley-Interscience.

Van de Ven, Andrew H., and William F. Joyce (eds.)
1981   Perspectives on Organization Design and Behavior. New York: Wiley-Interscience.

Van Maanen, John
1976   "Breaking In: Socialization to Work." In Robert Dubin (ed.), Handbook of Work, Organization, and Society: 67–130. Chicago: Rand McNally.

Van Maanen, John
1979a   "The Fact of Fiction in Organizational Ethnography." Administrative Science Quarterly, 24: 539–550.

Van Maanen, John
1979b   "Reclaiming Qualitative Methods for Organizational Research: A Preface." Administrative Science Quarterly, 24: 520–526.

Van Maanen, John
1979c   "On the Understanding of Interpersonal Relations." In Warren Bennis, John Van Maanen, and Edgar H. Schein (eds.), Essays in Interpersonal Relations: 13–42. Homewood, IL: Dorsey.

Villajero, Don
1962   "Stock Ownership and the Control of Corporations." New University Thought, 2: 33–77.

Vroom, Victor H
1964   Work and Motivation. New York: John Wiley.

Wachter, M. L., and O. E. Williamson
1978   "Obligational Markets and the Mechanics of Inflation." Bell
              Journal of Economics, 9: 549–571.

Wahba, Mahmoud A., and Lawrence G. Bridwell
1976   "Maslow Reconsidered: A Review of Research on the Need Hier-
              archy Theory." Organizational Behavior and Human Perfor-
              mance, 15: 212–240.

Webb, E. J., D. T. Campbell, R. D. Schwartz, and L. Sechrest
1966   Unobtrusive Measures. Chicago: Rand McNally.

Weber, Max
1947   The Theory of Social and Economic Organization. New York:
              Free Press.

Weick, Karl E.
1967   "Dissonance and Task Enhancement: A Problem for Compensa-
              tion Theory?" Organizational Behavior and Human Perfor-
              mance, 2: 189–208.

Weick, Karl E.
1969   The Social Psychology of Organizing. Reading, MA: Addison-
              Wesley.

Weick, Karl E.
1976   "Educational Organizations as Loosely Coupled Systems." Ad-
              ministrative Science Quarterly, 21: 1–19.

Weick, Karl E.
1979   "Cognitive Processes in Organizations." In Barry M. Staw (ed.)
              Research in Organizational Behavior, Vol. 1: 41–74. Greenwich,
              CT: JAI Press.

Weick, Karl E.
1980   "The Management of Eloquence." Executive, 6 (Summer): 18–21.

Weiner, Stephen S.
1976   "Participation, Deadlines, and Choice." In James G. March and
              Johan P. Olsen, Ambiguity and Choice in Organizations: 225–
              250. Bergen, Norway: Universitetsforlaget.

Weiss, Daniel S.
1979   "The Effects of Systematic Variations in Information on Judges'
          Descriptions of Personality." Journal of Personality and Social
          Psychology, 37: 2121–2136.

Weiss, Howard M., and James B. Shaw
1979   "Social Influences on Judgments about Tasks." Organizational
          Behavior and Human Performance, 24: 126–140.

Welch, Finis
1973   "Black-White Differences in Returns to Schooling." American
          Economic Review, 63: 893–907.

Wells, W. P., and D. C. Pelz
1966   "Groups." In D. C. Pelz and R. M. Andrews (eds.), Scientists in
          Organizations: Productive Climates for Research and Develop-
          ment. New York: John Wiley.

Wheeler, Stan
1966   "The Structure of Formally Organized Socialization Settings." In
          Orville G. Brim and Stan Wheeler (eds.), Socialization after
          Childhood: 53–116. New York: John Wiley.

White, J. Kenneth
1978   "Individual Differences and the Job Quality-Worker Response
          Relationship: Review, Integration, and Comments." Academy
          of Management Review, 3: 267–280.

White, Sam E., and Terence R. Mitchell
1979   "Job Enrichment versus Social Cues: A Comparison and Com-
          petitive Test." Journal of Applied Psychology, 64: 1–9.

White, Sam E., Terence R. Mitchell, and Cecil H. Bell, Jr.
1977   "Goal Setting, Evaluation Apprehension, and Social Cues as
          Determinants of Job Performance and Job Satisfaction in a Sim-
          ulated Organization." Journal of Applied Psychology, 62: 665–
          673.

Whitt, J. Allen
1979   "Toward a Class-Dialectic Model of Political Power: An Empiri-
          cal Assessment of Three Competing Models of Power." Ameri-
          can Sociological Review, 44: 81–100.

Whitt, J. Allen
1980   "Can Capitalists Organize Themselves?" In G. William Domhoff (ed.), Power Structure Research: 97–113. Beverly Hills, CA: Sage.

Wildavsky, Aaron
1979   The Politics of the Budgetary Process, 3rd ed. Boston: Little, Brown.

Williamson, Oliver E.
1966   "A Rational Theory of the Federal Budgetary Process." In Gordon Tullock (ed.), Papers on Non-Market Decision Making. Charlottesville, VA: Thomas Jefferson Center for Political Economy.

Williamson, Oliver E.
1975   Markets and Hierarchies: Analysis and Antitrust Implications. New York: Free Press.

Williamson, Oliver E.
1979   "Transaction-Cost Economics: The Governance of Contractual Relations." Journal of Law and Economics, 22: 233–261.

Williamson, Oliver E.
1981   "The Economics of Organization: The Transaction Cost Approach." Working Paper No. 96. Philadelphia: Center for the Study of Organizational Innovation, University of Pennsylvania.

Williamson, Oliver E., and William G. Ouchi
1981   "The Markets and Hierarchies Program of Research: Origins, Implications, Prospects." In A. H. Van de Ven and W. F. Joyce (eds.), Perspectives on Organization Design and Behavior: 347–370. New York: Wiley-Interscience.

Williamson, O. E., M. L. Wachter, and J. E. Harris
1975   "Understanding the Employment Relation: The Analysis of Idiosyncratic Exchange." Bell Journal of Economics, 6: 250–280.

Winter, Sidney G.
1975   "Optimization and Evolution in the Theory of the Firm." In Richard H. Day and Theodore Groves (eds.), Adaptive Economic Models: 73–118. New York: Academic Press.

Wofford, J. C.
1971   "The Motivational Basis of Job Satisfaction and Job Performance." Personnel Psychology, 24: 501–518.

Woodward, Joan
1965   Industrial Organization: Theory and Practice. London: Oxford University Press.

Woodward, Joan
1970   Industrial Organization: Behaviour and Control. London: Oxford University Press.

Yoels, William C.
1974   "The Structure of Scientific Fields and the Allocation of Editorships on Scientific Journals: Some Observations on the Politics of Knowledge." Sociological Quarterly, 15: 264–276.

Yukl, Gary, Kenneth N. Wexley, and James D. Seymore
1972   "Effectiveness of Pay Incentives under Variable Ratio and Continuous Reinforcement Schedules." Journal of Applied Psychology, 56: 19–23.

Zajonc, Robert B.
1965   "Social Facilitation." Science, 149: 269–274.

Zajonc, R. B.
1968   "Attitudinal Effects of Mere Exposure." Journal of Personality and Social Psychology, 9: 1–29.

Zald, Mayer N.
1965   "Who Shall Rule? A Political Analysis of Succession in a Large Welfare Organization." Pacific Sociological Review, 8: 52–60.

Zald, Mayer N.
1970a   Organizational Change: The Political Economy of the YMCA. Chicago: University of Chicago Press.

Zald, Mayer N.
1970b   "Political Economy: A Framework for Comparative Analysis." In Mayer N. Zald (ed.), Power in Organizations: 221–261. Nashville, TN: Vanderbilt University Press.

Zanna, Mark P.
1973   "On Inferring One's Belief from One's Behavior in a Low-Choice Setting." Journal of Personality and Social Psychology, 26: 386–394.

Zeitlin, Maurice
1974   "Corporate Ownership and Control: The Large Corporation and the Capitalist Class." American Journal of Sociology, 79: 1073–1119.

Zifferblatt, S. M.
1972   "The Effectiveness of Modes and Schedules of Reinforcement on
          Work and Social Behavior in Occupational Therapy." Behavior
          Therapy, 3: 567–578.

Zucker, Lynne G.
1977   "The Role of Institutionalization in Cultural Persistence." Amer-
          ican Sociological Review, 42: 726–743.

Zucker, Lynne G.
1980a   "Effect of Sudden Redefinition of Institutional Structure on 'De-
          mand Characteristics' in Experiments." Paper presented at the
          West Coast Conference for Small Group Research, San Fran-
          cisco, May 1980.

Zucker, Lynne G.
1980b   "Sources of Change in Institutionalized Systems: Generating and
          Testing a Theory of Occupational Mobility." Unpublished ms.,
          Department of Sociology, University of California-Los Angeles.

Zucker, Lynne G.
1980c   "Typifying Interaction: Action, Situation, and Role." Unpub-
          lished ms., Department of Sociology, University of California-
          Los Angeles.

Zucker, Lynne G.
1981a   "Institutional Structure and Organizational Processes: The Role
          of Evaluation Units in Schools." In Adrianne Bank and Richard
          C. Williams (eds.), Evaluation and Decision Making. CSE Mon-
          ograph Series, No. 10. Los Angeles: UCLA Center for the Study
          of Evaluation.

Zucker, Lynne G.
1981b   "Organizations as Institutions." In Samuel B. Bacharach (ed.),
          Perspectives in Organizational Sociology: Theory and Research.
          Greenwich, CT: JAI Press.

Zucker, Lynne G., and Carolyn Rosenstein
1981   "Taxonomies of Institutional Structure: Dual Economy Recon-
          sidered." American Sociological Review, 46: 869–884.

Zucker, Lynne G., and Pamela Tolbert
1981   "Institutional Sources of Change in the Formal Structure of Or-
          ganizations: The Diffusion of Civil Service Reform, 1880–1935."
          Paper presented at the Annual Meeting of the American Socio-
          logical Association, Toronto.

Zweigenhaft, R. L.
1976   "Personal Space in the Faculty Office: Desk Placement and the
         Student-Faculty Interaction." Journal of Applied Psychology,
         61: 529–532.

Zwerman, William L.
1970   New Perspectives on Organization Theory. Westport, CT:
         Greenwood.

AUTHOR INDEX

Abell, P., 155
Abelson, R. P., 221
Adam, E. E., Jr., 92
Adams, J. S., 85
Aiken, M., 20, 152, 275
Ajzen, I., 44
Alba, R. D., 257, 277
Alchian, A. A., 142
Aldag, R. J., 56, 57, 155, 156, 162
Alderfer, C. P., 17, 41, 54, 55
Aldrich, H. E., 26, 123, 157, 161,
   181, 182, 183, 184, 186, 187,
   190, 192, 198
Alexander, C. N., 247, 250
Alford, R. A., 277
Allen, A., 119
Allen, M. P., 201
Allen, R. W., 66
Allen, S. A., 141
Allison, G. T., 6, 63, 64, 133
Alport, F. H., 18, 84
Anderson, J. C., 52
Anderson, T. R., 150
Annett, J., 52
Arauz, C., 268
Argyris, C., 18, 26, 35
Armenakis, A. A., 100
Armour, H. O., 140, 147
Arnold, H. J., 46
Aronson, E., 105
Arvey, R. D., 51

Astley, W. G., 5, 12, 254, 255
Axelrod, R., 11, 217

Bacharach, S. B., 31
Back, K., 266
Bagazzi, R. P., 147
Baker, D., 128
Baker, S. H., 92
Baldes, J. J., 50, 52
Baldridge, J. V., 64
Bandura, A. 48–49, 52, 73, 86, 87,
   90, 93, 94, 95
Baritz, J. H., 31, 36
Barnard, C. I., 32
Baron, J. N., 167
Barwick, K. D., 91
Baty, G., 185, 290
Baumol, W., 128
Bavelas, A., 271
Beck, E. M., 166
Becker, F. D., 260, 261, 264, 265,
   267, 268, 270
Becker, H. S., 97
Bedeian, A. G., 100
Bell, C. H., Jr., 50, 102, 116
Bem, D. J., 50, 64, 73, 105, 107,
   119, 251
Berger, C. J., 88, 89
Berger, P. L., 209
Berle, A., Jr., 125, 127
Berlew, D. E., 97

Bernstein, R. J., 210
Bibb, R., 166
Bidwell, C. E., 14, 15
Bielby, W. T., 167
Biglan, A., 44, 45, 47
Binkhorst, D., 11, 216
Blai, B., Jr., 61
Blalock, H. M., Jr., 102, 103
Blau, P. M., 20, 23, 64, 83, 101,
    102, 130, 131, 149, 150, 190, 279
Blauner, R., 170
Block, F. E., 283
Blood, M. R., 56
Bloom, J. R., 60, 61, 63
Blumenfeld, W. E., 52
Blumer, H., 209
Boling, J. C., 51
Bonacich, F., 167, 168
Booker, G., 91
Bougon, M., 11, 216, 217
Bowers, K. S., 8
Brass, D. J., 267, 268
Braverman, 11, 27, 28–29, 44, 168,
    169, 210, 258, 264, 265, 293
Braybrooke, D., 7
Brayfield, A. H., 56
Brech, E. F. L., 28
Brehm, J. W., 108
Brewer, J. F., 91
Bridwell, L. G., 61
Brief, A. P., 56, 57
Britt, D. W., 15
Brittain, J. W., 182, 185
Brody, C., 249
Brookes, M. J., 266
Brown, C. A., 56
Brown, R., 243
Brown, R. E., 89
Brown, R. H., 9, 227, 228
Brown, W., 212
Bucher, R., 67
Burns, T., 20, 155

Burrell, G., 218, 254
Burroughs, W. A., 91
Burt, R. S., 102, 201, 206
Byrne, D., 223, 266

Calder, B. J., 36, 42, 63, 75, 78,
    81, 103, 110
Caldwell, D. F., 63, 109, 110, 113,
    116
Campbell, A., 26
Campbell, D. T., 183, 241, 269
Campbell, J. P., 101
Canty, D., 267
Caplan, R., 26
Carlsmith, J. M., 81, 250, 251
Carroll, S. J., 49, 51, 52
Cartwright, D., 27, 31
Chadwick-Jones, J. K., 56
Chaffee, E. E., 12, 71
Chambers, R., 268
Chandler, A. D., Jr., 157, 158, 188
Child, J., 150, 155, 159, 160
Chiu, J. S. Y., 128
Christman, K. P., 201
Cicourel, A. V., 209
Ciscel, D. H., 128
Clark, B. R., 232
Clarkson, G. P. E., 235
Clearwater, Y., 267
Clegg, S., 32, 74
Cohen, A. E., 108
Cohen, M. D., 9, 11, 235, 237
Coleman, J., 103
Collins, B. E., 250
Collins, R., 18–19, 20, 77, 166,
    169, 222, 223, 260
Comer, R., 108
Comstock, D. E., 124
Condry, J., 109
Connerton, M., 289, 290
Connerton, P., 210
Converse, P. E., 26

Conway, M., 105, 106
Coons, A. E., 101
Copeland, R. E., 89
Crecine, J. P., 235
Crockett, W. H., 56
Crozier, M., 65, 74
Cummings, L. L., 4, 41, 45, 56, 88, 89, 156, 254, 255
Curtis, M. I., 51
Cutler, N. E., 277
Cyert, R. M., 133, 190, 205, 235, 237

Dachler, H. P., 50, 51, 53
Daft, R. L., 11, 32, 254
Dahl, R. A., 64, 71
Daniel, W. W., 115
Darley, J., 52, 93
Davis, J. A., 102
Davis, J. H., 104
Davis, O. A., 238
Davis, T. R. V., 94, 95
Deci, E. L., 110
Delbevq, A. L., 104
Dempster, A. H., 238
Demsetz, H., 142
Deslauriers, B. C., 89
Dessler, G., 48
Deutsch, M., 85
DeVries, D. L., 87, 88
Dewhirst, H. D., 51
Dickson, W. J., 103
Diener, E., 11, 119
Domhoff, G. M., 71, 172
Dornbusch, S. M., 97, 130, 154, 190
Dossett, D. L., 51
Dowling, J., 245
Downey, H. K., 48, 155
Drucker, P., 292, 293
Dulaney, D. E., 47
Dunbar, R. L. M., 217

Duncan, R. B., 155, 156
Dunham, R. B., 60, 116
Dunkerley, D., 32
Dunn, M. G., 172
Dunnette, M. D., 101
Dutton, J. M., 217
Dyer, L., 46, 110
Dyer, W. G., 102

Easterlin, R. A., 30
Edelman, M., 62, 220, 221
Edstrom, A., 97, 199, 291
Edwards, R. C., 28, 29, 44, 122, 125, 164, 165, 166, 168, 265, 282
Edwards, W., 7
Elbing, A. O., 128
Emerson, R. M., 64, 83
Epstein, S., 119
Erez, M., 52
Evan, W., 185, 193, 290
Evans, M. G., 48
Everett, P. B., 89

Faber, H., 26
Faucheux, C., 275, 276
Fazio, R., 75
Featherman, D. L., 167
Feldman, D. C., 97, 190
Ferdinands, R., 266
Festinger, L., 59, 81, 85, 108, 250, 266
Fishbein, M., 44, 47
Flanagan, R. J., 170
Flanders, J. P., 94
Fleischman, E. F., 48
Fombrun, C., 271, 272, 273, 275
Form, W. H., 166
Fox, F. V., 30
Freeman, J. H., 8, 14, 15, 16, 23, 24, 150, 151, 180, 181, 182, 183, 185, 186, 187, 188, 189, 190, 191, 192, 198, 204

Freeman, R. B., 283, 289, 290
French, J., Jr., 65, 66, 102
Friedland, E. I., 6, 63
Friedman, I., 109
Friedman, M., 132, 134
Fromkin, H. L., 80
Funder, D. C., 119

Galbraith, J. K., 186
Galbraith, J. R., 45, 97, 148, 160, 199, 291
Galle, O., 15
Gamboa, V. U., 91
Ganster, D. C., 56, 57
Garfinkel, H., 209, 212, 213, 214
Geer, B., 97
Gephart, R. P., Jr., 212, 213, 214
Gerard, H., 85
Gergen, K. J., 33, 34, 35, 36, 37, 38, 294
Gerwin, D., 235
Glassman, R., 184
Glenn, N. D., 277
Glick, W., 59
Goffman, E., 209, 213
Goldberg, V. P., 144, 145, 146, 166, 168
Golding, D., 228
Goldman, P., 163, 164
Goldstein, A. P., 94
Gonos, G., 207
Goodman, P. S., 215, 216
Goodman, R. A., 61
Gordon, G., 227
Gordon, M. E., 36, 37, 277
Gordon, R. A., 32, 127
Graen, G., 45
Granovetter, M., 26
Greene, D., 109, 110
Griffin, R. W., 54, 57, 114, 115
Griffitt, W., 268
Gross, N., 99

Grusky, O., 212
Guetzkow, H., 271
Gulick, L., 32
Gusfield, J. R., 287
Gustafson, D. H., 104
Gutmann, M. P., 277

Haas, J. E., 150
Hackman, J. R., 17, 45, 55, 56, 57, 59, 62, 63, 113, 114
Hage, J., 20, 152, 275
Halaby, C. N., 291
Hall, D. T., 61, 97, 100
Hall, R. H., 50
Hall, R. V., 89, 91
Hamilton, H., 185
Hamner, E. P., 91
Hamner, W. C., 50, 52, 91
Hanada, M., 251, 252
Hanie, C. A., 36, 37
Hannan, M. T., 8, 15, 23, 151, 180, 181, 182, 183, 187, 188, 189
Harackiewicz, J. M., 109
Hargens, L. L., 67
Harre, R., 8
Harris, J. E., 137
Hauser, R. M., 17, 103, 167
Hawley, A. A., 186, 193
Heizer, J., 91
Hellriegel, D., 155
Helmich, D. L., 212, 285
Helmich, R. L., 250
Heneman, H. G., III, 88, 89, 130
Herman, J. B., 60, 116
Herzberg, F., 55
Hess, R. K., 110
Hickson, D. J., 17, 65, 148, 152, 203, 220, 275, 276
Hills, F. S., 64, 66
Hinings, C. R., 17, 65, 148, 275, 276
Hirschman, A. O., 170, 283

Hollingsworth, A. T., 56, 278
Holtzner, B., 209
Homans, G. C., 78, 267
Horan, D. M., 166
Horner, S. O., 56, 278
House, R. J., 7, 38, 48, 100
Howell, J. E., 32
Huber, G. P., 156
Hulin, C. L., 17, 25, 56, 60, 116
Hunter, F., 272
Hunter, J. E., 61
Hunstman, B., 128
Huson, C., 102

Ivancevich, J. M., 50, 51, 52
Ives, R. S., 266

Jablonsky, S. F., 87, 88
Jacobs, D., 194
Jacobs, R. C., 241
Jaeger, A. M., 31, 142, 143, 278,
    282, 285, 286
James, L. R., 113
Janis, I. L., 104
Jenkins, W. O., 87
Johns, G., 56
Johnson, G. E., 48, 150, 283
Joiner, D., 269
Jones, A. P., 113
Jones, E. E., 39, 62
Jonsson, S. A., 228, 229
Joyce, W. F., 254

Kahn, R. L., 26, 98, 99, 100, 142,
    193
Kanfer, F. H., 88
Kanter, R. M., 223, 277, 291
Kaplan, A., 266
Karpik, L., 74
Kasarda, J. D., 14, 15, 151
Katz, D., 142, 185, 285
Kaufman, H., 62, 186
Kay, E., 50, 52

Kelley, H. H., 39, 62, 84, 266
Kempen, R. W., 91
Kessel, J. H., 277
Keyfitz, N., 281
Khandwalla, P. N., 124, 156
Kiesler, C. A., 53, 59, 84, 101, 116
Kiesler, S. B., 59, 84, 101, 116
Kilburn, H. C., Jr., 201
Kim, J., 50, 52
Kimberley, J. R., 148, 151, 185
King, A. S., 115
Kinne, S. B., III, 50, 52
Kipnis, D., 68, 71
Kirk, R. J., 89
Kleiman, L. S., 36, 37
Knight, G. W., 249, 250, 251
Kolko, G., 127
Komaki, J., 91
Konda, S. L., 281, 291
Kotter, J. P., 10
Kraft, P., 168
Kreitner, R., 8, 86, 89
Kronenfeld, J. E., 150
Kruglanski, A. W., 109
Kuhn, T. S., 227, 228
Kuskin, M. S., 283

Ladd, E. C., 31
Laird, J. D., 108
Landau, M., 184
Langer, E. J., 35, 221
Lanzetta, J. T., 271
Larner, R. J., 127, 129
Latham, G. P., 50, 51, 52
Lawler, E. E., 31, 45, 46, 56, 59,
    62
Lawler, J., 108, 113
Lawrence, P. R., 10, 20, 56, 124,
    156, 184
Leavitt, H. J., 12, 24, 25, 271, 276
Leblebici, H., 64, 67, 156, 185,
    199, 290
Lecuyer, R., 269

Lee, C. A., 276
Leidy, T. E., 52
Lenneberg, E. H., 243
Leong, A., 64, 67
Leonard, D. W., 89
Lepper, M. R., 109, 110
Levin, M. L., 185
Levine, M. E., 67
Levinson, H., 26
Lewellan, W. G., 128, 129
Lieberman, S., 10, 100
Light, I. H., 136
Lincoln, J. R., 17, 251, 252
Lindblom, C. E., 7
Lipset, S. M., 31, 103
Lirtzman, S. I., 100
Locke, E. A., 2, 7, 41, 48, 49, 51,
    54, 78, 92, 93, 278
Lodahl, J., 67, 227
Logan, F. A., 88
London, M., 51, 52
Lorsch, J., 20, 124, 156, 184
Louis, M. R., 97
Luckmann, T., 209
Lundin, R. A., 228, 229
Luthans, F., 8, 86, 89, 92, 94, 95
Lynch, B. P., 154

Machlup, F., 132
Mackensie, K. D., 9, 38, 275, 276,
    277
Maguire, M. A., 160
Mahoney, T. A., 64, 66
Manns, C. L., 64
March, J. G., 9, 11, 22, 25, 63, 64,
    65, 66, 77, 85, 133, 146, 190,
    205, 233, 234, 235, 237, 238
Marris, R., 128
Martin, J., 78, 79, 85, 232
Marx, J. H., 209
Maslow, A. H., 18, 41, 55, 61, 268
Mason, W. S., 99
Masson, R. T., 128, 129

Matsui, T., 46
Mausner, B., 55
Mayhew, B. H., 20-21, 22, 38, 78,
    255
McCain, B. R., 280, 287, 288
McClelland, D. C., 55
McCue, G. M., 270
McDermott, T., 91
McEachern, W. A., 99, 126, 127,
    129
McElroy, J. C., 269
McGuire, J. W., 128
McNeil, K., 278, 286
Mead, G. H., 209
Means, G. C., 125, 127
Mechanic, D., 37
Medoff, J. L., 283, 289, 290
Meissner, M., 154
Merton, R. K., 1, 98, 99
Meyer, J. W., 11, 15, 239, 240,
    243, 244, 245, 246, 247, 252
Meyer, M. W., 16, 20, 149, 150,
    160, 190, 248
Miles, R. E., 158, 159, 160, 161
Miller, H., 51
Mills, C. W., 171
Mindlin, S., 157
Miner, J. B., 91
Mintz, M., 268
Mintzberg, H., 31
Mirvis, P., 255
Mischel, W., 119
Mitchell, J. C., 271
Mitchell, T., 4, 41, 44, 45, 46, 47,
    50, 51, 113, 116
Mobley, W. H., 50, 51, 53, 56, 278
Mohr, L., 152
Monteverde, K., 138, 139, 205
Moore, G., 172
Moore, L. F., 1
Moore, W. L., 65, 66, 238
Moorhead, G., 54, 57
Morgan, G., 218 254

Morris, S., 110, 292
Morrow, P. C., 269
Mowday, R. T., 56, 68, 71
Mulder, M., 271
Murray, A., 78, 79

Nadler, D. A., 52
Nagel, E., 132
Nagel, J., 65
Nehrbass, R. G., 36
Neisser, U., 74
Newcomb, J. E., 266
Newhams, T., 91
Newman, J. E., 114
Nicholson, N., 56
Nisbett, R. E., 39, 62, 109
Noble, D. F., 168
Nord, W. R., 86, 91
Nougaim, K. E., 61
Nowak, P., 199, 200

O'Connell, M. J., 156
O'Connor, J. F., 10
Ohtsuka, Y., 46
Oldham, G. R., 17, 51, 52, 55, 62, 113, 114, 267, 268
Olsen, J. P., 9, 11, 85, 234, 235, 238
Olson, J., 251, 252
O'Reilly, C. A., 52, 60, 61, 63, 90, 109, 110, 113, 116, 277, 280, 287, 288
Orne, M. T., 251
Orpen, C., 57, 58, 91
Ouchi, W. G., 26, 31, 142, 143, 144, 160, 175, 176, 192, 232, 278, 282, 285, 286

Padgett, J. F., 7, 12, 238
Pallak, M. S., 108
Palmer, D. A., 202, 206, 255
Palmer, J., 127

Parker, D. F., 46, 110
Parlette, G. N., 60, 61, 63
Parsons, T., 62, 78, 123
Patchen, M., 66, 67
Paul, R., 92
Payne, R., 275
Pearce, J. L., 57, 59
Pedalino, E., 91
Pelz, D. C., 285
Pennings, J. M., 16, 154, 162, 202, 276
Pepitone, A., 74
Perrow, C., 65, 130, 148, 152, 239
Peters, L. H., 46, 47, 48
Peters, T. J., 115
Pettigrew, A. M., 64, 67, 210, 212, 218, 276
Pfeffer, J., 6, 8, 10, 18, 31, 32, 55, 57, 58, 60, 62, 63, 64, 65, 66, 67, 73, 76, 82, 100, 101, 107, 108, 111, 113, 114, 115, 116, 117, 133, 156, 157, 159, 160, 161, 167, 170, 183, 185, 192, 193, 194, 196, 198, 199, 200, 201, 202, 203, 220, 223, 228, 238, 245, 279, 280, 283, 284, 287, 288, 290
Pheysey, D., 152, 275
Pinder, C., 1
Pipkin, R. M., 277
Platt, H., 150
Plott, C. R., 67
Polsby, N. W., 65
Pondy, L. R., 218, 219, 220
Porac, J. R., 110
Porter, L. W., 45, 56, 278
Pritchard, R. D., 51, 89
Pugh, D. S., 17, 36, 148, 152, 275

Randall, R., 195
Raphael, E., 150
Ratcliff, R. E., 173

Rauschenberger, J., 61
Raven, B., 65, 66
Regan, D., 75
Reibstein, D. J., 80
Reich, M., 167
Reid, S. R., 128
Ridgway, V. F., 131
Rindfuss, R. R., 78
Rivers, W. H. R., 78
Rizzo, J. R., 100
Roberts, D. R., 128
Roberts, K. H., 17, 25, 59, 60, 116
Roberts, K. W., 277
Robinson, W. S., 14
Roby, T. B., 271
Rodgers, W. L., 26
Roethlisberger, F. J., 103
Roistacher, R. C., 102
Rosenstein, C., 167
Ross, J., 30, 167, 283
Ross, L., 39
Ross, M., 78
Rothermel, T., 185, 290
Rounds, J., 229, 230, 231, 232, 233, 234
Rousseau, D. M., 17, 25
Rowan, B., 11, 239, 240, 243, 244, 245, 246, 247, 248, 252
Rumelt, R., 158
Rushing, W. A., 150, 151, 154
Ryder, N. B., 286

Salancik, G. R., 6, 8, 18, 53, 55, 57, 58, 62, 63, 64, 65, 66, 67, 73, 76, 82, 100, 101, 105, 106, 107, 110, 111, 113, 114, 115, 116, 157, 170, 190, 192, 193, 194, 196, 197, 198, 199, 200, 202, 203, 220, 223, 255, 257
Saloner, G., 147
Sampson, E. E., 43, 96
Sandelands, L. E., 110

Sandver, M. H., 130
Sarason, I. G., 11, 119
Sauser, W., 268
Schacter, S., 84, 86, 266
Schein, E. H., 97
Schelling, T. C., 19
Schmidt, F. L., 46
Schmidt, S., 68, 71
Schmitt, N., 61
Schneck, R. E., 276
Schnore, L. F., 277
Schoenherr, R., 149
Schoonhoven, C. B., 162
Schurr, P., 42, 63, 75, 81, 103
Schutz, A., 77, 209
Schwab, D. P., 56
Schwartz, R. D., 76
Scott, L. R., 91
Scott, W. E., Jr., 92
Scott, W. R., 4, 25, 102, 124, 125, 130, 131, 151, 152, 154, 162, 176, 204
Seashore, S. E., 103
Secord, P. F., 8
Sechrest, L., 76
Seeman, M., 170
Seligman, C., 52, 93
Selznick, P., 228, 239
Seymore, J. D., 89
Shearing, C. D., 39
Sheehan, R., 127
Sheldon, A., 228
Sheridan, J. E., 48
Sherif, M., 241
Shoup, L. H., 171
Simon, H. A., 6, 17, 25, 217, 233, 271
Sims, J. P., 57
Skinner, B. F., 86
Sloan, S., 268
Slocum, J. W., Jr., 48, 155
Smelser, N. J., 62, 123

Smircich, L., 218
Smith, P. B., 85
Smith, R. E., 11, 119
Snow, C. C., 158, 159, 161
Snyderman, B., 55
Sobel, M., 271
Sogin, S. R., 108
Solomons, L. M., 221
Sommer, R., 266, 267, 269, 270
Sorcher, M., 94
Spaeth, J. L., 102
Spangler, E., 277
Spence, M. A., 15
Spencer, D. G., 56, 57
Spenner, K., 169
Sproull, L. S., 211, 218, 227
Stalker, G. M., 20, 155
Stanley, J. C., 87
Stava, P., 237
Staw, B. M., 30, 53, 108, 110, 156, 190, 284
Stedry, A. C., 50, 52
Steele, F., 270
Steers, R. M., 50, 51, 52, 56, 57, 278
Stein, G., 221
Stephens, T. A., 91
Stewman, S., 281, 291
Stigler, G. J., 186
Stinchcombe, A. L., 184, 185
Stinson, J. E., 48
Stogdill, R. M., 1, 2, 47, 101
Stone, E. F., 56
Storey, R., 155, 162
Strauss, G., 55, 62, 170
Strehl, K., 67
Sweezy, P., 127
Szilagyi, A. D., 57
Szwajkowski, E., 156

Taylor, F. W., 42, 43
Teece, D. J., 138, 139, 140, 141,
147, 205, 246
Terborg, J., 50, 51
Thibaut, J. W., 266
Thompson, J. D., 4, 161, 194, 278, 286
Tichy, N. M., 271, 272, 273, 275
Tolbert, C. M., 166, 246, 247
Tosi, H. L., 49, 51, 52, 150, 155, 156, 162
Trow, M., 103
Tuggle, F. D., 5, 208
Turner, A. N., 56
Turner, C., 275
Turner, R. H., 290
Tushman, M. L., 272, 273, 276

Ulman, L., 170
Underwood, B. J., 88
Unger, R. M., 33
Urwick, L., 28, 32
Useem, M., 172, 173

Van de Ven, A. H., 5, 12, 39, 104, 254, 255
Van Maanen, J., 97, 212, 214, 254, 255
Van Zante, A., 108
Villajero, D., 127
Von Bergen, C. W., Jr., 89
Vroom, V. H., 41, 44, 46, 52, 56, 78, 88

Wachter, M. L., 137, 138
Wagner, A. R., 88
Wahba, M. A., 61
Warkov, S., 150
Webb, E. J., 76
Weber, M., 130, 148
Weick, K. E., 9, 11, 18, 19, 50, 73, 77, 84, 105, 108, 184, 189, 215, 216, 222, 224, 256, 271
Weiner, S. S., 237

Weiss, D. S., 119
Weiss, H. M., 114
Weitz, B. A., 90
Welch, F., 167
Wells, W. P., 285
Welsh, A., 54, 57
Wexby, K. N., 89
White, D., 86
White, J. K., 56, 120
White, S. E., 50, 113, 116
Whitt, J. A., 171
Wiginton, J. C., 11, 254
Wildavsky, A., 7, 71, 238
Wilkinson, O. E., 68, 70
Williamson, O. E., 7, 27, 71, 122,
    134, 135, 136, 137, 138, 139,
    140, 141, 142, 144, 146, 147,
    162, 165, 166, 173, 175, 188,
    191, 192, 238, 259
Winter, S. G., 132, 133, 186

Wofford, J. C., 61
Wolfe, J. C., 57, 59
Woodward, J., 124, 152, 154

Yoels, W. C., 67
Youmans, K. C., 283
Youngblood, S. A., 80
Yukl, G. A., 50, 51, 52, 89

Zajonc, R. B., 263, 266
Zanna, M. P., 108
Zeevi, G., 109
Zeitlin, M., 125, 127
Zeitz, G., 17
Zifferblatt, S. M., 89
Zucker, L. G., 167, 209, 240, 241,
    242, 243, 246, 247, 248, 249,
    251
Zweigenhaft, R. L., 269
Zwerman, W. L., 152

SUBJECT INDEX

Absenteeism, 50, 56, 91, 92, 163
Adaptation, 73
Administrative action, 10–11, 115;
    see also Manager
Affect-based process, 221, 222, 223
Affirmative action, 196, 197
Age, of group, 282, 283, 284, 285
Agenda, 67
Aggregation bias, 14, 15, 20, 41,
    78, 79
Alienation, 170
Ambiguity, 48, 85, 100, 234, 238
American Psychological Associa-
    tion, 24
Analysis, covariance, 17
Analysis, job, 29
"As if" argument, 131, 132, 133
Attitude, job, 2, 4, 60, 116
Attitude-behavior link, 47
Attitudinal homogenization, 103
Attributional analysis, 272

Behavior, individual, 5, 6, 18, 19,
    26, 48, 83, 89, 90, 102–105
Behavior, interorganizational, 170,
    173, 293
Behavior-consequence sequence, 86
Behavior modification, 90, 91; *see*
    also Operant conditioning
Behaviorism, 179
Bounded rationality, 6, 7, 71, 135,
    173, 238

Budget allocation, 64, 66–67
Bureaucracy, and control, 28, 29,
    130, 131, 142, 143, 144, 155,
    165–166, 190

Capital allocation, 140
Carnegie Council on Higher Educa-
    tion, 108
Case study, validity and reliability,
    237
Centralization, 149, 150
Chameleon, 71
Change, 229, 230, 233
Coalignment, 10
Coalition, 3, 67, 133
Cognitive dissonance theory, 250
Cohort, 278, 286, 287, 288, 289,
    290, 291, 293
Commitment, 53, 190, 278
Compensation, 128, 129, 130, 140,
    145, 146
Competition, 156, 186, 187, 191,
    195, 206, 291
Conformity, 59, 60, 74, 84, 101,
    103, 104, 116, 221
Consistency, cross-situational, 119,
    120
Consonance hypothesis, 148, 152
Consultant, 115
Context, social, 2, 3, 26, 33, 79,
    83, 118
Contingency management, 86

Control, 4, 27, 28, 29, 131, 144,
    147, 156, 160, 264, 265, 275
  bureaucratic, 28, 29, 130, 131,
    142, 143, 144
  clan, 142, 143, 144
  and demography, 282, 285, 286
  and markets, 143, 144
  mechanisms of, 149, 150, 176,
    286
  vs. ownership, 125, 126, 127,
    161, 171
  process, 28, 29
  propositional, 47, 67
  and reporting systems, 136, 137
  and work force, 165, 168, 169,
    170
Cooptation, 67
Critical theory, 32, 210, 214

Decentralization, 17, 20
Decision analysis, 272
Decision making, 6, 7, 12, 49, 179
Decision process theory, 7, 9, 11,
    12, 49, 68, 226, 233, 235, 237,
    238, 252
Decision structure, 235, 236
Decoupling, 245
Design, physical, 260, 263, 264,
    265, 266, 268, 269, 270, 271
Design, task, 59, 61, 114, 115
Deskilling, 168, 169, 170, 175, 265
Differentiation, 20, 23, 149, 150,
    156
Discipline, 1, 90, 91, 141, 142

Economic order quantity inventory
    planning, 10
Economy, dual, 166, 167
Efficiency, internal, 139, 140
Efficient boundary, 134, 137–139
Emergent process, 7, 9–10
Employee relation, 141, 163, 164,
    165, 167, 175, 206

Environment:
  and institutionalization, 245,
    251, 252
  and organizational structure, 16,
    17, 155, 156, 157, 182, 186,
    203
  perception of, 113, 114, 115,
    116, 155, 156, 160, 161
  and population ecology, 198
  and resource dependency, 198
  and strategic choice, 159, 160,
    202
  and strategic contingency theory,
    162, 175
Equilibrium analysis, 192
Equity theory, 78, 85
Ethnomethodology, 209, 211, 212,
    213, 225, 255
Evaluation, job, 62
Exchange theory, 83–85, 101, 118
Expectancy theory, 7, 41, 43, 44–
    47, 48, 52, 54, 58, 72, 78, 87,
    88, 89, 94, 95, 96, 212, 257
External constraint, 8–9, 10, 11,
    25, 80, 81–82, 86, 104, 111,
    117, 193–197, 205, 234

Falsifiability, 58, 259
Federal Trade Commission, 156–
    157
Feedback, 4, 52, 56, 81
Force activation model, 66
Free will, 5
Functionalism, 224

Generalist, 181, 182, 183
Generative theory, 35
Gini index, 279
Goal:
  acceptance, 51, 53, 54
  commitment, 51
  congruence, 128, 144, 160
  difficulty, 49–50, 51, 52, 54

homogeneity, 63
and performance, 51, 52, 53
retrospective, 50
setting, 49, 50, 51, 52, 53, 73, 92
specificity, 49, 54, 67
Goal-setting theory, 7, 41, 48, 49, 51, 52, 53, 54, 78
Group, as unit of analysis, 63, 84–85, 103, 104
Groupthink, 104
Growth need strength, 81
Growth rate, in industry, 281
Growth rate, in organization, 280–281

Heterogeneity, index of, 279
Hierarchy, 17, 27, 28

Ideology, 2, 33, 34, 35, 36, 37, 62
Incentive, 50–51, 52; *see also* Motivation
Incrementalism, 6–7, 71, 238
Inculturation, 81
Individualist, 18, 21, 22
Individualist-structuralist controversy, 18
Influence, informational social, 59, 60, 85–86, 96, 118, 286
Influence, personal, 67–68
Influence, social, 113, 114, 115
Influence tactics, 68, 69, 70
Information processing, 7, 42, 48, 49, 77, 79, 111, 112, 113, 114, 115, 116, 117, 118, 179, 221
Information saliency, 105, 106, 108, 113
Institutionalization theory, 226, 239–240, 249, 251, 252, 256
determinants of, 241–244
and innovation, 246, 247, 248, 249
and organizational structure, 244–246

Instrumentality theory, 44, 47, 48, 54
Interaction, social, 249, 251, 260, 266–267
Interactional analysis, 272–273
Interactionist, 209
Integration, vertical, 138, 139, 173, 204, 205, 206
Interdependence, 149, 193–194, 196, 198, 199, 200, 201, 206, 208
Interlock, 199, 200, 201, 202, 206, 207
Internal contracting, 27

Job characteristics, perceptions of, 59, 60, 61, 63, 76, 113, 114, 117
Job classification system, 264
Job ladder, 29
Joint venture, 199, 200
Justification, insufficient, 107, 108, 109, 118, 250

Labor laws, 29
Language, 218–220, 225
Leader Behavior Description Questionnaire, 101
Leadership, 1, 2, 4, 29, 31, 36, 218, 219, 228, 269, 270
path-goal theory of, 7, 43, 47–48
Learning, symbolically, 94
Linear programming, 10

Map cognitive, 215, 216, 217, 218, 220, 225
Market failures theory, 122, 134, 146, 147, 162, 173, 174, 175, 176, 199, 204, 205, 206, 255
Marxist analysis, 7–8, 122, 162, 163, 164, 165, 167, 168, 170–173, 174, 175–176, 206, 207, 255

Mayo, Elton, 36
M-form hypothesis, 139, 140, 141, 147
Mobility, occupational, 249, 291, 292, 293
Modeling, 93, 94
Motivation, 4, 17, 30, 31, 44, 52, 53, 59, 110, 284–285
Multidivisional structure, 157, 158, 188
Multiple regression analysis, 52

Natural selection, 183, 204
Need fulfillment theory, 7, 41, 43, 54, 55, 56, 59, 60, 61, 62, 63
Need-satisfaction model, 55, 62
Network, 23, 201, 271, 272, 273, 274, 275, 276
Network analysis, 102, 201, 256, 271, 276, 277
Niche, 181, 182, 183

Operant conditioning, 8, 43, 52, 73, 82, 86, 87, 88, 89, 90, 91, 92, 93, 94, 96, 98, 105, 117, 118
Opportunism, 135, 136, 137
Organization set, 193
Organizational disappearance, 187, 188, 189
Organizing, as process, 18
Overjustification, 109–111, 118
Ownership-control separation, 126–128

Paradigm, organization, and change, 227–228, 229–230, 232, 252, 255
Parsimony, 39, 259
Performance, job, 48, 50, 52, 54, 56, 57, 90, 91, 114, 145, 160, 233, 235, 238, 276
Personnel, movement of, 199, 290,

291, 293
Phenomenology, 255
Political theory, 41, 63, 64–65, 72, 78
Polymorphism, 182, 183
Population ecology, 8, 23, 39, 179, 180, 186, 187, 191, 198, 204, 205, 255, 256
Positional analysis, 272
Power, 64–65, 66, 67, 71, 83, 195, 202, 203, 206, 209, 220, 232, 264, 265, 270, 276, 287
Preference expectancy, 208
Probit analysis, 138
Product market strategy, 158
Production cost efficiency, 134
Promotion, 281
Psychology, industrial, 24, 28, 29, 31, 36, 37, 41

Qualitative analysis, 254
Quality control, 92
Quality of working life, 62

Rationality, organizational, 63, 71, 73, 74
Rationality, retrospective, 8, 75, 77, 79, 82, 105, 107, 109, 111, 118, 119, 257
Reality, social construct of, 9, 11, 82, 111, 112, 113, 257
Recruitment, executive, 199, 200, 291
Redesign, job, 62
Reductionism, 21, 22
Reference group theory, 85
Regeneration, 278, 279, 286
Regulation, 29
Reinforcement, 81, 82, 87, 88, 89, 91, 92, 95, 117
Relative deprivation theory, 85
Reputational analysis, 272
Resource dependence theory, 9,

164, 180, 192–197, 198, 199, 203, 204, 205, 206, 207, 219, 220, 255
Role, 82, 98, 99, 100, 101, 102, 118, 193, 241, 243, 244
Role theory, 9, 98, 117, 118

Safety, occupational, 91–92
Satellite, 71
Satisfaction, job, 2, 48, 52, 54, 55, 268, 276, 278
Satisficing, 6, 7
Segmentation, 167
Selection process, of organizational structure, 180, 181, 186–189, 233
Self-perception theory, 50, 105, 107
Self-reinforcement, 95
Similarity, attitudinal, 233, 266
Situationism, 8
Social constructionist theory, 209, 210, 211, 214, 220, 221, 225, 226, 238, 256
Social influence theory, 9
Social learning theory, 52, 82, 93–96, 118
Socialization, 9, 82, 96, 97, 98, 118, 144, 176, 190, 286
Space, and organizational structure, 256, 261–263
Specialist, 181, 182, 183
Specialization, task, 149
Sponsorship, 287, 290
Stability, 227, 229
Status degradation, 213, 214
Stimulus-response theory, 12, 208
Strategic choice, 160, 161, 163, 168, 173, 175
Strategic contingencies, 74, 203, 219, 220
Strategy, 10, 157, 158, 159, 160, 161

Stratification, 23, 31
Structural choice, 258
Structural contingencies, 255
Structural contingency theory, 7, 8, 122, 147, 148, 149, 161, 162–163, 173, 174, 175, 176
Structuralism, 21–22, 23, 209
Subjective utility maximization theory, 43
Subsidiary, 17
Subsidy, 110
Subunit membership, 66, 116, 117, 156
Succession, executive, 64, 212–213, 285, 293

Task design theory, 7, 59, 61
Tautology, 77
Technology, and organizational structure, 4, 7, 28, 151, 152, 153, 154, 162, 168, 175, 264, 265, 274–275, 281–282
Temporary National Economic Committee, 127
Tenure, 278, 279, 284–285, 286
Testing, in field settings, 35
"Theory Z" management, 232
Transactions costs theory, 7, 134, 135, 136, 146, 147, 162, 175, 176; see also Market failures theory
Transactions dependence, 196
Turnover, 50, 56, 91, 163, 280, 287, 288, 289, 290

Unionization, 282–284

Variation, 183–186, 189

Wilcox matched pairs test, 141
Workforce, internalization of, 164, 165
Work in America, 170